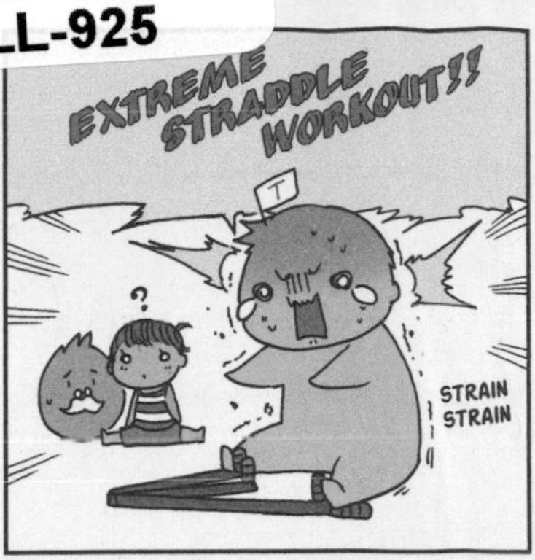
EXTREME STRADDLE WORKOUT!!
T
?
STRAIN STRAIN

This is Tsutsui.

Welcome to the long-awaited eighth volume!
Thank you for supporting us to volume number infinity!

So...what is that indispensable item that helps you stave off sleepiness while waiting for the coffee to brew after a bath?

That's right! It's the straddle-stretch machine!

The straddle-stretching device I bought on an impulse is actually strangely popular at the office!

Yes, moderate exercise and stretching is essential for maintaining good health!

Whether you have the flexible body of a toddler with a perfect 180-degree straddle or you overdo it a bit by pushing past 90 degrees and screaming the whole time (injuring your joints slightly but still insisting that you're ever so happy with your purchase), why not kick back with this romantic comedy manga every now and then to stretch out your tired heart?

• Taishi Tsutsui •

We Never Learn

We Never Learn

Volume 8 • SHONEN JUMP Manga Edition

STORY AND ART Taishi Tsutsui

TRANSLATION Camellia Nieh
SHONEN JUMP SERIES LETTERING Snir Aharon
GRAPHIC NOVEL TOUCH-UP ART & LETTERING Erika Terriquez
DESIGN Shawn Carrico
SHONEN JUMP SERIES EDITOR John Bae
GRAPHIC NOVEL EDITOR David Brothers

BOKUTACHI WA BENKYOU GA DEKINAI © 2017 by Taishi Tsutsui
All rights reserved.
First published in Japan in 2017 by SHUEISHA Inc., Tokyo.
English translation rights arranged by SHUEISHA Inc.

The stories, characters and incidents mentioned in this publication are entirely fictional.

Printed in the U.S.A.

Published by VIZ Media, LLC
P.O. Box 77010
San Francisco, CA 94107

10 9 8 7 6 5 4 3 2 1
First printing, February 2020

viz.com

shonenjump.com

PARENTAL ADVISORY
WE NEVER LEARN is rated T+ for Older
Teen and is recommended for ages 16
and up. This volume contains mild
language and sexual themes.

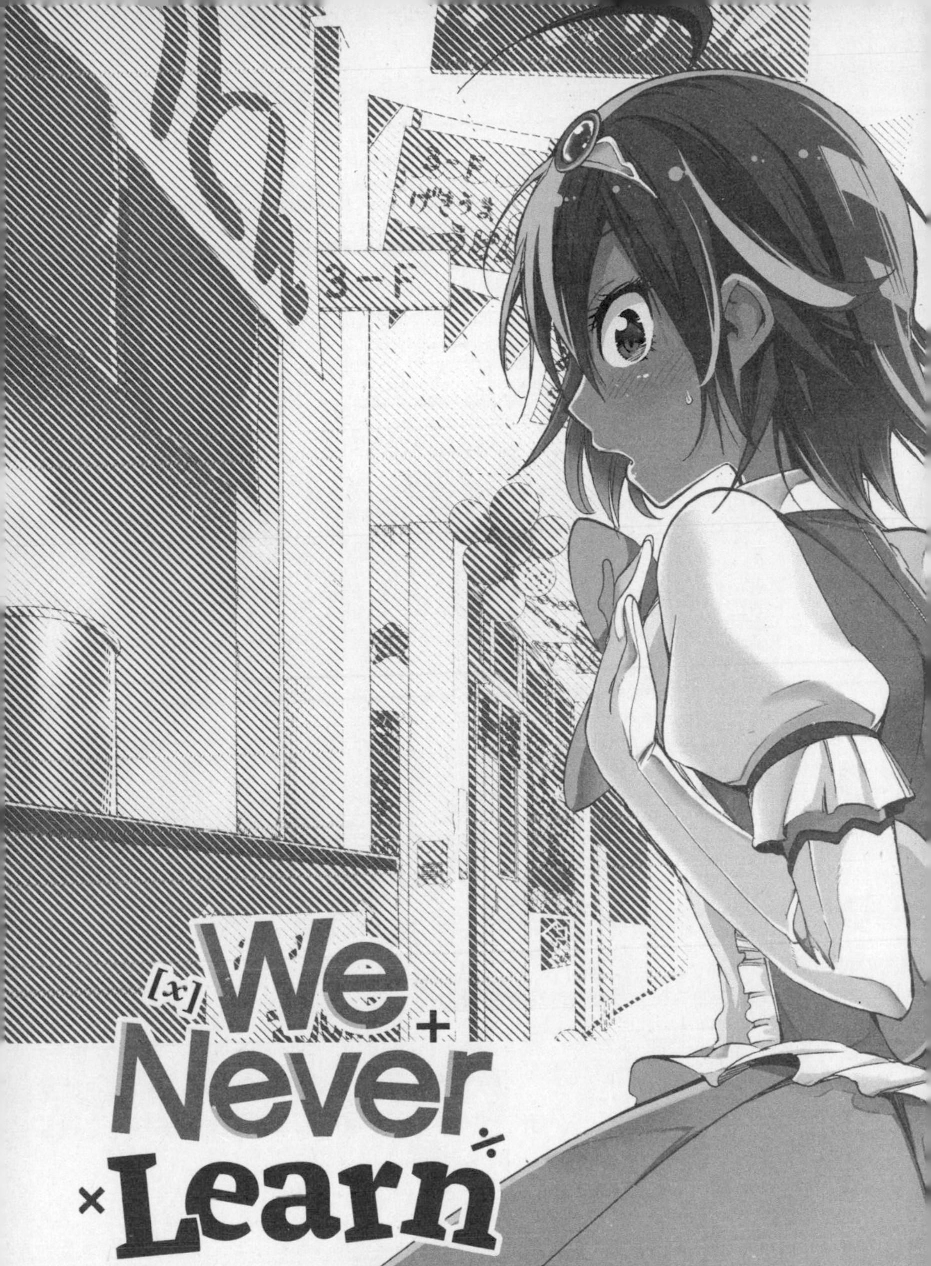
3ーF

[x] We + Never ÷ × Learn

8

As the Festival Unfolds Mysteriously, [X] Dance in Full Splendor

Taishi Tsutsui

We Never Learn

Characters & Story

Nariyuki Yuiga and his family have led a humble life since his father passed away, with Yuiga doing everything he can to support his siblings. So when the principal of his school agrees to grant Nariyuki the school's special VIP recommendation for a full scholarship to college, he leaps at the opportunity. However, the principal's offer comes with one condition: Yuiga must serve as the tutor of Rizu Ogata, Fumino Furuhashi and Uruka Takemoto, the three girl geniuses who are the pride of Ichinose Academy! Unfortunately, the girls, while extremely talented in certain ways, all have subjects where their grades are absolutely rock-bottom. How will these three struggling students ever manage to pass their college entrance exams?!

When Nariyuki and Uruka accidentally see Kobayashi and Umihara kissing, they start to feel oddly self-conscious around each other. Later, Fumino is depressed on a stormy day, and Nariyuki offers support. Then, Nariyuki rushes to help both Kirisu Sensei when she loses the key to her house and Asumi when she is injured!

NARIYUKI YUIGA

CLASS:3-B

☺ Liberal Arts
☺ STEM
☹ Athletics

A bright student from an ordinary family. Nariyuki lacks genius in any one subject but manages to maintain stellar grades through hard work. Agrees to take on the role of tutor in return for the school's special VIP recommendation.

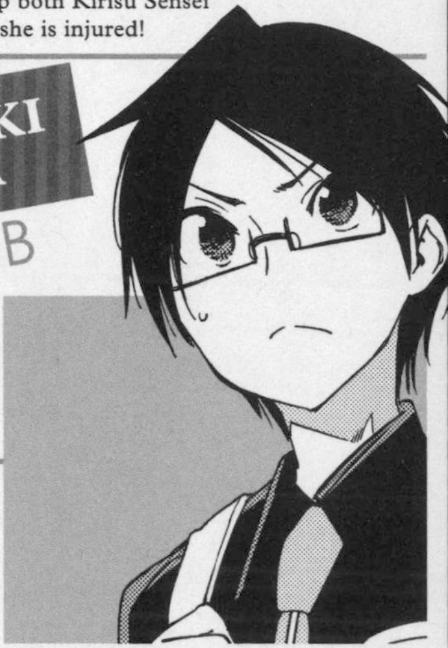

The Yuiga Family

A family of five consisting of Nariyuki, his mother and his siblings, Mizuki, Hazuki and Kazuki.

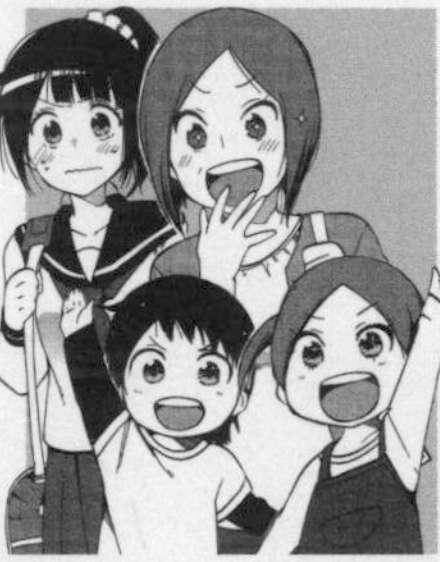

Kobayashi and Omori

Nariyuki's friends.

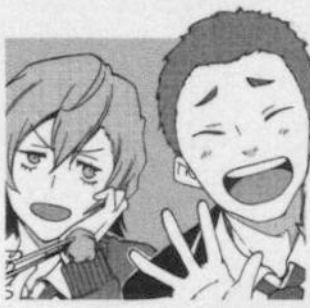

Inomori, Kashima and Chono

Members of the Thorn Club, Fumino's fan club!

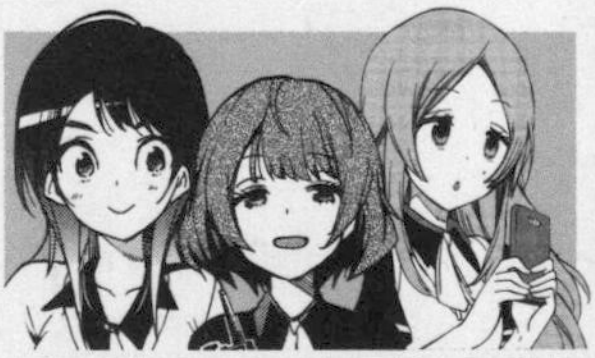

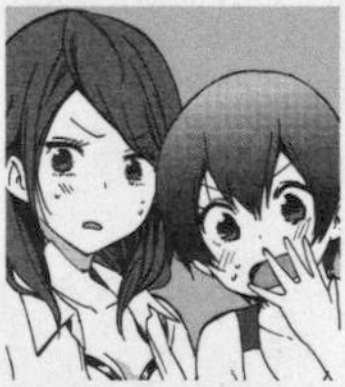

Kawase and Umihara

Uruka's friends.

Sawako Sekijo

The head of the science club and a rival of Rizu's, but in fact she adores Rizu.

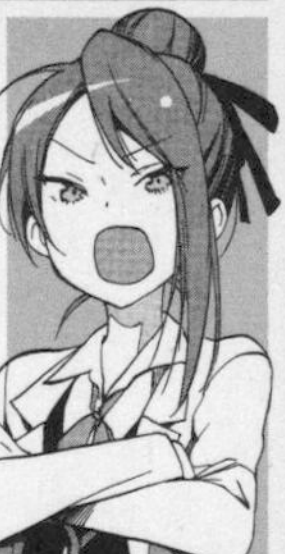

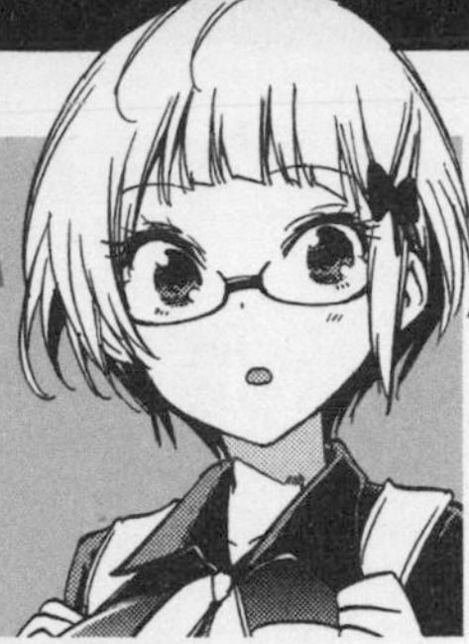

RIZU OGATA

Known as the Thumbelina Supercomputer, Rizu is a math and science genius, but she's a dunce at literature, especially when human emotions come into play. She chooses a literary path to learn about human psychology—partially because she wants to become better at board games.

CLASS:3-F

☹ Liberal Arts 😀 STEM ☹ Athletics

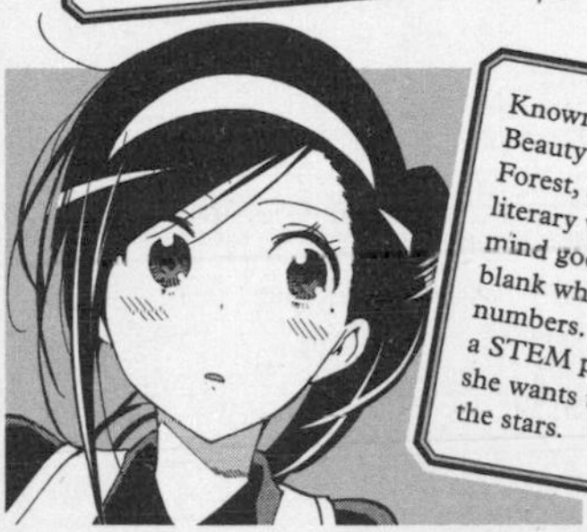

FUMINO FURUHASHI

Known as the Sleeping Beauty of the Literary Forest, Fumino is a literary wiz whose mind goes completely blank when she sees numbers. She chooses a STEM path because she wants to study the stars.

CLASS:3-A

😀 Liberal Arts ☹ STEM ☺ Athletics

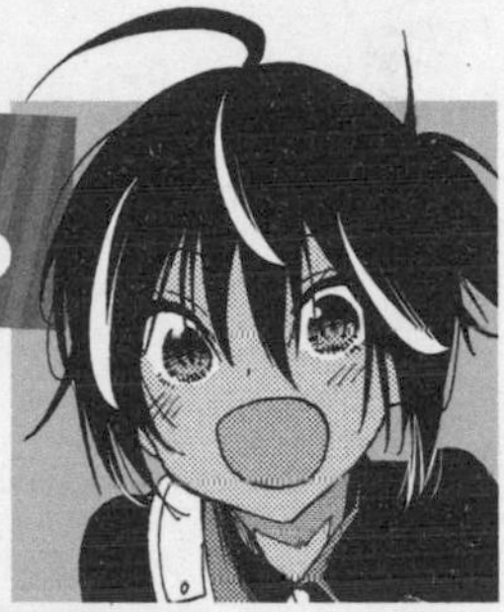

URUKA TAKEMOTO

Known as the Shimmering Ebony Mermaid Princess, Uruka is a swimming prodigy but is terrible at academics. In order to get an athletic scholarship, she needs to meet certain academic standards. She's had a crush on Nariyuki since junior high.

CLASS:3-D

☹ Liberal Arts ☹ STEM 😀 Athletics

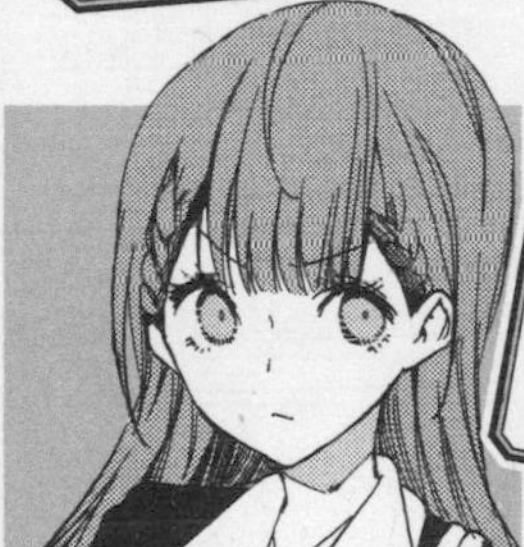

MAFUYU KIRISU

A teacher at Ichinose Academy, and Rizu and Fumino's previous tutor. She believes people should choose their path according to their talents.

TEACHER

😀 Pedagogy ☹ Home Economics

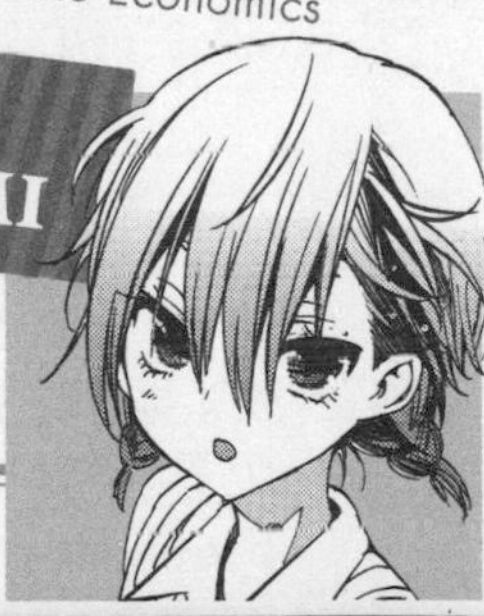

ASUMI KOMINAMI

A graduate of Ichinose Academy. Works at a maid cafe and attends cram school in order to get into medical school and take over her father's clinic one day.

OG

☹ Science ☺ Service

VOLUME **8** As the Festival Unfolds Mysteriously, [X] Dance in Full Splendor

NAME **Taishi Tsutsui**

QUESTION
61 Wherefore Might They Fathom the Aspirations of the Immediate [X]? 7

QUESTION
62 A Best Friend Illustrates [X] for a Genius 29

QUESTION
63 After a Dream, [X] Respond to a Certain Form 49

QUESTION
64 Excitement and Busyness in Anticipation of [X] 69

QUESTION
65 [X] Descends like Wildfire at the Festival's Beginning 89

QUESTION
66 As the Festival Unfolds Mysteriously, [X] Dance in Full Splendor 109

QUESTION
67 The [X] Tread a Thorny Path as the Festivities Continue... 129

QUESTION
68 At the Festival's Climax, Each Frantically Strives for [X] 149

QUESTION
69 A Post-Festival Celebration of [X], both Dazzling and Lonely 171

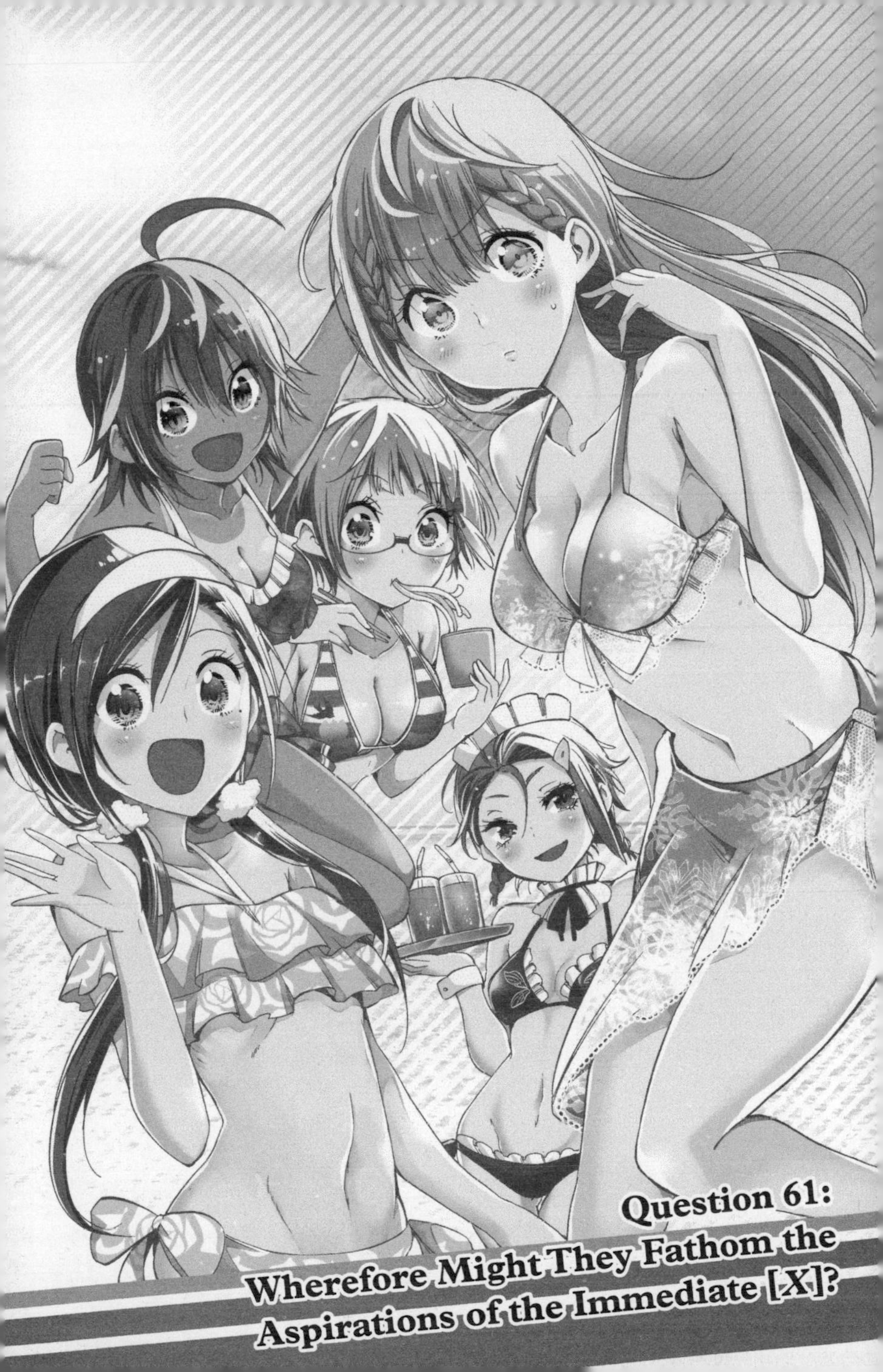

Question 61: Wherefore Might They Fathom the Aspirations of the Immediate [X]?

[x] We Never Learn

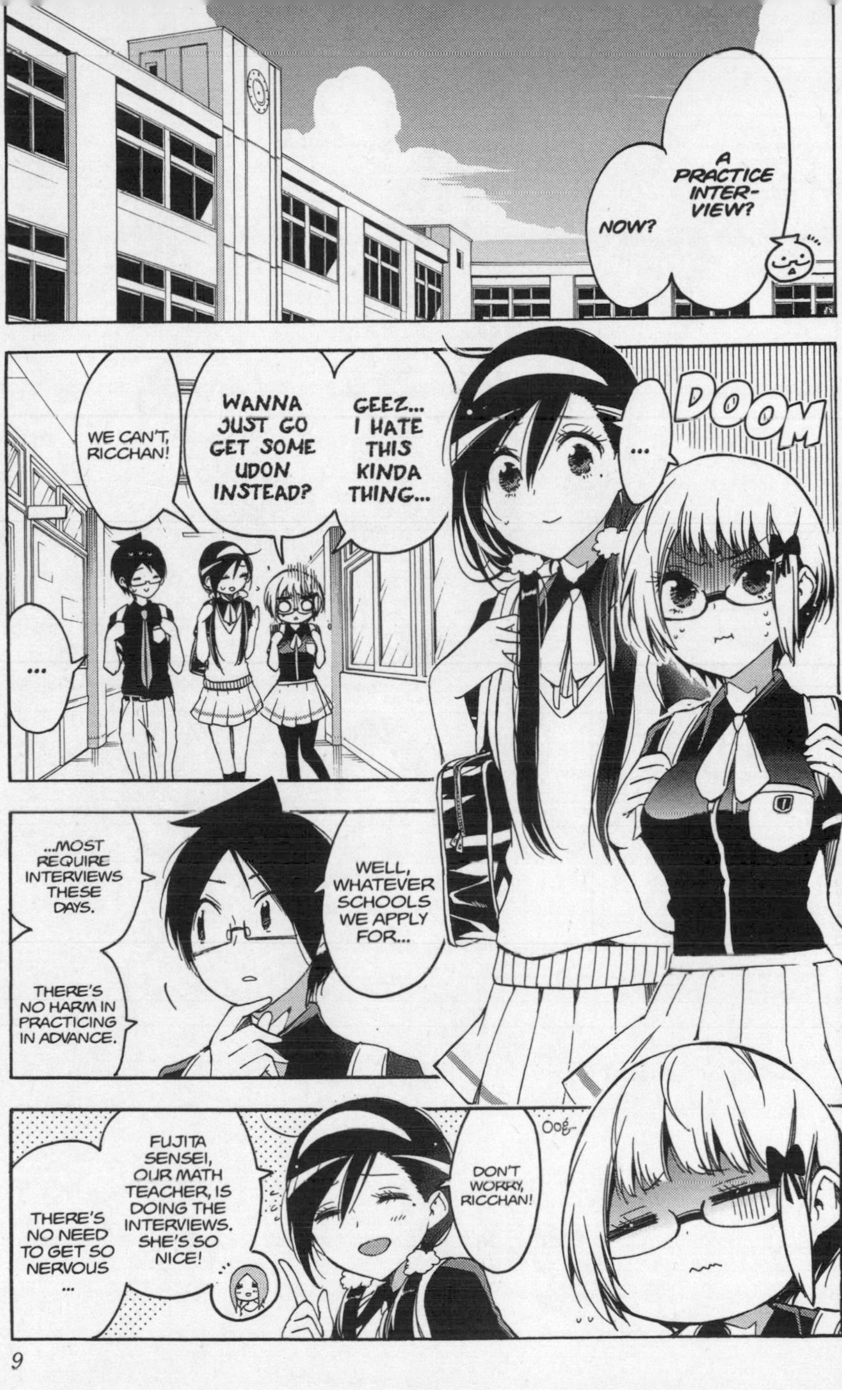
A PRACTICE INTER-VIEW?
NOW?
DOOM
...
GEEZ... I HATE THIS KINDA THING...
WANNA JUST GO GET SOME UDON INSTEAD?
WE CAN'T, RICCHAN!
...
WELL, WHATEVER SCHOOLS WE APPLY FOR...
...MOST REQUIRE INTERVIEWS THESE DAYS.
THERE'S NO HARM IN PRACTICING IN ADVANCE.
Oog...
DON'T WORRY, RICCHAN!
FUJITA SENSEI, OUR MATH TEACHER, IS DOING THE INTERVIEWS. SHE'S SO NICE!
THERE'S NO NEED TO GET SO NERVOUS...

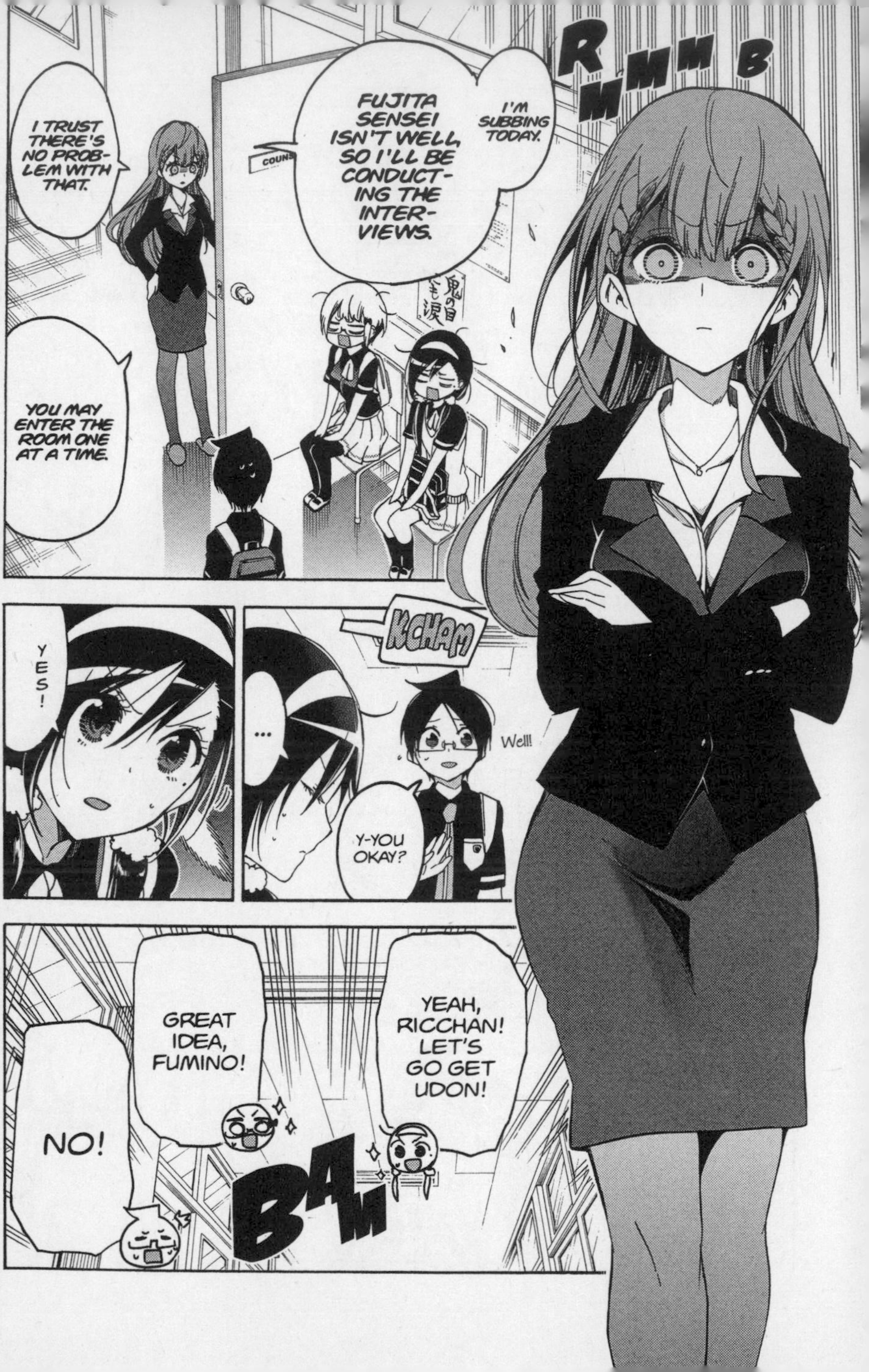
RMMMB
I'M SUBBING TODAY.
FUJITA SENSEI ISN'T WELL, SO I'LL BE CONDUCTING THE INTERVIEWS.
COUNS
鬼の目にも涙
I TRUST THERE'S NO PROBLEM WITH THAT.
YOU MAY ENTER THE ROOM ONE AT A TIME.
KCHAM
Well!
...
Y-YOU OKAY?
YES!
YEAH, RICCHAN! LET'S GO GET UDON!
GREAT IDEA, FUMINO!
NO!
BAM

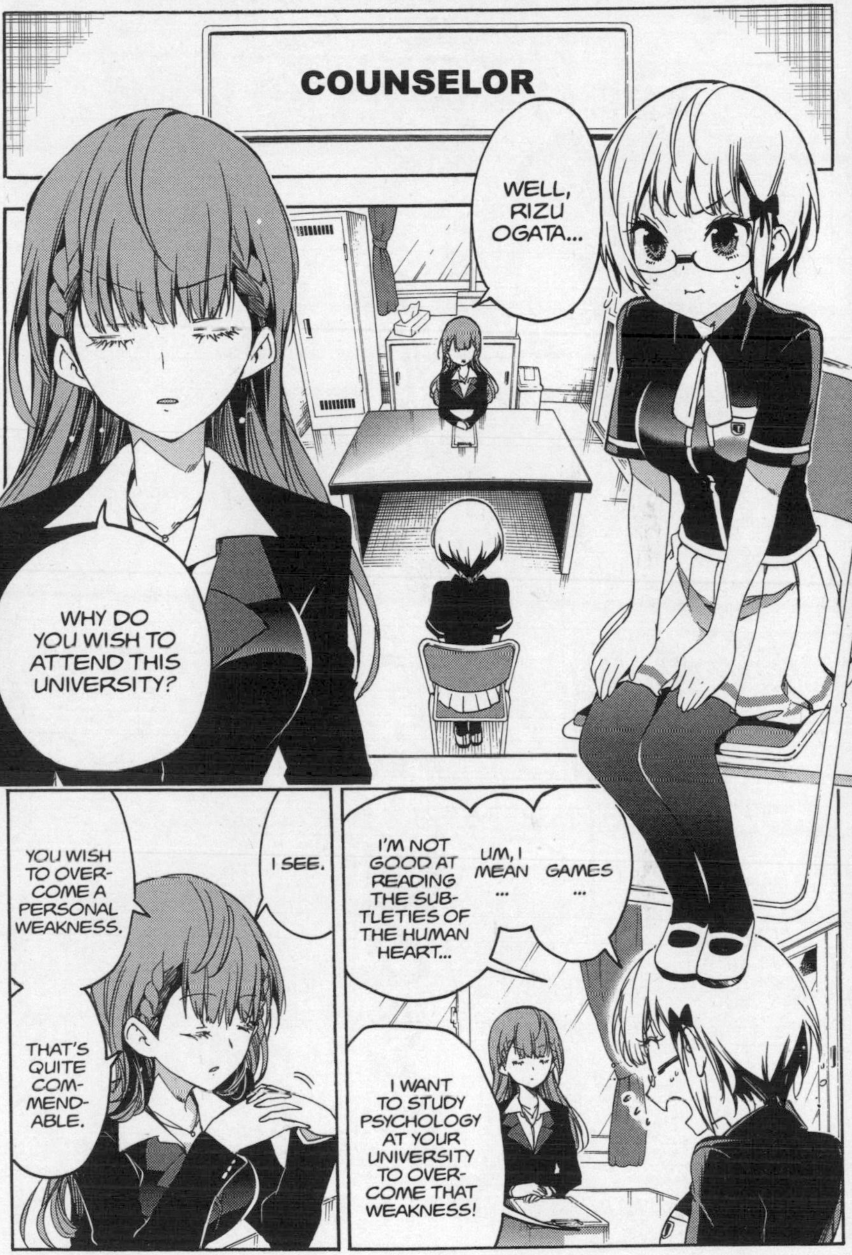

COUNSELOR
WELL, RIZU OGATA...
WHY DO YOU WISH TO ATTEND THIS UNIVERSITY?
GAMES ...
UM, I MEAN ...
I'M NOT GOOD AT READING THE SUBTLETIES OF THE HUMAN HEART...
I WANT TO STUDY PSYCHOLOGY AT YOUR UNIVERSITY TO OVERCOME THAT WEAKNESS!
I SEE.
YOU WISH TO OVERCOME A PERSONAL WEAKNESS.
THAT'S QUITE COMMENDABLE.

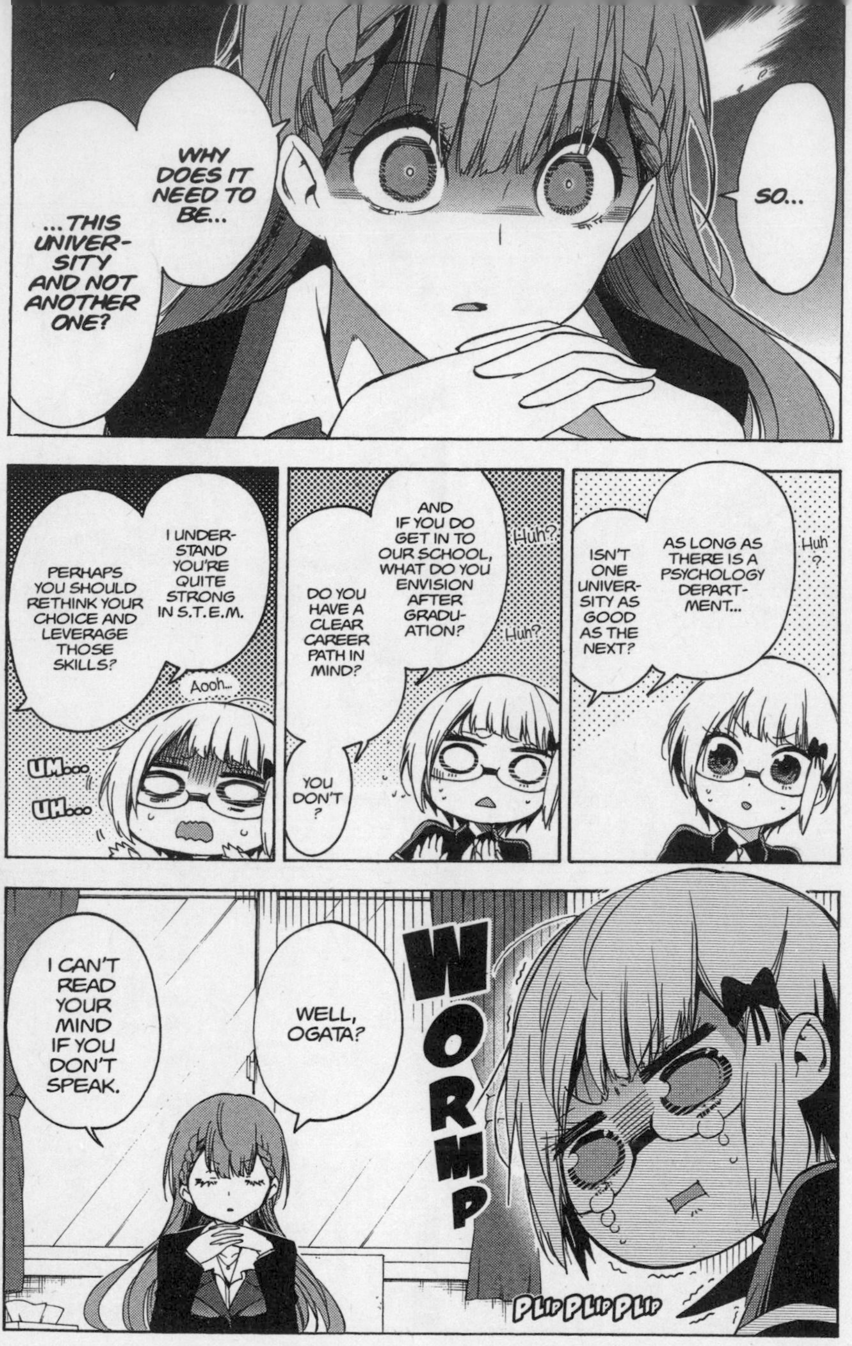
SO...
WHY DOES IT NEED TO BE...
...THIS UNIVERSITY AND NOT ANOTHER ONE?
AS LONG AS THERE IS A PSYCHOLOGY DEPARTMENT...
Huh?
ISN'T ONE UNIVERSITY AS GOOD AS THE NEXT?
AND IF YOU DO GET IN TO OUR SCHOOL, WHAT DO YOU ENVISION AFTER GRADUATION?
Huh?
Huh?
DO YOU HAVE A CLEAR CAREER PATH IN MIND?
YOU DON'T?
I UNDERSTAND YOU'RE QUITE STRONG IN S.T.E.M.
PERHAPS YOU SHOULD RETHINK YOUR CHOICE AND LEVERAGE THOSE SKILLS?
Aooh...
UM...
UH...
WORMP
WELL, OGATA?
I CAN'T READ YOUR MIND IF YOU DON'T SPEAK.
PLIP PLIP PLIP

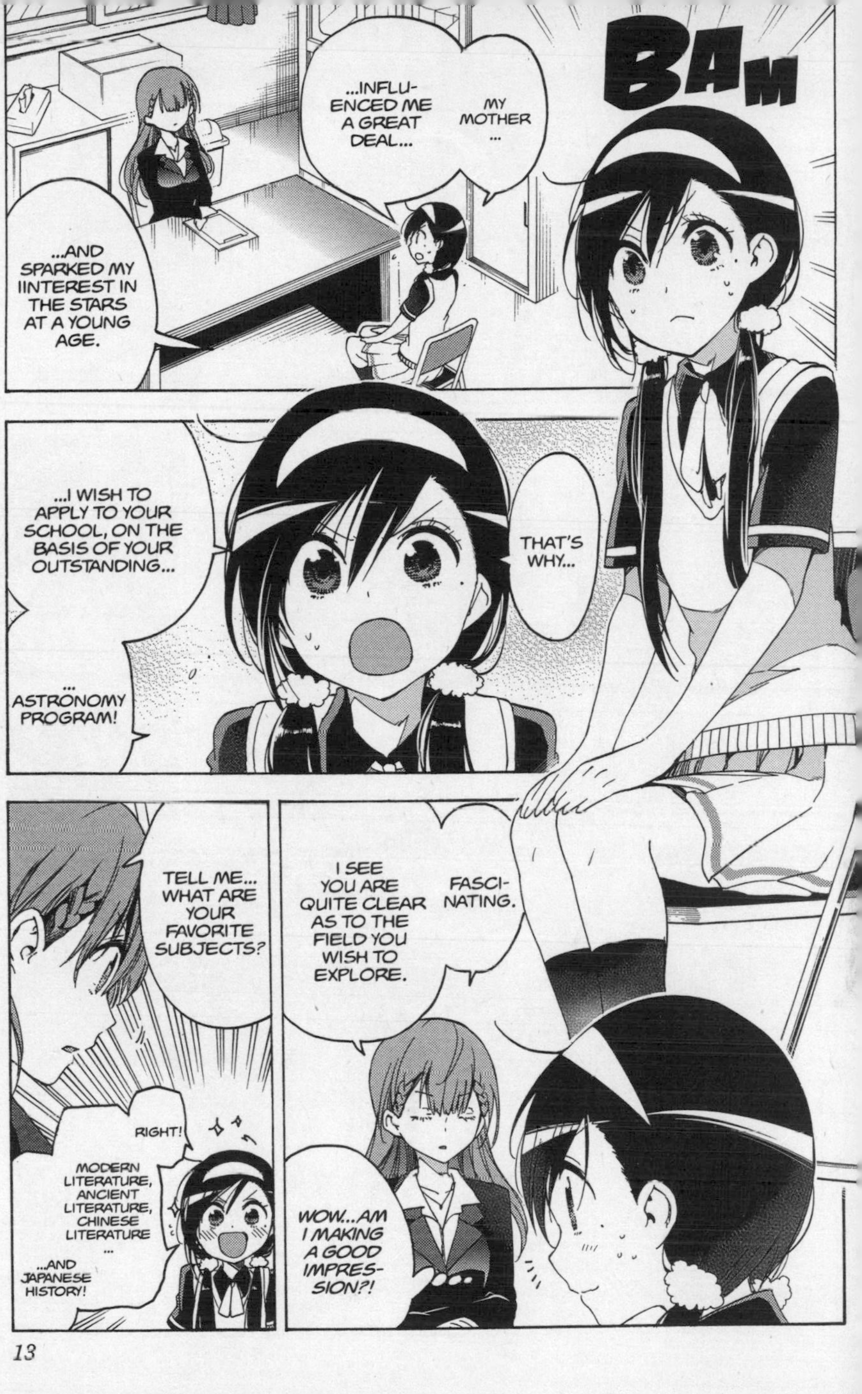
BAM
MY MOTHER ...
...INFLU-ENCED ME A GREAT DEAL...
...AND SPARKED MY IINTEREST IN THE STARS AT A YOUNG AGE.
THAT'S WHY...
...I WISH TO APPLY TO YOUR SCHOOL, ON THE BASIS OF YOUR OUTSTANDING...
... ASTRONOMY PROGRAM!
FASCI-NATING.
I SEE YOU ARE QUITE CLEAR AS TO THE FIELD YOU WISH TO EXPLORE.
WOW...AM I MAKING A GOOD IMPRES-SION?!
TELL ME... WHAT ARE YOUR FAVORITE SUBJECTS?
RIGHT!
MODERN LITERATURE, ANCIENT LITERATURE, CHINESE LITERATURE ...
...AND JAPANESE HISTORY!

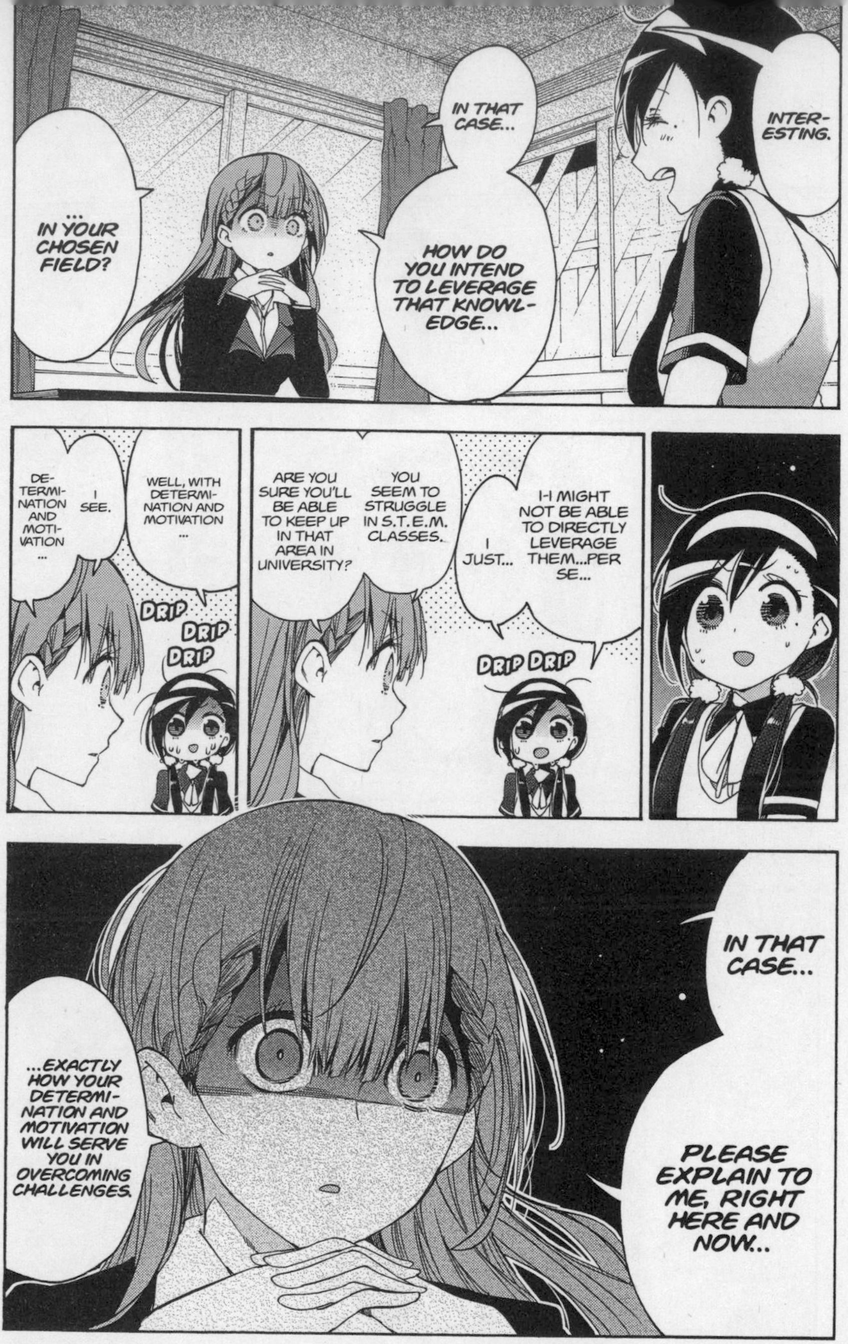
INTER-ESTING.
IN THAT CASE...
HOW DO YOU INTEND TO LEVERAGE THAT KNOWL-EDGE...
... IN YOUR CHOSEN FIELD?
I-I MIGHT NOT BE ABLE TO DIRECTLY LEVERAGE THEM...PER SE...
I JUST...
DRIP DRIP
YOU SEEM TO STRUGGLE IN S.T.E.M. CLASSES.
ARE YOU SURE YOU'LL BE ABLE TO KEEP UP IN THAT AREA IN UNIVERSITY?
WELL, WITH DETERMI-NATION AND MOTIVATION ...
I SEE.
DE-TERMI-NATION AND MOTI-VATION ...
DRIP DRIP DRIP
IN THAT CASE...
PLEASE EXPLAIN TO ME, RIGHT HERE AND NOW...
...EXACTLY HOW YOUR DETERMI-NATION AND MOTIVATION WILL SERVE YOU IN OVERCOMING CHALLENGES.

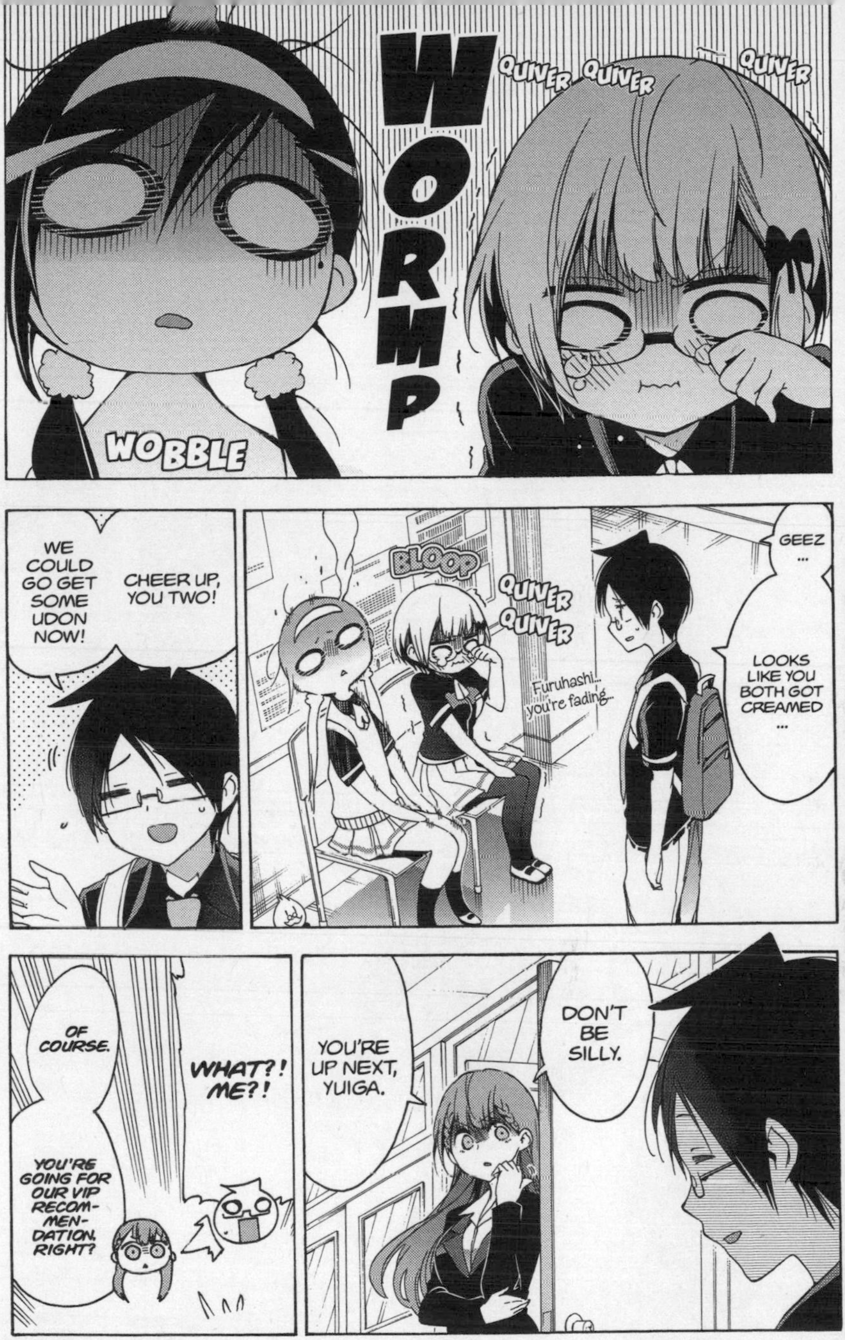
QUIVER QUIVER
QUIVER
WORMP
WOBBLE
GEEZ...
LOOKS LIKE YOU BOTH GOT CREAMED...
QUIVER QUIVER
BLOOP
Furuhashi... you're fading...
CHEER UP, YOU TWO!
WE COULD GO GET SOME UDON NOW!
DON'T BE SILLY.
YOU'RE UP NEXT, YUIGA.
WHAT?! ME?!
OF COURSE.
YOU'RE GOING FOR OUR VIP RECOMMEN-DATION. RIGHT?

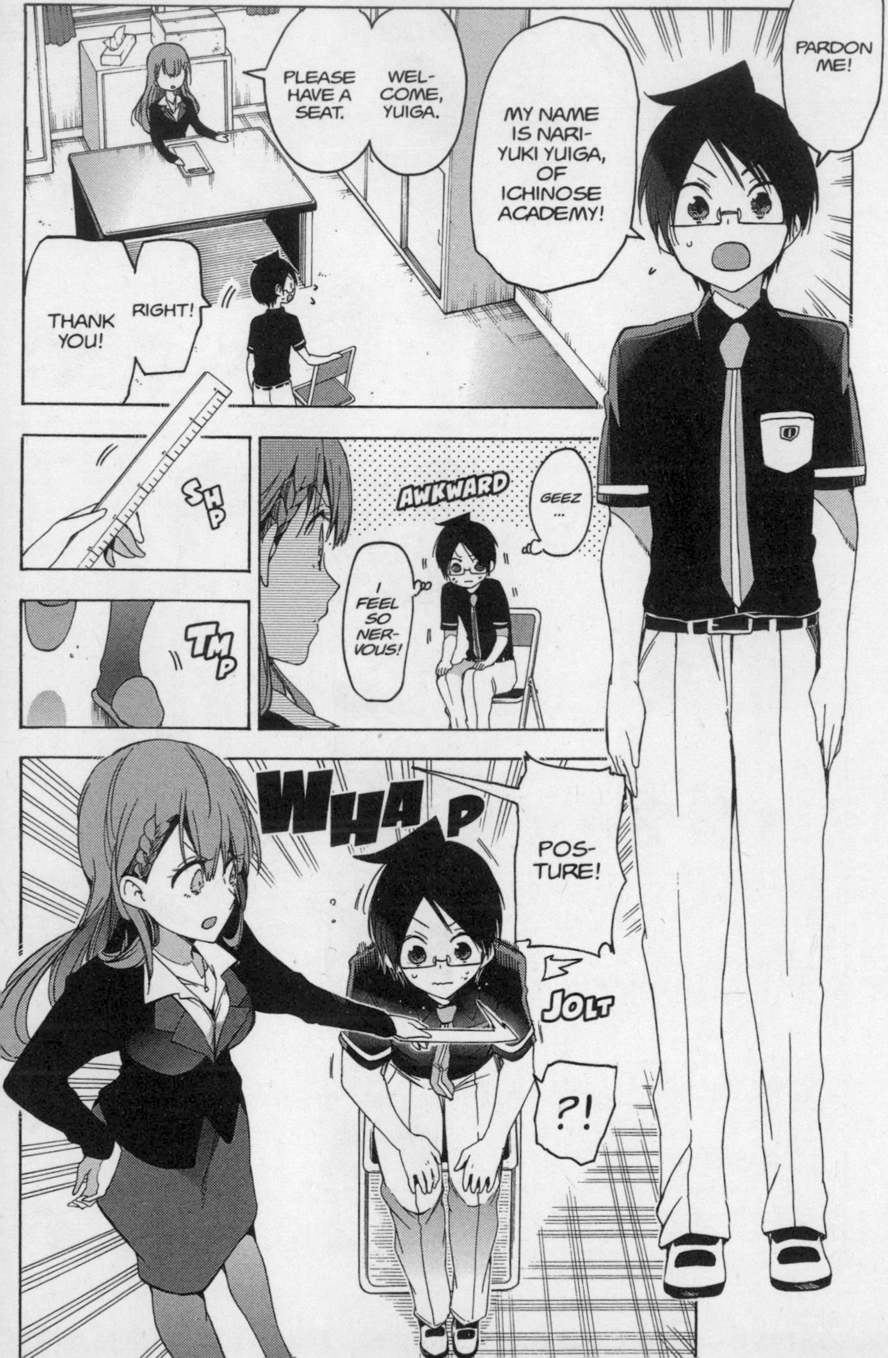
PARDON ME!
MY NAME IS NARI-YUKI YUIGA, OF ICHINOSE ACADEMY!
WEL-COME, YUIGA.
PLEASE HAVE A SEAT.
RIGHT!
THANK YOU!
AWKWARD
GEEZ ...
I FEEL SO NER-VOUS!
SHP
TMP
WHAP
POS-TURE!
JOLT
?!

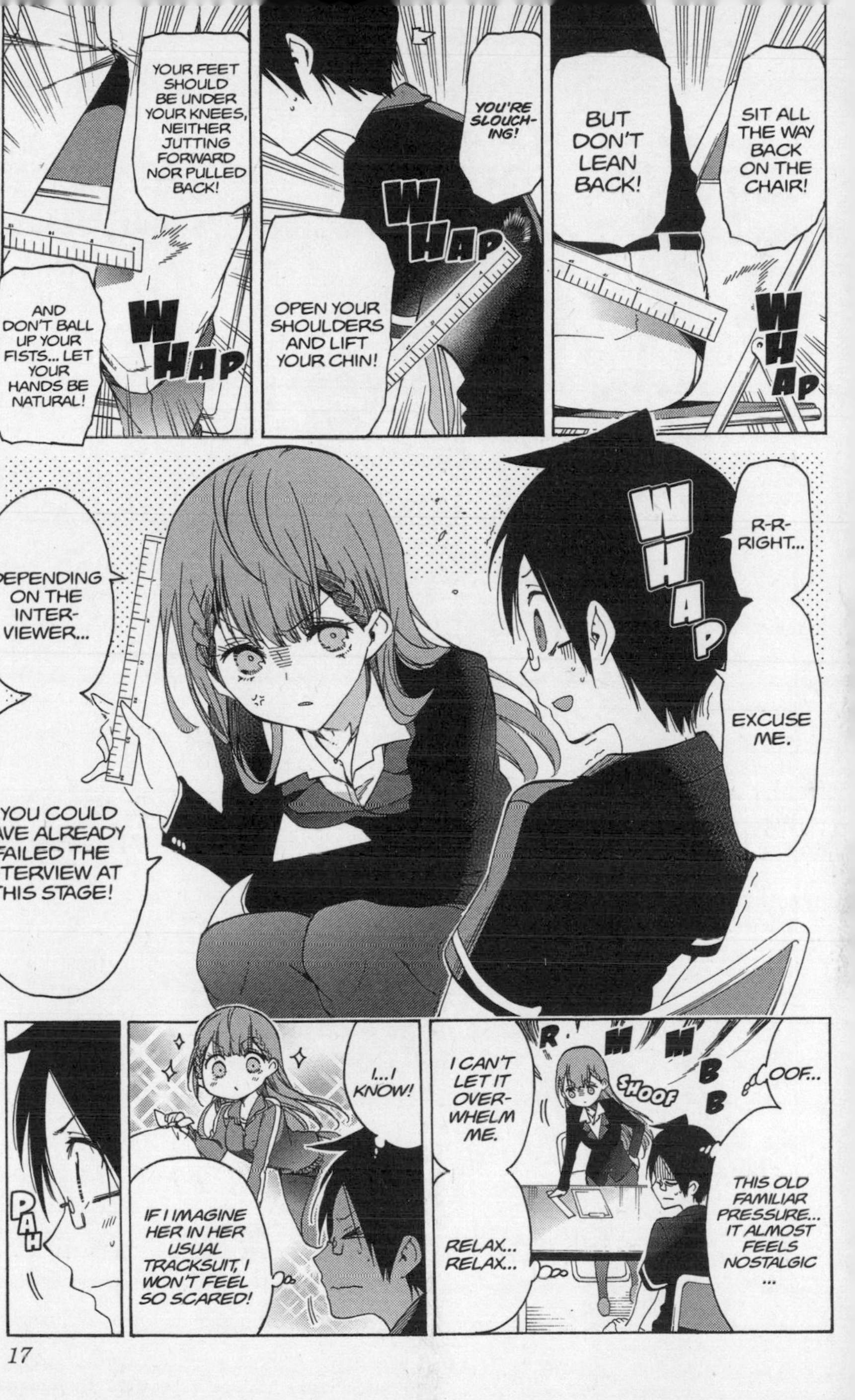
SIT ALL THE WAY BACK ON THE CHAIR!
BUT DON'T LEAN BACK!
WHAP
YOU'RE SLOUCHING!
WHAP
OPEN YOUR SHOULDERS AND LIFT YOUR CHIN!
YOUR FEET SHOULD BE UNDER YOUR KNEES, NEITHER JUTTING FORWARD NOR PULLED BACK!
WHAP
AND DON'T BALL UP YOUR FISTS... LET YOUR HANDS BE NATURAL!
WHAP
R-R-RIGHT...
EXCUSE ME.
DEPENDING ON THE INTERVIEWER...
...YOU COULD HAVE ALREADY FAILED THE INTERVIEW AT THIS STAGE!
RMMMBB
SHOOF
OOF...
THIS OLD FAMILIAR PRESSURE... IT ALMOST FEELS NOSTALGIC...
I CAN'T LET IT OVERWHELM ME.
RELAX... RELAX...
I...I KNOW!
IF I IMAGINE HER IN HER USUAL TRACKSUIT, I WON'T FEEL SO SCARED!
PAH

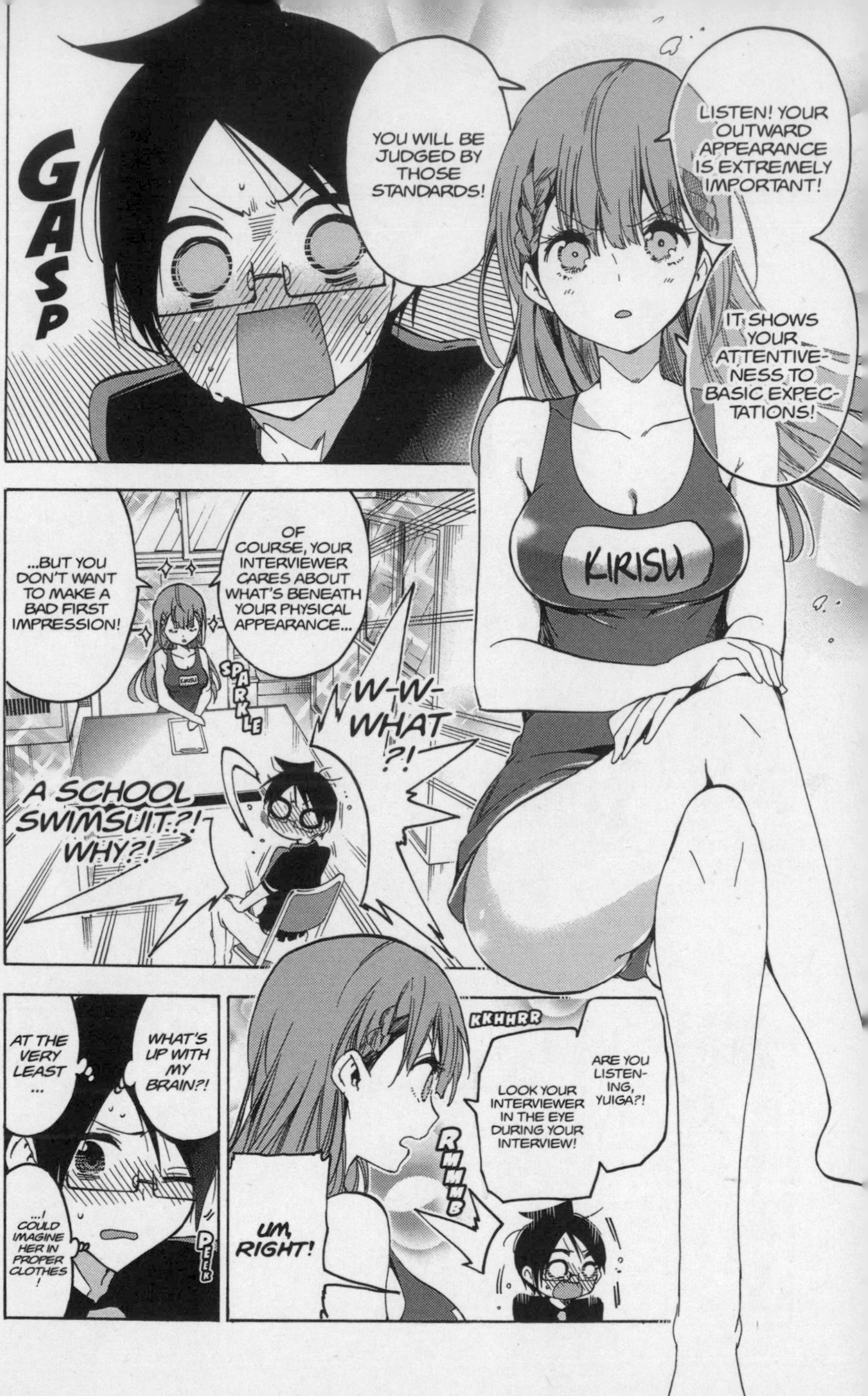
LISTEN! YOUR OUTWARD APPEARANCE IS EXTREMELY IMPORTANT!
IT SHOWS YOUR ATTENTIVENESS TO BASIC EXPECTATIONS!
YOU WILL BE JUDGED BY THOSE STANDARDS!
GASP
KIRISU
OF COURSE, YOUR INTERVIEWER CARES ABOUT WHAT'S BENEATH YOUR PHYSICAL APPEARANCE...
...BUT YOU DON'T WANT TO MAKE A BAD FIRST IMPRESSION!
SPARKLE
W-W-WHAT?!
A SCHOOL SWIMSUIT?! WHY?!
KKHHRR
ARE YOU LISTENING, YUIGA?!
LOOK YOUR INTERVIEWER IN THE EYE DURING YOUR INTERVIEW!
RMMMB
UM, RIGHT!
WHAT'S UP WITH MY BRAIN?!
AT THE VERY LEAST...
...I COULD IMAGINE HER IN PROPER CLOTHES!
PEEK

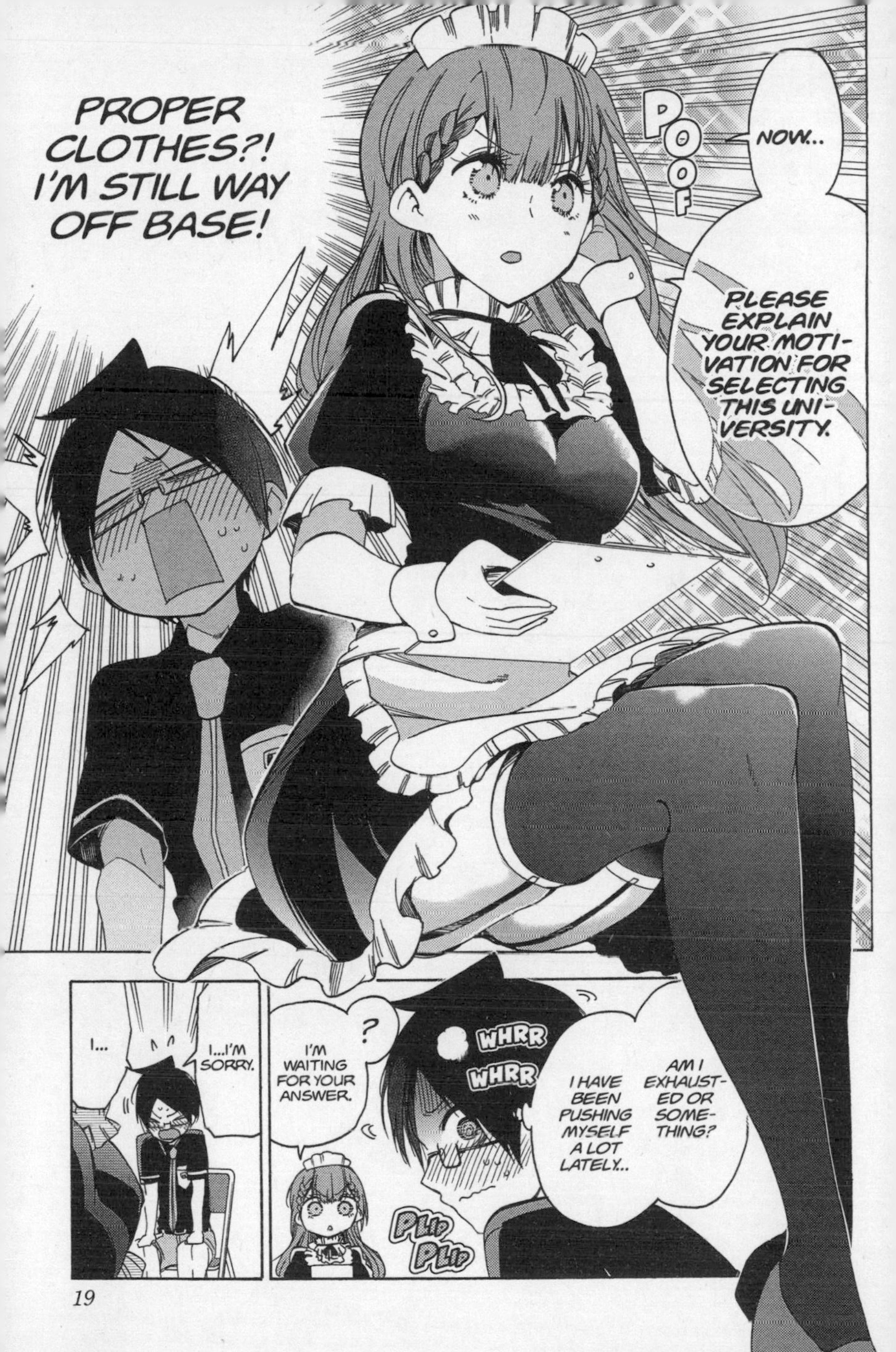
NOW...
PLEASE EXPLAIN YOUR MOTIVATION FOR SELECTING THIS UNIVERSITY.
POOF
PROPER CLOTHES?! I'M STILL WAY OFF BASE!
WHRR
WHRR
AM I EXHAUSTED OR SOMETHING?
I HAVE BEEN PUSHING MYSELF A LOT LATELY...
?
I'M WAITING FOR YOUR ANSWER.
PLIP
PLIP
I...
I...I'M SORRY.

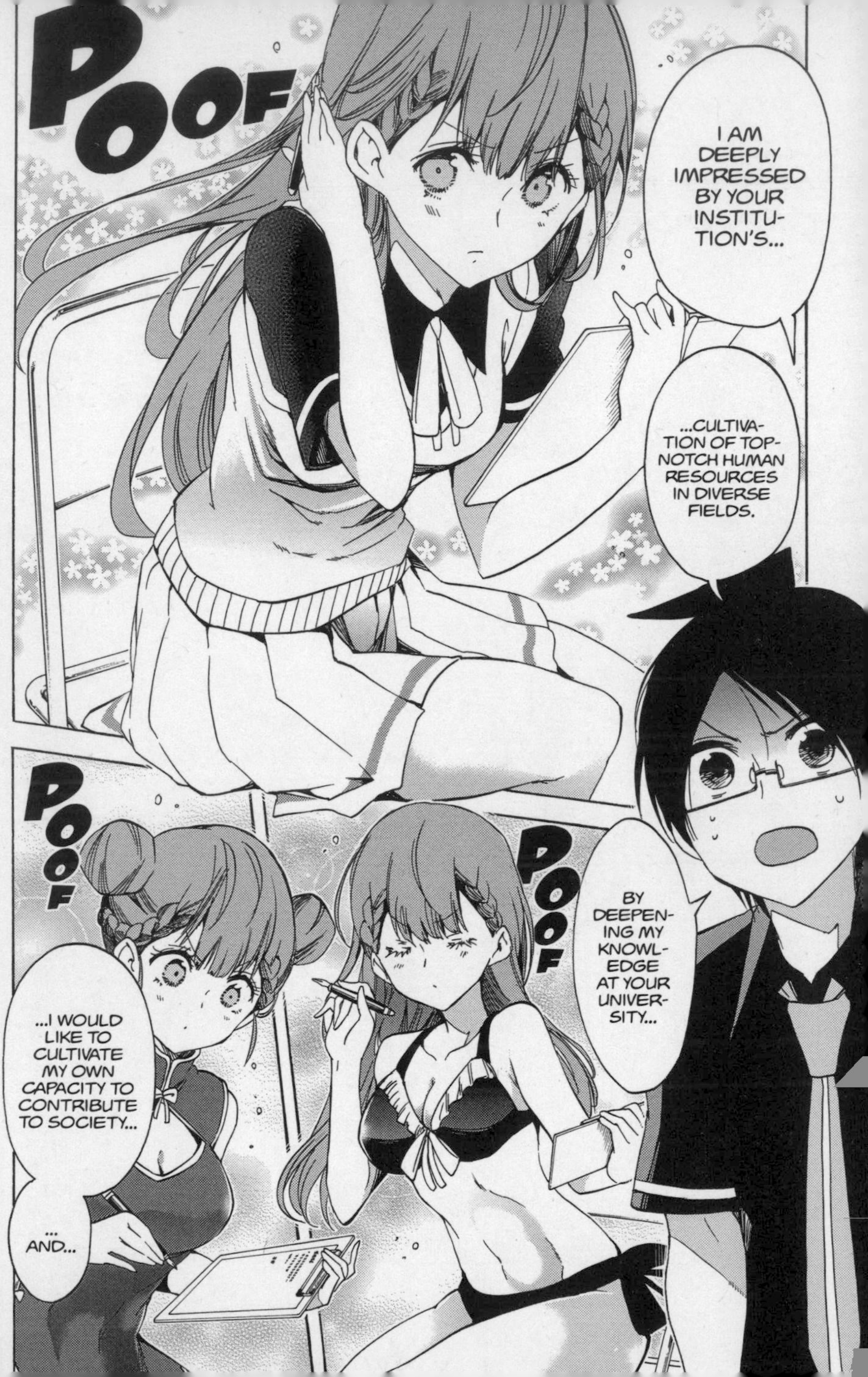
POOF
I AM DEEPLY IMPRESSED BY YOUR INSTITUTION'S...
...CULTIVATION OF TOP-NOTCH HUMAN RESOURCES IN DIVERSE FIELDS.
POOF
BY DEEPENING MY KNOWLEDGE AT YOUR UNIVERSITY...
POOF
...I WOULD LIKE TO CULTIVATE MY OWN CAPACITY TO CONTRIBUTE TO SOCIETY...
... AND...

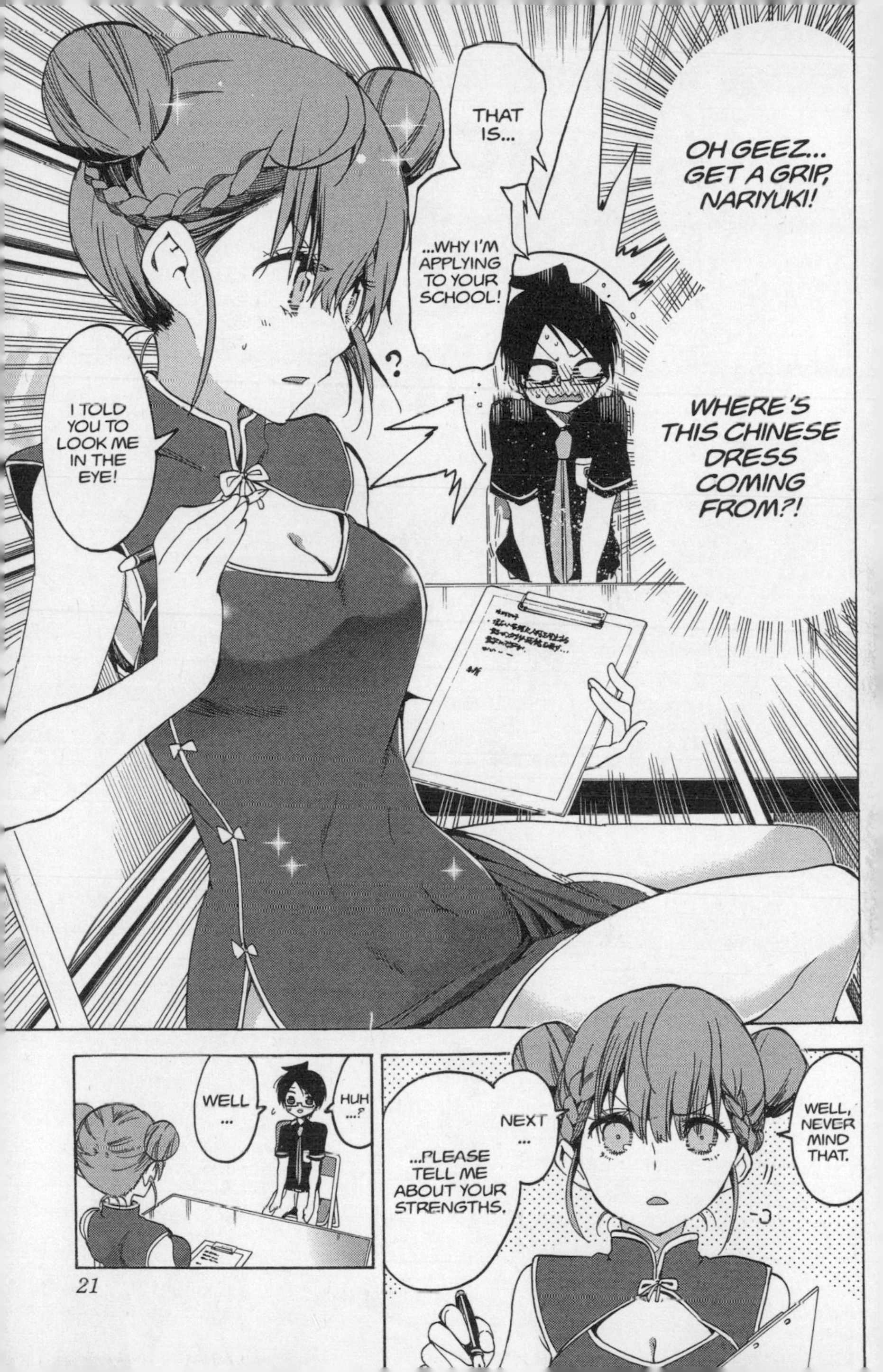
OH GEEZ... GET A GRIP, NARIYUKI!
WHERE'S THIS CHINESE DRESS COMING FROM?!
THAT IS...
...WHY I'M APPLYING TO YOUR SCHOOL!
I TOLD YOU TO LOOK ME IN THE EYE!
WELL, NEVER MIND THAT.
NEXT...
...PLEASE TELL ME ABOUT YOUR STRENGTHS.
HUH...?
WELL...

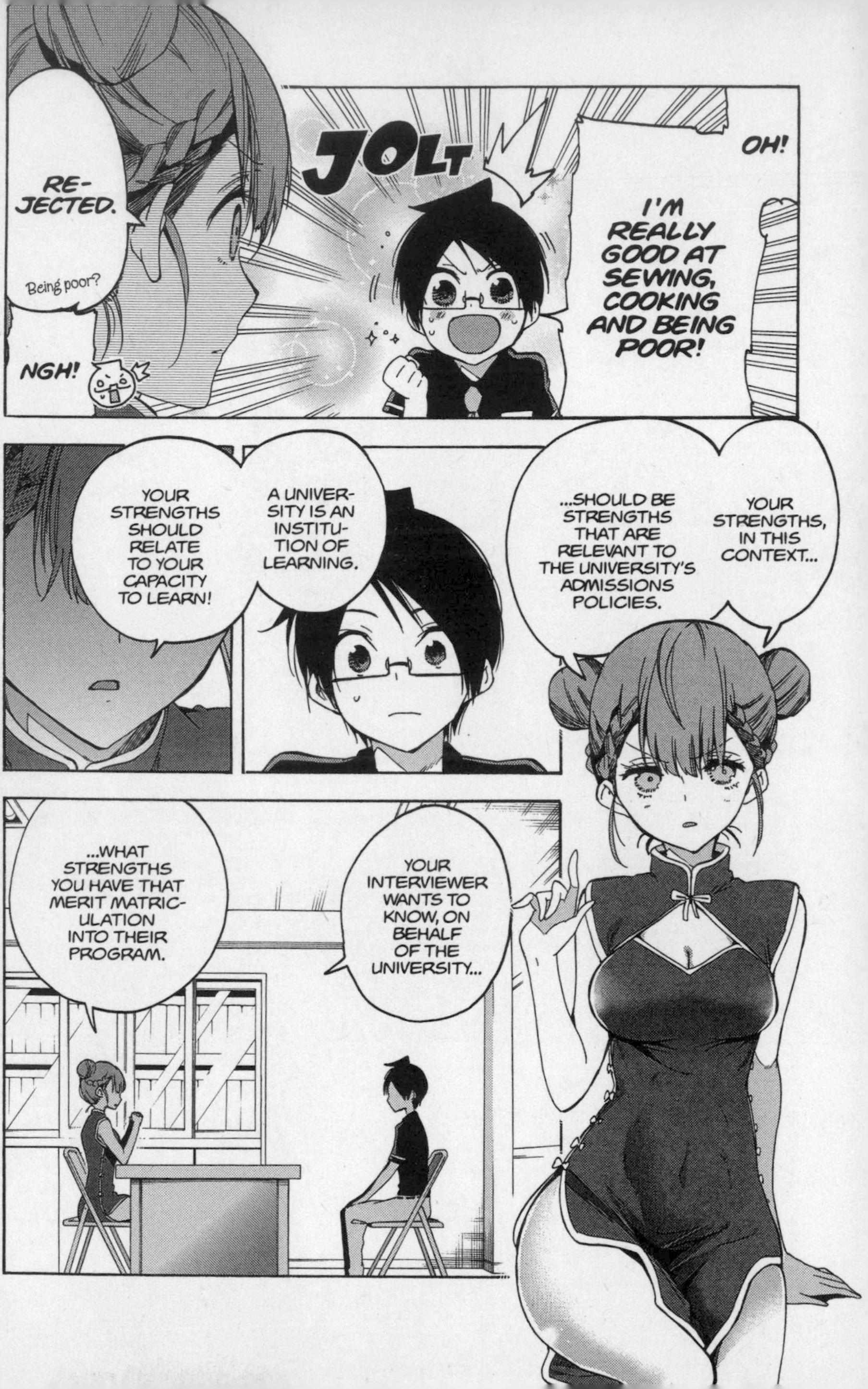
OH!
I'M REALLY GOOD AT SEWING, COOKING AND BEING POOR!
JOLT
RE-JECTED.
Being poor?
NGH!
YOUR STRENGTHS, IN THIS CONTEXT...
...SHOULD BE STRENGTHS THAT ARE RELEVANT TO THE UNIVERSITY'S ADMISSIONS POLICIES.
A UNIVER-SITY IS AN INSTITU-TION OF LEARNING.
YOUR STRENGTHS SHOULD RELATE TO YOUR CAPACITY TO LEARN!
YOUR INTERVIEWER WANTS TO KNOW, ON BEHALF OF THE UNIVERSITY...
...WHAT STRENGTHS YOU HAVE THAT MERIT MATRIC-ULATION INTO THEIR PROGRAM.

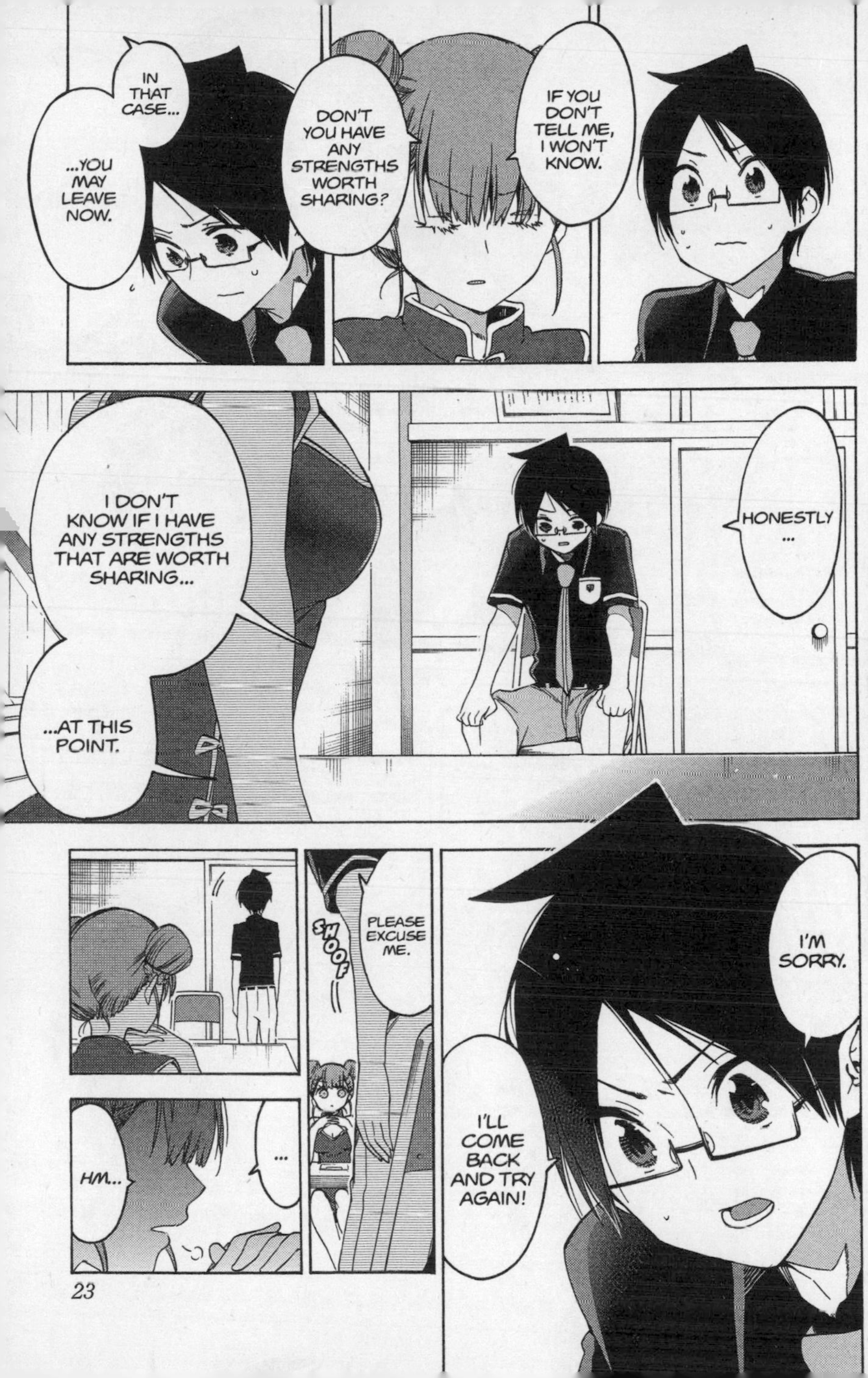

IF YOU DON'T TELL ME, I WON'T KNOW.
DON'T YOU HAVE ANY STRENGTHS WORTH SHARING?
IN THAT CASE...
...YOU MAY LEAVE NOW.
HONESTLY ...
I DON'T KNOW IF I HAVE ANY STRENGTHS THAT ARE WORTH SHARING...
...AT THIS POINT.
I'M SORRY.
I'LL COME BACK AND TRY AGAIN!
PLEASE EXCUSE ME.
SHOOF
...
HM...

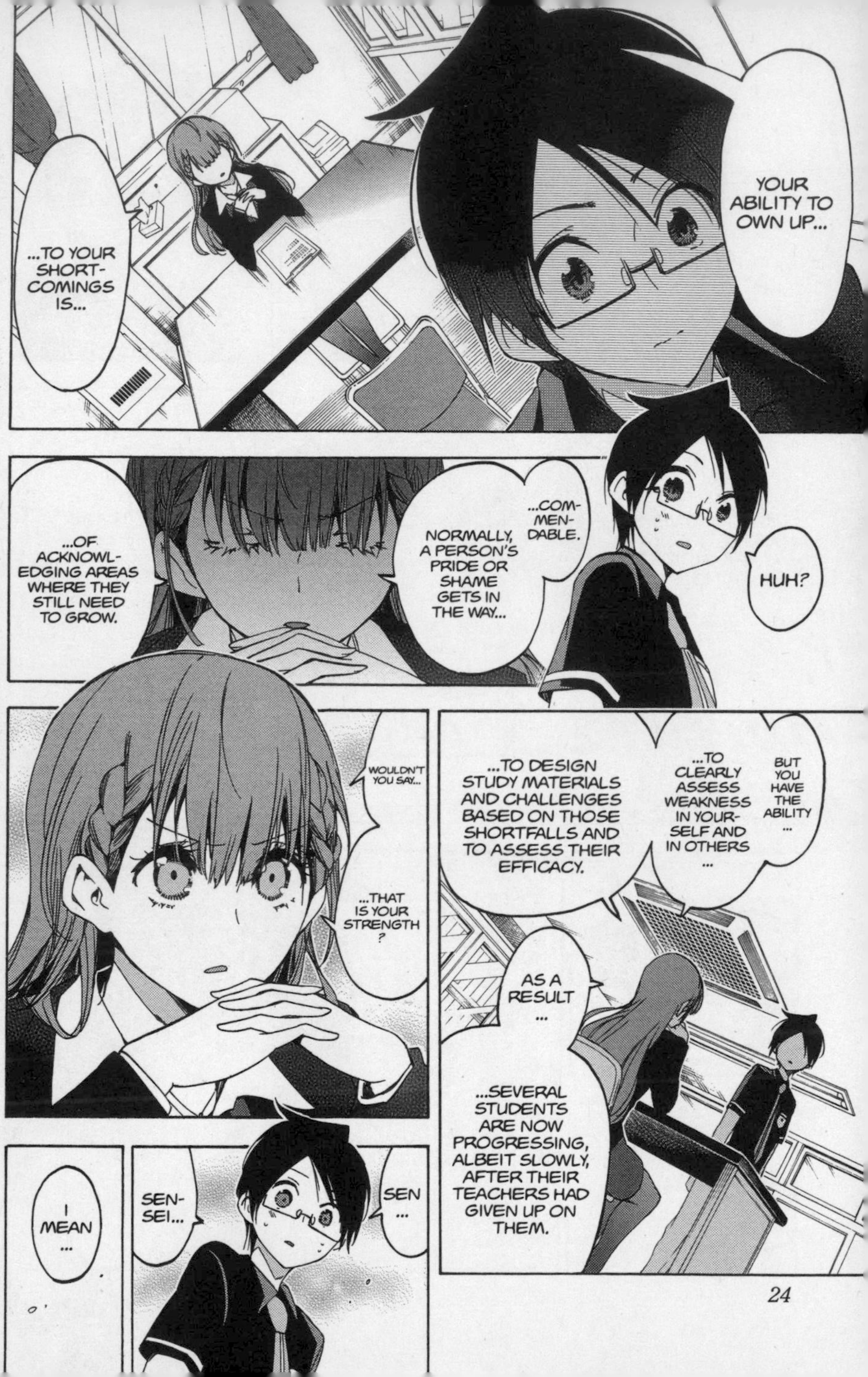
YOUR ABILITY TO OWN UP...
...TO YOUR SHORT-COMINGS IS...
...COM-MEN-DABLE.
HUH?
NORMALLY, A PERSON'S PRIDE OR SHAME GETS IN THE WAY...
...OF ACKNOWL-EDGING AREAS WHERE THEY STILL NEED TO GROW.
BUT YOU HAVE THE ABILITY...
...TO CLEARLY ASSESS WEAKNESS IN YOUR-SELF AND IN OTHERS...
...TO DESIGN STUDY MATERIALS AND CHALLENGES BASED ON THOSE SHORTFALLS AND TO ASSESS THEIR EFFICACY.
AS A RESULT...
...SEVERAL STUDENTS ARE NOW PROGRESSING, ALBEIT SLOWLY, AFTER THEIR TEACHERS HAD GIVEN UP ON THEM.
WOULDN'T YOU SAY...
...THAT IS YOUR STRENGTH?
SEN...
SEN-SEI...
I MEAN...

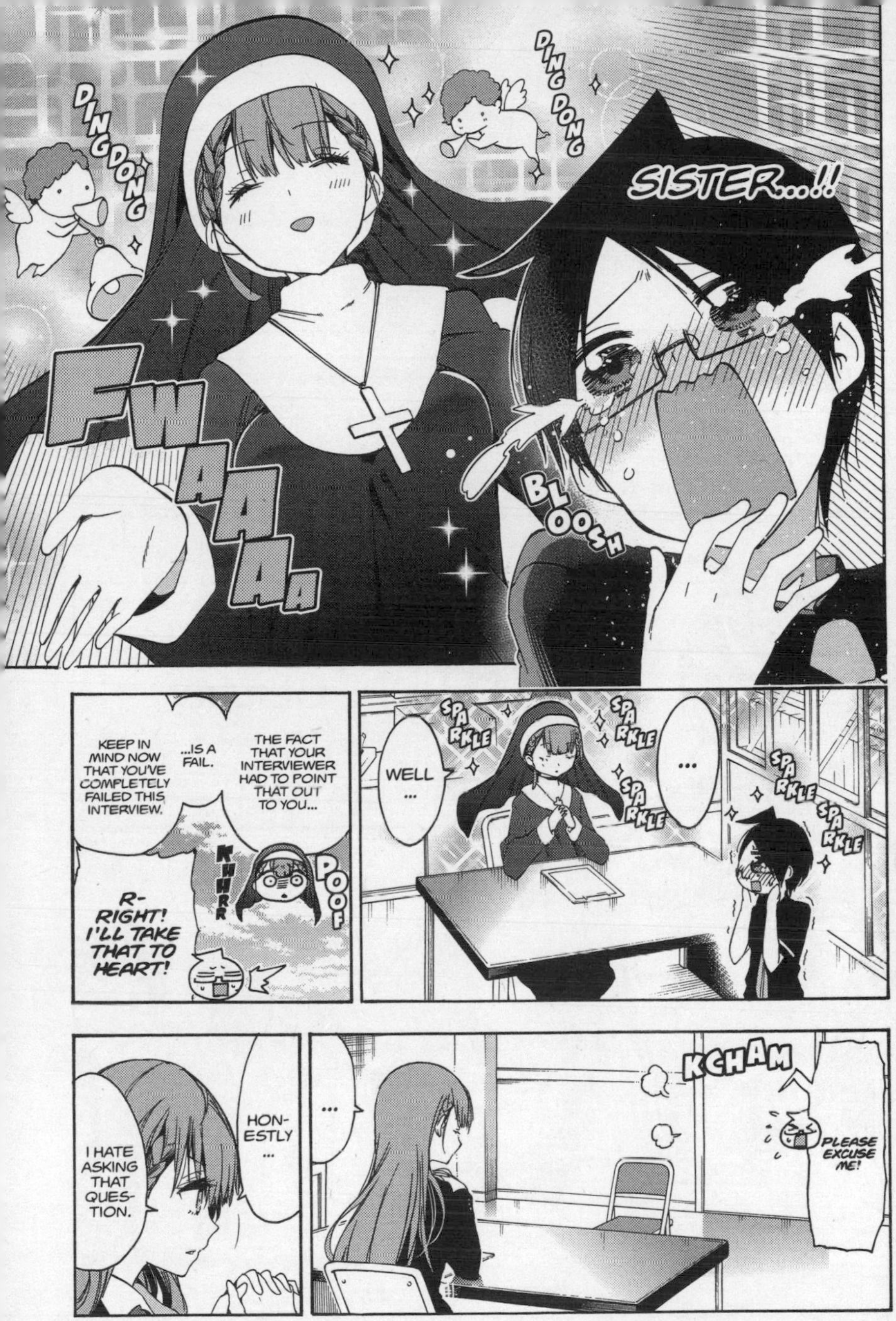
DING DONG
SISTER...!!
DING DONG
FWAAAAA
BLOOSH
SPARKLE
SPARKLE
SPARKLE
SPARKLE
SPARKLE
...
WELL ...
THE FACT THAT YOUR INTERVIEWER HAD TO POINT THAT OUT TO YOU...
...IS A FAIL.
KEEP IN MIND NOW THAT YOU'VE COMPLETELY FAILED THIS INTERVIEW.
POOF
KHHRR
R-RIGHT! I'LL TAKE THAT TO HEART!
KCHAM
PLEASE EXCUSE ME!
HON-ESTLY ...
...
I HATE ASKING THAT QUES-TION.

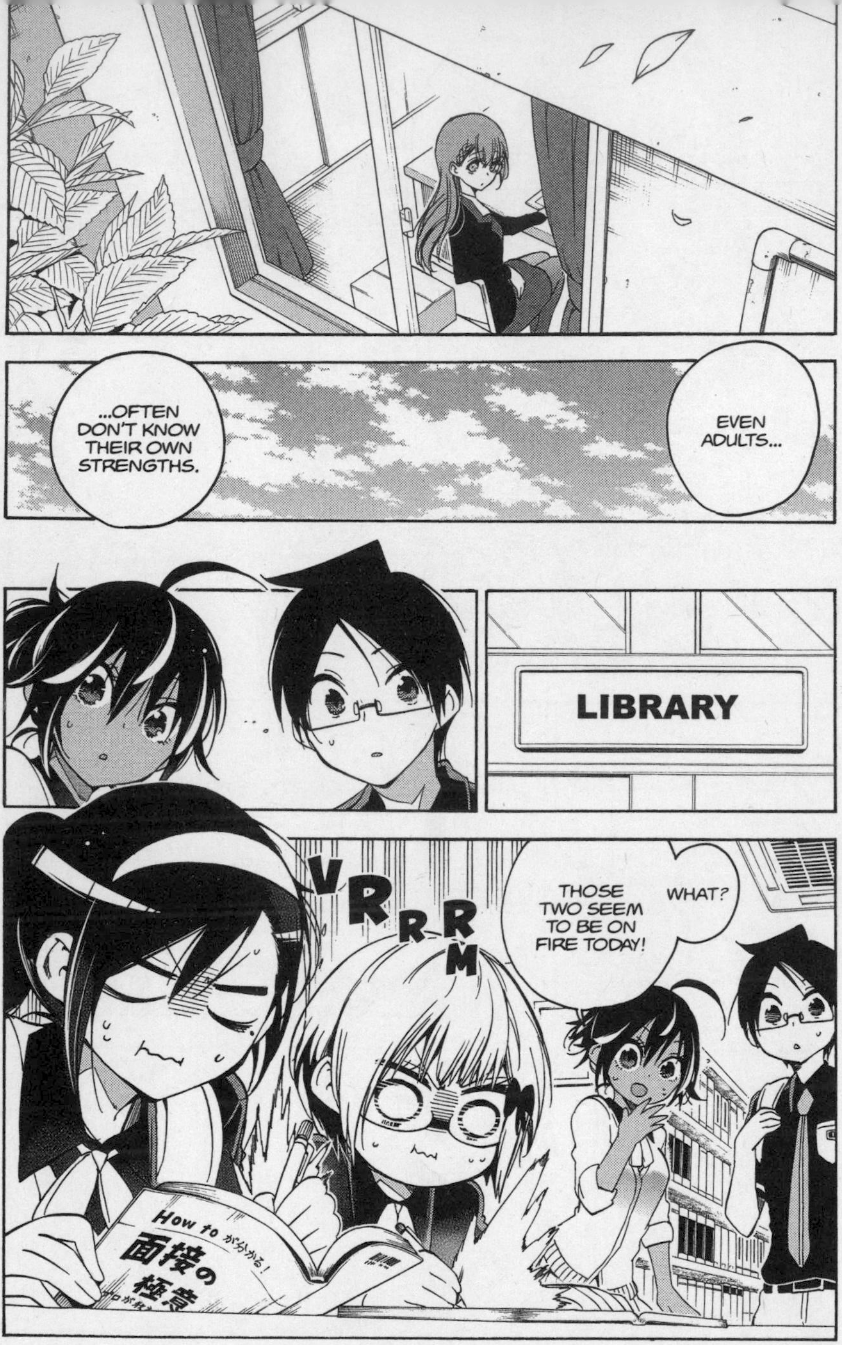
EVEN ADULTS...
...OFTEN DON'T KNOW THEIR OWN STRENGTHS.
LIBRARY
...
WHAT?
THOSE TWO SEEM TO BE ON FIRE TODAY!
VRRRM
How to
面接の極意

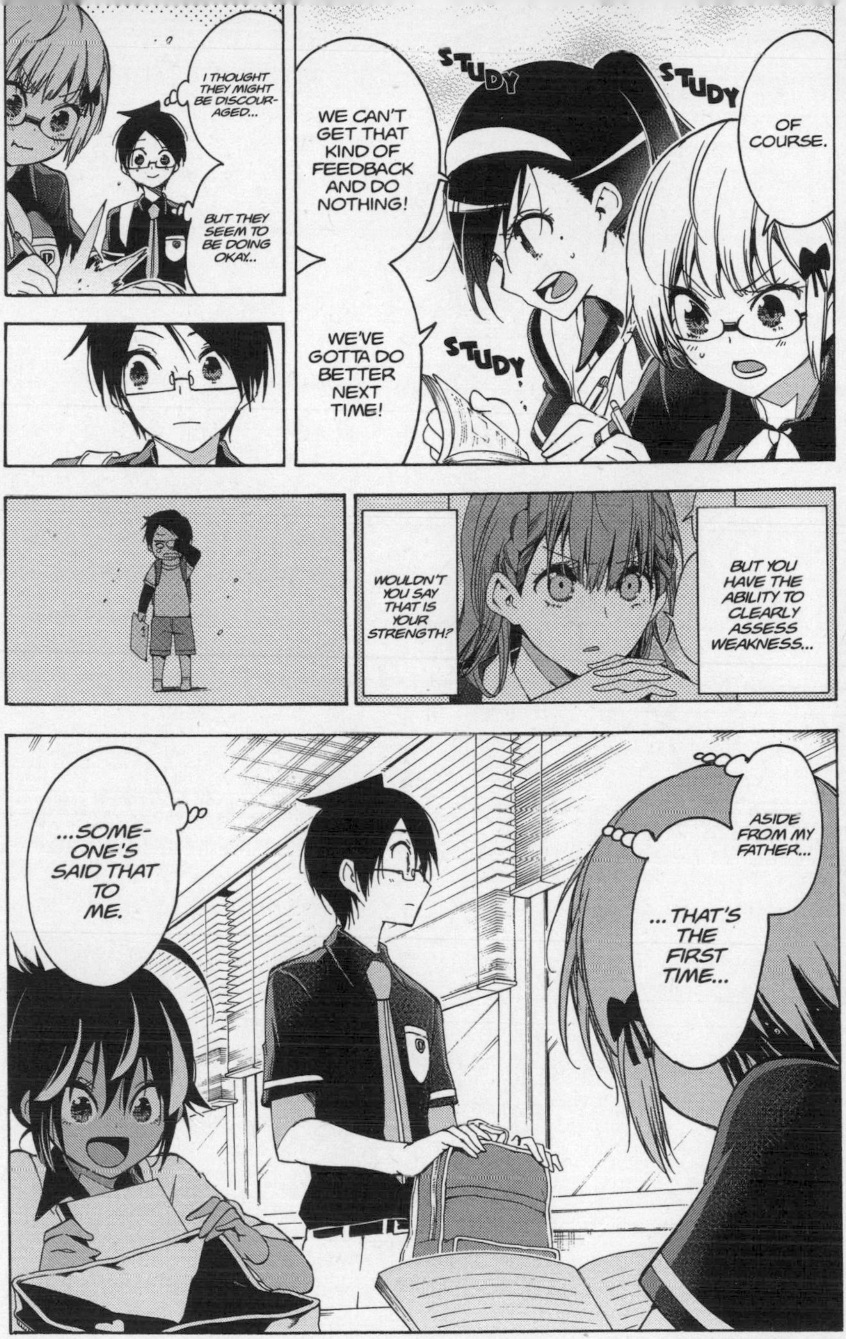
STUDY
STUDY
OF COURSE.
WE CAN'T GET THAT KIND OF FEEDBACK AND DO NOTHING!
STUDY
WE'VE GOTTA DO BETTER NEXT TIME!
I THOUGHT THEY MIGHT BE DISCOUR-AGED...
BUT THEY SEEM TO BE DOING OKAY...
BUT YOU HAVE THE ABILITY TO CLEARLY ASSESS WEAKNESS...
WOULDN'T YOU SAY THAT IS YOUR STRENGTH?
ASIDE FROM MY FATHER...
...THAT'S THE FIRST TIME...
...SOME-ONE'S SAID THAT TO ME.

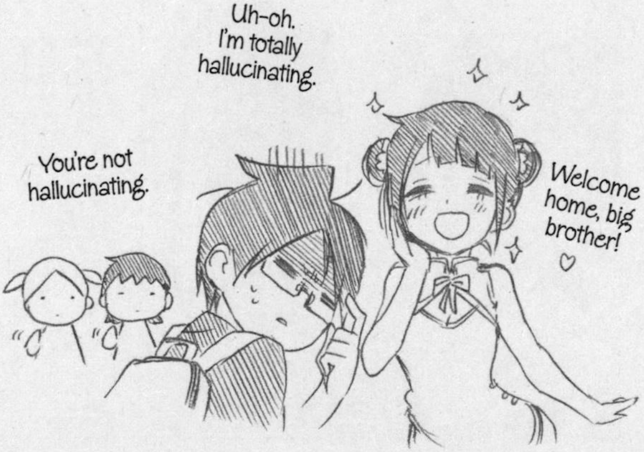
Welcome home, big brother! ♡
Uh-oh. I'm totally hallucinating.
You're not hallucinating.

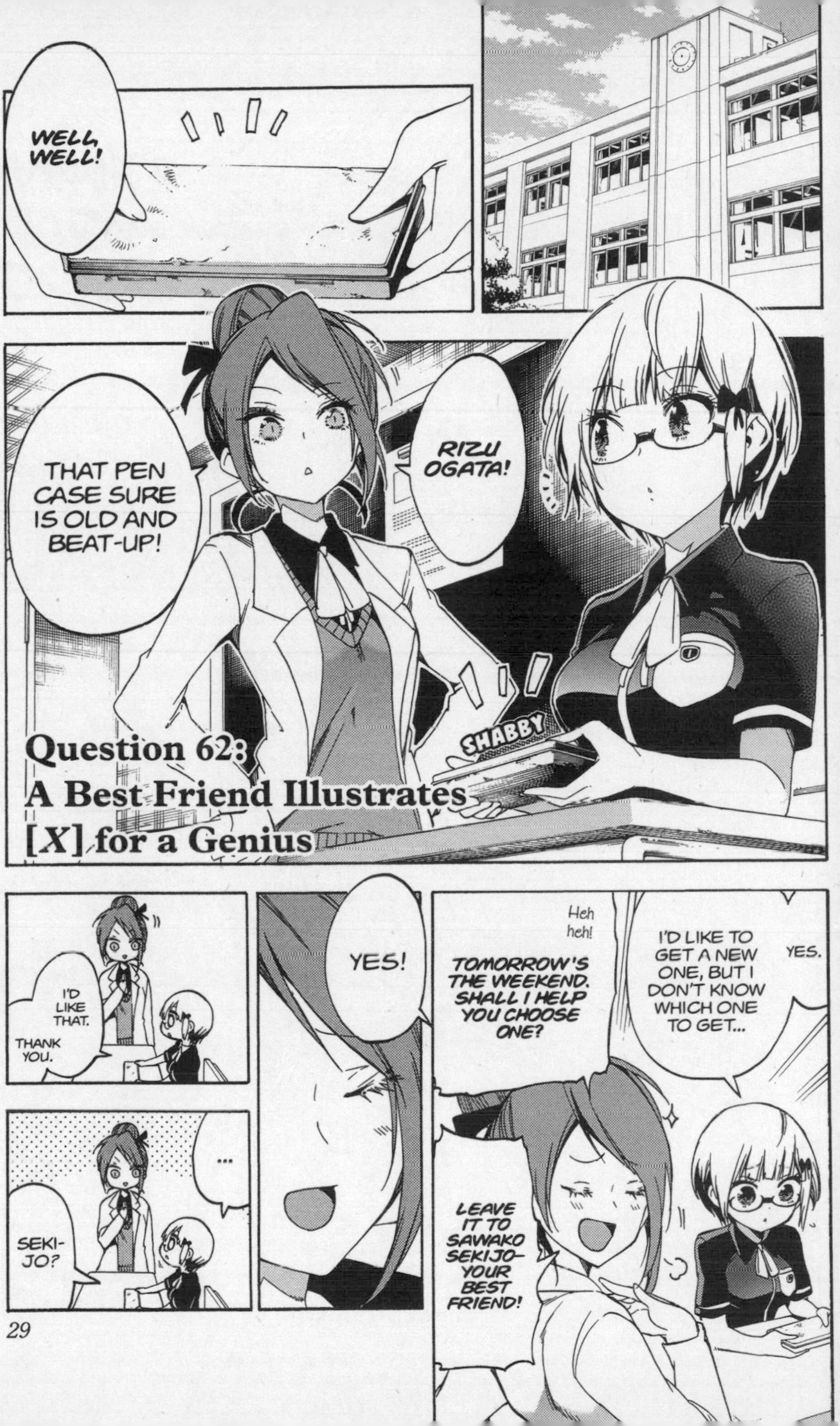
WELL, WELL!
RIZU OGATA!
THAT PEN CASE SURE IS OLD AND BEAT-UP!
SHABBY
Question 62: A Best Friend Illustrates [X] for a Genius
YES.
I'D LIKE TO GET A NEW ONE, BUT I DON'T KNOW WHICH ONE TO GET...
Heh heh!
TOMORROW'S THE WEEKEND. SHALL I HELP YOU CHOOSE ONE?
LEAVE IT TO SAWAKO SEKIJO—YOUR BEST FRIEND!
YES!
I'D LIKE THAT.
THANK YOU.
...
SEKI-JO?

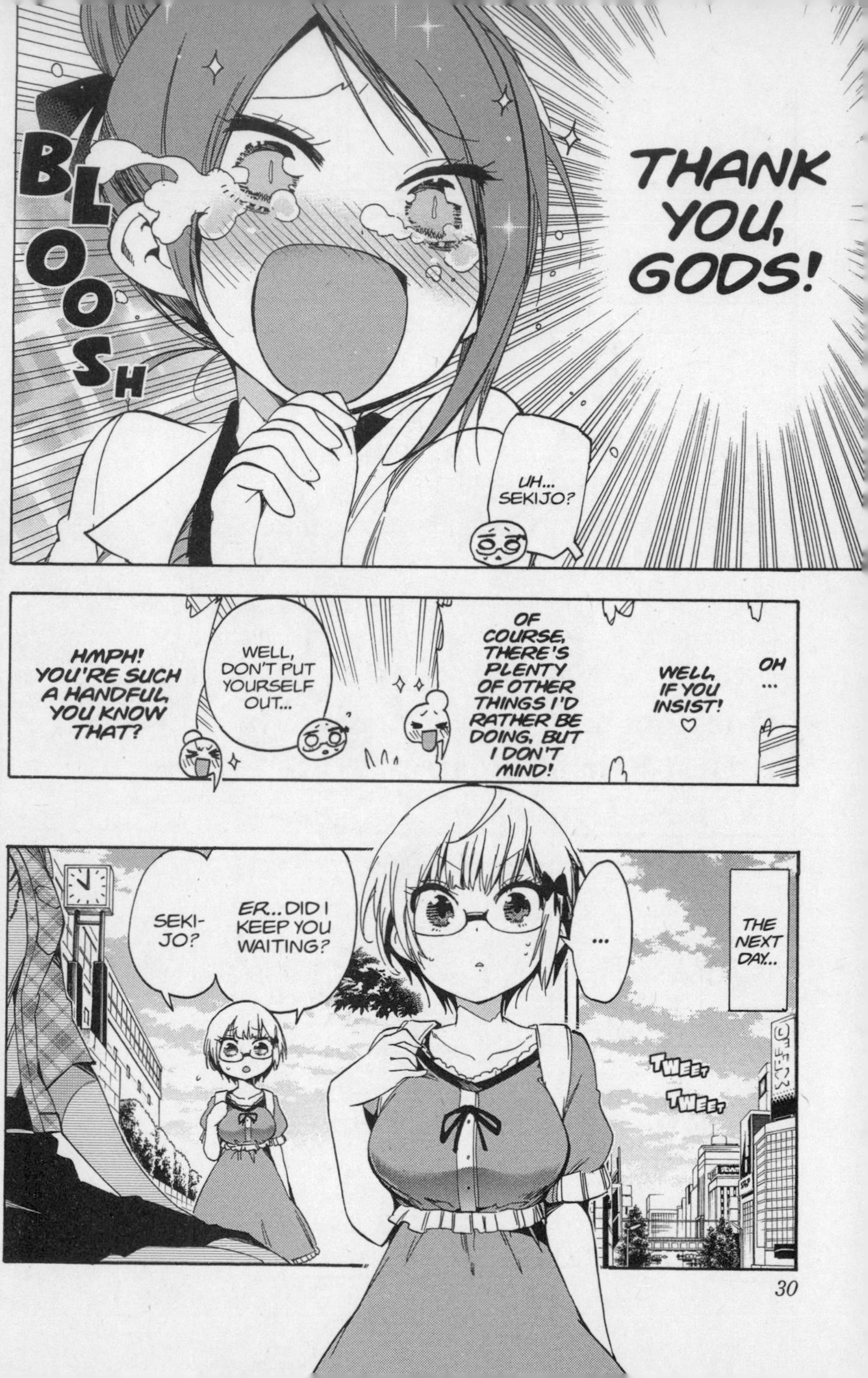
THANK YOU, GODS!
BLOOSH
UH... SEKIJO?
OH...
WELL, IF YOU INSIST! ♡
OF COURSE, THERE'S PLENTY OF OTHER THINGS I'D RATHER BE DOING, BUT I DON'T MIND!
WELL, DON'T PUT YOURSELF OUT...
HMPH! YOU'RE SUCH A HANDFUL, YOU KNOW THAT?
THE NEXT DAY...
TWEET
TWEET
...
ER...DID I KEEP YOU WAITING?
SEKI-JO?

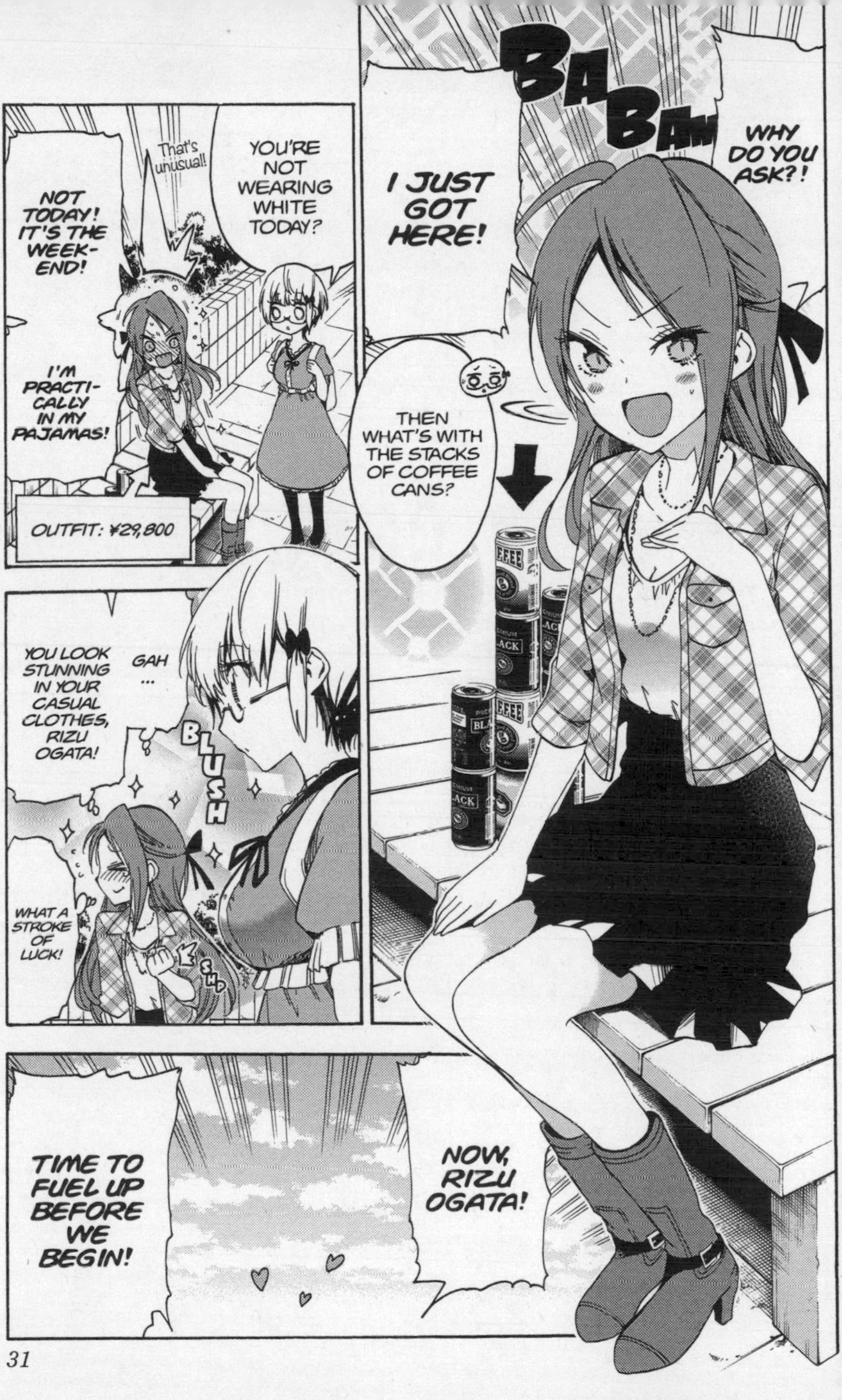
BA BAM
WHY DO YOU ASK?!
I JUST GOT HERE!
THEN WHAT'S WITH THE STACKS OF COFFEE CANS?
YOU'RE NOT WEARING WHITE TODAY?
That's unusual!
NOT TODAY! IT'S THE WEEK-END!
I'M PRACTI-CALLY IN MY PAJAMAS!
OUTFIT: ¥29,800
GAH ...
YOU LOOK STUNNING IN YOUR CASUAL CLOTHES, RIZU OGATA!
BLUSH
WHAT A STROKE OF LUCK!
SHP
NOW, RIZU OGATA!
TIME TO FUEL UP BEFORE WE BEGIN!

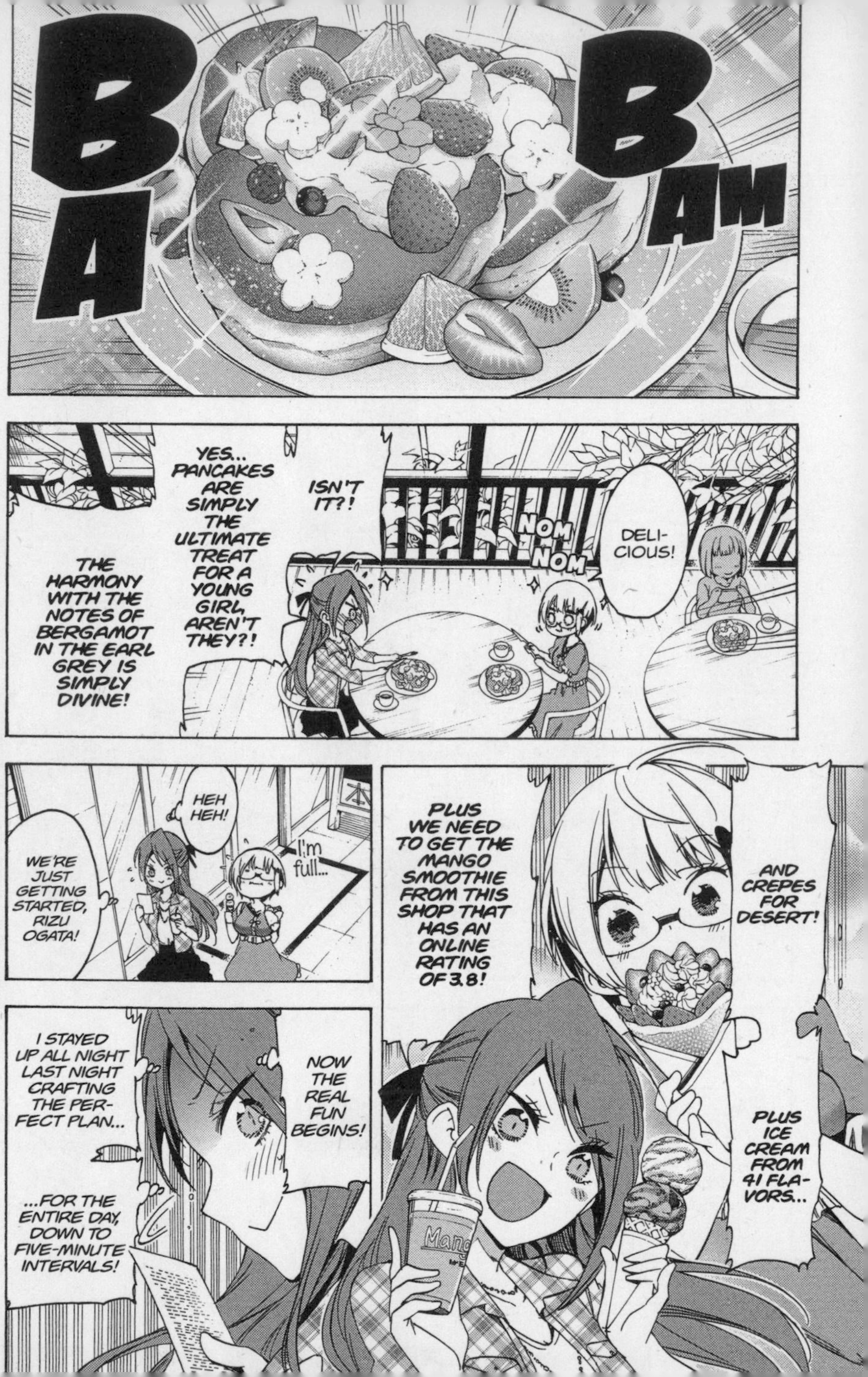
BAM
BA
DELICIOUS!
NOM NOM
ISN'T IT?!
YES... PANCAKES ARE SIMPLY THE ULTIMATE TREAT FOR A YOUNG GIRL, AREN'T THEY?!
THE HARMONY WITH THE NOTES OF BERGAMOT IN THE EARL GREY IS SIMPLY DIVINE!
AND CREPES FOR DESERT!
PLUS WE NEED TO GET THE MANGO SMOOTHIE FROM THIS SHOP THAT HAS AN ONLINE RATING OF 3.8!
HEH HEH!
I'm full...
WE'RE JUST GETTING STARTED, RIZU OGATA!
PLUS ICE CREAM FROM 41 FLAVORS...
NOW THE REAL FUN BEGINS!
I STAYED UP ALL NIGHT LAST NIGHT CRAFTING THE PERFECT PLAN...
...FOR THE ENTIRE DAY, DOWN TO FIVE-MINUTE INTERVALS!

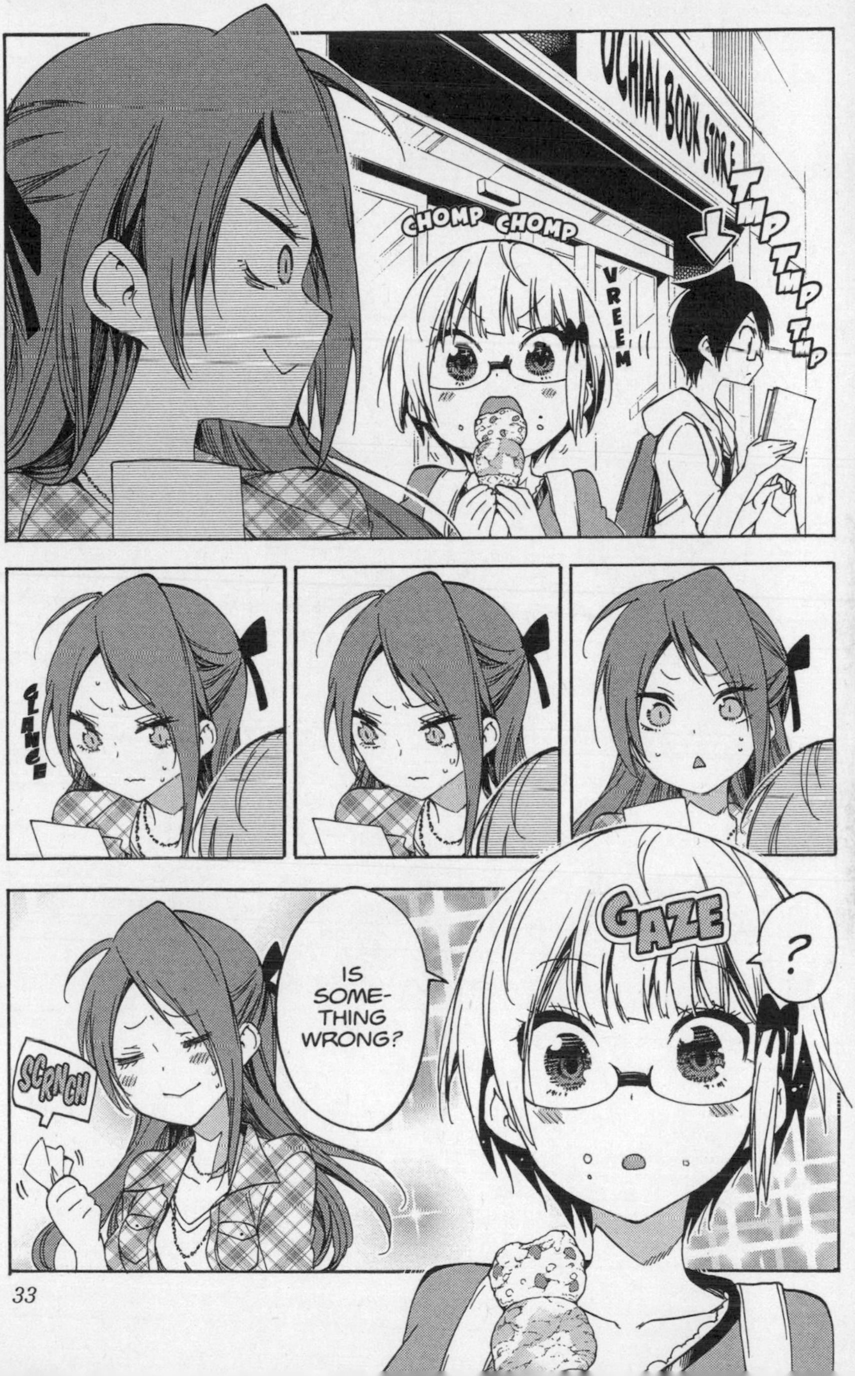
UCHIAI BOOK STORE
TMP TMP TMP TMP
VREEM
CHOMP CHOMP
GLANCE
GAZE
?
IS SOMETHING WRONG?
SCRNCH

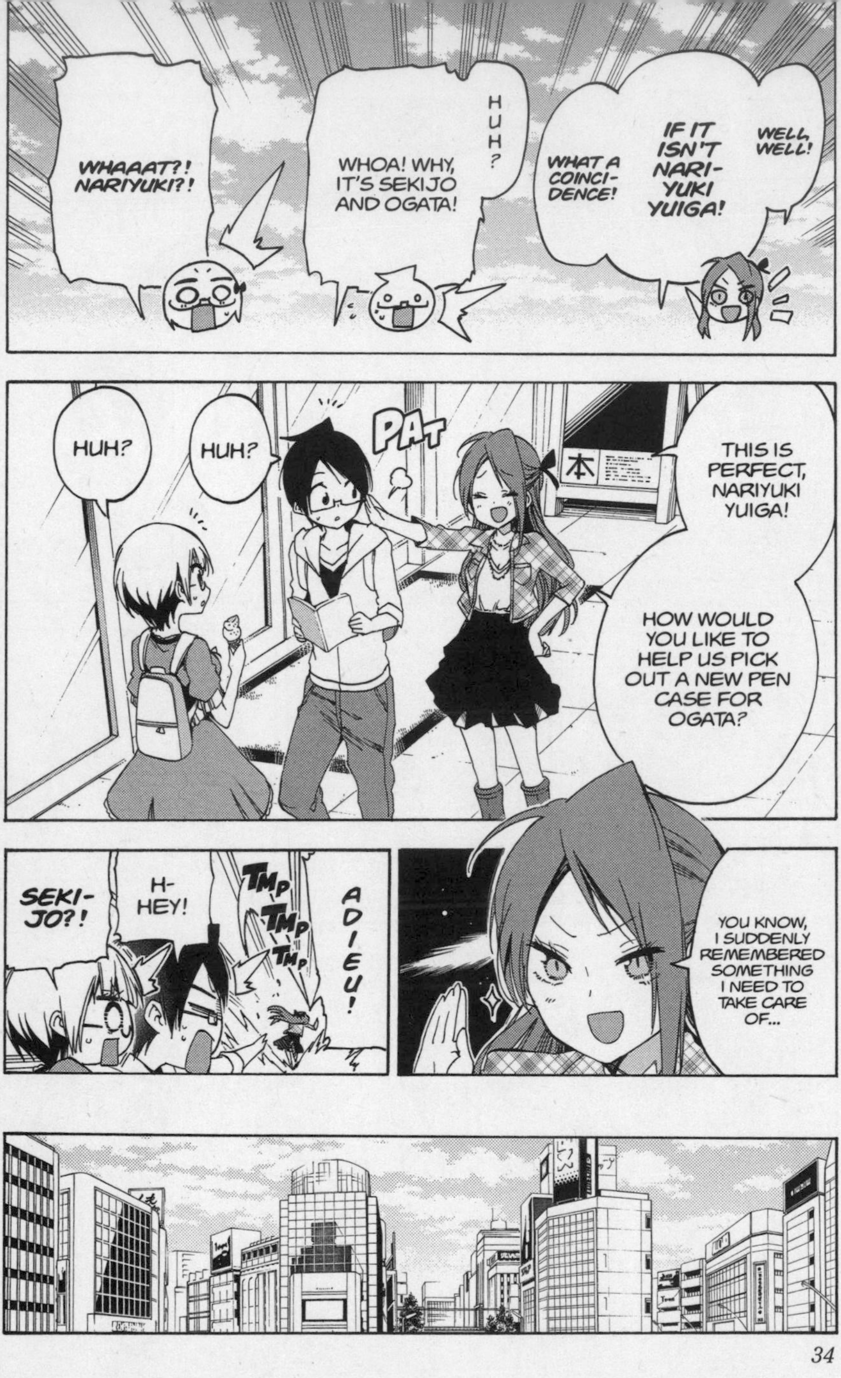
WELL, WELL!
IF IT ISN'T NARI-YUKI YUIGA!
WHAT A COINCI-DENCE!
HUH?
WHOA! WHY, IT'S SEKIJO AND OGATA!
WHAAAT?! NARIYUKI?!
THIS IS PERFECT, NARIYUKI YUIGA!
HOW WOULD YOU LIKE TO HELP US PICK OUT A NEW PEN CASE FOR OGATA?
PAT
HUH?
HUH?
YOU KNOW, I SUDDENLY REMEMBERED SOMETHING I NEED TO TAKE CARE OF...
ADIEU!
TMP TMP TMP
H-HEY!
SEKI-JO?!

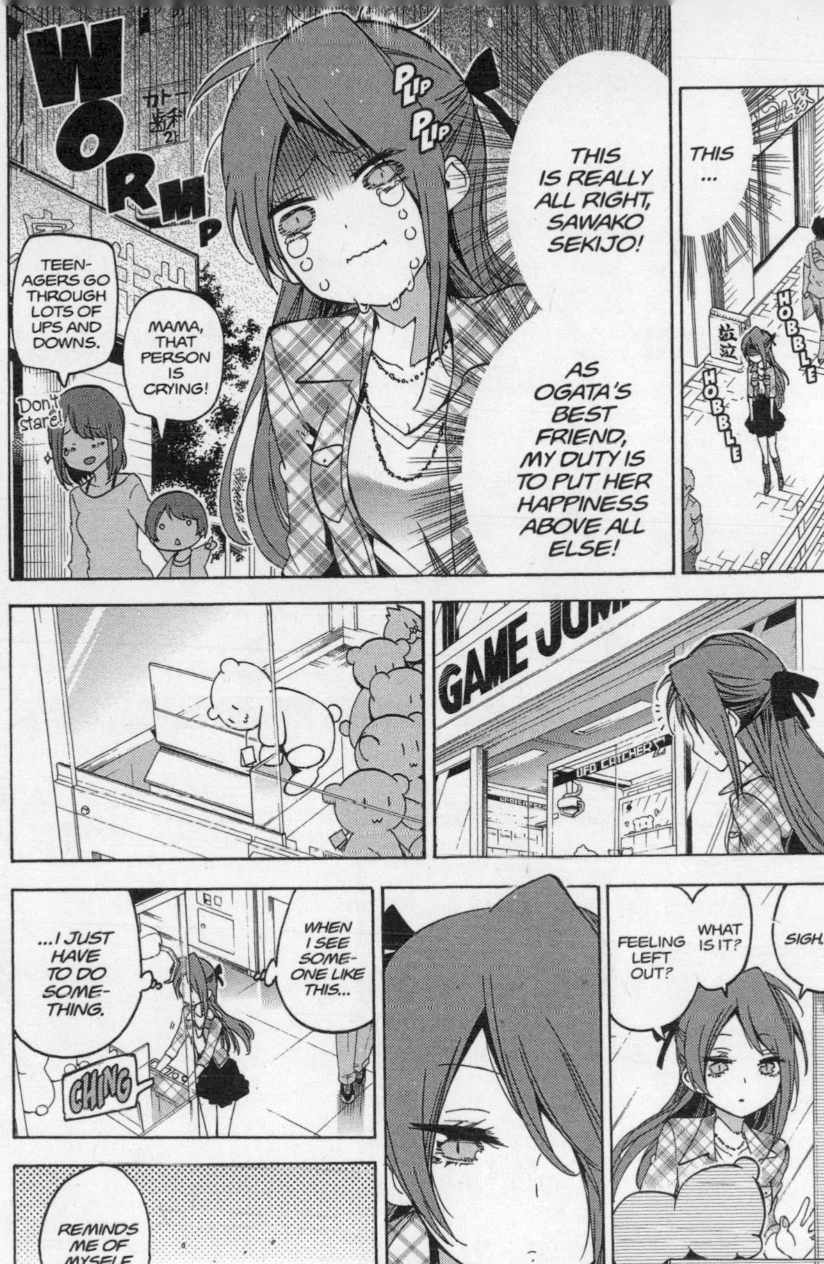
THIS ...
HOBBLE
HOBBLE
THIS IS REALLY ALL RIGHT, SAWAKO SEKIJO!
AS OGATA'S BEST FRIEND, MY DUTY IS TO PUT HER HAPPINESS ABOVE ALL ELSE!
PLIP
PLIP
WORMP
MAMA, THAT PERSON IS CRYING!
TEEN-AGERS GO THROUGH LOTS OF UPS AND DOWNS.
Don't stare!
GAME JUM
UFO CATCHER
SIGH...
WHAT IS IT?
FEELING LEFT OUT?
WHEN I SEE SOME-ONE LIKE THIS...
...I JUST HAVE TO DO SOME-THING.
CHING
REMINDS ME OF MYSELF.

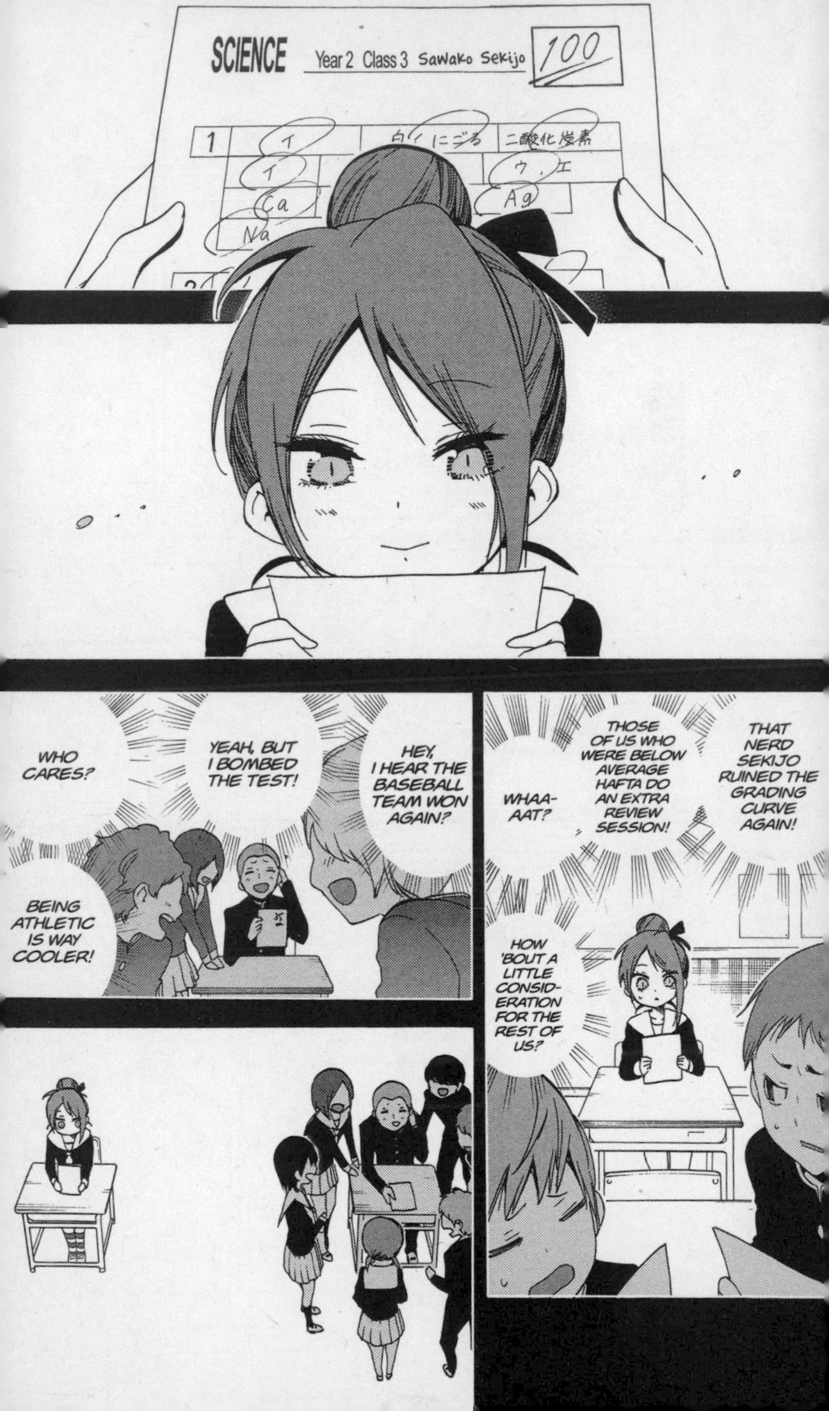
SCIENCE
Year 2 Class 3 Sawako Sekijo
100
1
イ
白くにごる
二酸化炭素
イ
ウ,エ
Ca
Ag
Na
THAT NERD SEKIJO RUINED THE GRADING CURVE AGAIN!
THOSE OF US WHO WERE BELOW AVERAGE HAFTA DO AN EXTRA REVIEW SESSION!
WHAA-AAT?
HOW 'BOUT A LITTLE CONSID-ERATION FOR THE REST OF US?
HEY, I HEAR THE BASEBALL TEAM WON AGAIN?
YEAH, BUT I BOMBED THE TEST!
WHO CARES?
BEING ATHLETIC IS WAY COOLER!

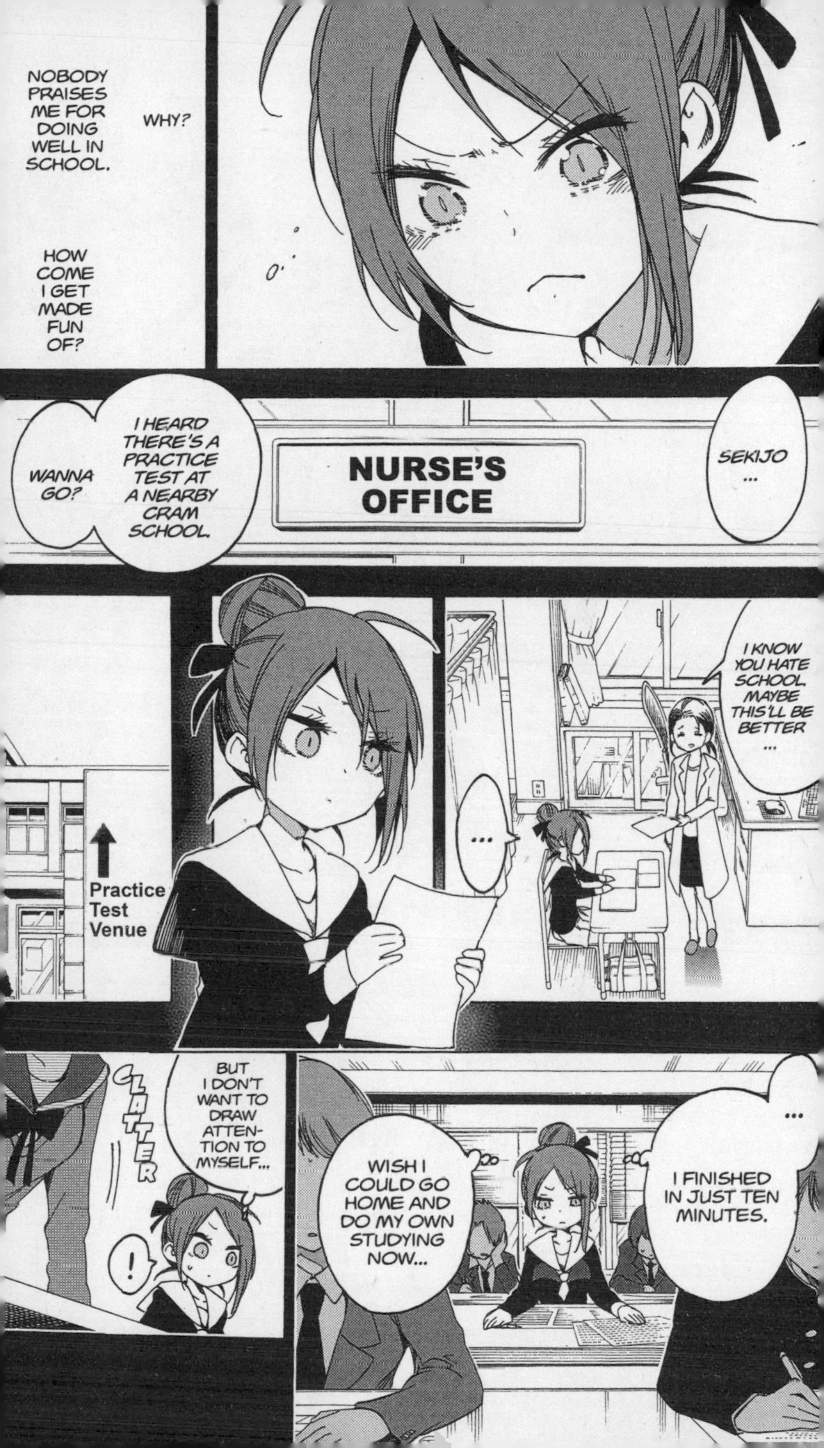
WHY?
NOBODY PRAISES ME FOR DOING WELL IN SCHOOL.
HOW COME I GET MADE FUN OF?
SEKIJO...
NURSE'S OFFICE
I HEARD THERE'S A PRACTICE TEST AT A NEARBY CRAM SCHOOL.
WANNA GO?
I KNOW YOU HATE SCHOOL. MAYBE THIS'LL BE BETTER...
...
Practice Test Venue
...
I FINISHED IN JUST TEN MINUTES.
WISH I COULD GO HOME AND DO MY OWN STUDYING NOW...
BUT I DON'T WANT TO DRAW ATTENTION TO MYSELF...
CLATTER
!

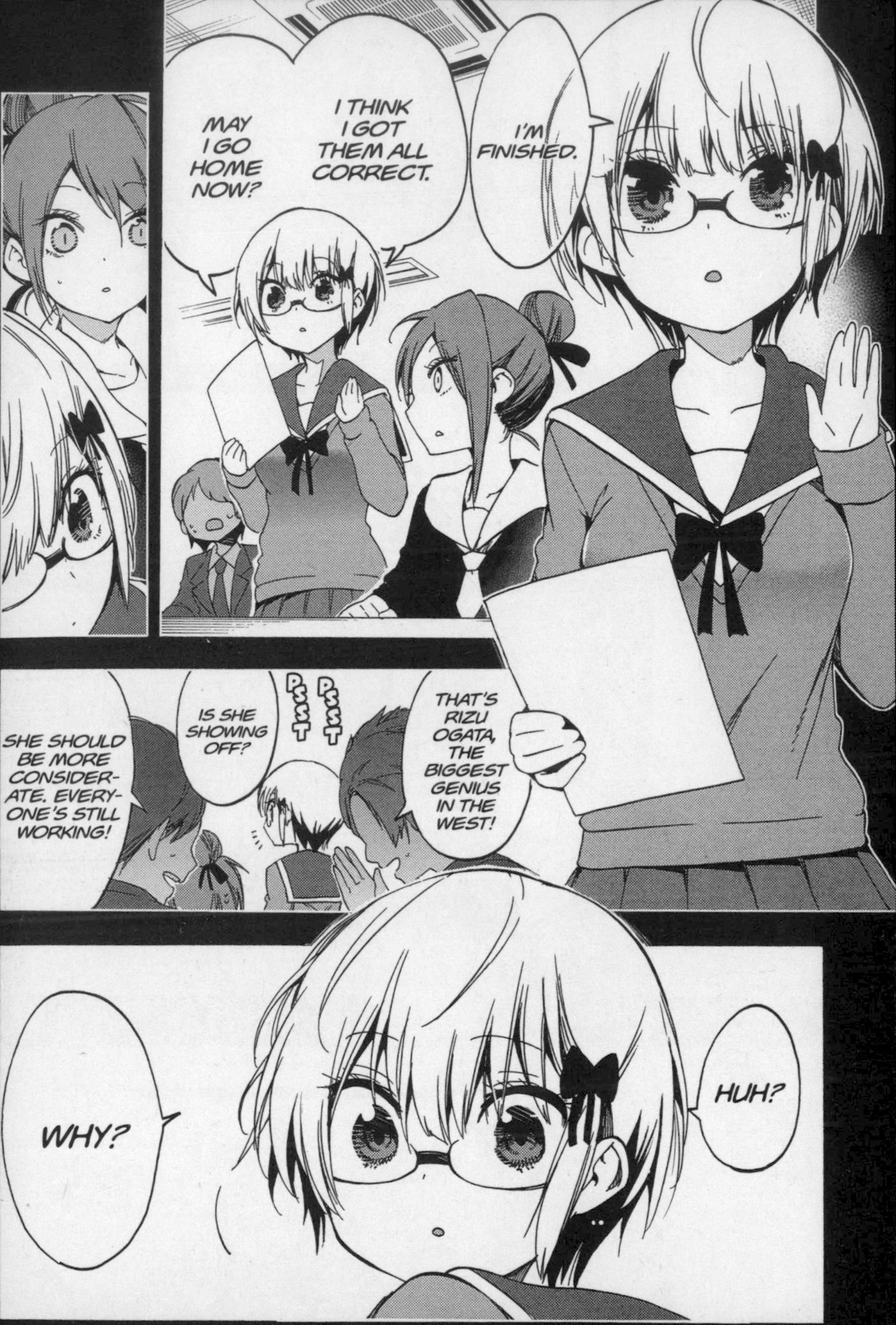
I'M FINISHED.
I THINK I GOT THEM ALL CORRECT.
MAY I GO HOME NOW?
THAT'S RIZU OGATA, THE BIGGEST GENIUS IN THE WEST!
PSST PSST
IS SHE SHOWING OFF?
SHE SHOULD BE MORE CONSIDER-ATE. EVERY-ONE'S STILL WORKING!
HUH?
WHY?

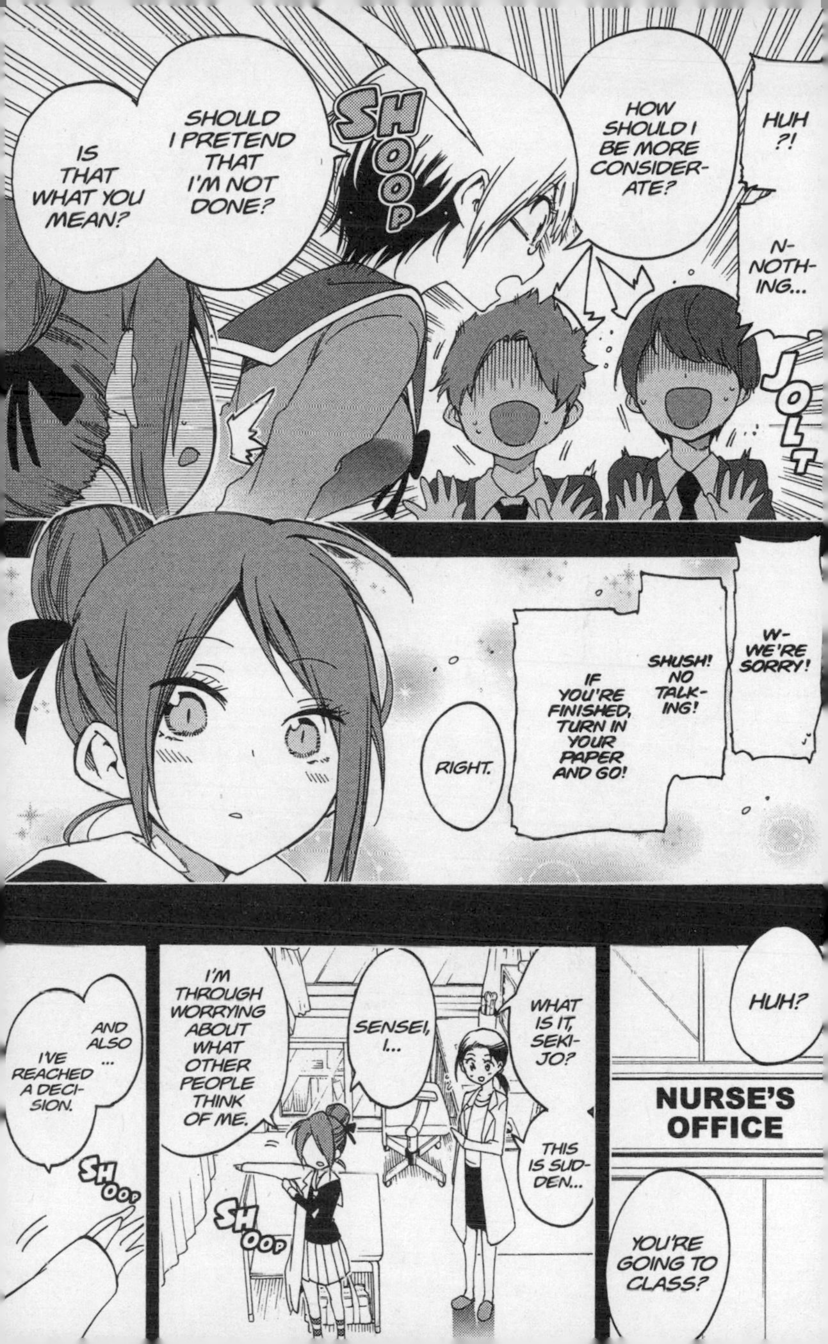
HUH?!
HOW SHOULD I BE MORE CONSIDERATE?
SHOOP
SHOULD I PRETEND THAT I'M NOT DONE?
IS THAT WHAT YOU MEAN?
N-NOTHING...
JOLT
W-WE'RE SORRY!
SHUSH! NO TALKING!
IF YOU'RE FINISHED, TURN IN YOUR PAPER AND GO!
RIGHT.
HUH?
NURSE'S OFFICE
YOU'RE GOING TO CLASS?
WHAT IS IT, SEKIJO?
SENSEI, I...
THIS IS SUDDEN...
I'M THROUGH WORRYING ABOUT WHAT OTHER PEOPLE THINK OF ME.
SHOOP
AND ALSO ...
I'VE REACHED A DECISION.
SHOOP

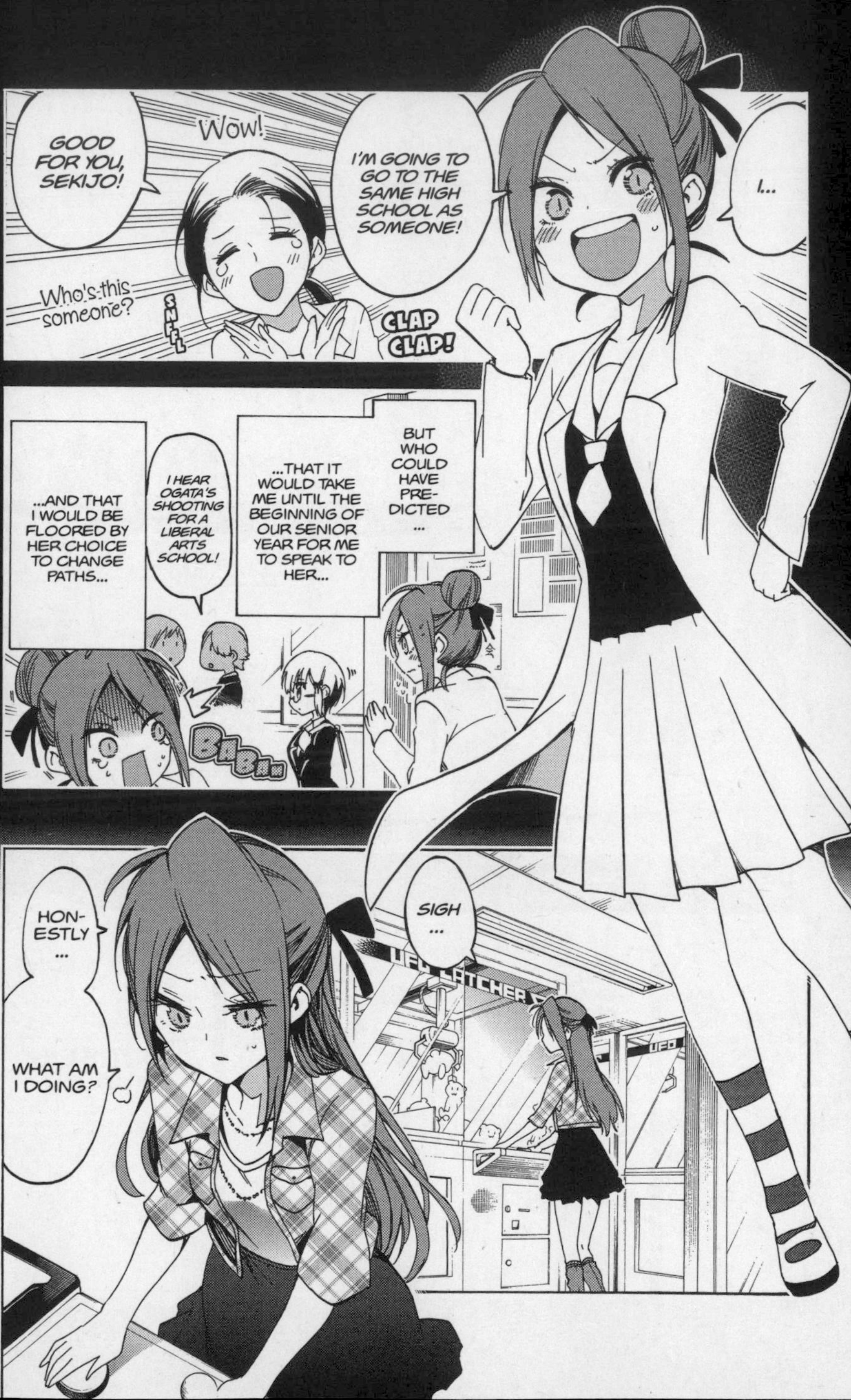
I...
I'M GOING TO GO TO THE SAME HIGH SCHOOL AS SOMEONE!
CLAP CLAP!
Wow!
GOOD FOR YOU, SEKIJO!
SNFFL
Who's this someone?
BUT WHO COULD HAVE PREDICTED...
...THAT IT WOULD TAKE ME UNTIL THE BEGINNING OF OUR SENIOR YEAR FOR ME TO SPEAK TO HER...
I HEAR OGATA'S SHOOTING FOR A LIBERAL ARTS SCHOOL!
...AND THAT I WOULD BE FLOORED BY HER CHOICE TO CHANGE PATHS...
SIGH...
HONESTLY...
WHAT AM I DOING?

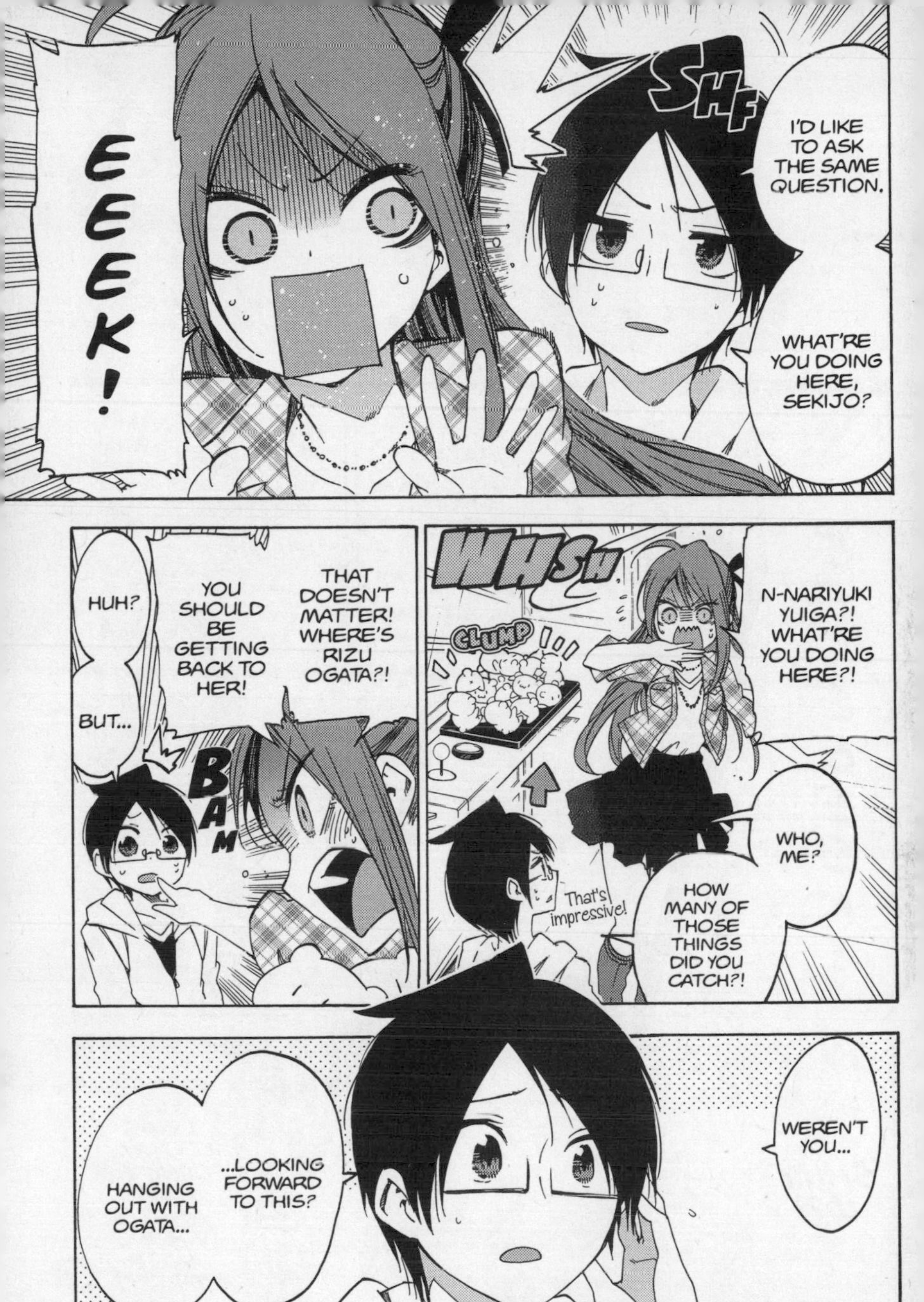
SHF
I'D LIKE TO ASK THE SAME QUESTION.
WHAT'RE YOU DOING HERE, SEKIJO?
EEEK!
WHSH
N-NARIYUKI YUIGA?! WHAT'RE YOU DOING HERE?!
CLUMP
WHO, ME?
HOW MANY OF THOSE THINGS DID YOU CATCH?!
That's impressive!
THAT DOESN'T MATTER! WHERE'S RIZU OGATA?!
YOU SHOULD BE GETTING BACK TO HER!
HUH?
BUT...
BAM
WEREN'T YOU...
...LOOKING FORWARD TO THIS?
HANGING OUT WITH OGATA...

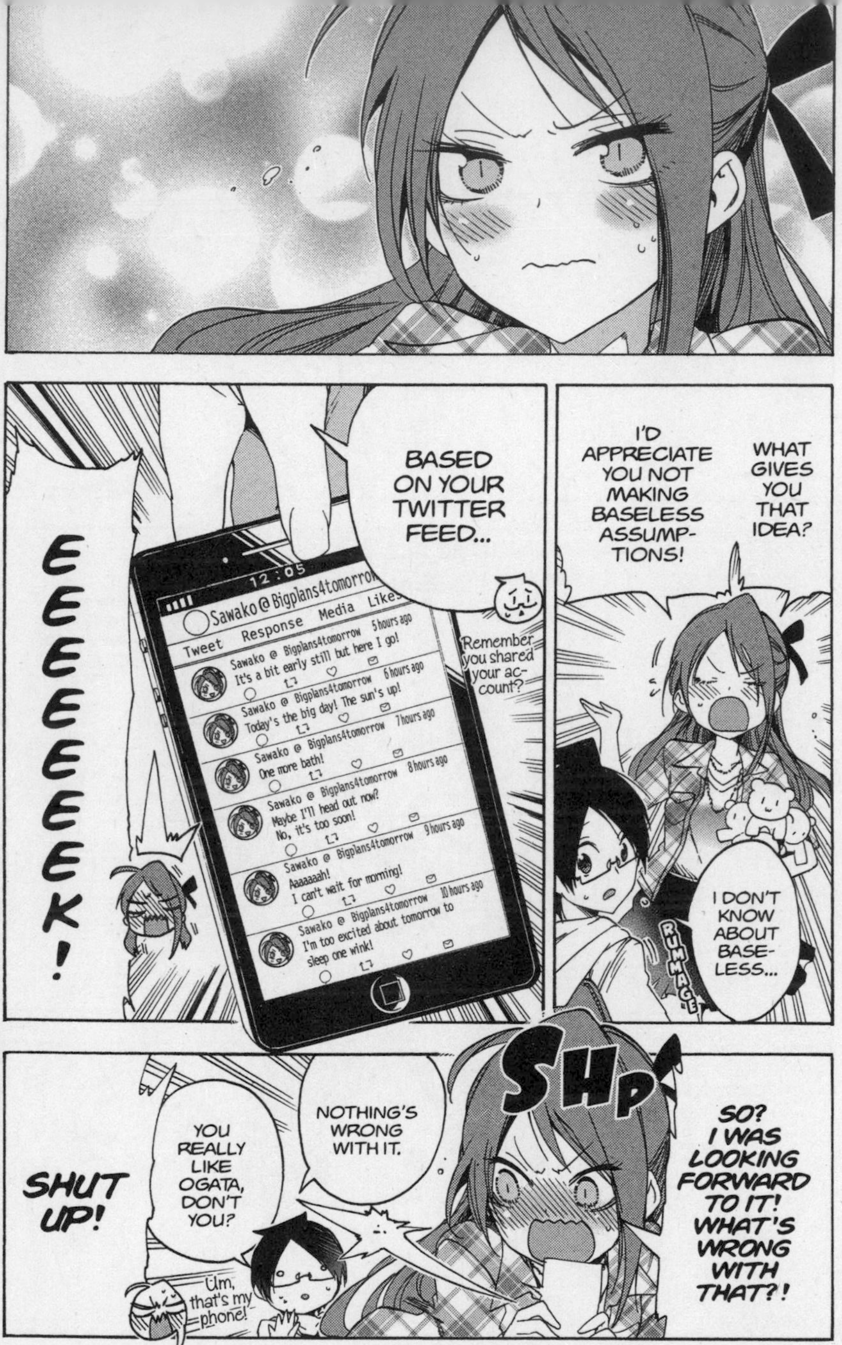
WHAT GIVES YOU THAT IDEA?
I'D APPRECIATE YOU NOT MAKING BASELESS ASSUMPTIONS!
I DON'T KNOW ABOUT BASELESS...
RUMMAGE
BASED ON YOUR TWITTER FEED...
Remember you shared your account?
12:05
Sawako @ Bigplans4tomorrow
Tweet Response Media Likes
Sawako @ Bigplans4tomorrow 5 hours ago
It's a bit early still but here I go!
Sawako @ Bigplans4tomorrow 6 hours ago
Today's the big day! The sun's up!
Sawako @ Bigplans4tomorrow 7 hours ago
One more bath!
Sawako @ Bigplans4tomorrow 8 hours ago
Maybe I'll head out now?
No, it's too soon!
Sawako @ Bigplans4tomorrow 9 hours ago
Aaaaaaah!
I can't wait for morning!
Sawako @ Bigplans4tomorrow 10 hours ago
I'm too excited about tomorrow to sleep one wink!
EEEEEEEEK!
SHP
SO? I WAS LOOKING FORWARD TO IT! WHAT'S WRONG WITH THAT?!
NOTHING'S WRONG WITH IT.
YOU REALLY LIKE OGATA, DON'T YOU?
SHUT UP!
Um, that's my phone!

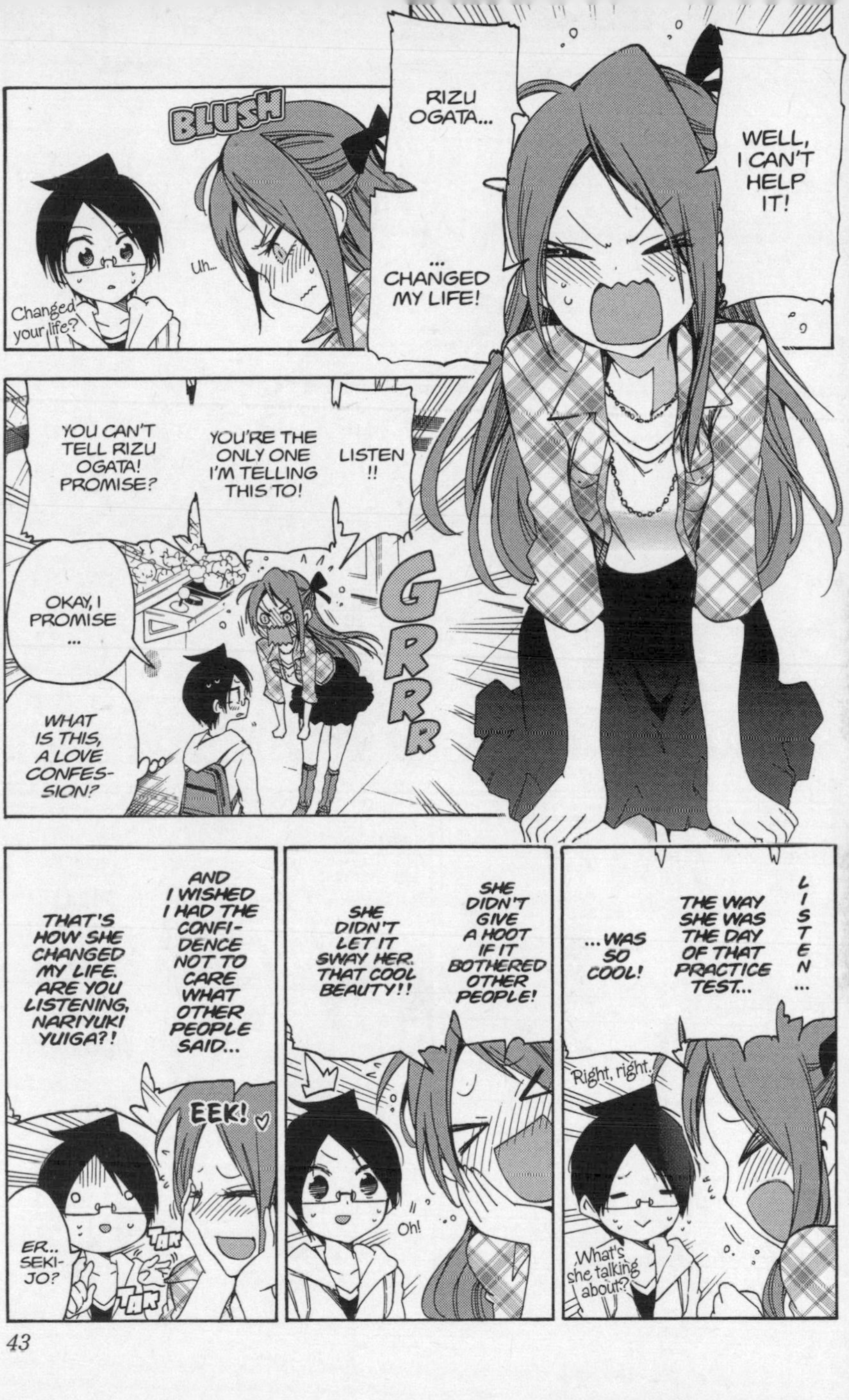
WELL, I CAN'T HELP IT!
RIZU OGATA...
...CHANGED MY LIFE!
BLUSH
Uh...
Changed your life?
LISTEN!!
YOU'RE THE ONLY ONE I'M TELLING THIS TO!
YOU CAN'T TELL RIZU OGATA! PROMISE?
GRRR
OKAY, I PROMISE...
WHAT IS THIS, A LOVE CONFESSION?
LISTEN...
THE WAY SHE WAS THE DAY OF THAT PRACTICE TEST...
...WAS SO COOL!
Right, right.
What's she talking about?
SHE DIDN'T GIVE A HOOT IF IT BOTHERED OTHER PEOPLE!
SHE DIDN'T LET IT SWAY HER. THAT COOL BEAUTY!!
Oh!
AND I WISHED I HAD THE CONFIDENCE NOT TO CARE WHAT OTHER PEOPLE SAID...
THAT'S HOW SHE CHANGED MY LIFE. ARE YOU LISTENING, NARIYUKI YUIGA?!
EEK!
TAK
TAK
ER... SEKIJO?

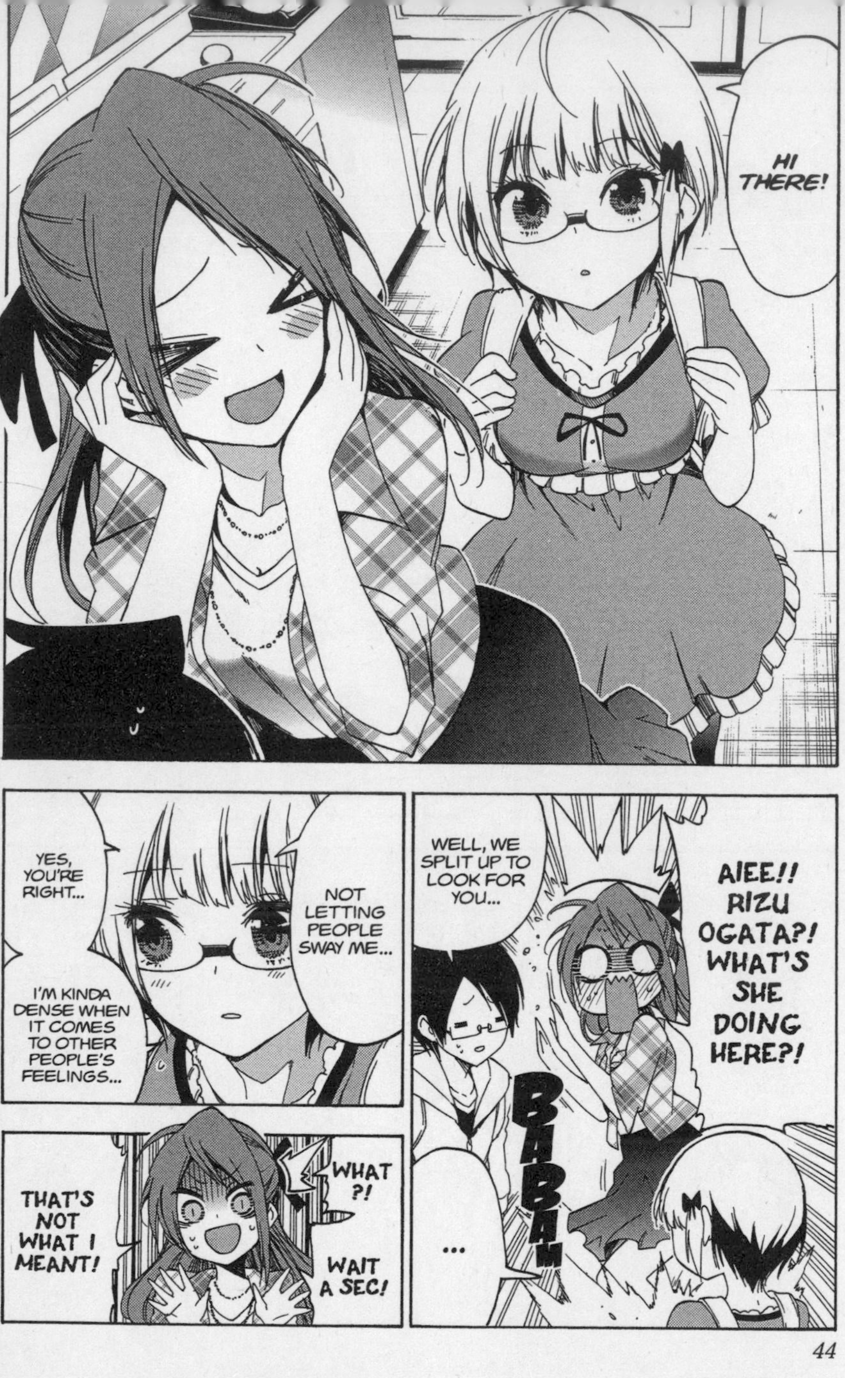
HI THERE!
AIEE!! RIZU OGATA?! WHAT'S SHE DOING HERE?!
WELL, WE SPLIT UP TO LOOK FOR YOU...
BABAM
...
NOT LETTING PEOPLE SWAY ME...
YES, YOU'RE RIGHT...
I'M KINDA DENSE WHEN IT COMES TO OTHER PEOPLE'S FEELINGS...
WHAT?!
WAIT A SEC!
THAT'S NOT WHAT I MEANT!

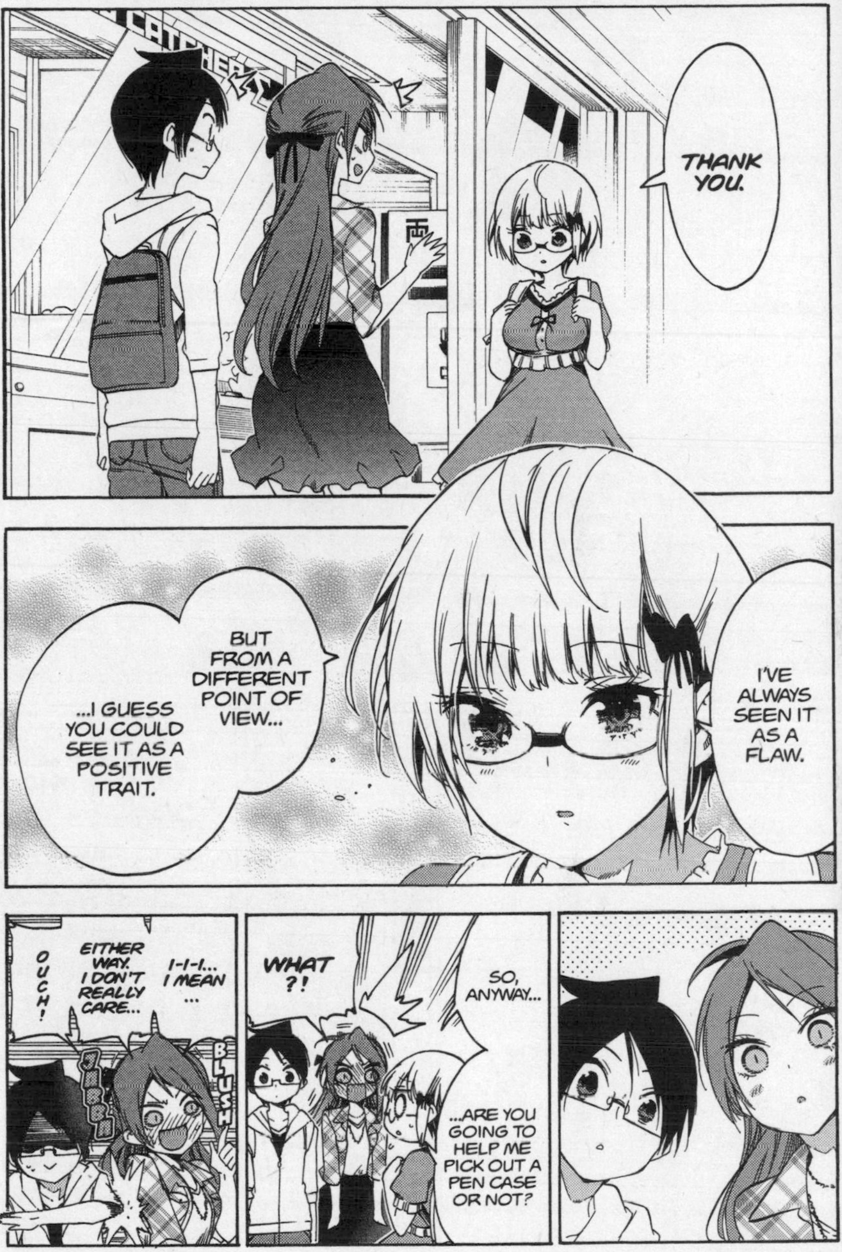
THANK YOU.
I'VE ALWAYS SEEN IT AS A FLAW.
BUT FROM A DIFFERENT POINT OF VIEW...
...I GUESS YOU COULD SEE IT AS A POSITIVE TRAIT.
SO, ANYWAY...
...ARE YOU GOING TO HELP ME PICK OUT A PEN CASE OR NOT?
WHAT?!
I-I-I... I MEAN ...
EITHER WAY. I DON'T REALLY CARE...
BLUSH
OUCH!

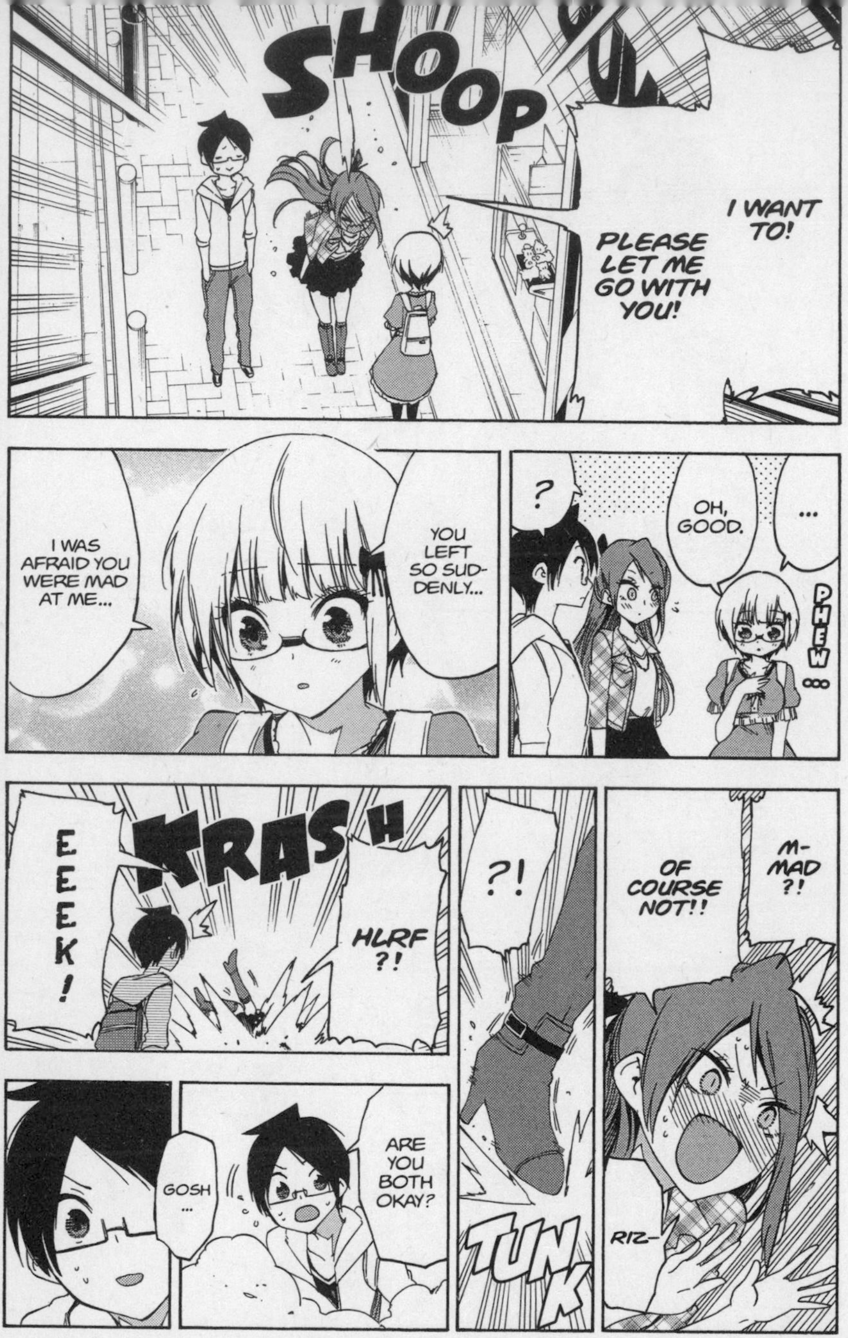
SHOOP
I WANT TO!
PLEASE LET ME GO WITH YOU!
...
OH, GOOD.
?
PHEW...
YOU LEFT SO SUDDENLY...
I WAS AFRAID YOU WERE MAD AT ME...
M-MAD?!
OF COURSE NOT!!
RIZ-
?!
TUNK
KRASH
HLRF?!
EEEK!
ARE YOU BOTH OKAY?
GOSH...

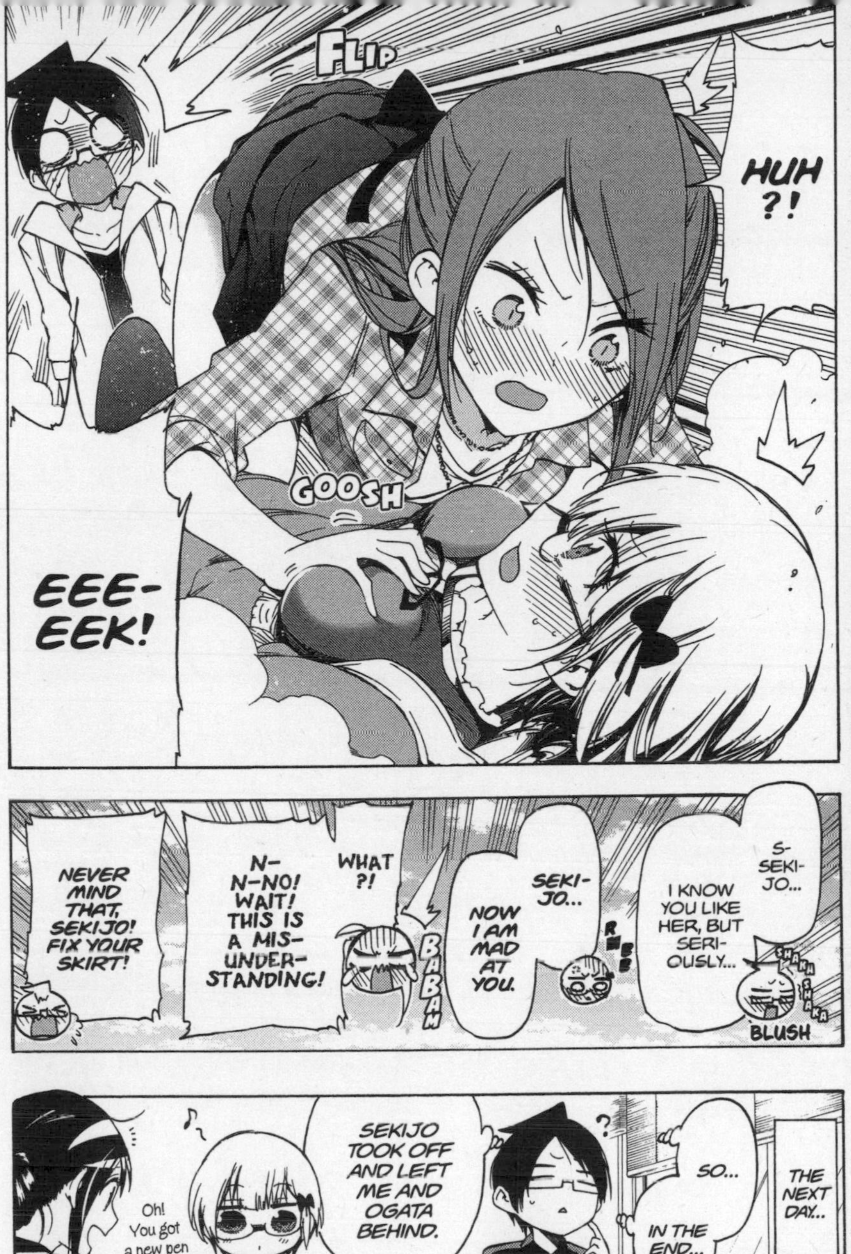
FLIP
HUH ?!
GOOSH
EEE-EEK!
S-SEKI-JO...
I KNOW YOU LIKE HER, BUT SERI-OUSLY...
BLUSH
SEKI-JO...
NOW I AM MAD AT YOU.
WHAT ?!
BABAM
N-N-NO! WAIT! THIS IS A MIS-UNDER-STANDING!
NEVER MIND THAT, SEKIJO! FIX YOUR SKIRT!
THE NEXT DAY...
SO...
IN THE END...
SEKIJO TOOK OFF AND LEFT ME AND OGATA BEHIND.
Oh! You got a new pen case! It's cute!

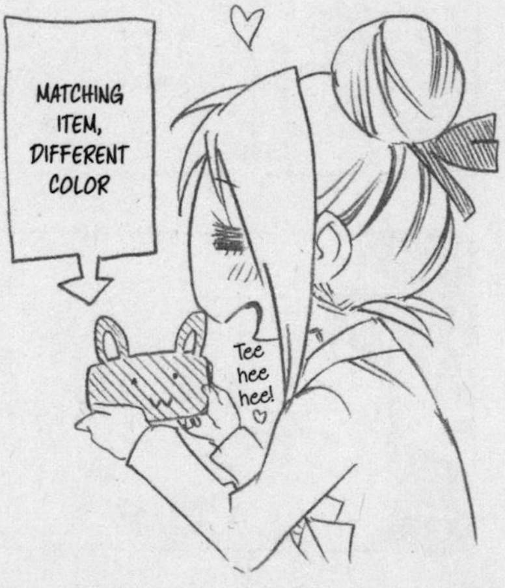
MATCHING ITEM, DIFFERENT COLOR
Tee hee hee!

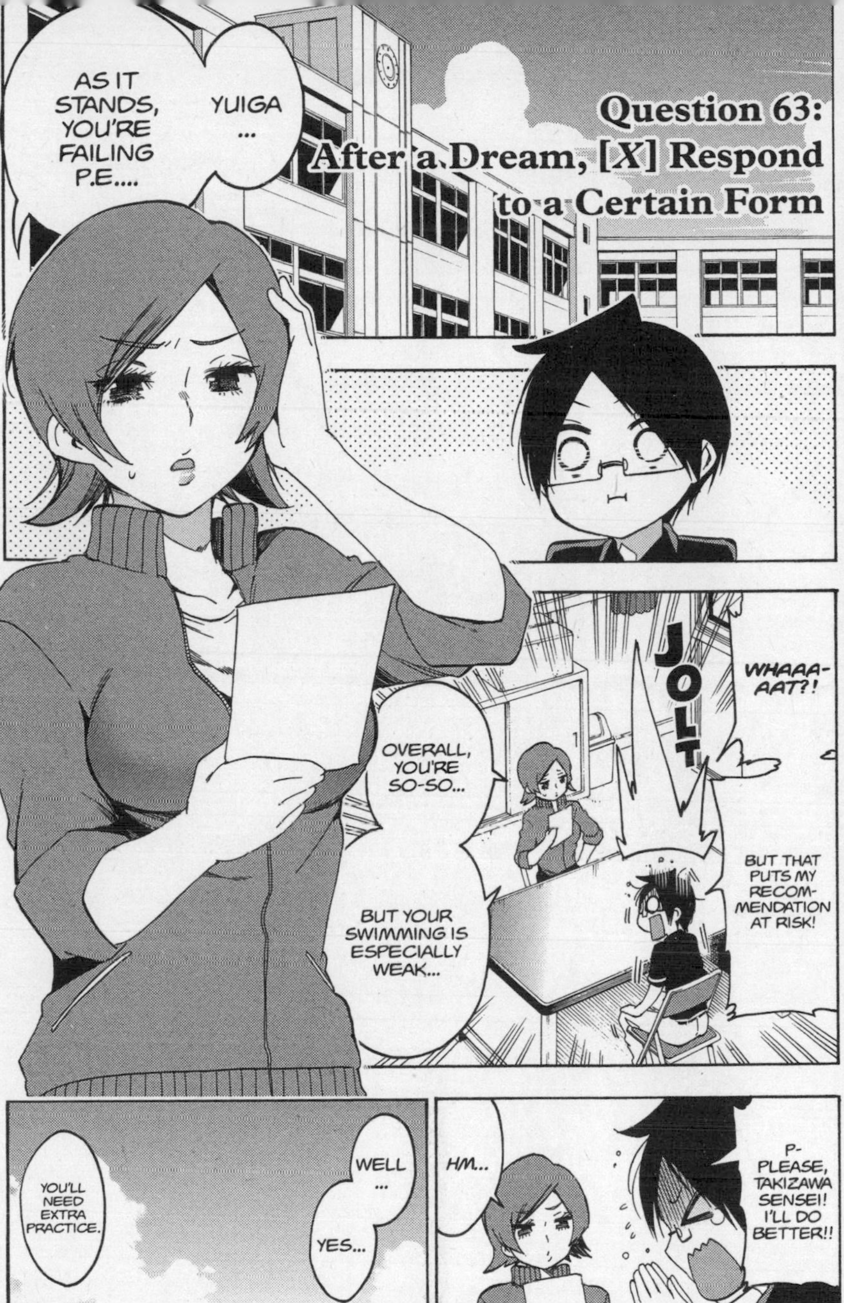
Question 63: After a Dream, [X] Respond to a Certain Form
YUIGA ...
AS IT STANDS, YOU'RE FAILING P.E....
OVERALL, YOU'RE SO-SO...
BUT YOUR SWIMMING IS ESPECIALLY WEAK...
JOLT
WHAAA-AAT?!
BUT THAT PUTS MY RECOM-MENDATION AT RISK!
P-PLEASE, TAKIZAWA SENSEI! I'LL DO BETTER!!
HM...
WELL ...
YES...
YOU'LL NEED EXTRA PRACTICE.

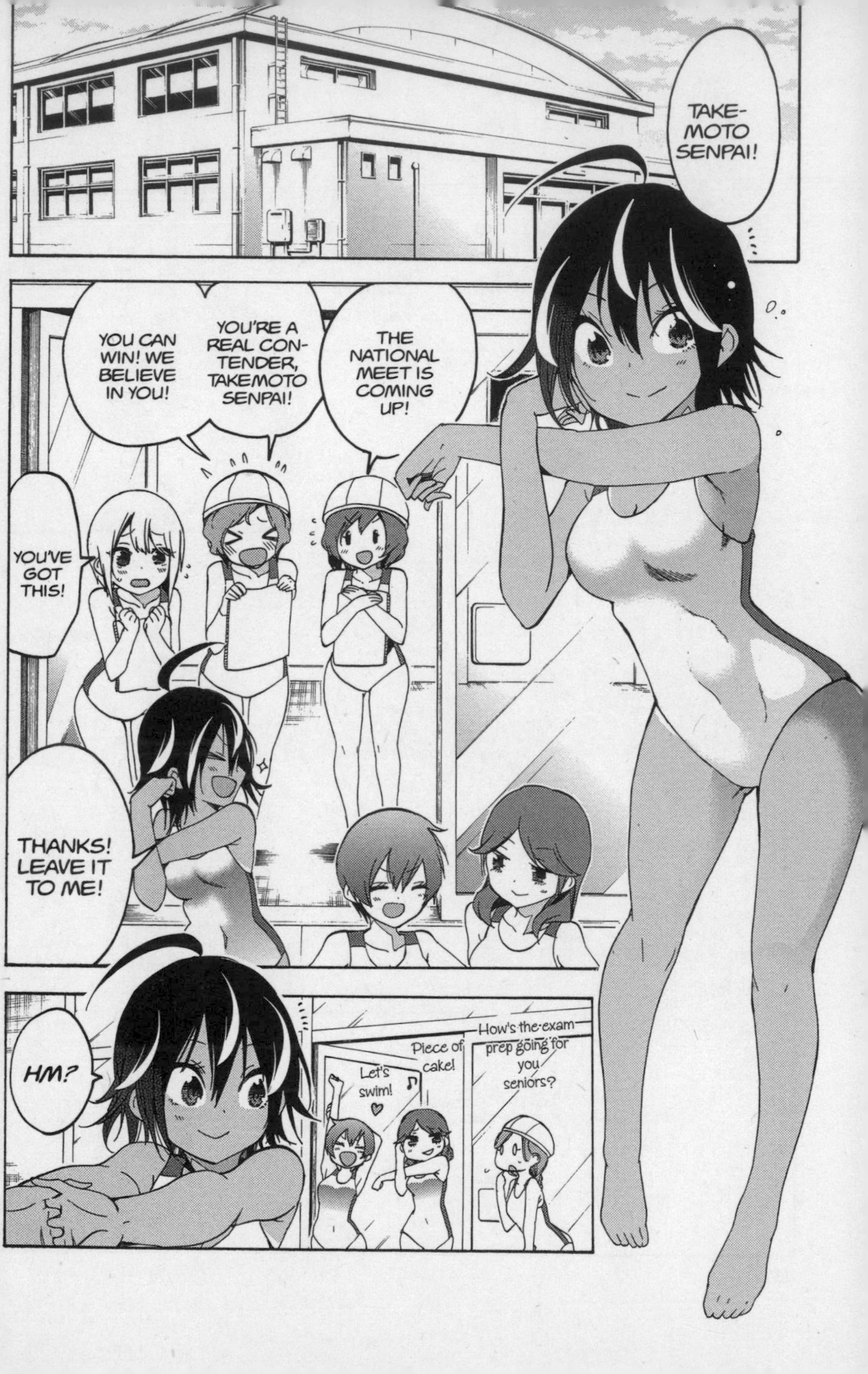
TAKE-MOTO SENPAI!
THE NATIONAL MEET IS COMING UP!
YOU'RE A REAL CON-TENDER, TAKEMOTO SENPAI!
YOU CAN WIN! WE BELIEVE IN YOU!
YOU'VE GOT THIS!
THANKS! LEAVE IT TO ME!
How's the exam prep going for you seniors?
Piece of cake!
Let's swim!
HM?

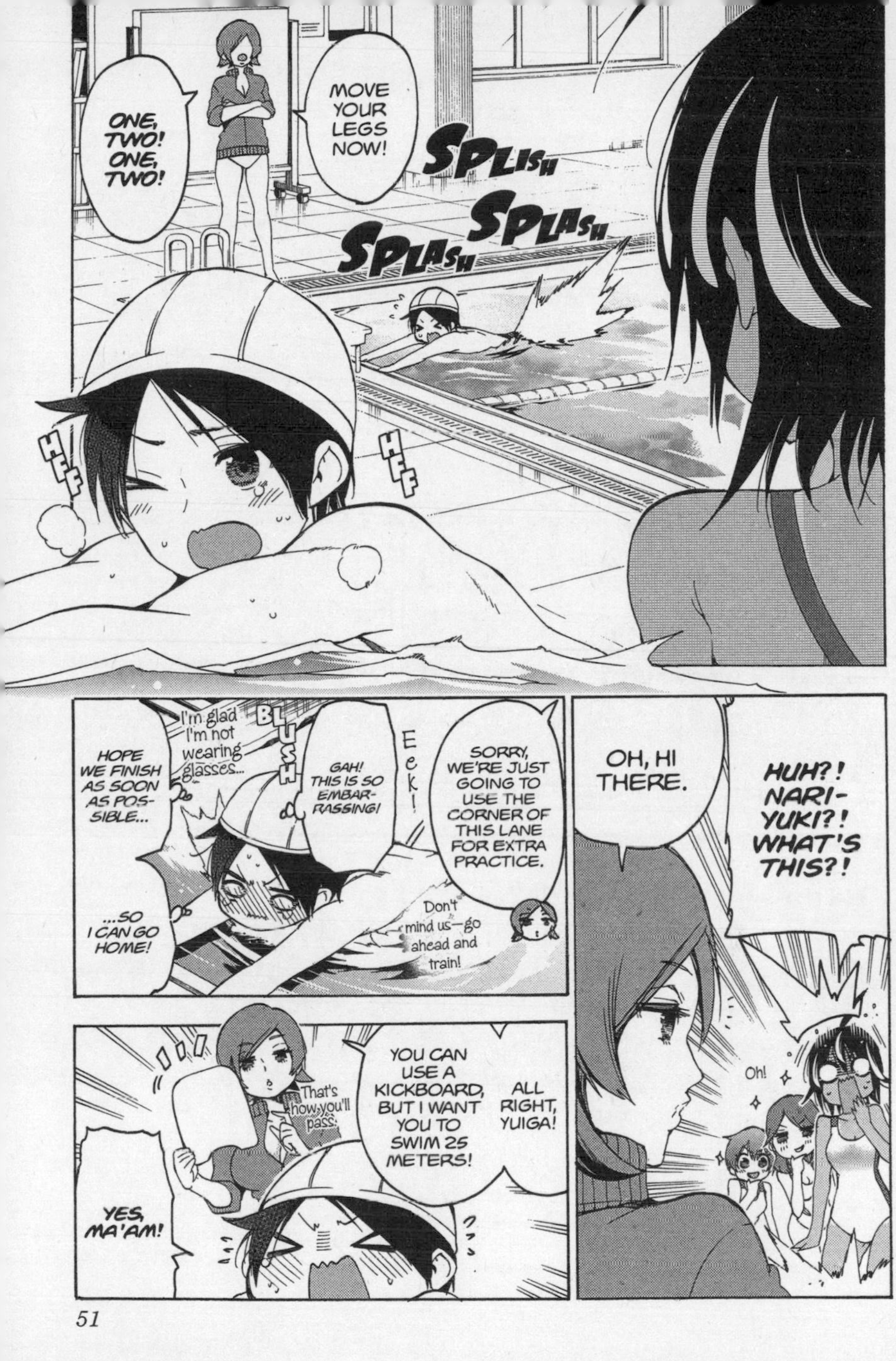
SPLISH
SPLASH
SPLASH
MOVE YOUR LEGS NOW!
ONE, TWO! ONE, TWO!
HEFF
HEFF
HUH?! NARI-YUKI?! WHAT'S THIS?!
OH, HI THERE.
Oh!
SORRY, WE'RE JUST GOING TO USE THE CORNER OF THIS LANE FOR EXTRA PRACTICE.
Eek!
GAH! THIS IS SO EMBARRASSING!
BLUSH
I'm glad I'm not wearing glasses...
HOPE WE FINISH AS SOON AS POSSIBLE...
Don't mind us—go ahead and train!
...SO I CAN GO HOME!
ALL RIGHT, YUIGA!
YOU CAN USE A KICKBOARD, BUT I WANT YOU TO SWIM 25 METERS!
That's how you'll pass.
YES, MA'AM!

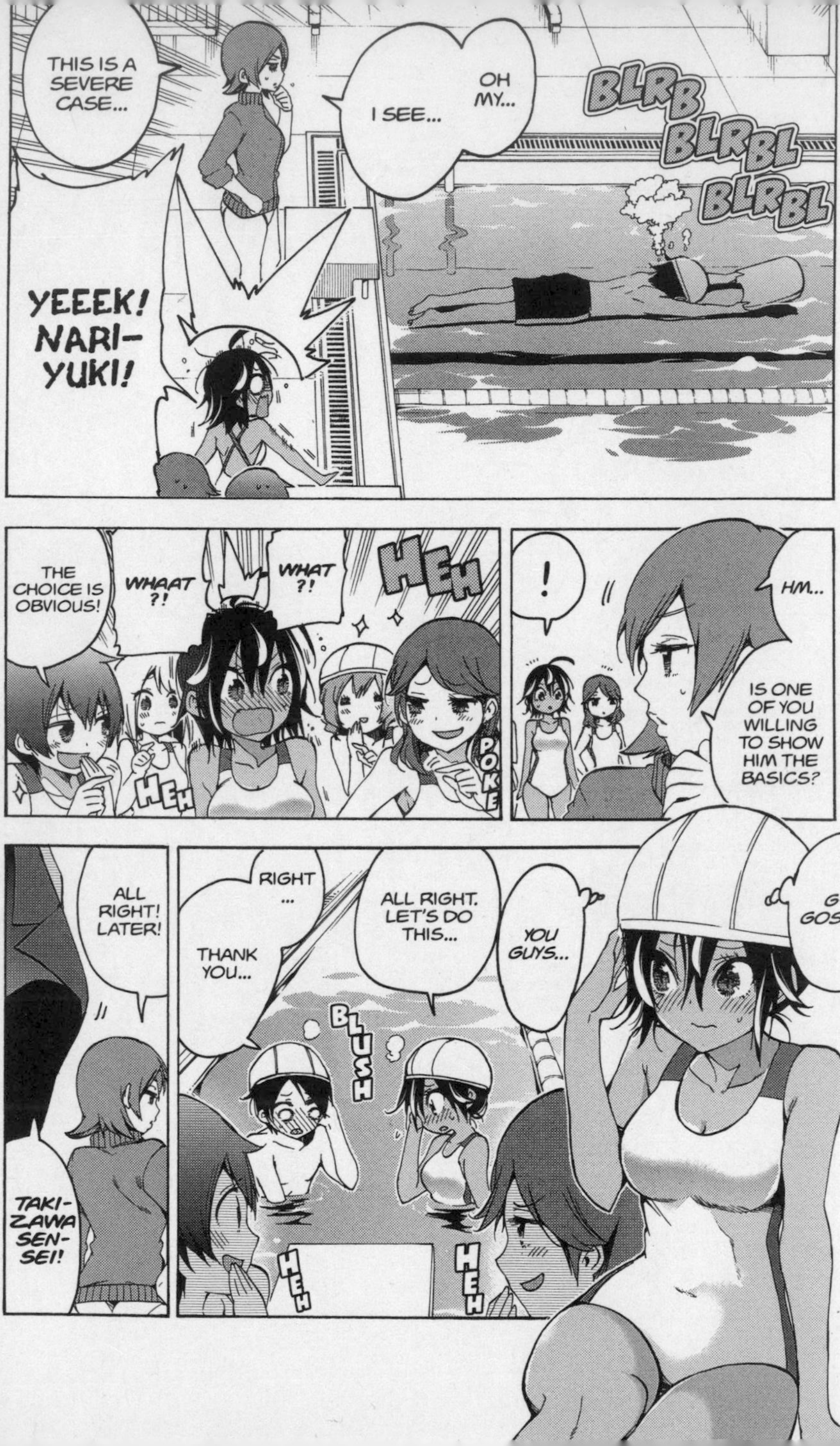
BLRB BLRBL BLRBL
OH MY... I SEE...
THIS IS A SEVERE CASE...
YEEEK! NARI-YUKI!
HM...
!
IS ONE OF YOU WILLING TO SHOW HIM THE BASICS?
HEH
WHAT ?!
WHAAT ?!
THE CHOICE IS OBVIOUS!
POKE
HEH
G-GOSH...
YOU GUYS...
ALL RIGHT. LET'S DO THIS...
RIGHT ...
THANK YOU...
BLUSH
HEH
HEH
ALL RIGHT! LATER!
TAKI-ZAWA SEN-SEI!

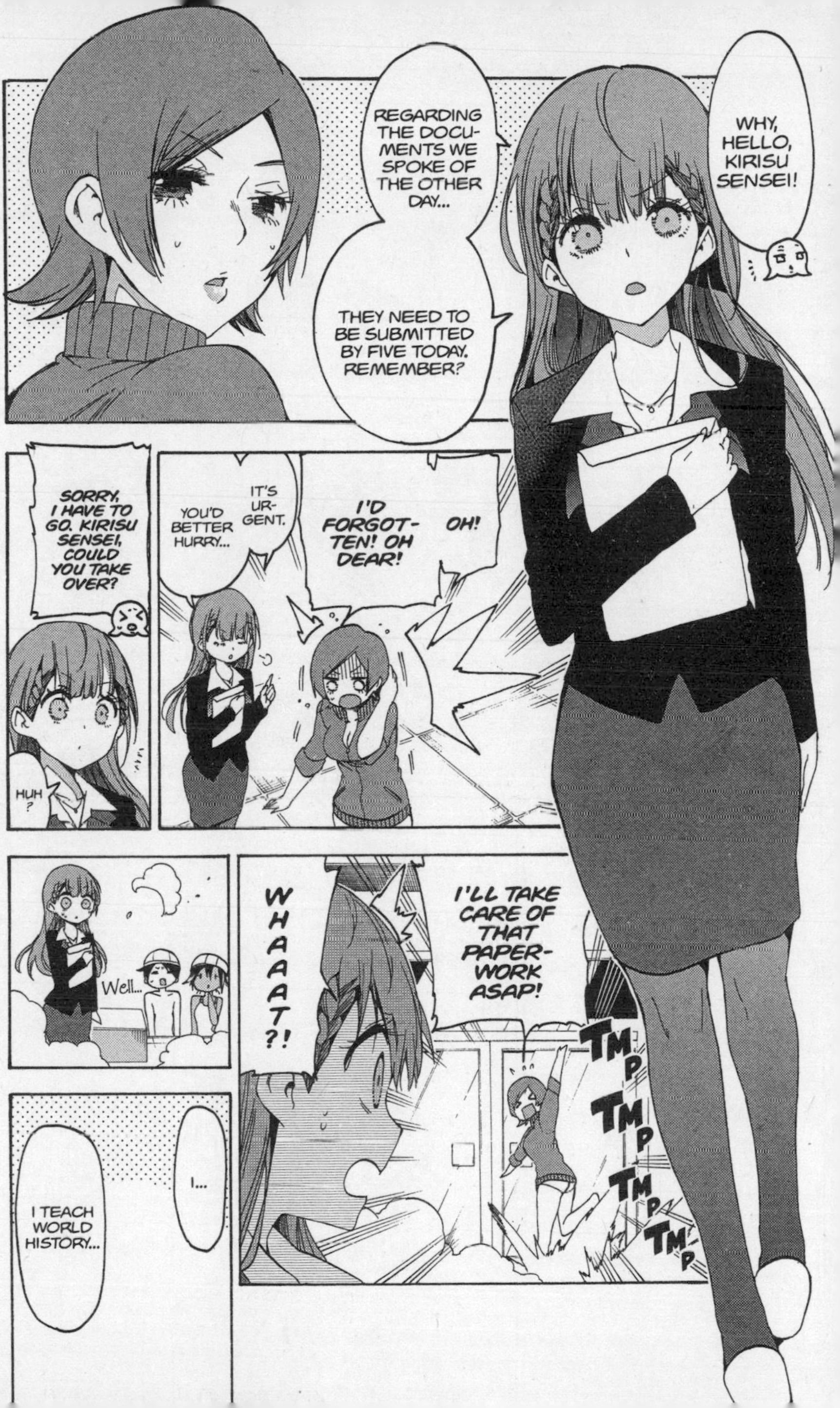
WHY, HELLO, KIRISU SENSEI!
REGARDING THE DOCU-MENTS WE SPOKE OF THE OTHER DAY...
THEY NEED TO BE SUBMITTED BY FIVE TODAY. REMEMBER?
OH!
I'D FORGOT-TEN! OH DEAR!
IT'S UR-GENT.
YOU'D BETTER HURRY...
SORRY, I HAVE TO GO. KIRISU SENSEI, COULD YOU TAKE OVER?
HUH ?
I'LL TAKE CARE OF THAT PAPER-WORK ASAP!
TMP TMP TMP TMP TMP
WHAAAAT?!
Well...
I...
I TEACH WORLD HISTORY...

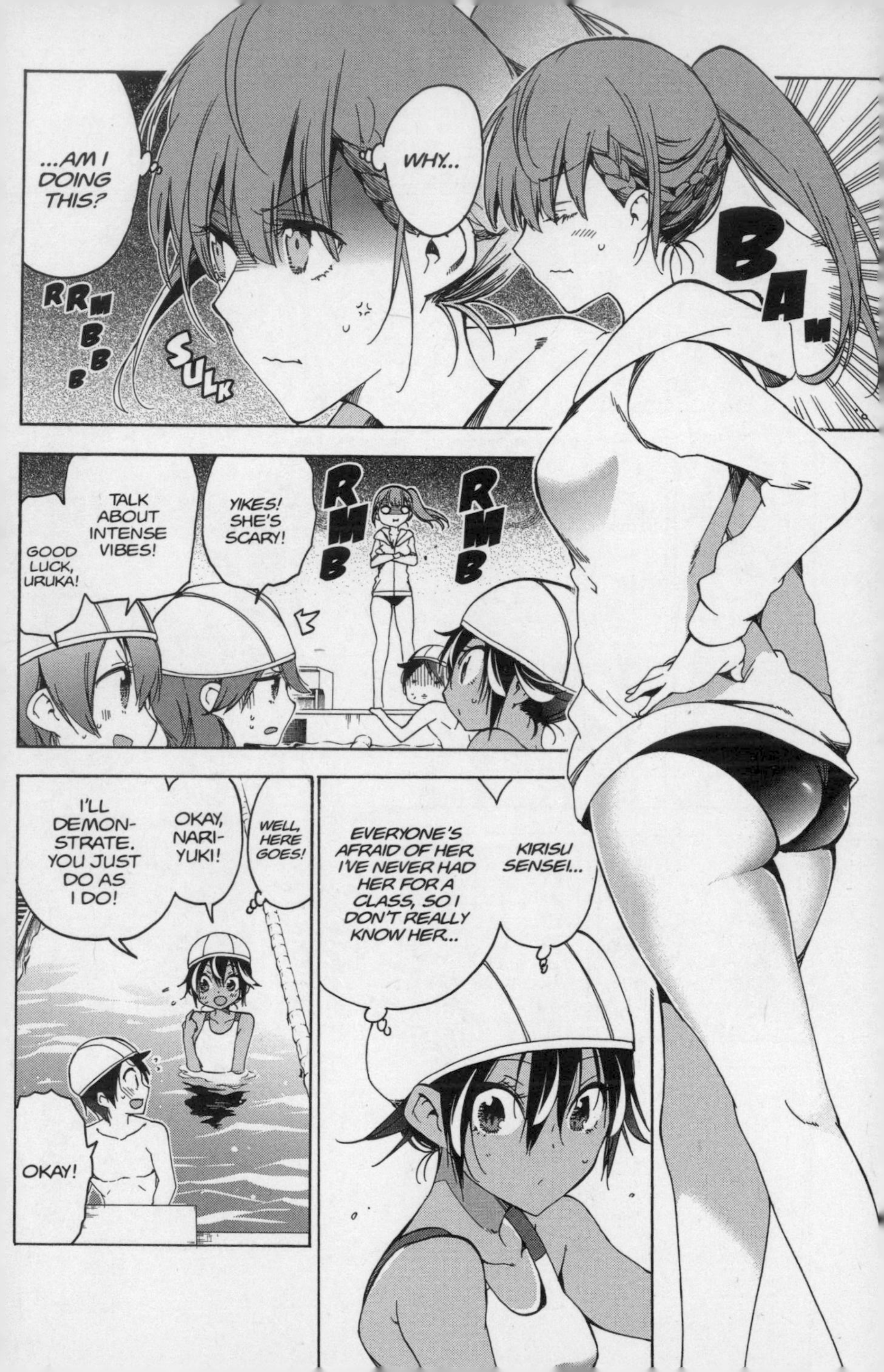
BAM
WHY...
...AM I DOING THIS?
RRMBBB
SULK
RMB
RMB
YIKES! SHE'S SCARY!
TALK ABOUT INTENSE VIBES!
GOOD LUCK, URUKA!
KIRISU SENSEI...
EVERYONE'S AFRAID OF HER I'VE NEVER HAD HER FOR A CLASS, SO I DON'T REALLY KNOW HER...
WELL, HERE GOES!
OKAY, NARI-YUKI!
I'LL DEMON-STRATE. YOU JUST DO AS I DO!
OKAY!

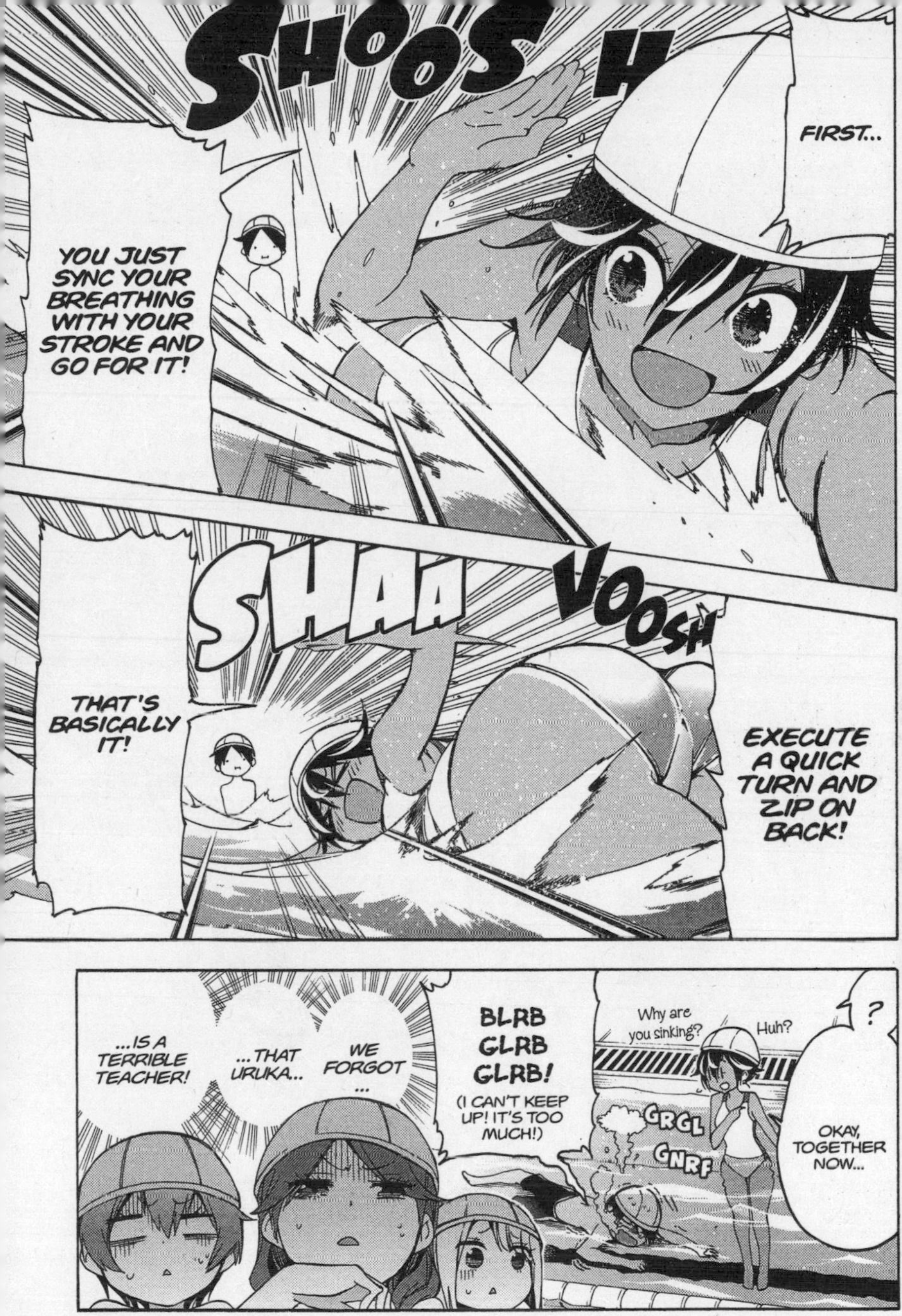
SHOOSH
FIRST...
YOU JUST SYNC YOUR BREATHING WITH YOUR STROKE AND GO FOR IT!
SHAA
VOOSH
EXECUTE A QUICK TURN AND ZIP ON BACK!
THAT'S BASICALLY IT!
?
OKAY, TOGETHER NOW...
Huh?
Why are you sinking?
GRGL
GNRF
BLRB GLRB GLRB!
(I CAN'T KEEP UP! IT'S TOO MUCH!)
WE FORGOT...
...THAT URUKA...
...IS A TERRIBLE TEACHER!

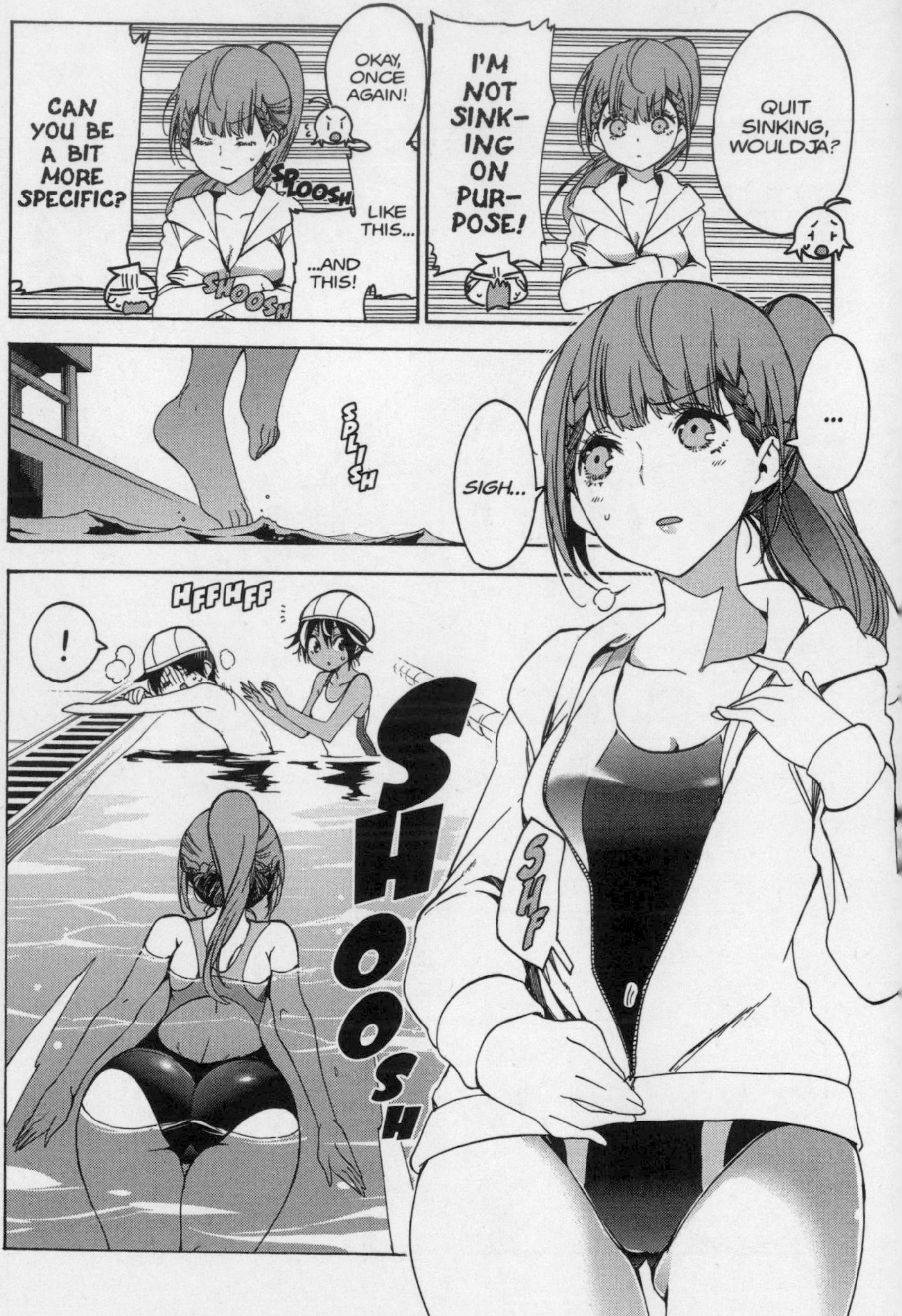
QUIT SINKING, WOULDJA?
I'M NOT SINKING ON PURPOSE!
OKAY, ONCE AGAIN!
SPLOOSH
LIKE THIS...
...AND THIS!
SHOOSH
CAN YOU BE A BIT MORE SPECIFIC?
...
SIGH...
SHF
SPLISH
HFF HFF
!
SHOOOOSH

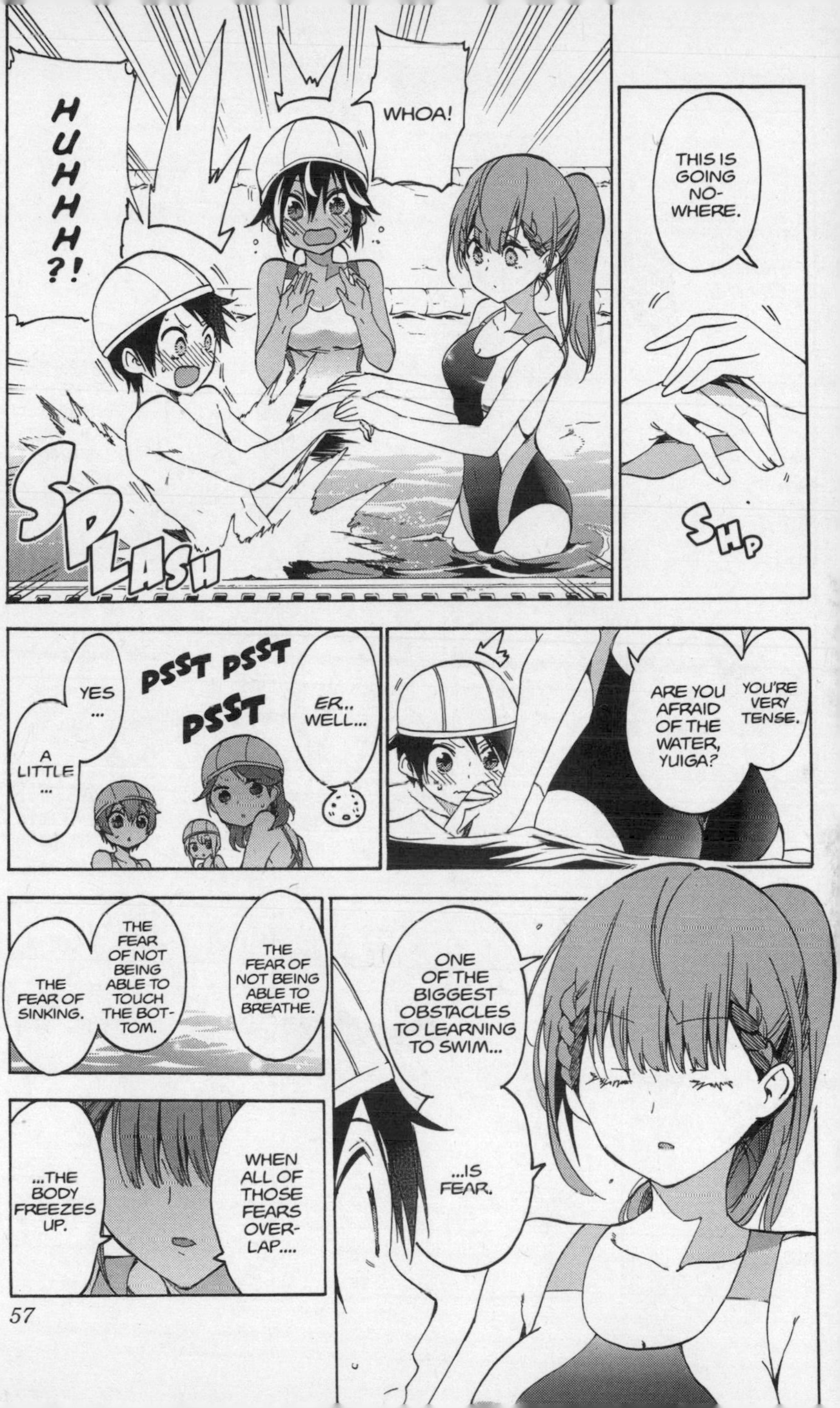
THIS IS GOING NO-WHERE.
SHP
WHOA!
HUHHHH?!
SPLASH
YOU'RE VERY TENSE.
ARE YOU AFRAID OF THE WATER, YUIGA?
ER.. WELL...
PSST PSST PSST
YES ... A LITTLE ...
ONE OF THE BIGGEST OBSTACLES TO LEARNING TO SWIM...
...IS FEAR.
THE FEAR OF NOT BEING ABLE TO BREATHE.
THE FEAR OF NOT BEING ABLE TO TOUCH THE BOT-TOM.
THE FEAR OF SINKING.
WHEN ALL OF THOSE FEARS OVER-LAP....
...THE BODY FREEZES UP.

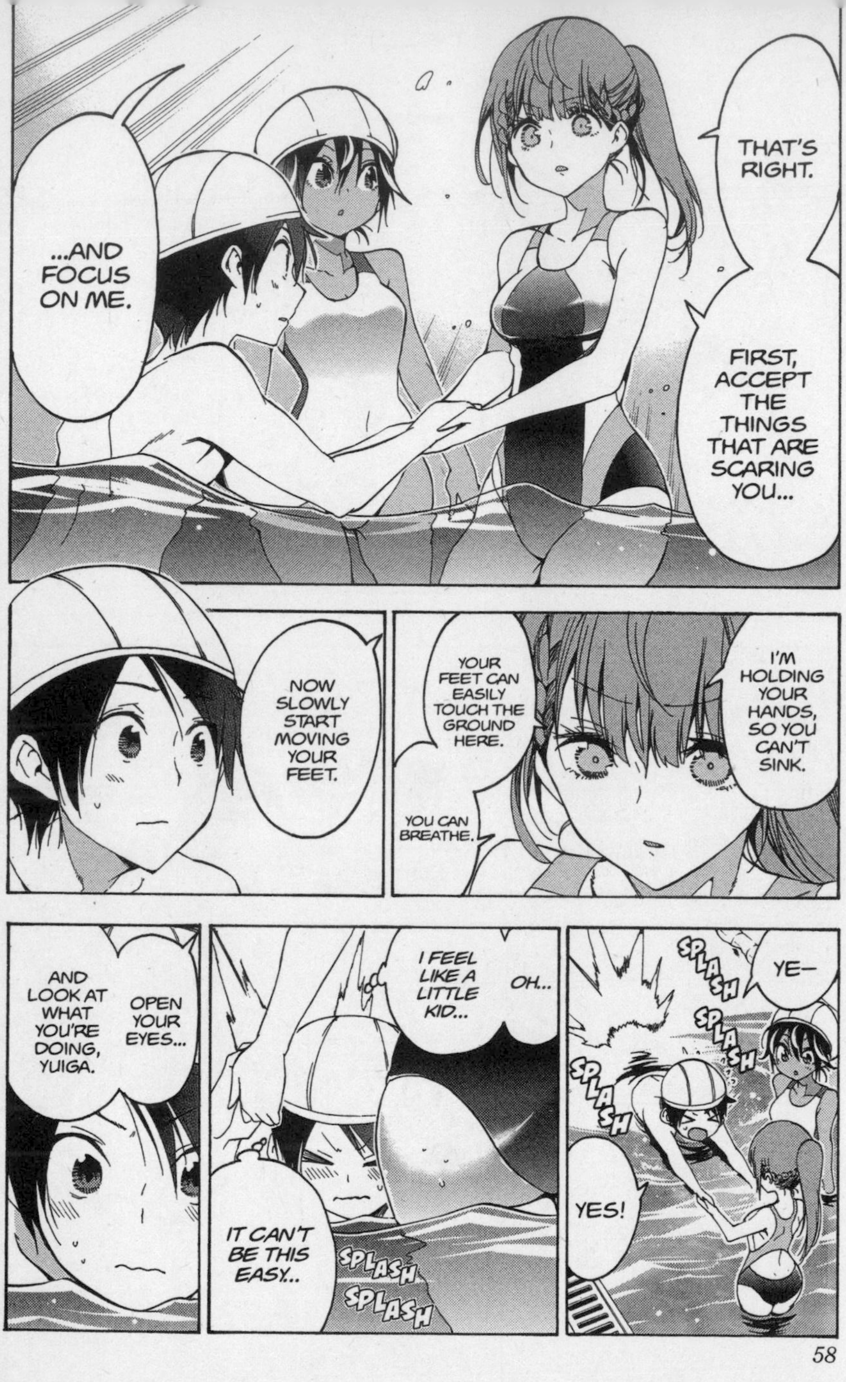
THAT'S RIGHT.
FIRST, ACCEPT THE THINGS THAT ARE SCARING YOU...
...AND FOCUS ON ME.
I'M HOLDING YOUR HANDS, SO YOU CAN'T SINK.
YOUR FEET CAN EASILY TOUCH THE GROUND HERE.
YOU CAN BREATHE.
NOW SLOWLY START MOVING YOUR FEET.
YE—
SPLASH
SPLASH
SPLASH
YES!
OH...
I FEEL LIKE A LITTLE KID...
IT CAN'T BE THIS EASY...
SPLASH
SPLASH
OPEN YOUR EYES...
AND LOOK AT WHAT YOU'RE DOING, YUIGA.

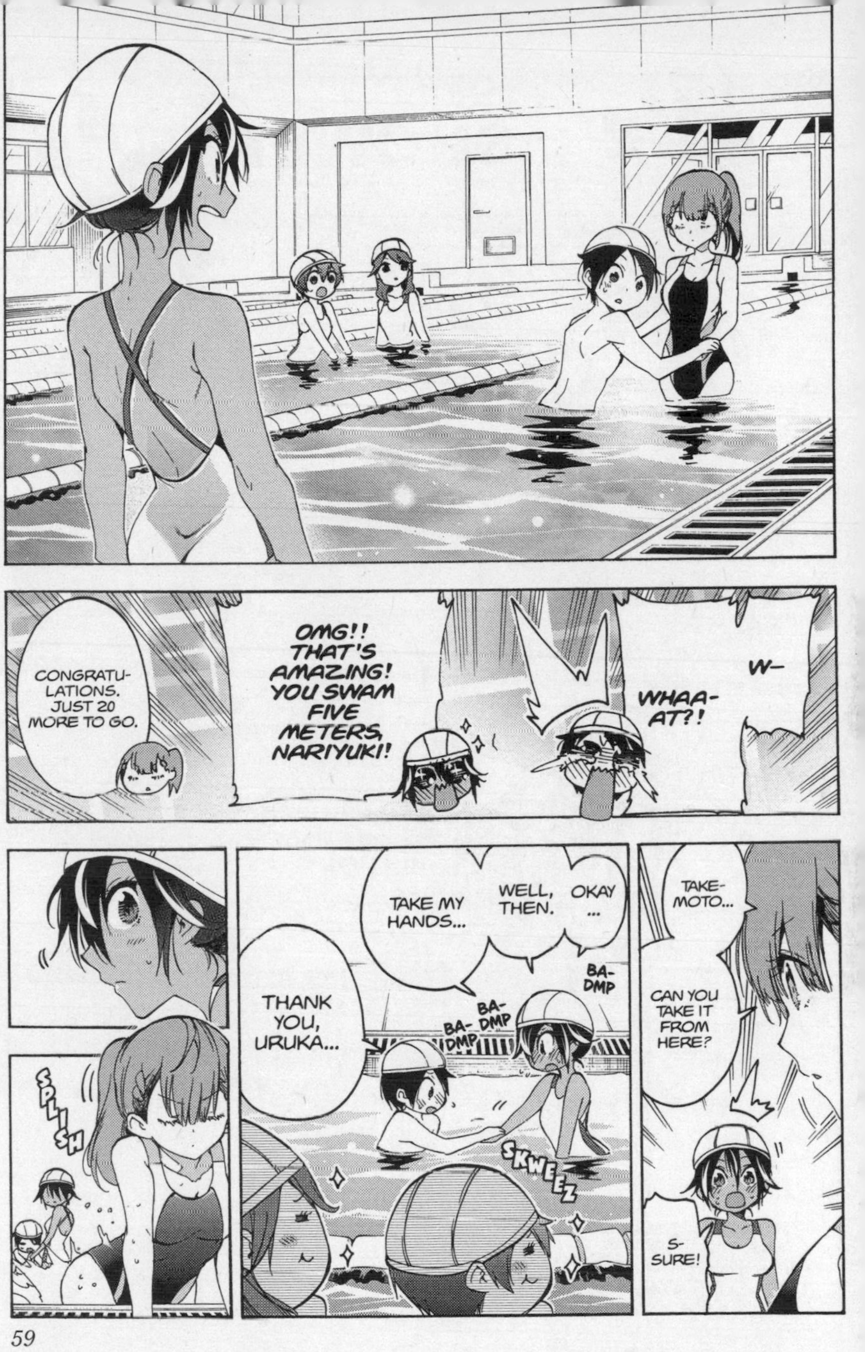
W-
WHAA-AT?!
OMG!! THAT'S AMAZING! YOU SWAM FIVE METERS, NARIYUKI!
CONGRATULATIONS. JUST 20 MORE TO GO.
TAKE-MOTO...
CAN YOU TAKE IT FROM HERE?
S-SURE!
OKAY ...
WELL, THEN.
TAKE MY HANDS...
BA-DMP
BA-DMP
BA-DMP
THANK YOU, URUKA...
SKWEEZ
SPLISH

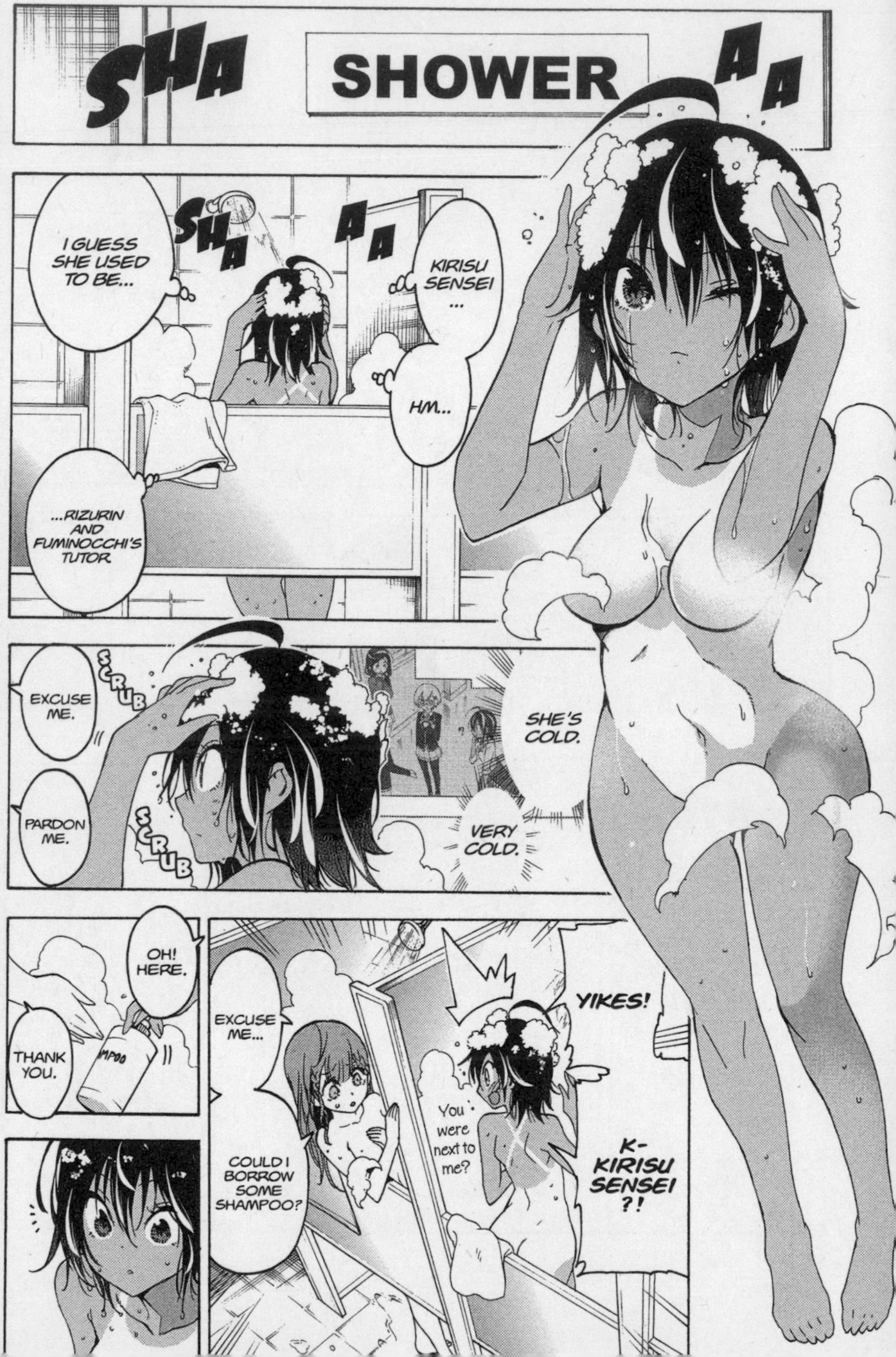
SHA
SHOWER
AA
SHA
AA
KIRISU SENSEI ...
HM...
I GUESS SHE USED TO BE...
...RIZURIN AND FUMINOCCHI'S TUTOR.
SHE'S COLD.
VERY COLD.
SCRUB
SCRUB
EXCUSE ME.
PARDON ME.
YIKES!
K-KIRISU SENSEI ?!
You were next to me?
EXCUSE ME...
COULD I BORROW SOME SHAMPOO?
OH! HERE.
THANK YOU.
MPOO

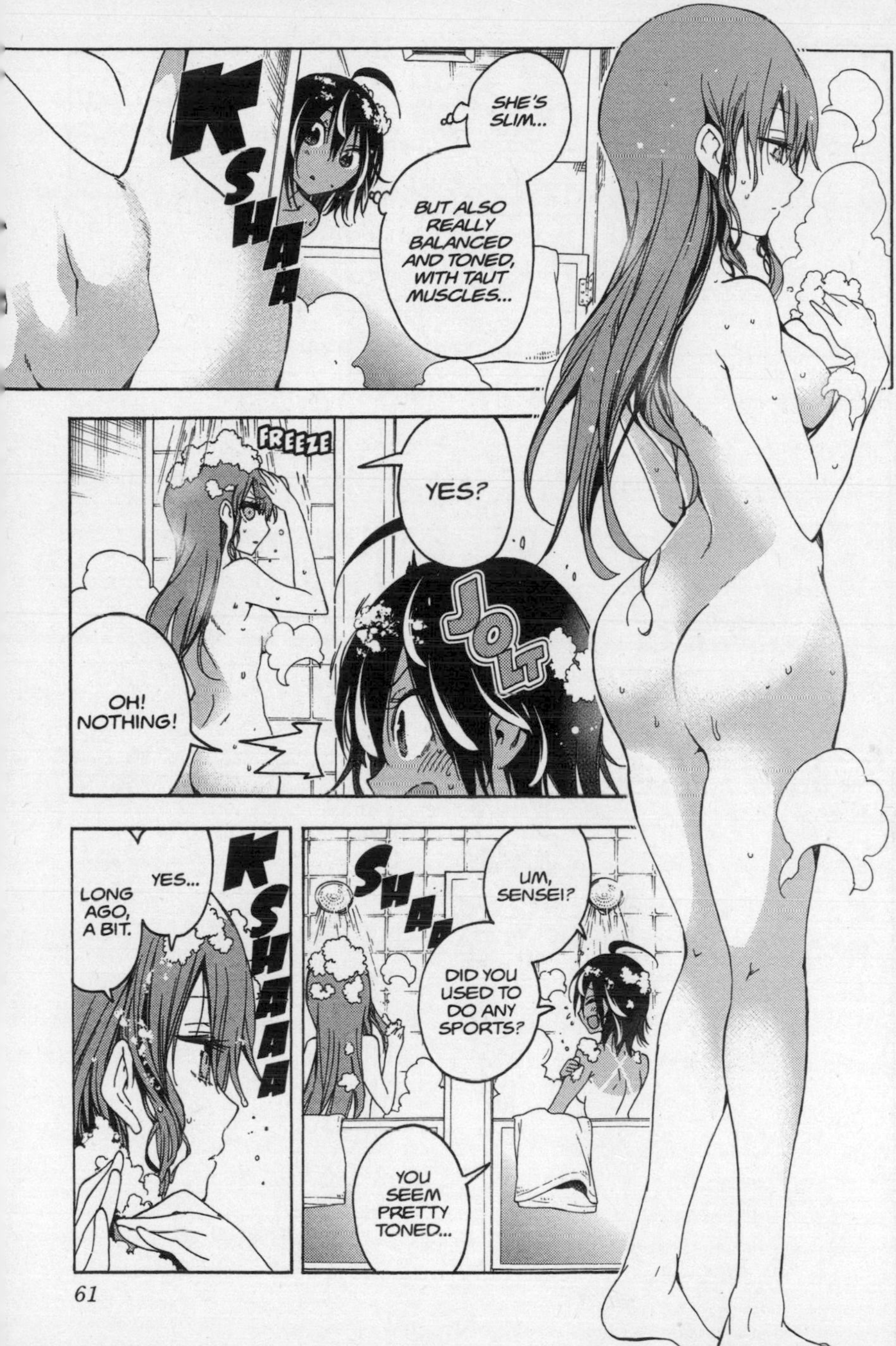

SHE'S SLIM...
BUT ALSO REALLY BALANCED AND TONED, WITH TAUT MUSCLES...
KSHAA
YES?
FREEZE
JOLT
OH! NOTHING!
UM, SENSEI?
SHAA
DID YOU USED TO DO ANY SPORTS?
YOU SEEM PRETTY TONED...
KSHAAA
YES...
LONG AGO, A BIT.

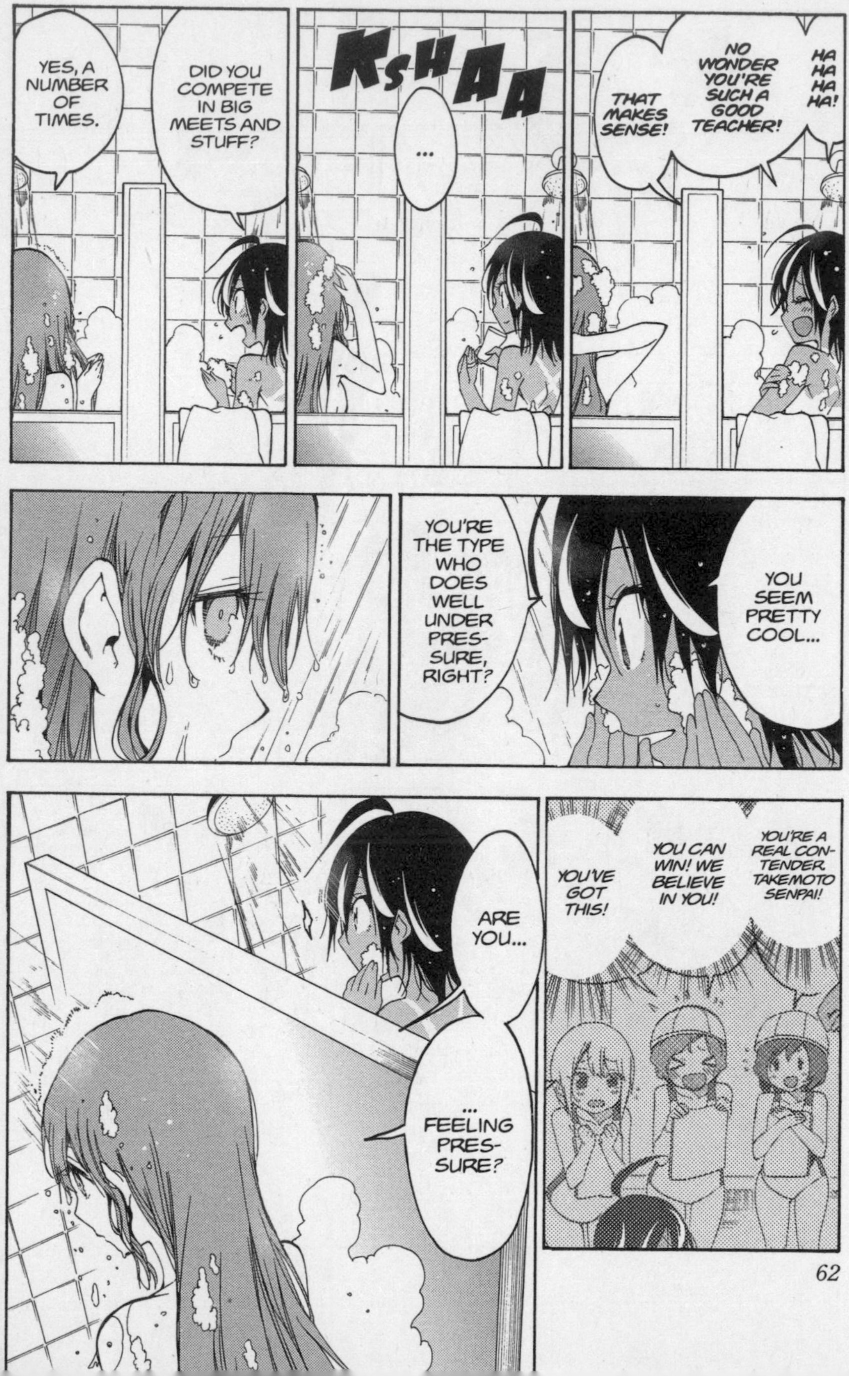
HA HA HA HA!
NO WONDER YOU'RE SUCH A GOOD TEACHER!
THAT MAKES SENSE!
KSHAA
...
DID YOU COMPETE IN BIG MEETS AND STUFF?
YES, A NUMBER OF TIMES.
YOU SEEM PRETTY COOL...
YOU'RE THE TYPE WHO DOES WELL UNDER PRES-SURE, RIGHT?
YOU'RE A REAL CON-TENDER, TAKEMOTO SENPAI!
YOU CAN WIN! WE BELIEVE IN YOU!
YOU'VE GOT THIS!
ARE YOU...
...FEELING PRES-SURE?

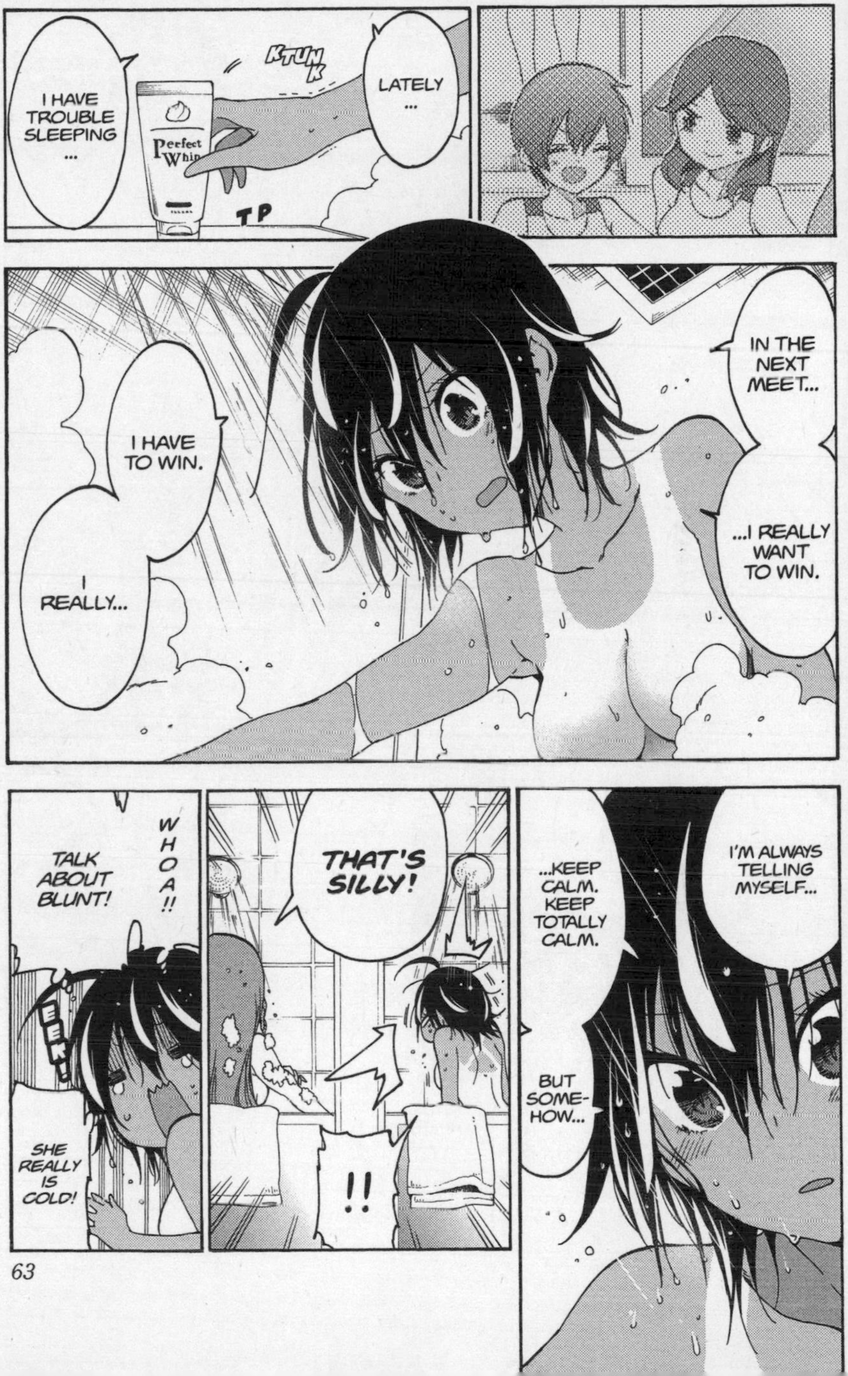

LATELY ...
KTUNK
I HAVE TROUBLE SLEEPING ...
Perfect Whip
TP
IN THE NEXT MEET...
...I REALLY WANT TO WIN.
I HAVE TO WIN.
I REALLY...
I'M ALWAYS TELLING MYSELF...
...KEEP CALM. KEEP TOTALLY CALM.
BUT SOMEHOW...
THAT'S SILLY!
!!
WHOA!!
TALK ABOUT BLUNT!
EEK!
SHE REALLY IS COLD!

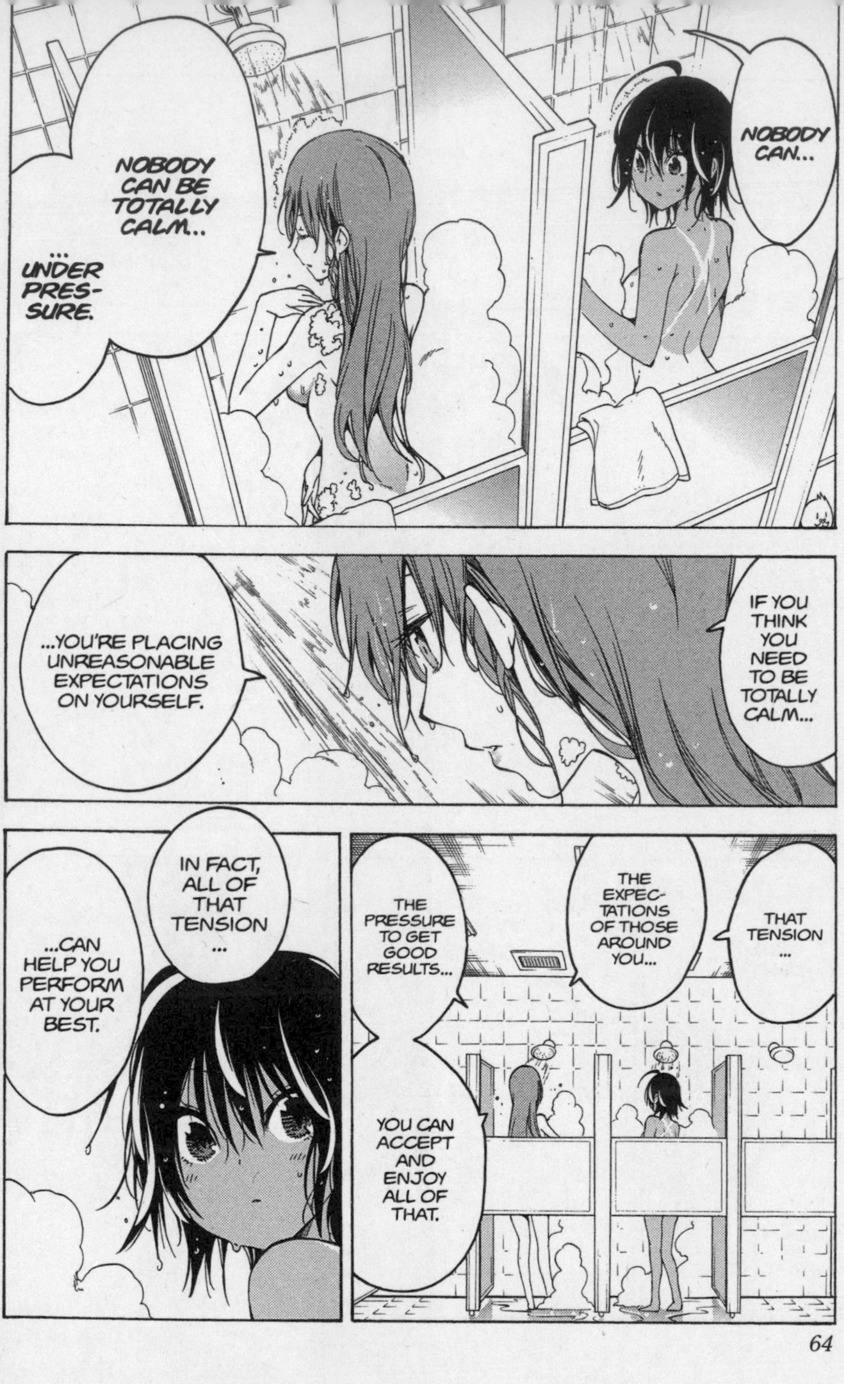
NOBODY CAN...
NOBODY CAN BE TOTALLY CALM...
... UNDER PRESSURE.
IF YOU THINK YOU NEED TO BE TOTALLY CALM...
...YOU'RE PLACING UNREASONABLE EXPECTATIONS ON YOURSELF.
THAT TENSION ...
THE EXPECTATIONS OF THOSE AROUND YOU...
THE PRESSURE TO GET GOOD RESULTS...
YOU CAN ACCEPT AND ENJOY ALL OF THAT.
IN FACT, ALL OF THAT TENSION ...
...CAN HELP YOU PERFORM AT YOUR BEST.

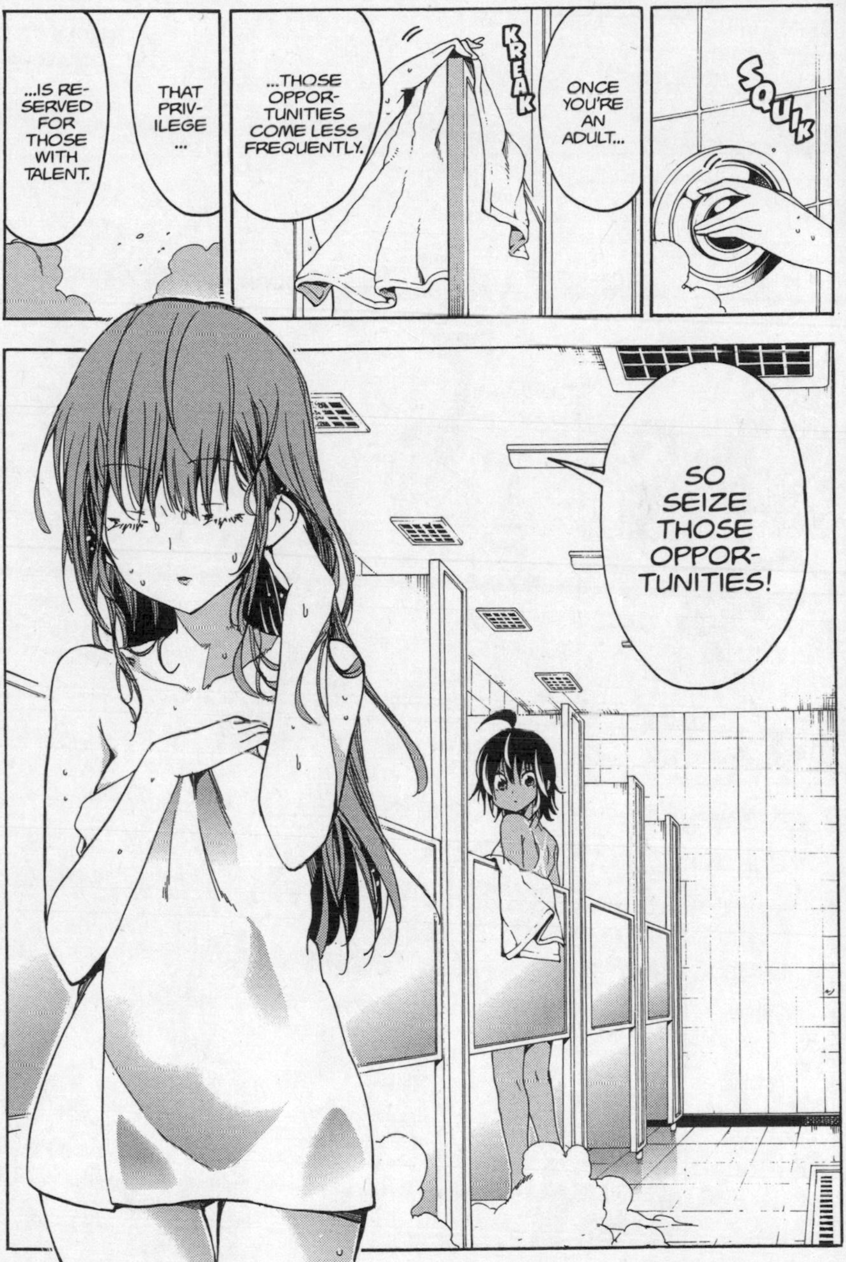
SQUIK
ONCE YOU'RE AN ADULT...
KREAK
...THOSE OPPORTUNITIES COME LESS FREQUENTLY.
THAT PRIVILEGE...
...IS RESERVED FOR THOSE WITH TALENT.
SO SEIZE THOSE OPPORTUNITIES!

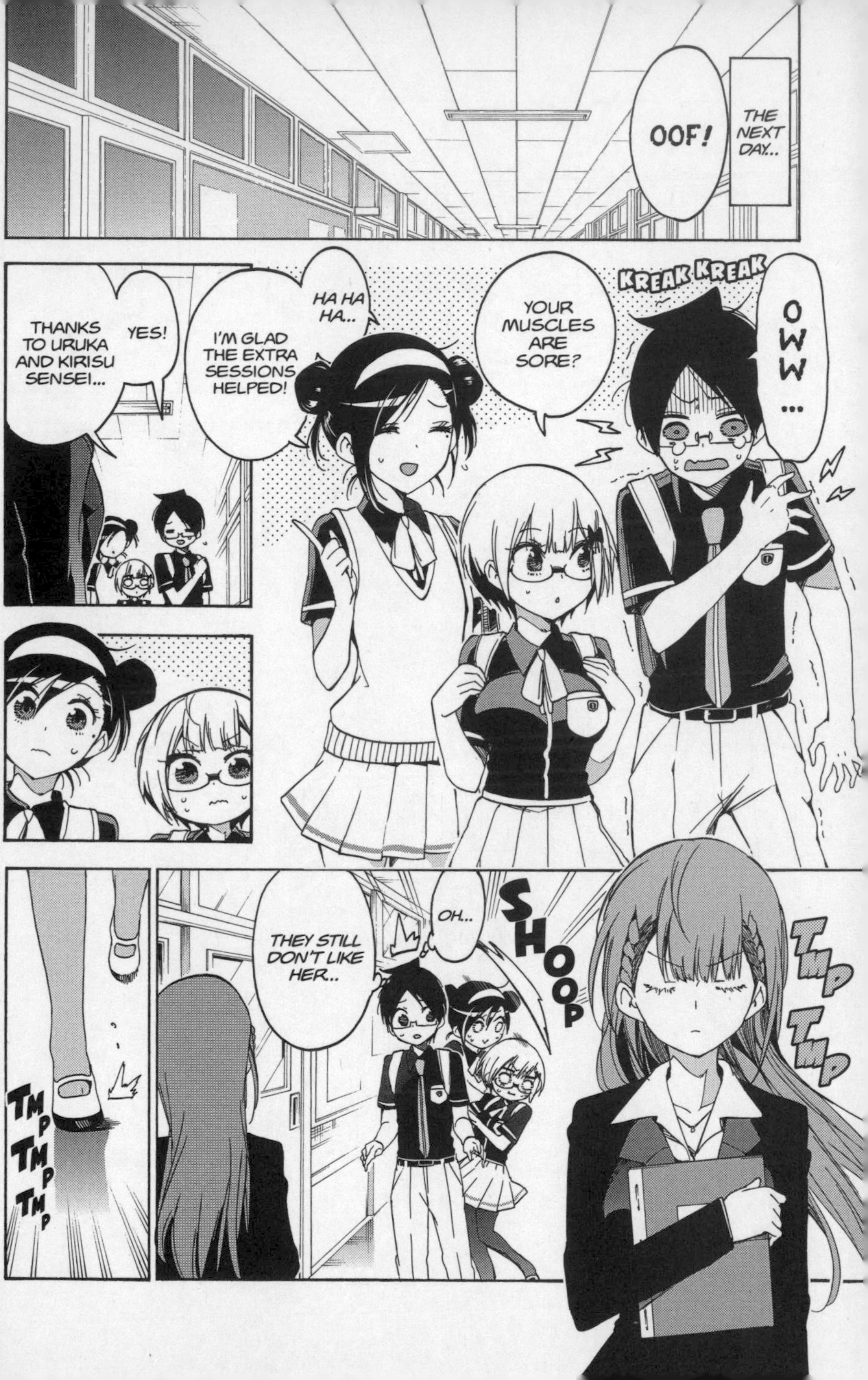
THE NEXT DAY...
OOF!
KREAK KREAK
OWW...
YOUR MUSCLES ARE SORE?
HA HA HA...
I'M GLAD THE EXTRA SESSIONS HELPED!
YES!
THANKS TO URUKA AND KIRISU SENSEI...
SHOOP
TMP TMP TMP
OH...
THEY STILL DON'T LIKE HER...
TMP TMP TMP

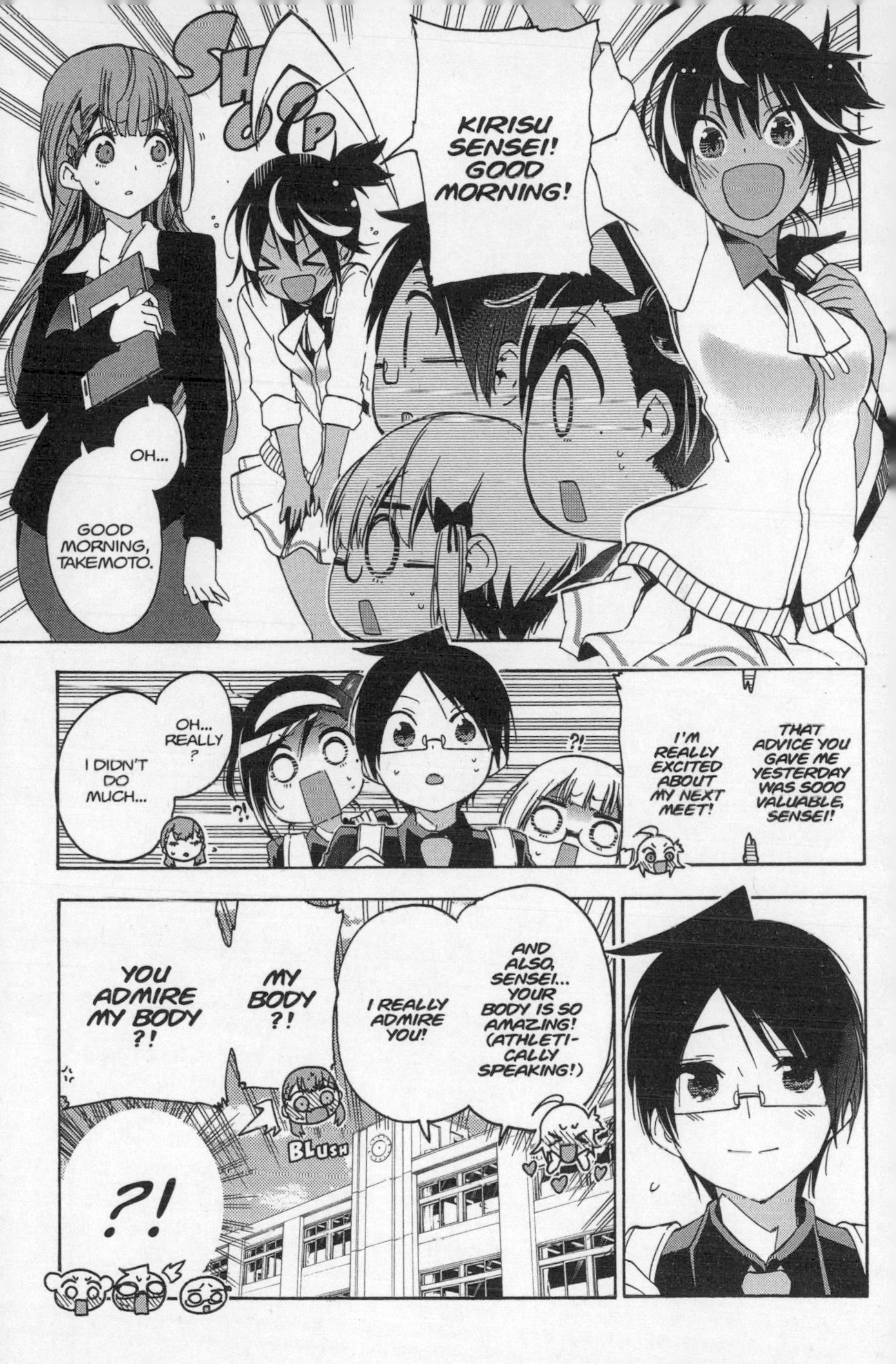
KIRISU SENSEI! GOOD MORNING!
SHOOP
OH...
GOOD MORNING, TAKEMOTO.
THAT ADVICE YOU GAVE ME YESTERDAY WAS SOOO VALUABLE, SENSEI!
I'M REALLY EXCITED ABOUT MY NEXT MEET!
?!
OH... REALLY?
I DIDN'T DO MUCH...
?!
AND ALSO, SENSEI... YOUR BODY IS SO AMAZING! (ATHLETI-CALLY SPEAKING!)
I REALLY ADMIRE YOU!
MY BODY?!
YOU ADMIRE MY BODY?!
BLUSH
?!

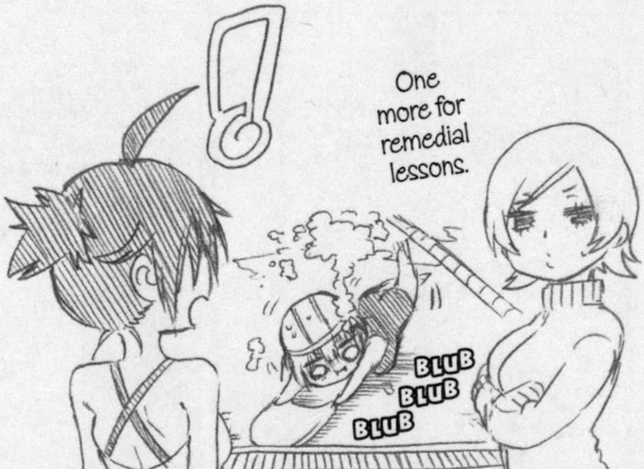
One more for remedial lessons.
BLUB
BLUB
BLUB

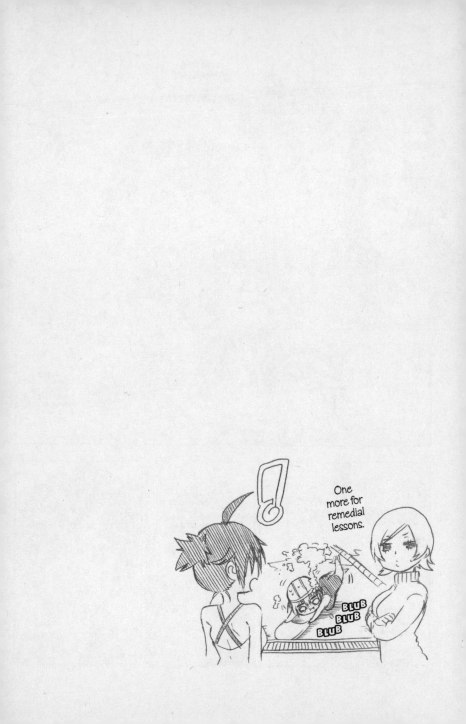

Question 64: Excitement and Busyness in Anticipation of [X]

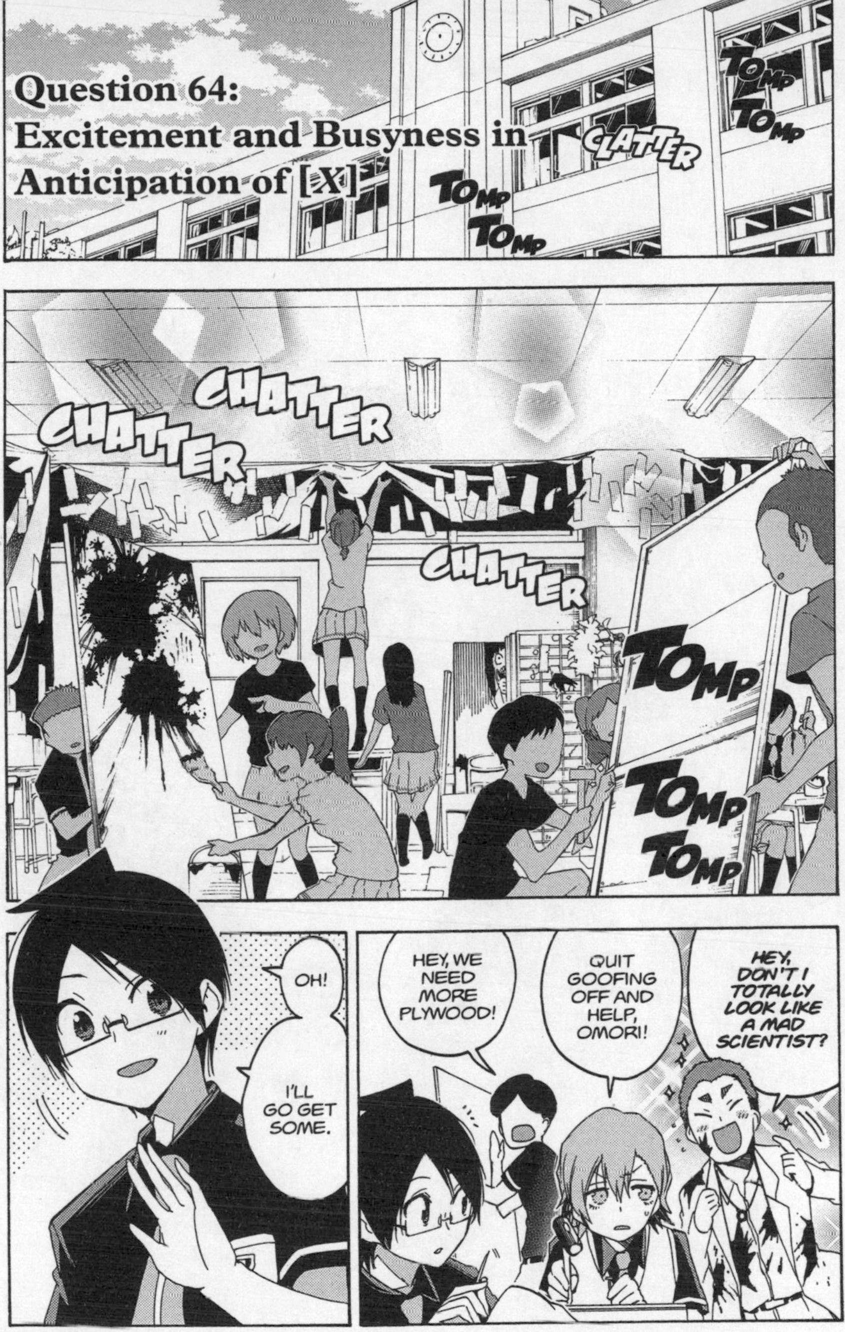
TOMP TOMP
CLATTER
TOMP TOMP
CHATTER
CHATTER
CHATTER
TOMP
TOMP TOMP
HEY, DON'T I TOTALLY LOOK LIKE A MAD SCIENTIST?
QUIT GOOFING OFF AND HELP, OMORI!
HEY, WE NEED MORE PLYWOOD!
OH!
I'LL GO GET SOME.

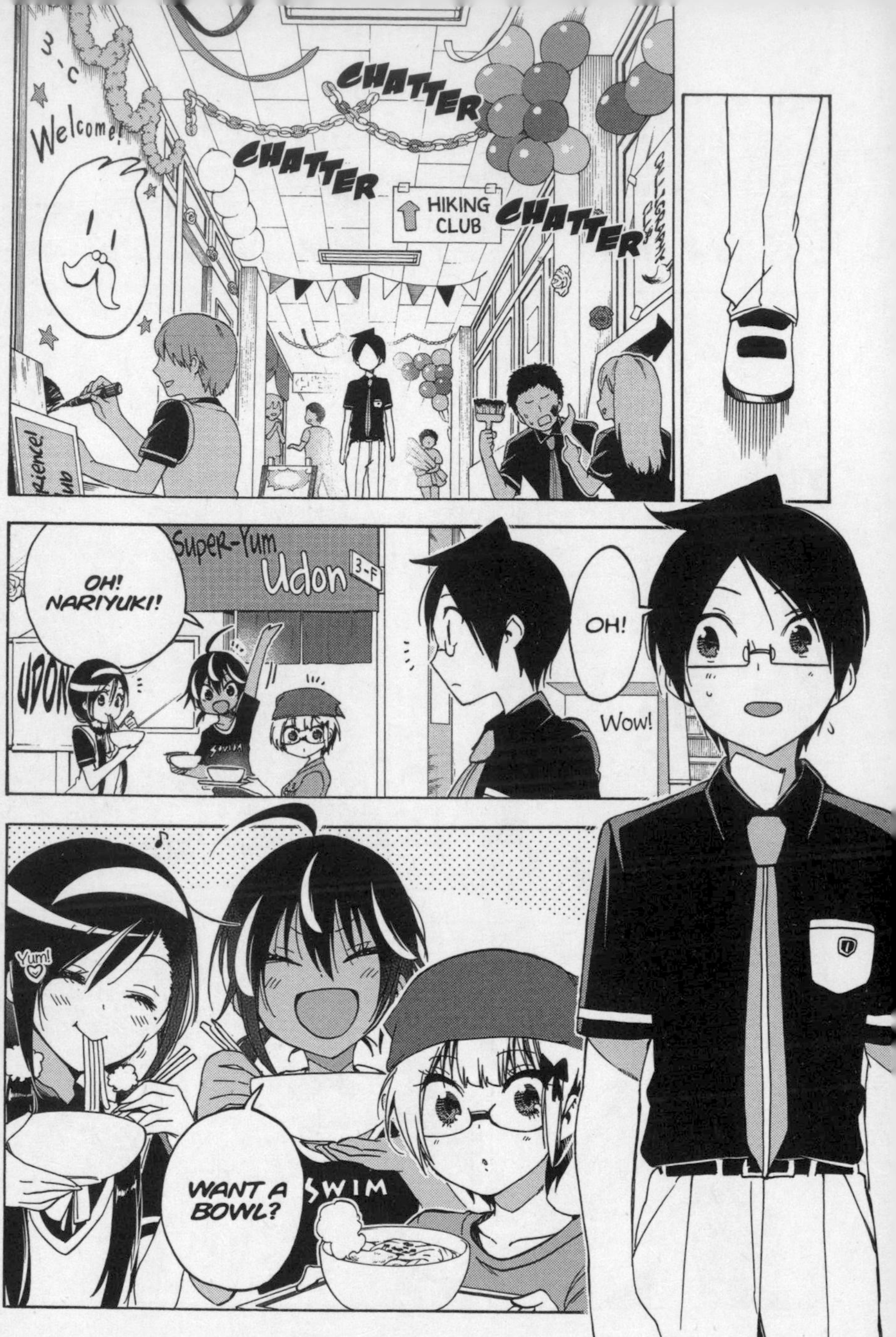
3-C
Welcome!
CHATTER
CHATTER
HIKING CLUB
CHATTER
OH!
Wow!
Super-Yum Udon
3-F
OH! NARIYUKI!
UDON
WANT A BOWL?
SWIM
Yum!

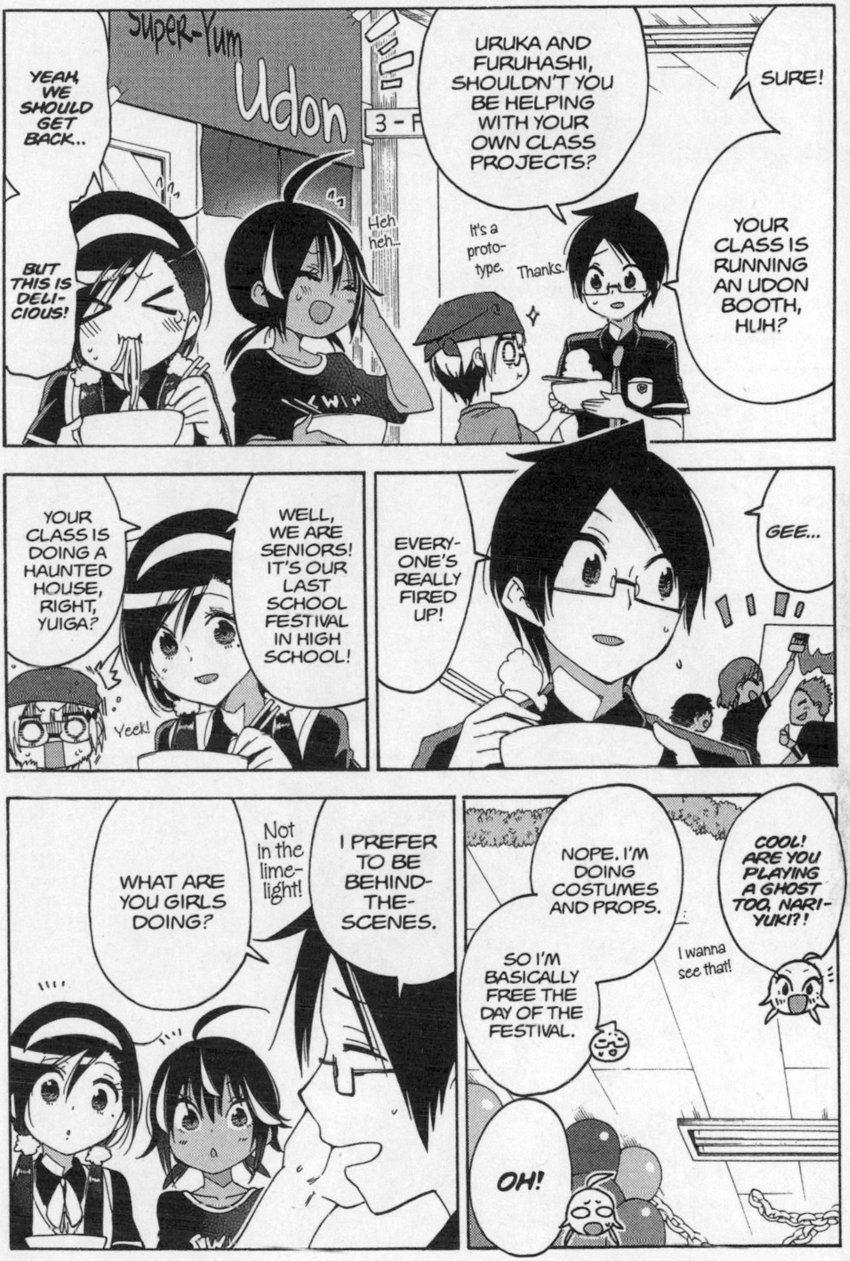

SURE!
URUKA AND FURUHASHI, SHOULDN'T YOU BE HELPING WITH YOUR OWN CLASS PROJECTS?
YOUR CLASS IS RUNNING AN UDON BOOTH, HUH?
Thanks.
It's a prototype.
3-F
Super-Yum Udon
Heh heh...
YEAH, WE SHOULD GET BACK...
BUT THIS IS DELICIOUS!
GEE...
EVERYONE'S REALLY FIRED UP!
WELL, WE ARE SENIORS! IT'S OUR LAST SCHOOL FESTIVAL IN HIGH SCHOOL!
YOUR CLASS IS DOING A HAUNTED HOUSE, RIGHT, YUIGA?
Yeek!
COOL! ARE YOU PLAYING A GHOST TOO, NARI-YUKI?!
I wanna see that!
NOPE. I'M DOING COSTUMES AND PROPS.
SO I'M BASICALLY FREE THE DAY OF THE FESTIVAL.
OH!
I PREFER TO BE BEHIND-THE-SCENES.
Not in the limelight!
WHAT ARE YOU GIRLS DOING?

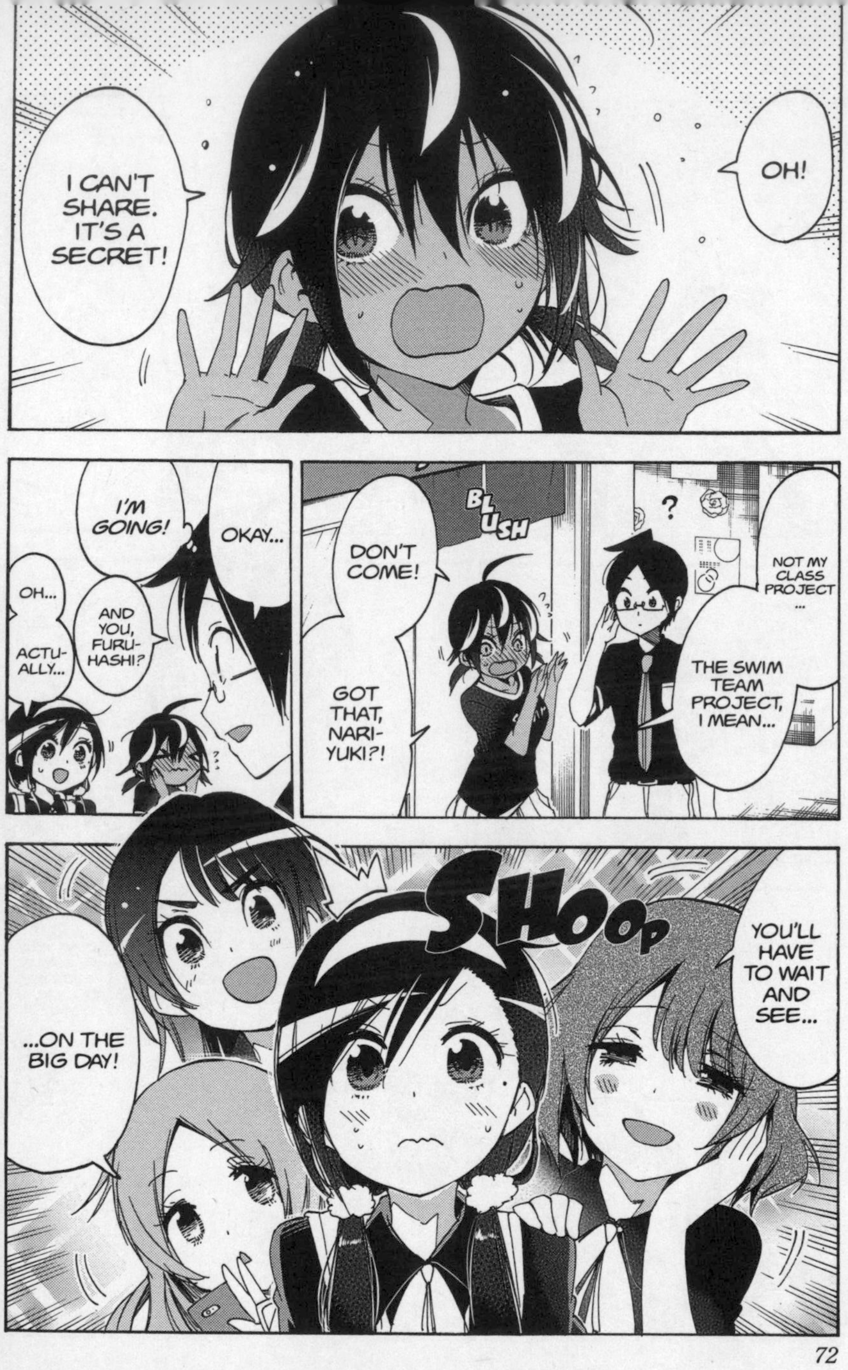
OH!
I CAN'T SHARE. IT'S A SECRET!
NOT MY CLASS PROJECT ...
THE SWIM TEAM PROJECT, I MEAN...
?
BLUSH
DON'T COME!
GOT THAT, NARI-YUKI?!
OKAY...
I'M GOING!
AND YOU, FURU-HASHI?
OH... ACTU-ALLY...
YOU'LL HAVE TO WAIT AND SEE...
SHOOP
...ON THE BIG DAY!

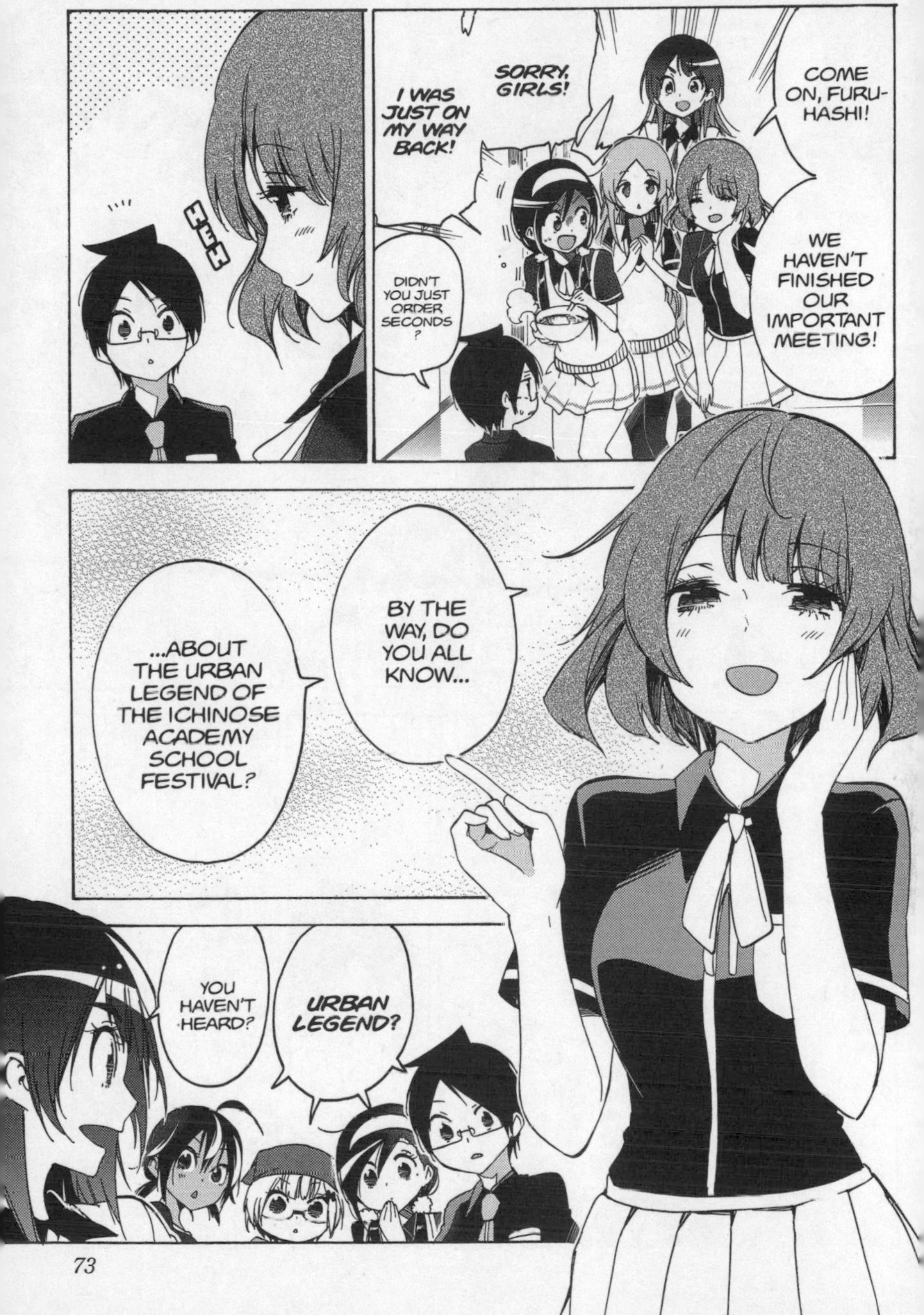
COME ON, FURU-HASHI!
WE HAVEN'T FINISHED OUR IMPORTANT MEETING!
SORRY, GIRLS!
I WAS JUST ON MY WAY BACK!
DIDN'T YOU JUST ORDER SECONDS?
HEH
BY THE WAY, DO YOU ALL KNOW...
...ABOUT THE URBAN LEGEND OF THE ICHINOSE ACADEMY SCHOOL FESTIVAL?
URBAN LEGEND?
YOU HAVEN'T HEARD?

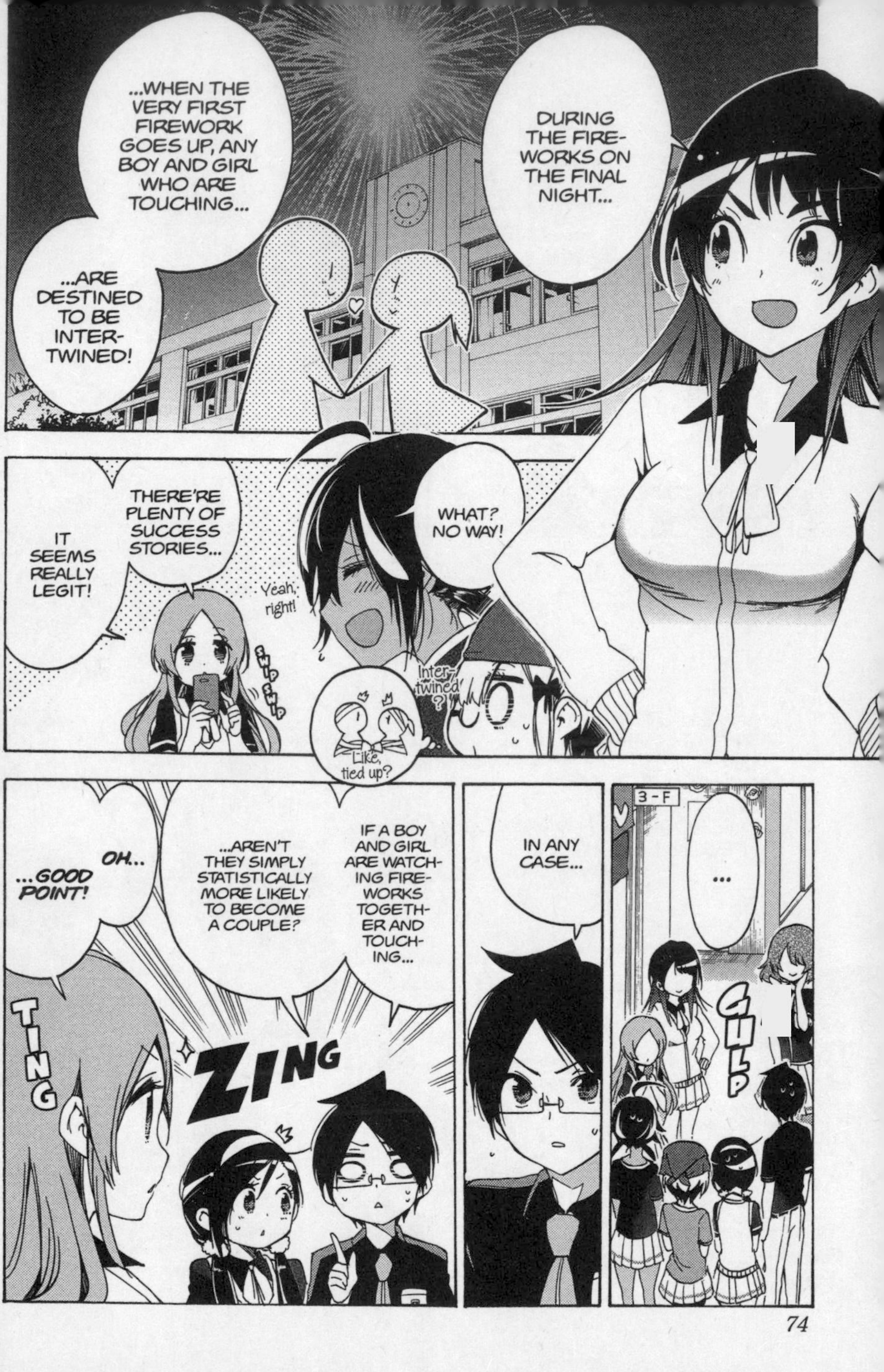
DURING THE FIRE-WORKS ON THE FINAL NIGHT...
...WHEN THE VERY FIRST FIREWORK GOES UP, ANY BOY AND GIRL WHO ARE TOUCHING...
...ARE DESTINED TO BE INTER-TWINED!
WHAT? NO WAY!
Yeah, right!
THERE'RE PLENTY OF SUCCESS STORIES...
IT SEEMS REALLY LEGIT!
SWIP SWIP
Inter-twined?
Like, tied up?
3-F
...
GULP
IN ANY CASE...
IF A BOY AND GIRL ARE WATCHING FIRE-WORKS TOGETH-ER AND TOUCH-ING...
...AREN'T THEY SIMPLY STATISTICALLY MORE LIKELY TO BECOME A COUPLE?
ZING
OH...
...GOOD POINT!
TING

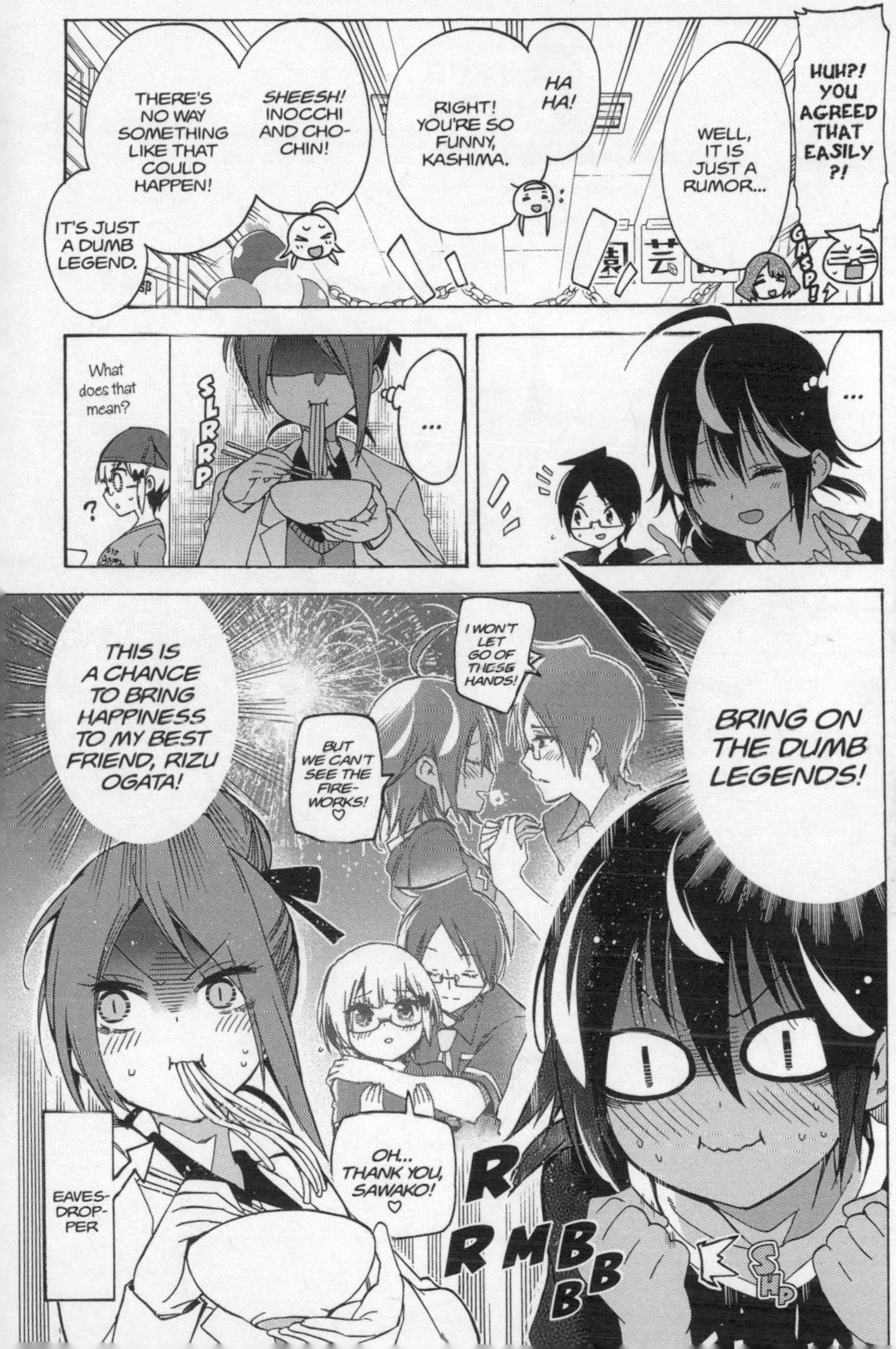
HUH?! YOU AGREED THAT EASILY?!
WELL, IT IS JUST A RUMOR...
HA HA!
RIGHT! YOU'RE SO FUNNY, KASHIMA.
SHEESH! INOCCHI AND CHO-CHIN!
THERE'S NO WAY SOMETHING LIKE THAT COULD HAPPEN!
IT'S JUST A DUMB LEGEND.
GASP!
...
...
SLRRP
What does that mean?
?
BRING ON THE DUMB LEGENDS!
I WON'T LET GO OF THESE HANDS!
THIS IS A CHANCE TO BRING HAPPINESS TO MY BEST FRIEND, RIZU OGATA!
BUT WE CAN'T SEE THE FIRE-WORKS! ♡
SHP
OH... THANK YOU, SAWAKO! ♡
RRMBBBB
EAVES-DROPPER

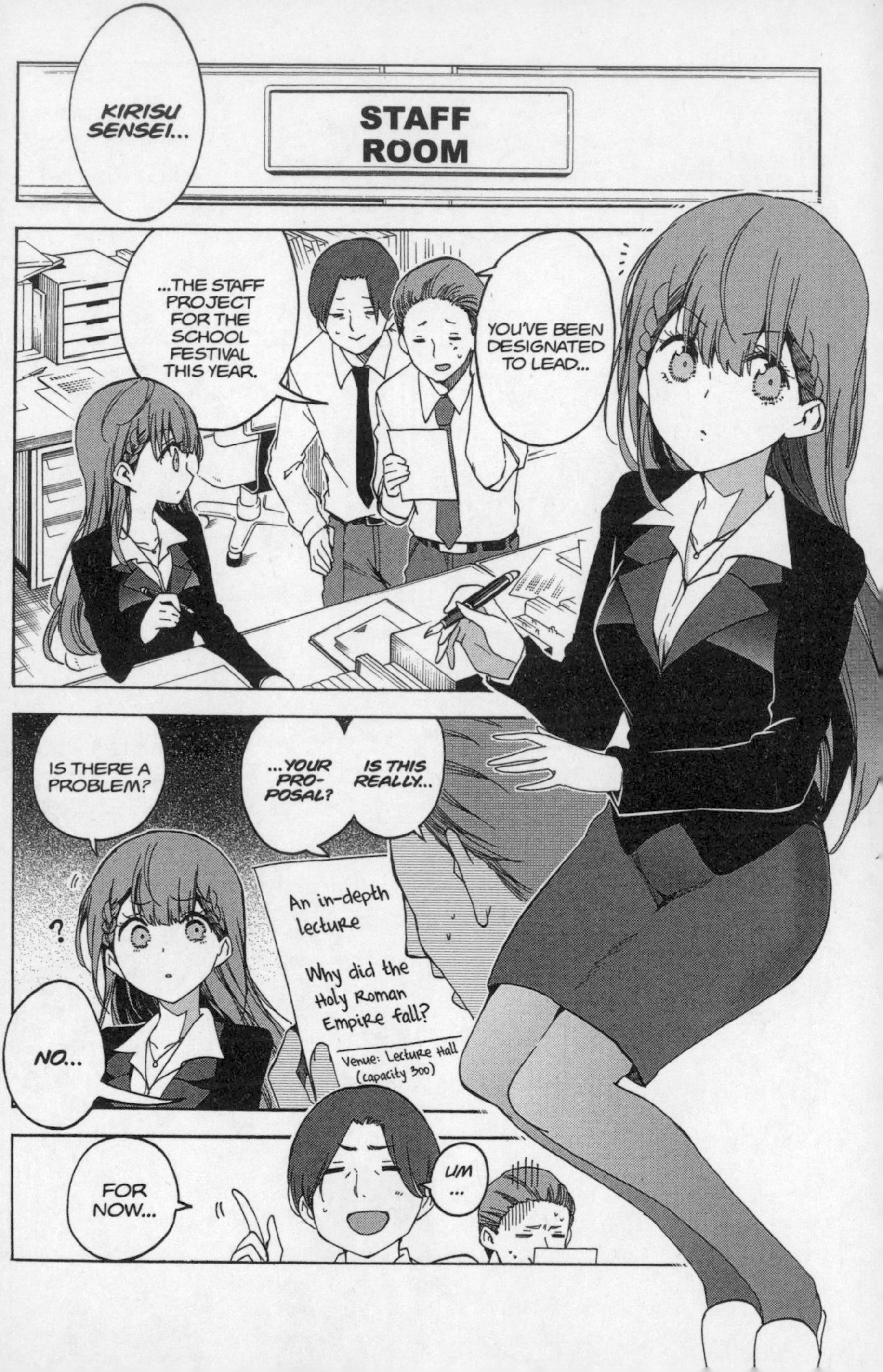
STAFF ROOM
KIRISU SENSEI...
YOU'VE BEEN DESIGNATED TO LEAD...
...THE STAFF PROJECT FOR THE SCHOOL FESTIVAL THIS YEAR.
IS THIS REALLY...
...YOUR PRO-POSAL?
IS THERE A PROBLEM?
An in-depth lecture
Why did the Holy Roman Empire fall?
Venue: Lecture Hall (capacity 300)
NO...
UM ...
FOR NOW...

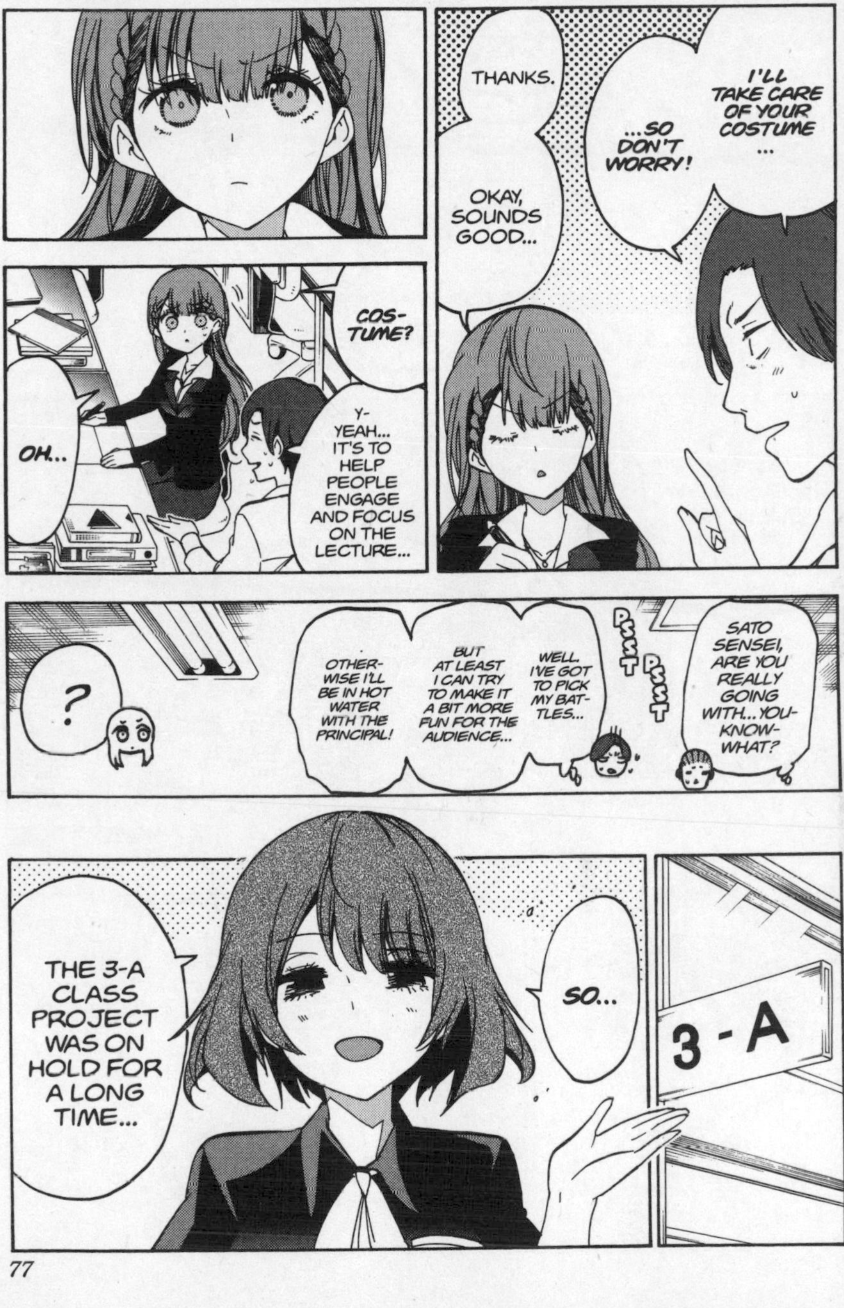
I'LL TAKE CARE OF YOUR COSTUME ...
...SO DON'T WORRY!
THANKS.
OKAY, SOUNDS GOOD...
COS-TUME?
Y-YEAH... IT'S TO HELP PEOPLE ENGAGE AND FOCUS ON THE LECTURE...
OH...
SATO SENSEI, ARE YOU REALLY GOING WITH... YOU-KNOW-WHAT?
PSST PSST
WELL. I'VE GOT TO PICK MY BAT-TLES...
BUT AT LEAST I CAN TRY TO MAKE IT A BIT MORE FUN FOR THE AUDIENCE...
OTHER-WISE I'LL BE IN HOT WATER WITH THE PRINCIPAL!
?
3 - A
SO...
THE 3-A CLASS PROJECT WAS ON HOLD FOR A LONG TIME...

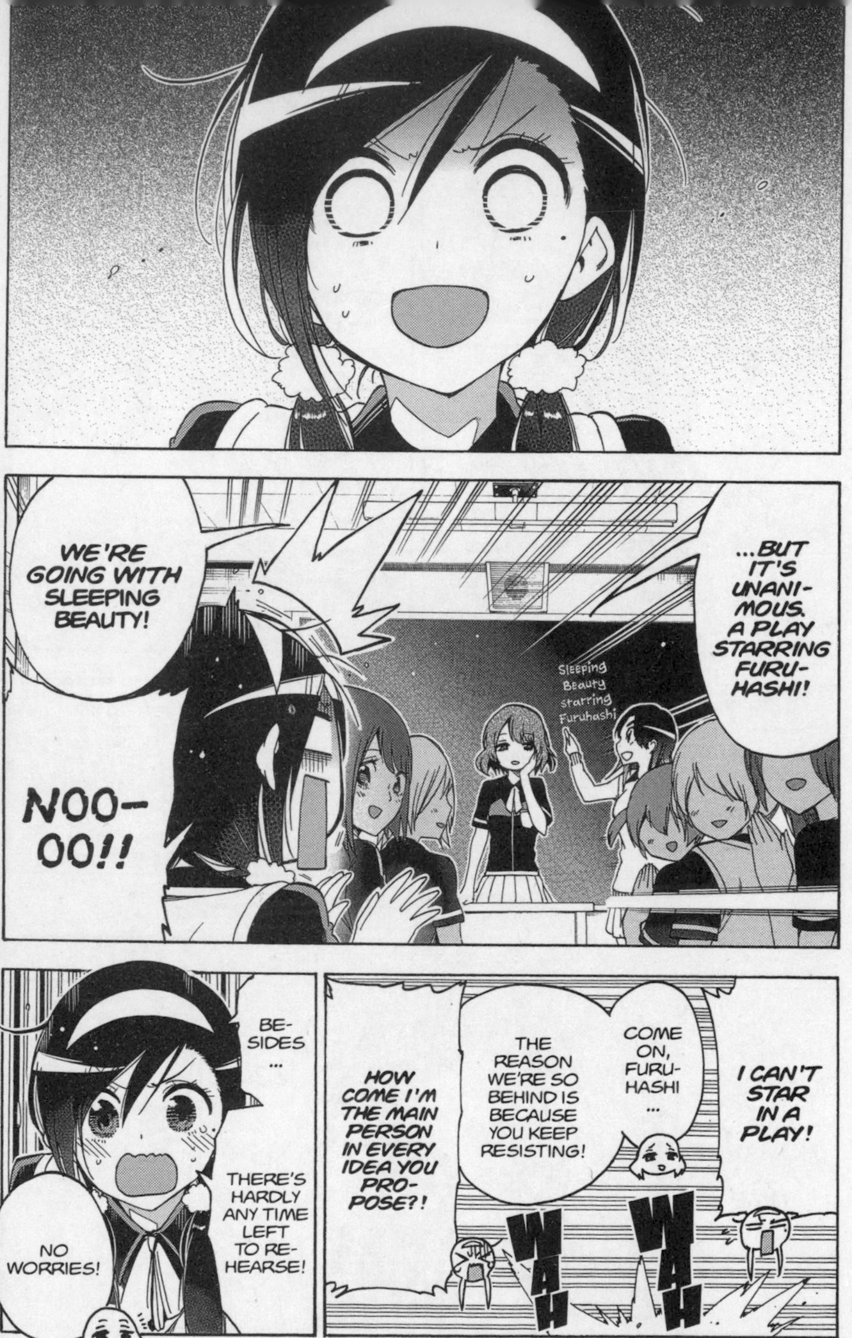
...BUT IT'S UNANI-MOUS. A PLAY STARRING FURU-HASHI!
Sleeping Beauty starring Furuhashi
WE'RE GOING WITH SLEEPING BEAUTY!
NOO-OO!!
I CAN'T STAR IN A PLAY!
COME ON, FURU-HASHI ...
THE REASON WE'RE SO BEHIND IS BECAUSE YOU KEEP RESISTING!
HOW COME I'M THE MAIN PERSON IN EVERY IDEA YOU PRO-POSE?!
WAH
WAH
BE-SIDES ...
THERE'S HARDLY ANY TIME LEFT TO RE-HEARSE!
NO WORRIES!

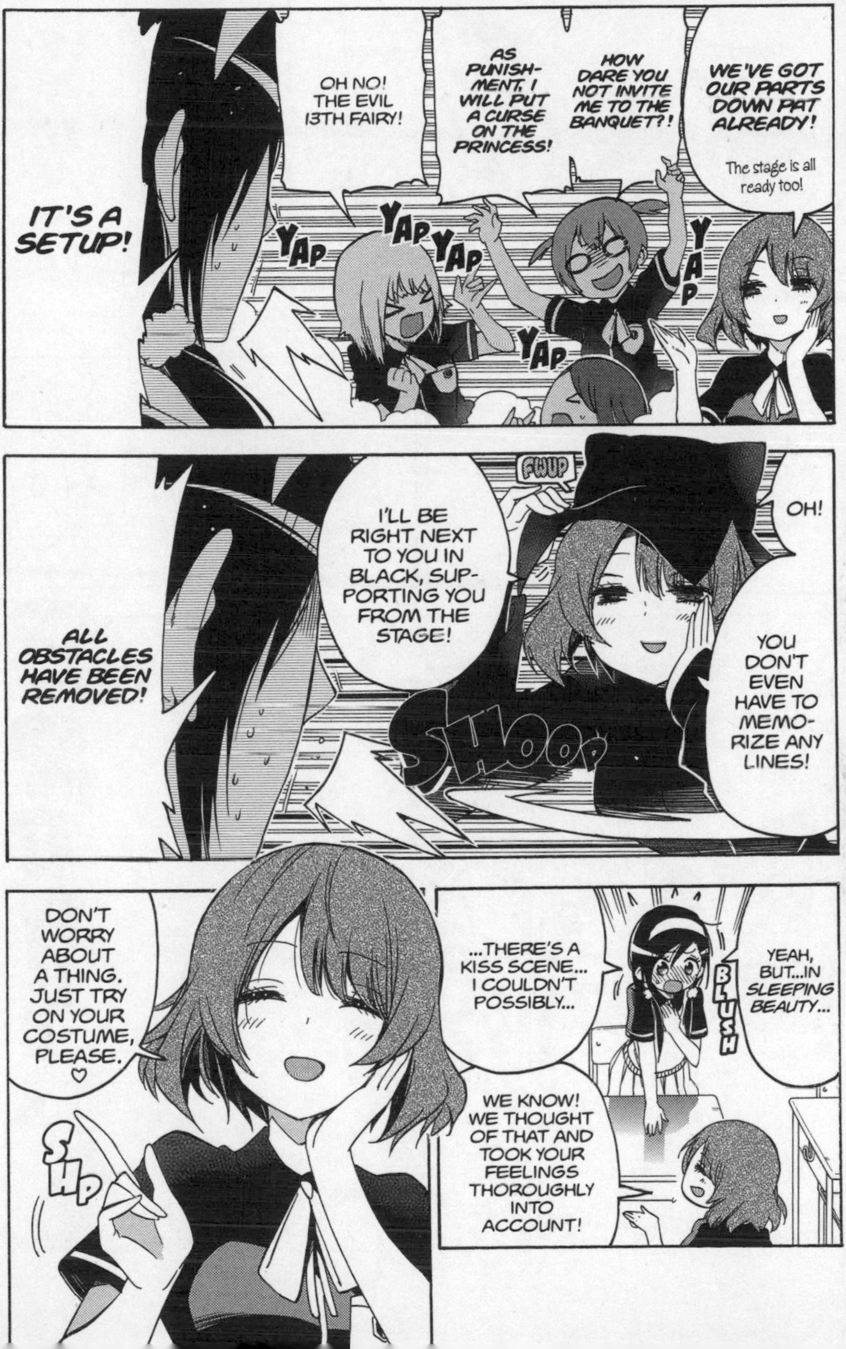
WE'VE GOT OUR PARTS DOWN PAT ALREADY!
The stage is all ready too!
HOW DARE YOU NOT INVITE ME TO THE BANQUET?!
AS PUNISH-MENT, I WILL PUT A CURSE ON THE PRINCESS!
OH NO! THE EVIL 13TH FAIRY!
YAP
YAP
YAP YAP
YAP
IT'S A SETUP!
OH!
YOU DON'T EVEN HAVE TO MEMO-RIZE ANY LINES!
FWUP
I'LL BE RIGHT NEXT TO YOU IN BLACK, SUP-PORTING YOU FROM THE STAGE!
SHOOP
ALL OBSTACLES HAVE BEEN REMOVED!
YEAH, BUT...IN SLEEPING BEAUTY...
BLUSH
...THERE'S A KISS SCENE... I COULDN'T POSSIBLY...
WE KNOW! WE THOUGHT OF THAT AND TOOK YOUR FEELINGS THOROUGHLY INTO ACCOUNT!
DON'T WORRY ABOUT A THING. JUST TRY ON YOUR COSTUME, PLEASE. ♡
SHP

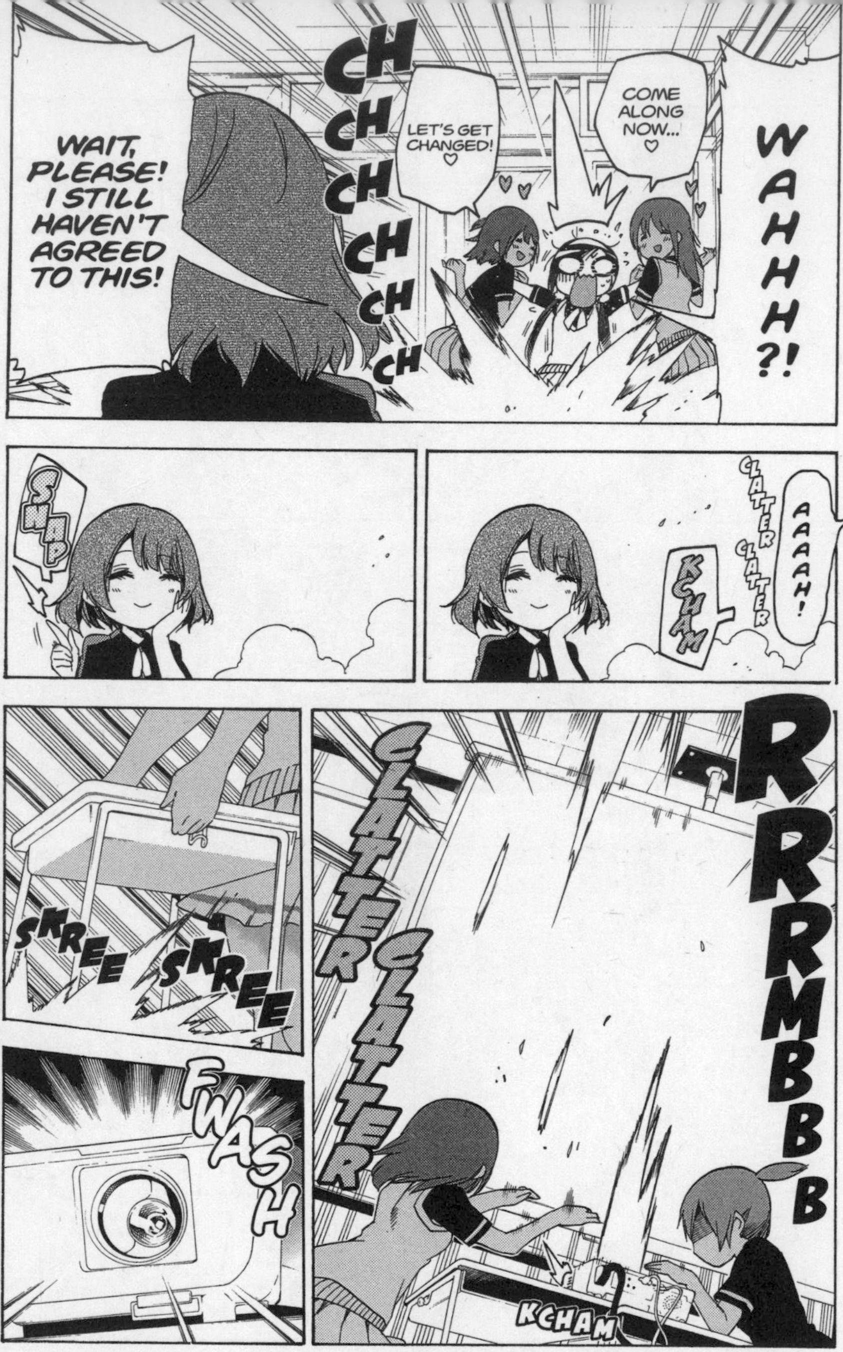
WAHHHH?!
COME ALONG NOW... ♡
LET'S GET CHANGED! ♡
CH CH CH CH CH CH CH
WAIT, PLEASE! I STILL HAVEN'T AGREED TO THIS!
AAAAH!
CLATTER CLATTER
KCHAM
SNAP
RRRMBBB
CLATTER CLATTER
KCHAM
SKREE SKREE
FWASH

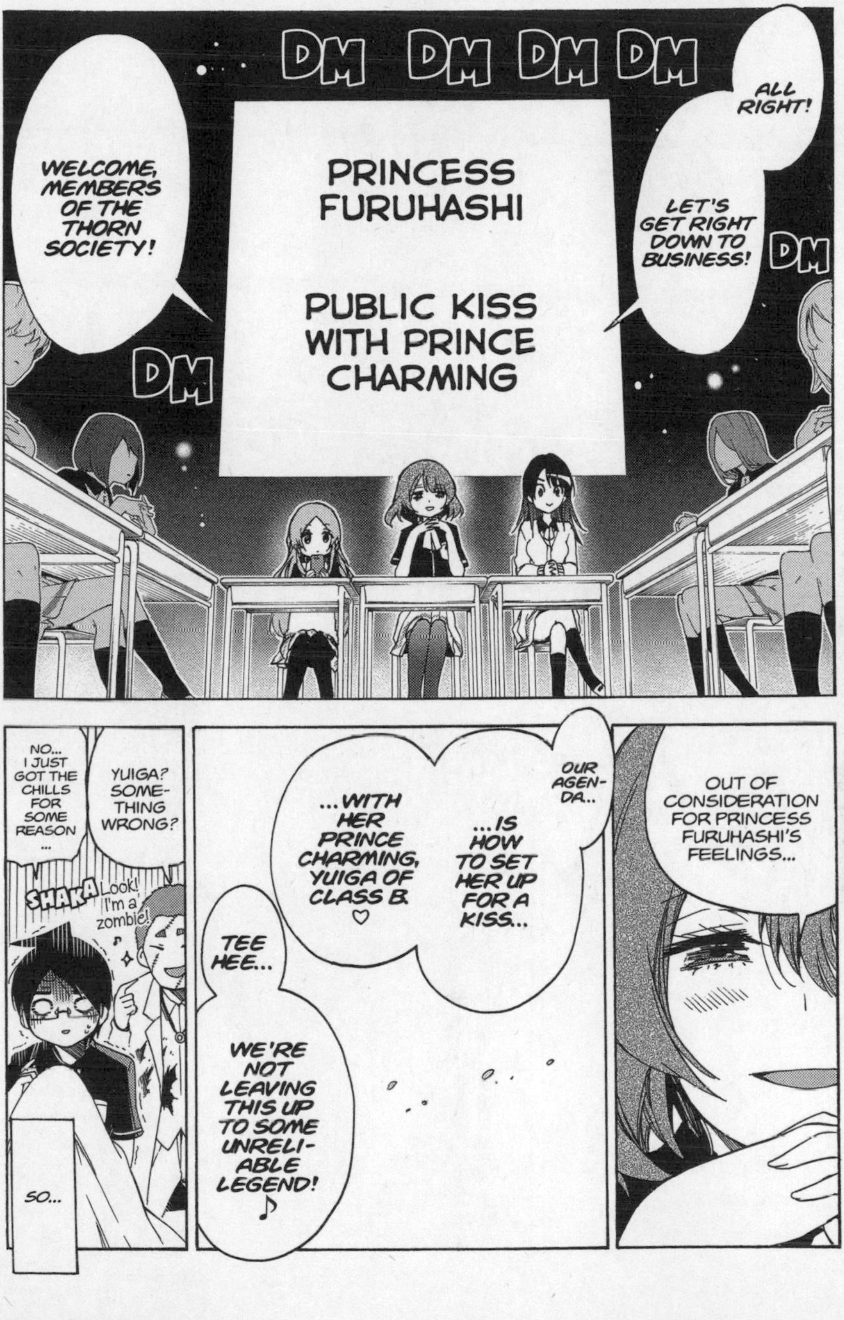
DM DM DM DM
ALL RIGHT!
LET'S GET RIGHT DOWN TO BUSINESS!
DM
PRINCESS FURUHASHI
PUBLIC KISS WITH PRINCE CHARMING
WELCOME, MEMBERS OF THE THORN SOCIETY!
DM
OUT OF CONSIDERATION FOR PRINCESS FURUHASHI'S FEELINGS...
OUR AGENDA...
...IS HOW TO SET HER UP FOR A KISS...
...WITH HER PRINCE CHARMING, YUIGA OF CLASS B. ♡
TEE HEE...
WE'RE NOT LEAVING THIS UP TO SOME UNRELIABLE LEGEND! ♪
YUIGA? SOMETHING WRONG?
NO... I JUST GOT THE CHILLS FOR SOME REASON...
SHAKA
Look! I'm a zombie!
SO...

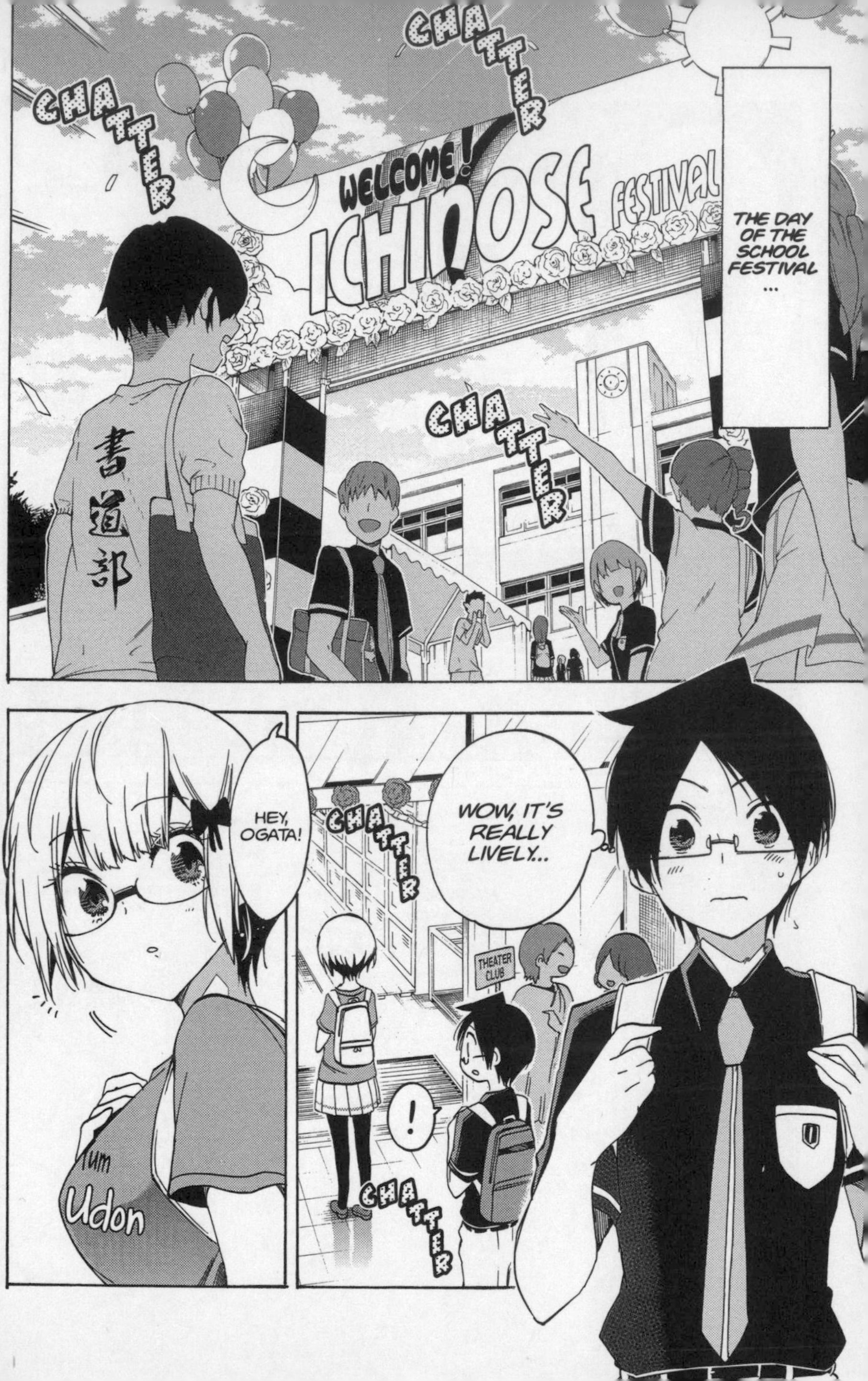
THE DAY OF THE SCHOOL FESTIVAL ...
CHATTER
WELCOME! ICHINOSE FESTIVAL
CHATTER
CHATTER
書道部
WOW, IT'S REALLY LIVELY...
CHATTER
THEATER CLUB
!
CHATTER
HEY, OGATA!
Yum
Udon

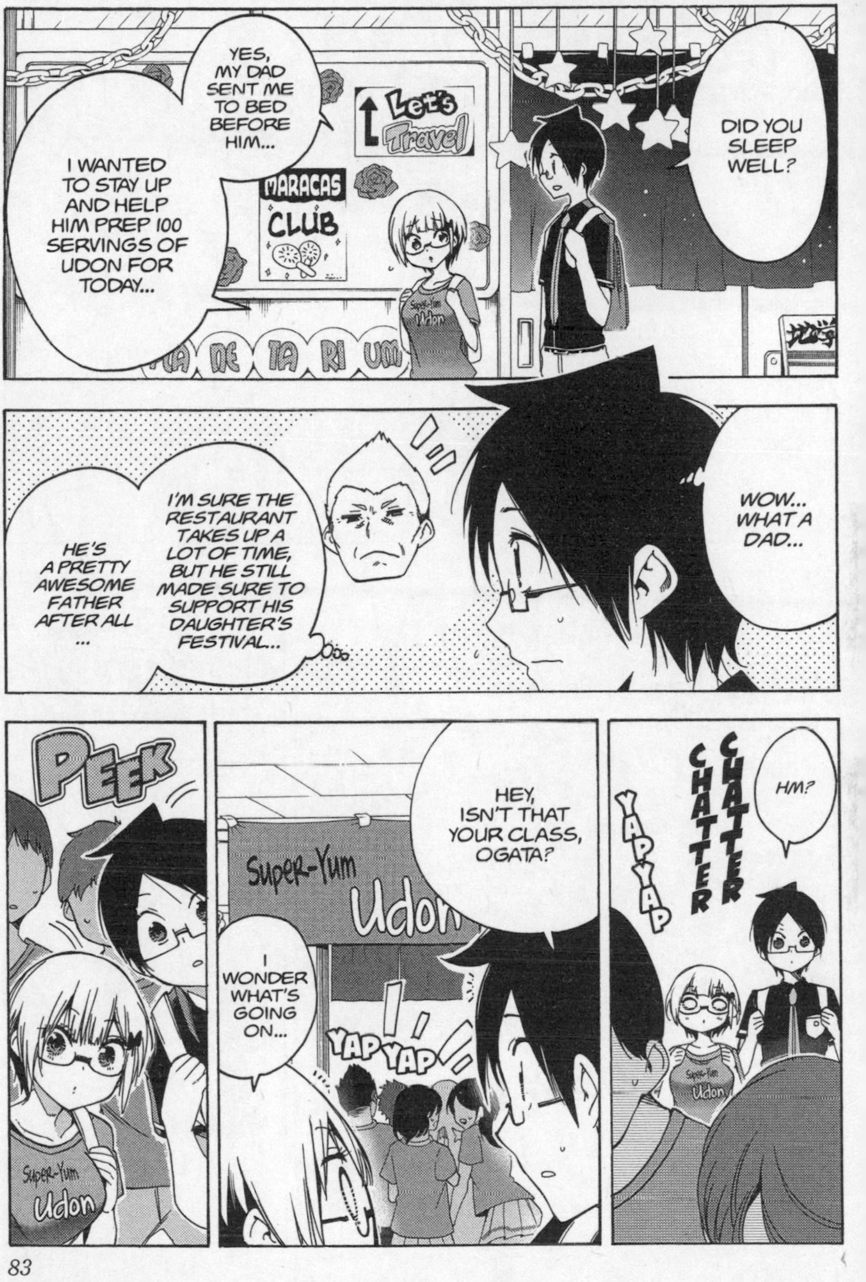
DID YOU SLEEP WELL?
YES, MY DAD SENT ME TO BED BEFORE HIM...
I WANTED TO STAY UP AND HELP HIM PREP 100 SERVINGS OF UDON FOR TODAY...
Let's Travel
MARACAS CLUB
Super-Yum Udon
WOW... WHAT A DAD...
I'M SURE THE RESTAURANT TAKES UP A LOT OF TIME, BUT HE STILL MADE SURE TO SUPPORT HIS DAUGHTER'S FESTIVAL...
HE'S A PRETTY AWESOME FATHER AFTER ALL ...
CHATTER CHATTER
YAP YAP
HM?
Super-Yum Udon
HEY, ISN'T THAT YOUR CLASS, OGATA?
Super-Yum Udon
I WONDER WHAT'S GOING ON...
YAP YAP
PEEK
Super-Yum Udon

BABAM

RMBB

Huff
Huff

HERE'S... THE DE-LIVERY... AS PROM-ISED...

HEY... RIZU-RIN...

DAD ?!

SHOOP

THIS IS WAY MORE THAN 100 OR 200 SERV-INGS!!

WHAT'S WITH THIS UDON MOUN-TAIN?!

OOF ...

!!

GLEAM
GLEAM

ORDER

Product		Quantity
Udon noodles.	×	100.
	×	
	×	

A THOUSAND ORDERS OF UDON!

84

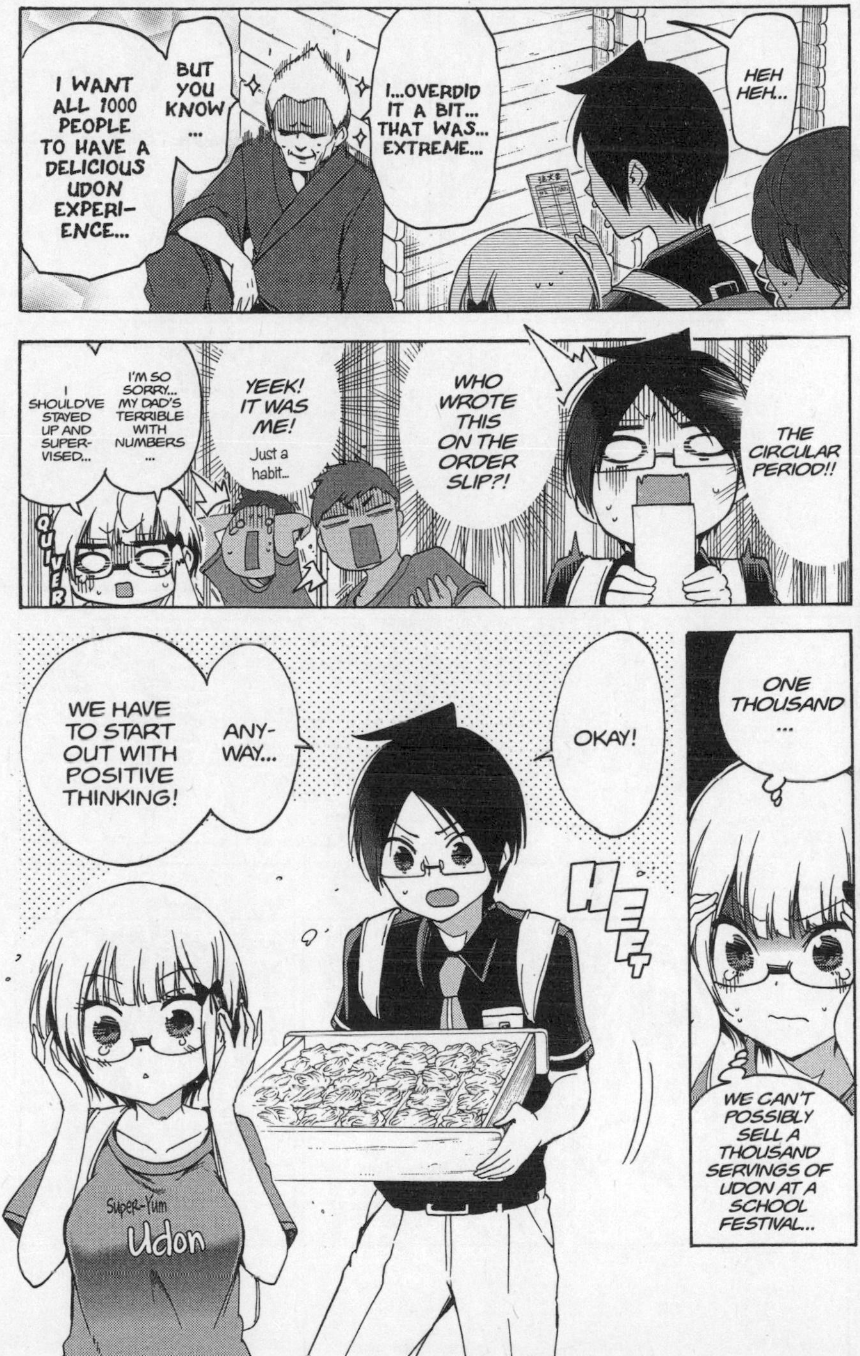
HEH HEH...
I...OVERDID IT A BIT... THAT WAS... EXTREME...
BUT YOU KNOW...
I WANT ALL 1000 PEOPLE TO HAVE A DELICIOUS UDON EXPERIENCE...
THE CIRCULAR PERIOD!!
WHO WROTE THIS ON THE ORDER SLIP?!
YEEK! IT WAS ME!
Just a habit...
I'M SO SORRY... MY DAD'S TERRIBLE WITH NUMBERS...
I SHOULD'VE STAYED UP AND SUPERVISED...
QUIVER
ONE THOUSAND...
WE CAN'T POSSIBLY SELL A THOUSAND SERVINGS OF UDON AT A SCHOOL FESTIVAL...
OKAY!
HEFT
ANYWAY...
WE HAVE TO START OUT WITH POSITIVE THINKING!
Super-Yum Udon

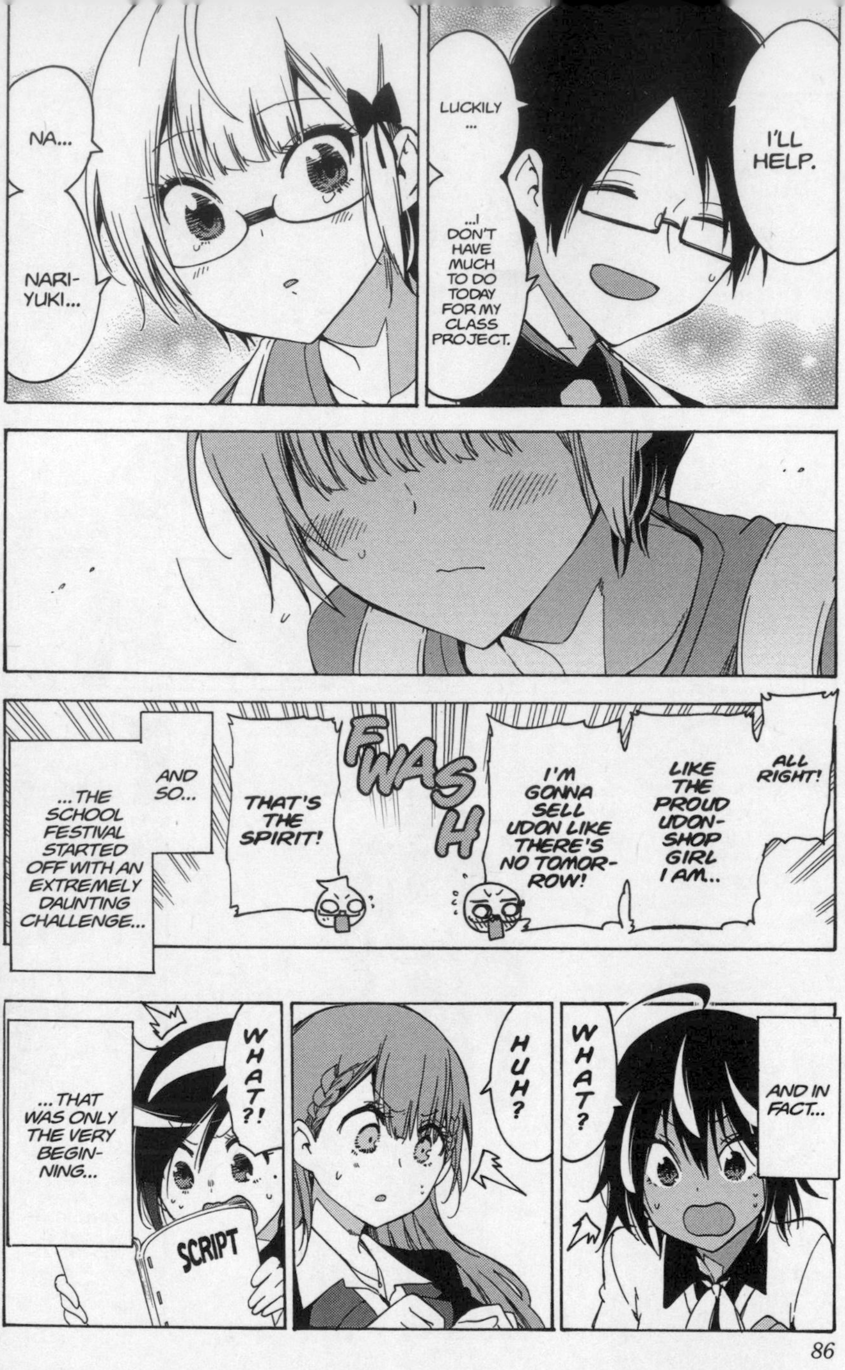
I'LL HELP.
LUCKILY...
...I DON'T HAVE MUCH TO DO TODAY FOR MY CLASS PROJECT.
NA...
NARI-YUKI...
ALL RIGHT!
LIKE THE PROUD UDON-SHOP GIRL I AM...
I'M GONNA SELL UDON LIKE THERE'S NO TOMORROW!
FWASH
THAT'S THE SPIRIT!
AND SO...
...THE SCHOOL FESTIVAL STARTED OFF WITH AN EXTREMELY DAUNTING CHALLENGE...
AND IN FACT...
WHAT?
HUH?
WHAT?!
...THAT WAS ONLY THE VERY BEGINNING...
SCRIPT

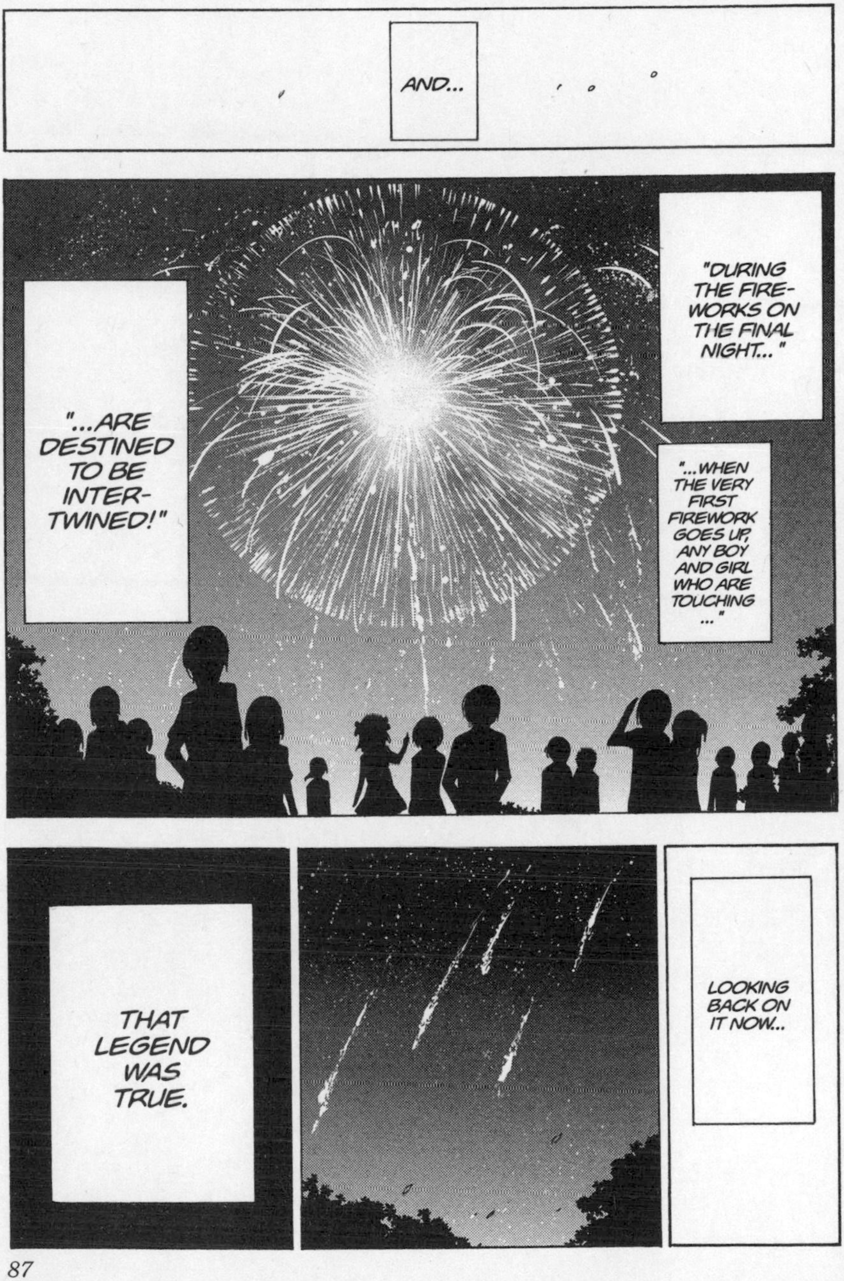
AND...
"DURING THE FIREWORKS ON THE FINAL NIGHT..."
"...WHEN THE VERY FIRST FIREWORK GOES UP, ANY BOY AND GIRL WHO ARE TOUCHING..."
"...ARE DESTINED TO BE INTERTWINED!"
LOOKING BACK ON IT NOW...
THAT LEGEND WAS TRUE.

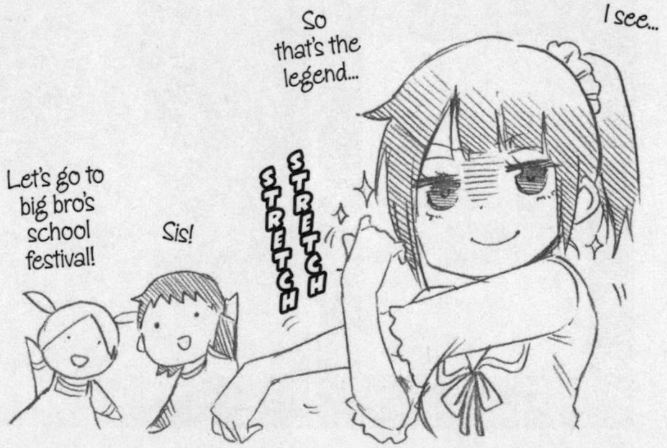
I see...
So that's the legend...
STRETCH
STRETCH
Sis!
Let's go to big bro's school festival!

Question 65: [X] Descends like Wildfire at the Festival's Beginning

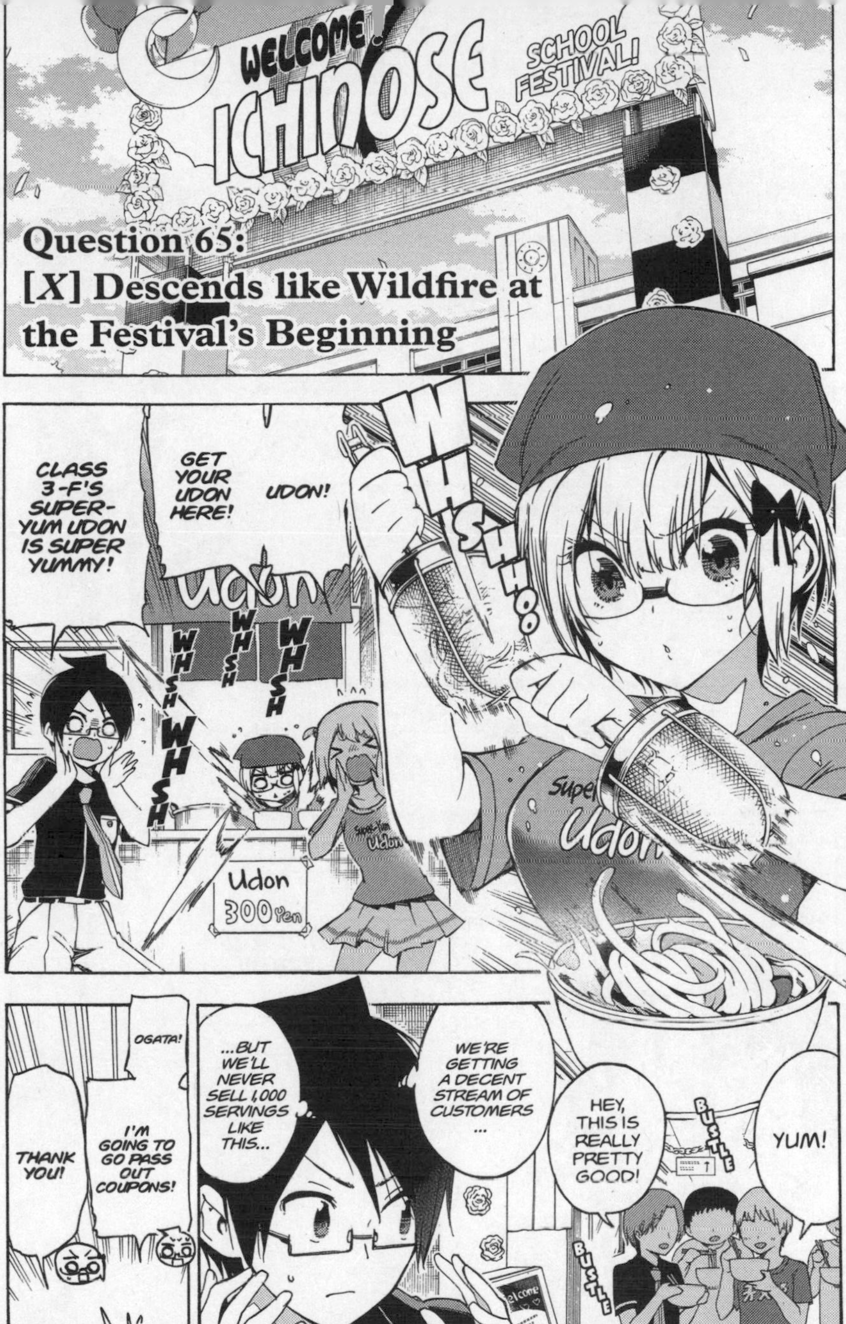
WELCOME! ICHINOSE SCHOOL FESTIVAL!
WHSHHOO
UDON!
GET YOUR UDON HERE!
CLASS 3-F'S SUPER-YUM UDON IS SUPER YUMMY!
Udon
WHSH WHSH WHSH WHSH WHSH
Super-Yum Udon
Udon 300 Yen
YUM!
HEY, THIS IS REALLY PRETTY GOOD!
BUSTLE BUSTLE
WE'RE GETTING A DECENT STREAM OF CUSTOMERS...
...BUT WE'LL NEVER SELL 1,000 SERVINGS LIKE THIS...
OGATA!
I'M GOING TO GO PASS OUT COUPONS!
THANK YOU!

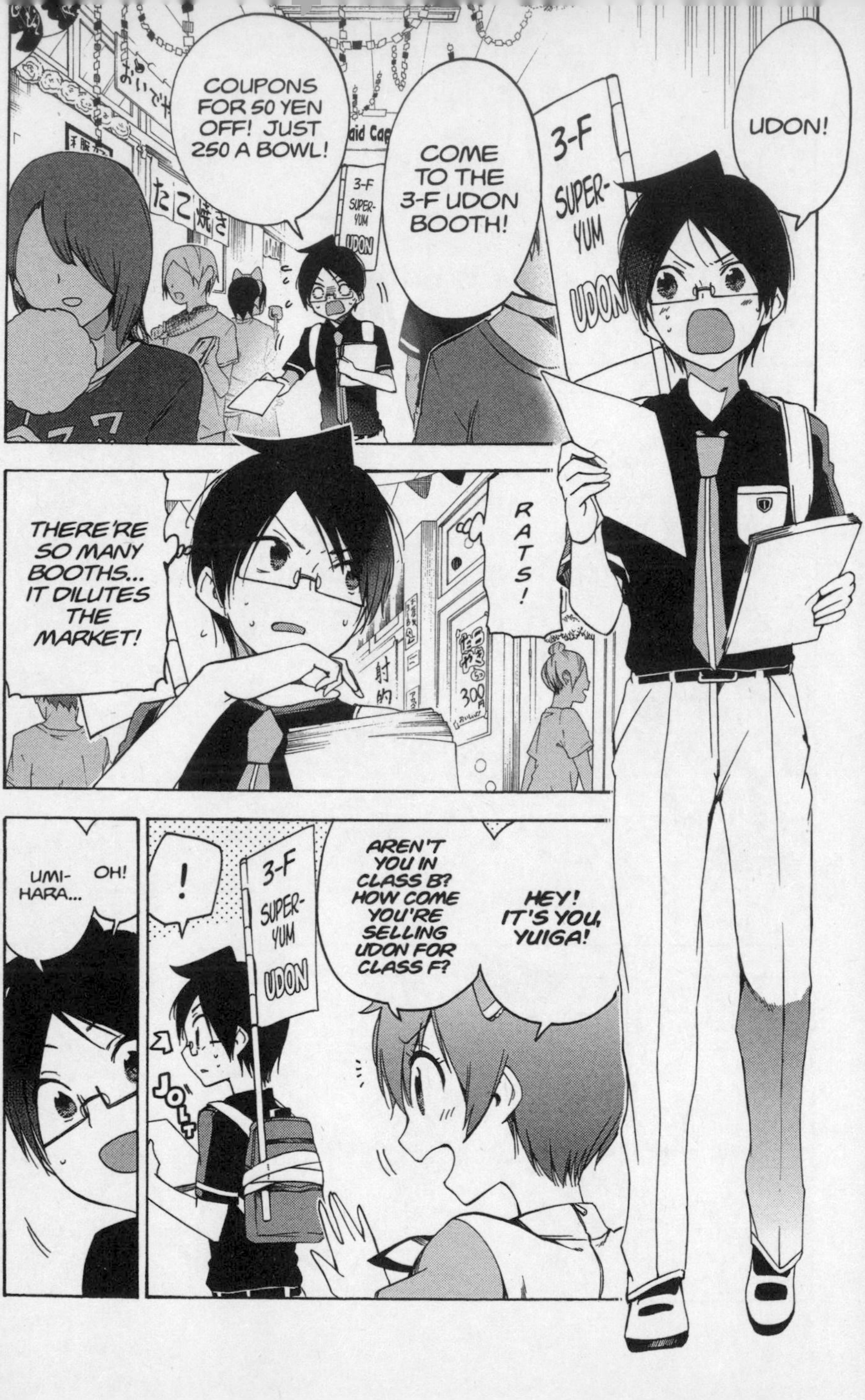

UDON!
3-F
SUPER-YUM
UDON
COME TO THE 3-F UDON BOOTH!
COUPONS FOR 50 YEN OFF! JUST 250 A BOWL!
3-F
SUPER-YUM
UDON
たこ焼き
RATS!
THERE'RE SO MANY BOOTHS... IT DILUTES THE MARKET!
300円
HEY! IT'S YOU, YUIGA!
AREN'T YOU IN CLASS B? HOW COME YOU'RE SELLING UDON FOR CLASS F?
!
3-F
SUPER-YUM
UDON
JOLT
OH!
UMI-HARA...

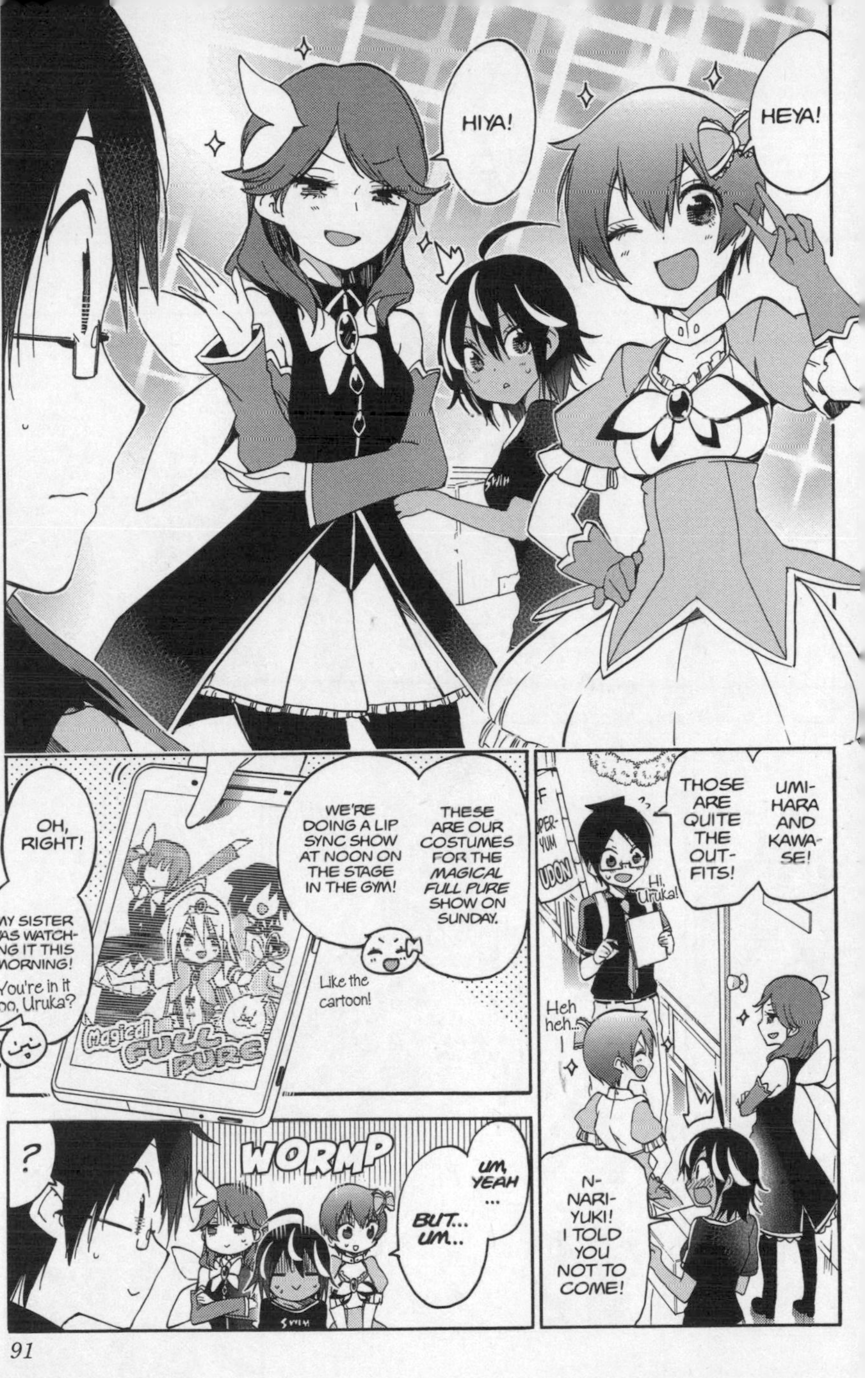
HEYA!
HIYA!
UMI-HARA AND KAWA-SE!
THOSE ARE QUITE THE OUT-FITS!
Hi, Uruka!
UDON
Heh heh...!
N-NARI-YUKI! I TOLD YOU NOT TO COME!
THESE ARE OUR COSTUMES FOR THE MAGICAL FULL PURE SHOW ON SUNDAY.
WE'RE DOING A LIP SYNC SHOW AT NOON ON THE STAGE IN THE GYM!
Like the cartoon!
OH, RIGHT!
Magical FULL PURE
MY SISTER WAS WATCHING IT THIS MORNING!
You're in it too, Uruka?
UM, YEAH...
BUT... UM...
WORMP
?

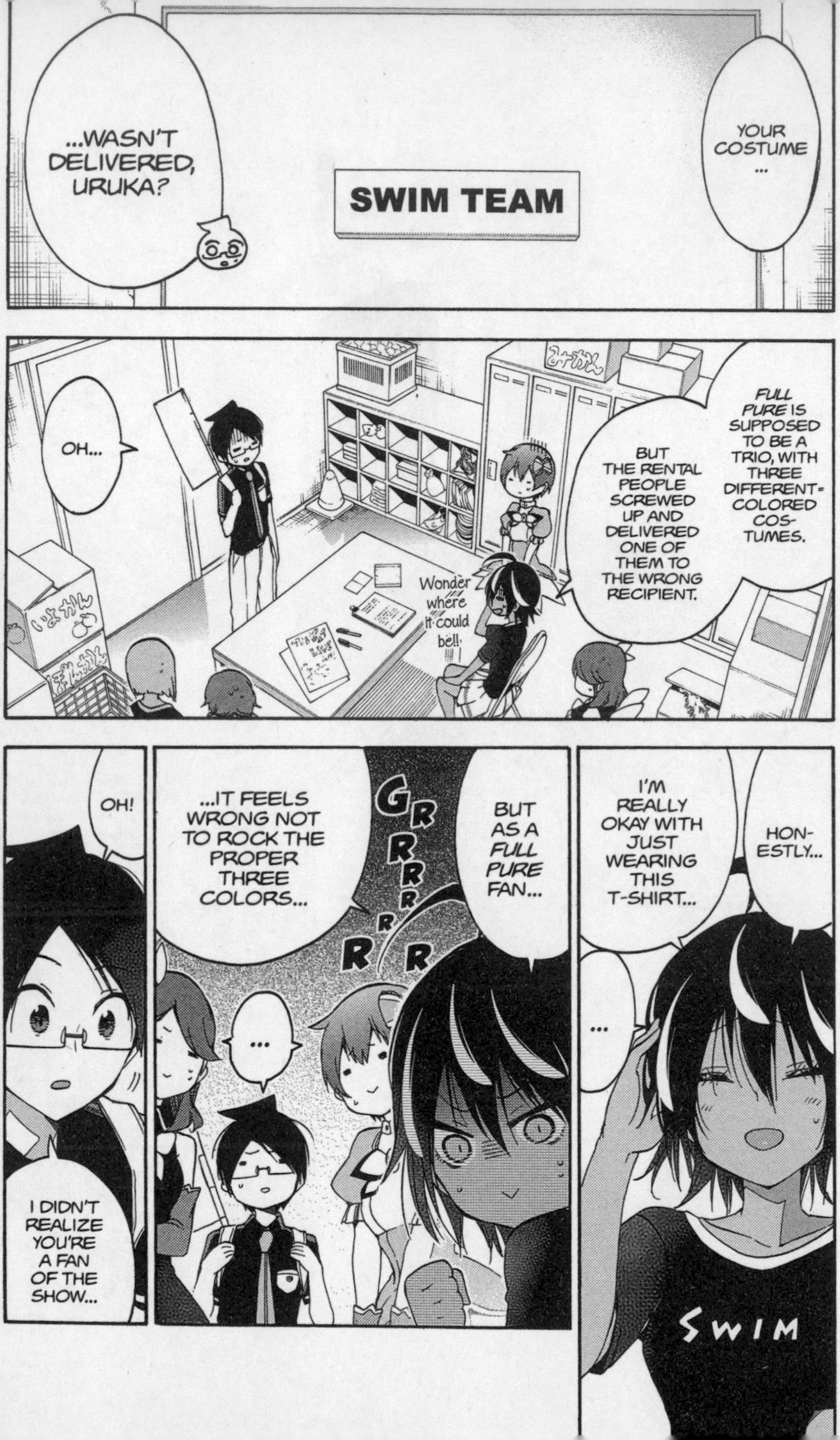
YOUR COSTUME ...
SWIM TEAM
...WASN'T DELIVERED, URUKA?
FULL PURE IS SUPPOSED TO BE A TRIO, WITH THREE DIFFERENT-COLORED COS-TUMES.
BUT THE RENTAL PEOPLE SCREWED UP AND DELIVERED ONE OF THEM TO THE WRONG RECIPIENT.
Wonder where it could be!!
OH...
HON-ESTLY...
I'M REALLY OKAY WITH JUST WEARING THIS T-SHIRT...
...
SWIM
BUT AS A *FULL PURE* FAN...
GRRRRRRR
...IT FEELS WRONG NOT TO ROCK THE PROPER THREE COLORS...
...
OH!
I DIDN'T REALIZE YOU'RE A FAN OF THE SHOW...

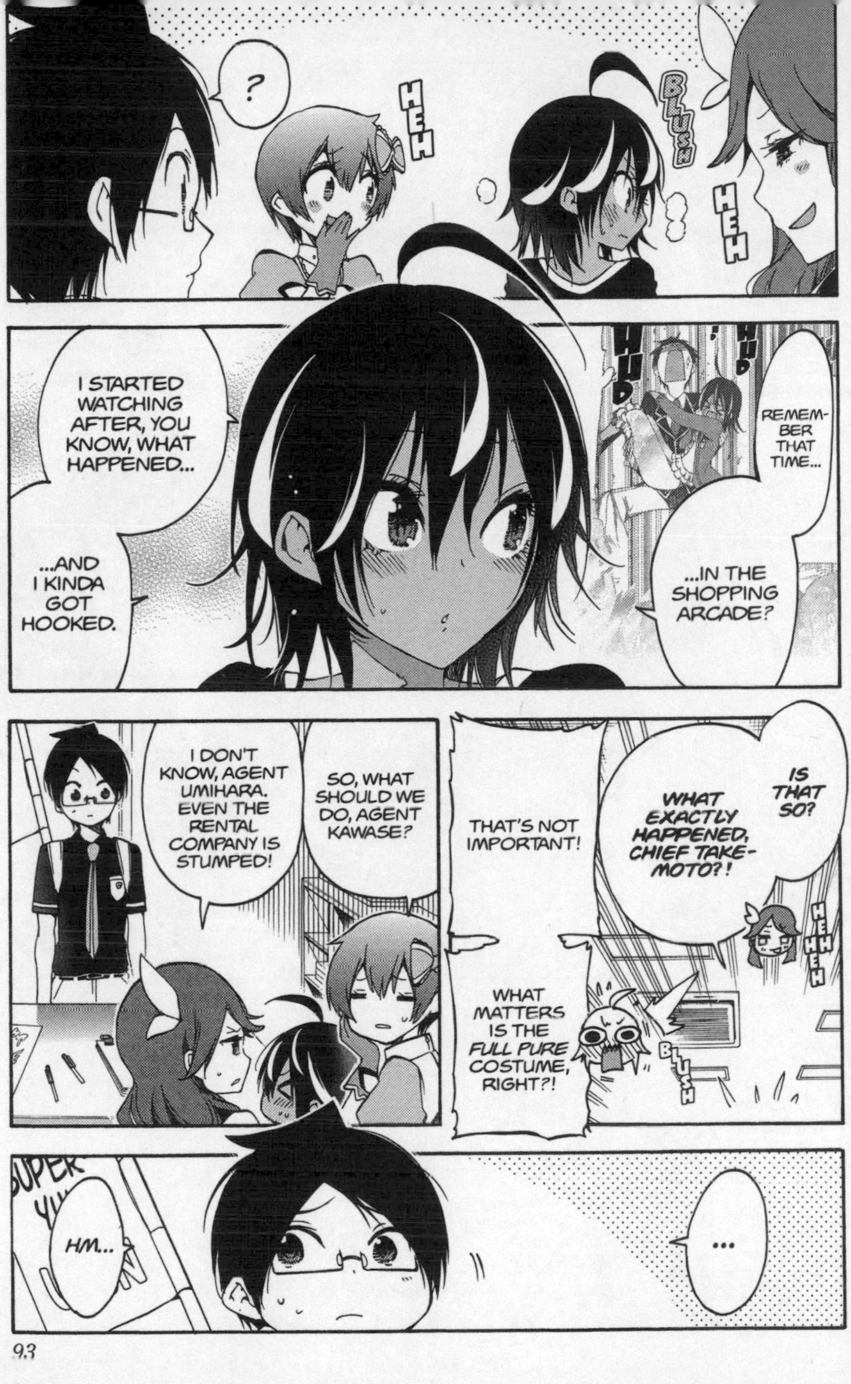
BLUSH
HEH HEH
HEH
?
HUD HUD
REMEMBER THAT TIME...
...IN THE SHOPPING ARCADE?
I STARTED WATCHING AFTER, YOU KNOW, WHAT HAPPENED...
...AND I KINDA GOT HOOKED.
IS THAT SO?
WHAT EXACTLY HAPPENED, CHIEF TAKEMOTO?!
HEH HEH HEH
THAT'S NOT IMPORTANT!
WHAT MATTERS IS THE *FULL PURE* COSTUME, RIGHT?!
BLUSH
SO, WHAT SHOULD WE DO, AGENT KAWASE?
I DON'T KNOW, AGENT UMIHARA. EVEN THE RENTAL COMPANY IS STUMPED!
...
HM...

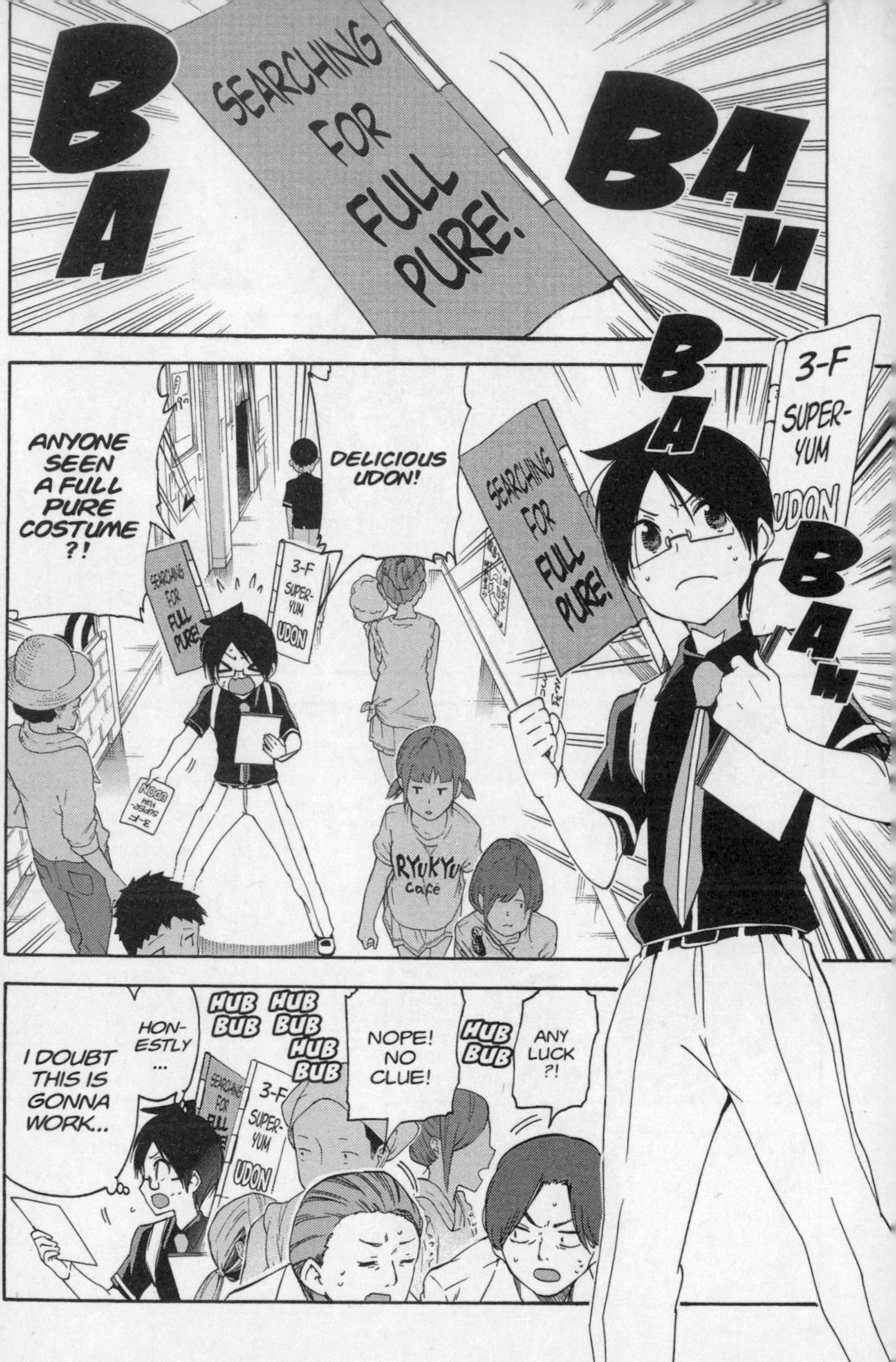
SEARCHING FOR FULL PURE!
BAM
BA
BA
BA
3-F SUPER-YUM UDON
SEARCHING FOR FULL PURE!
BAM
BAM
DELICIOUS UDON!
3-F SUPER-YUM UDON
SEARCHING FOR FULL PURE!
ANYONE SEEN A FULL PURE COSTUME?!
3-F SUPER-YUM UDON
RYUKYU Café
ANY LUCK?!
HUB BUB
NOPE! NO CLUE!
HUB BUB HUB BUB
HUB BUB
HON-ESTLY...
I DOUBT THIS IS GONNA WORK...
3-F SUPER-YUM UDON
SEARCHING FOR FULL

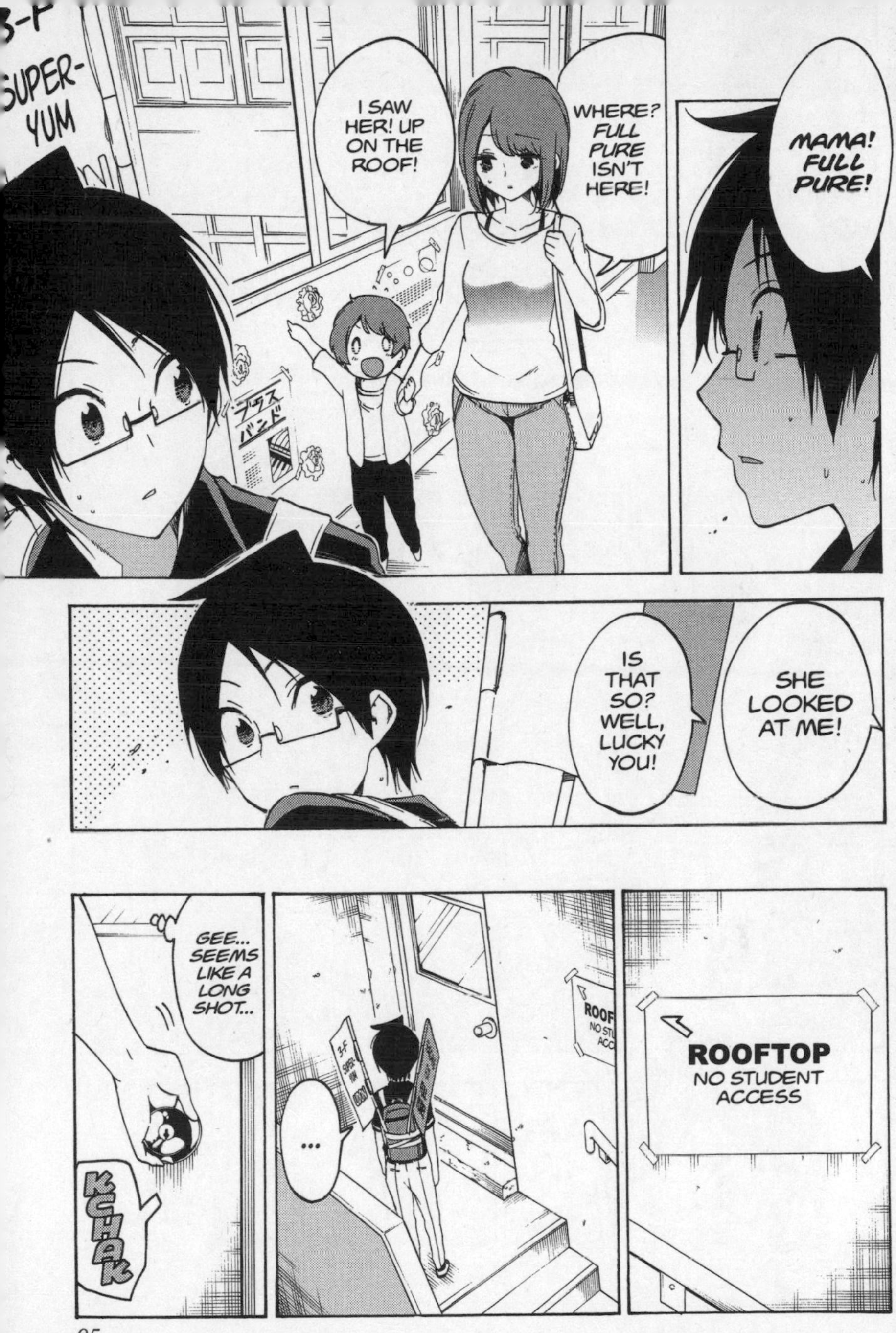
MAMA! FULL PURE!
WHERE? FULL PURE ISN'T HERE!
I SAW HER! UP ON THE ROOF!
SUPER-YUM
ブラスバンド
SHE LOOKED AT ME!
IS THAT SO? WELL, LUCKY YOU!
ROOFTOP
NO STUDENT ACCESS
...
GEE... SEEMS LIKE A LONG SHOT...
KCHAK

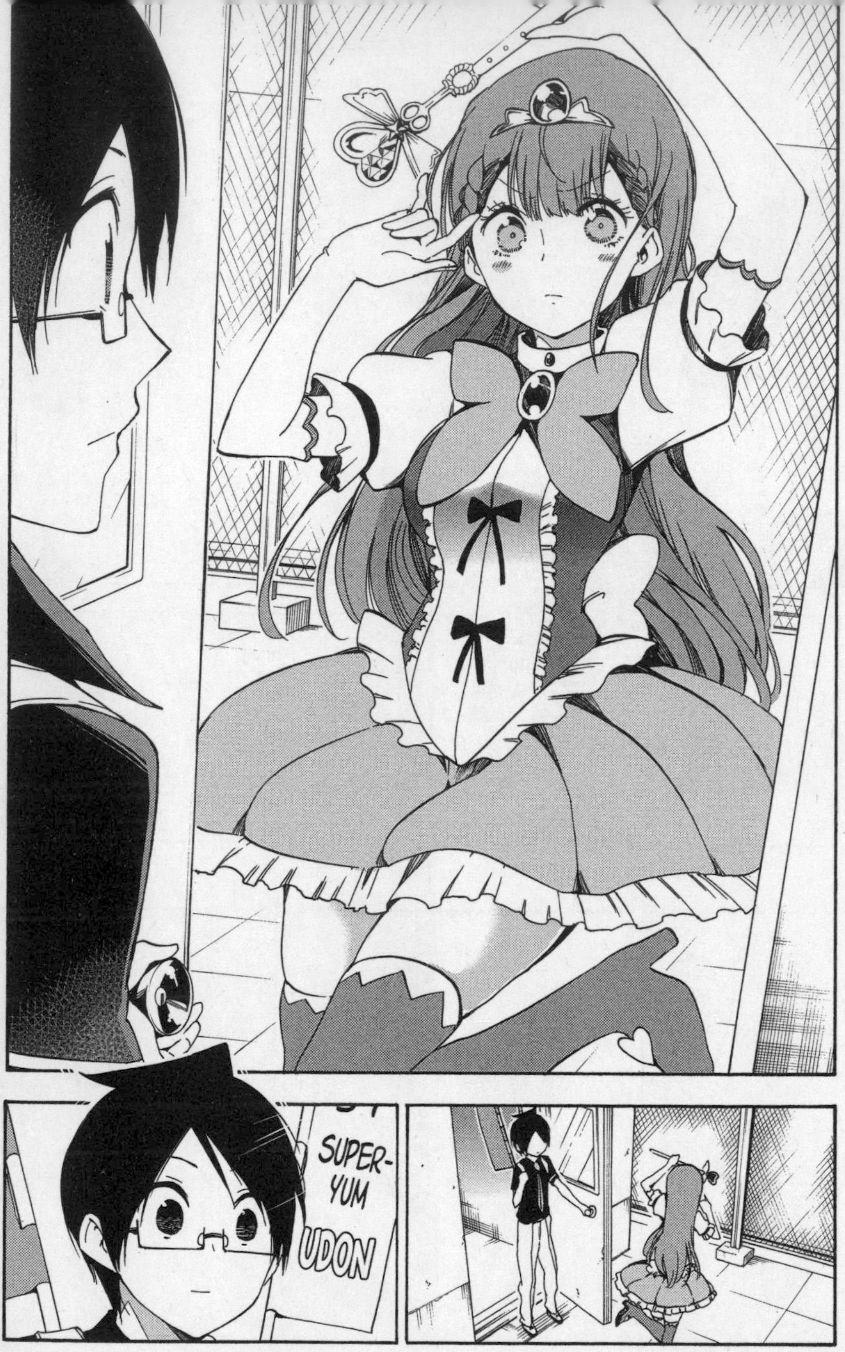
SUPER-
YUM
UDON

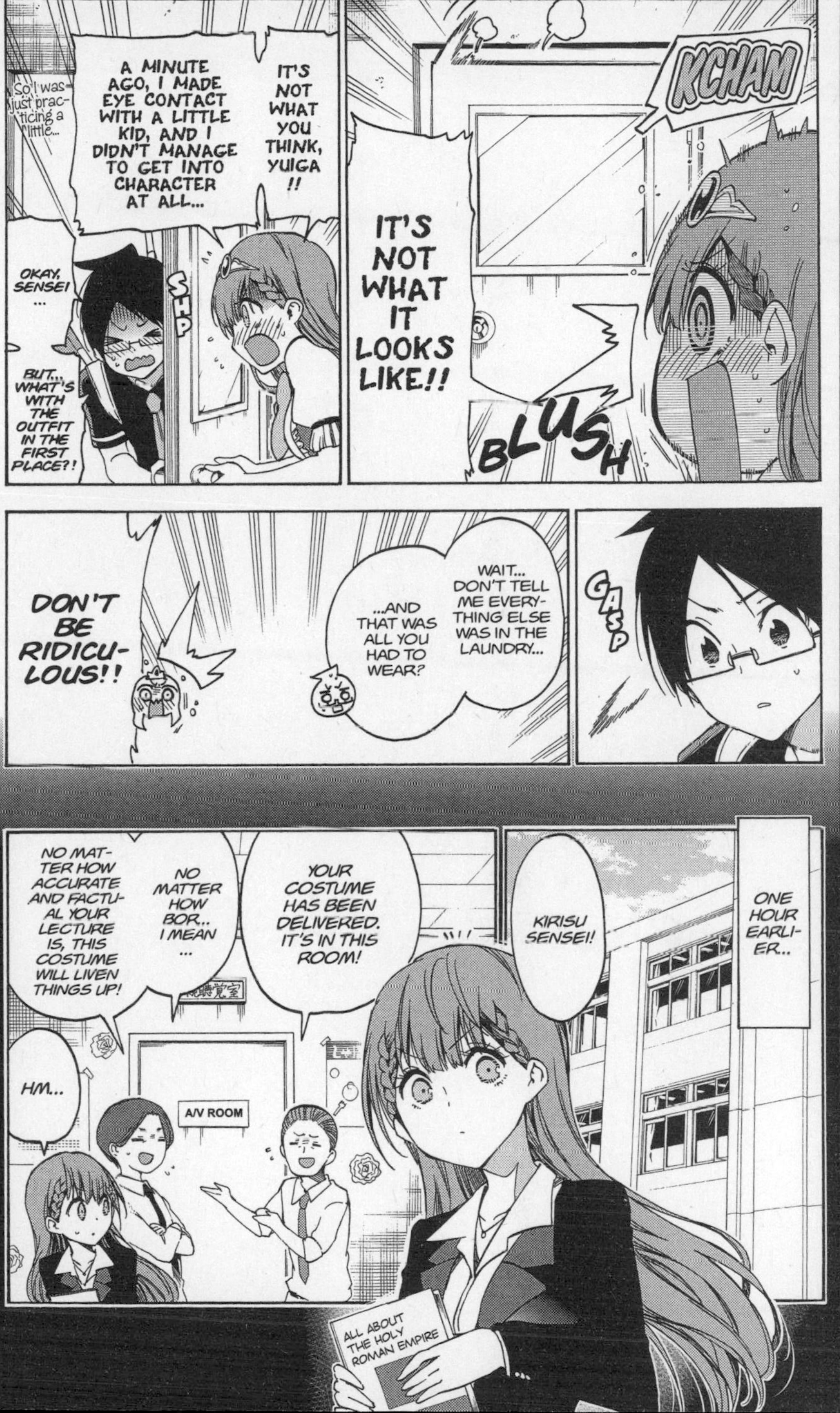
KCHAM
IT'S NOT WHAT IT LOOKS LIKE!!
BLUSH
IT'S NOT WHAT YOU THINK, YUIGA!!
A MINUTE AGO, I MADE EYE CONTACT WITH A LITTLE KID, AND I DIDN'T MANAGE TO GET INTO CHARACTER AT ALL...
So I was just practicing a little...
SHP
OKAY, SENSEI...
BUT... WHAT'S WITH THE OUTFIT IN THE FIRST PLACE?!
GASP
WAIT... DON'T TELL ME EVERYTHING ELSE WAS IN THE LAUNDRY...
...AND THAT WAS ALL YOU HAD TO WEAR?
DON'T BE RIDICULOUS!!
ONE HOUR EARLIER...
KIRISU SENSEI!
YOUR COSTUME HAS BEEN DELIVERED. IT'S IN THIS ROOM!
NO MATTER HOW BOR... I MEAN...
NO MATTER HOW ACCURATE AND FACTUAL YOUR LECTURE IS, THIS COSTUME WILL LIVEN THINGS UP!
A/V ROOM
HM...
ALL ABOUT THE HOLY ROMAN EMPIRE

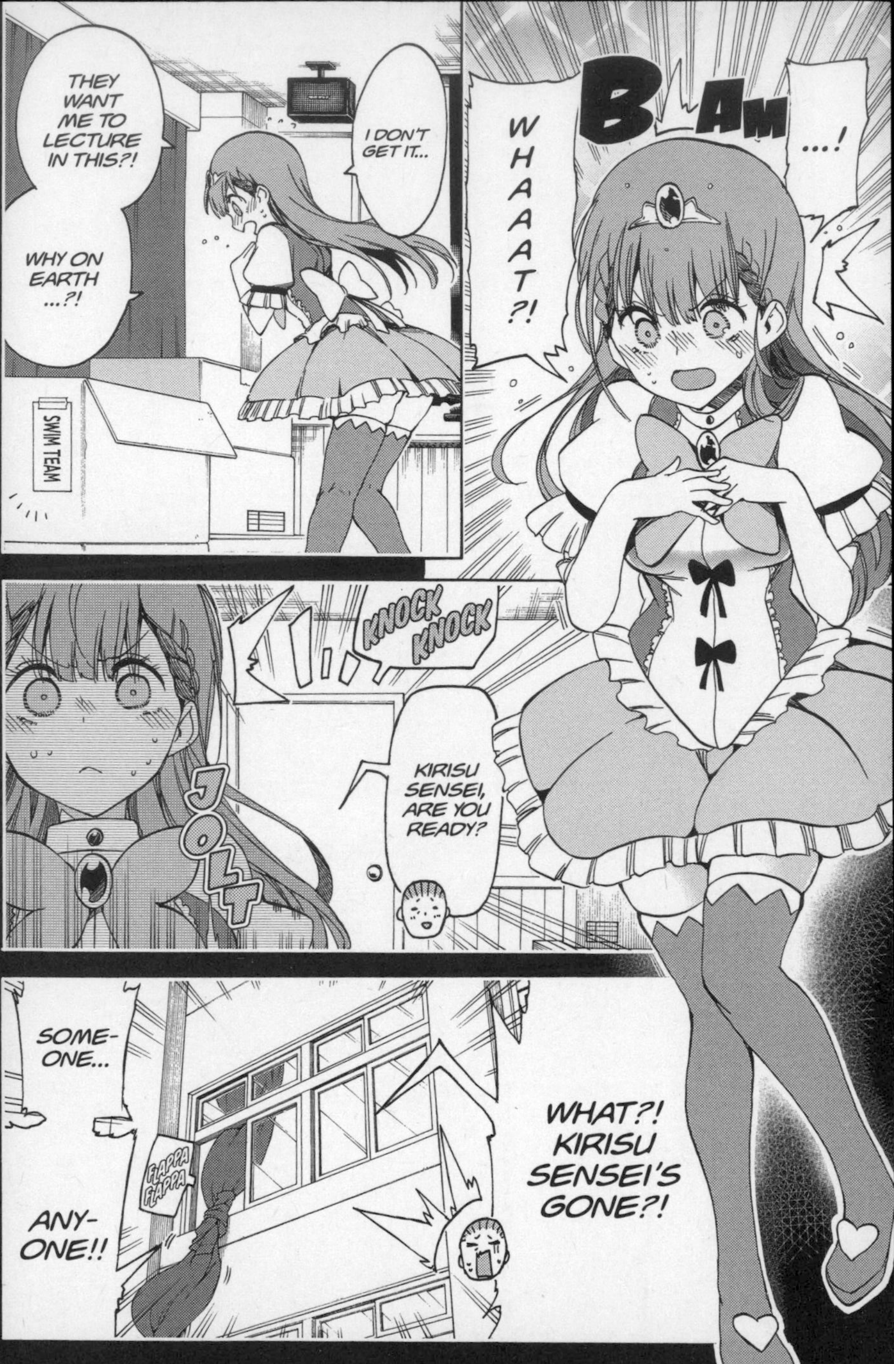

BAM ...!
WHAAAAT?!
I DON'T GET IT...
THEY WANT ME TO LECTURE IN THIS?!
WHY ON EARTH ...?!
SWIM TEAM
KNOCK KNOCK
KIRISU SENSEI, ARE YOU READY?
JOLT
WHAT?! KIRISU SENSEI'S GONE?!
FLAPPA FLAPPA
SOME-ONE...
ANY-ONE!!

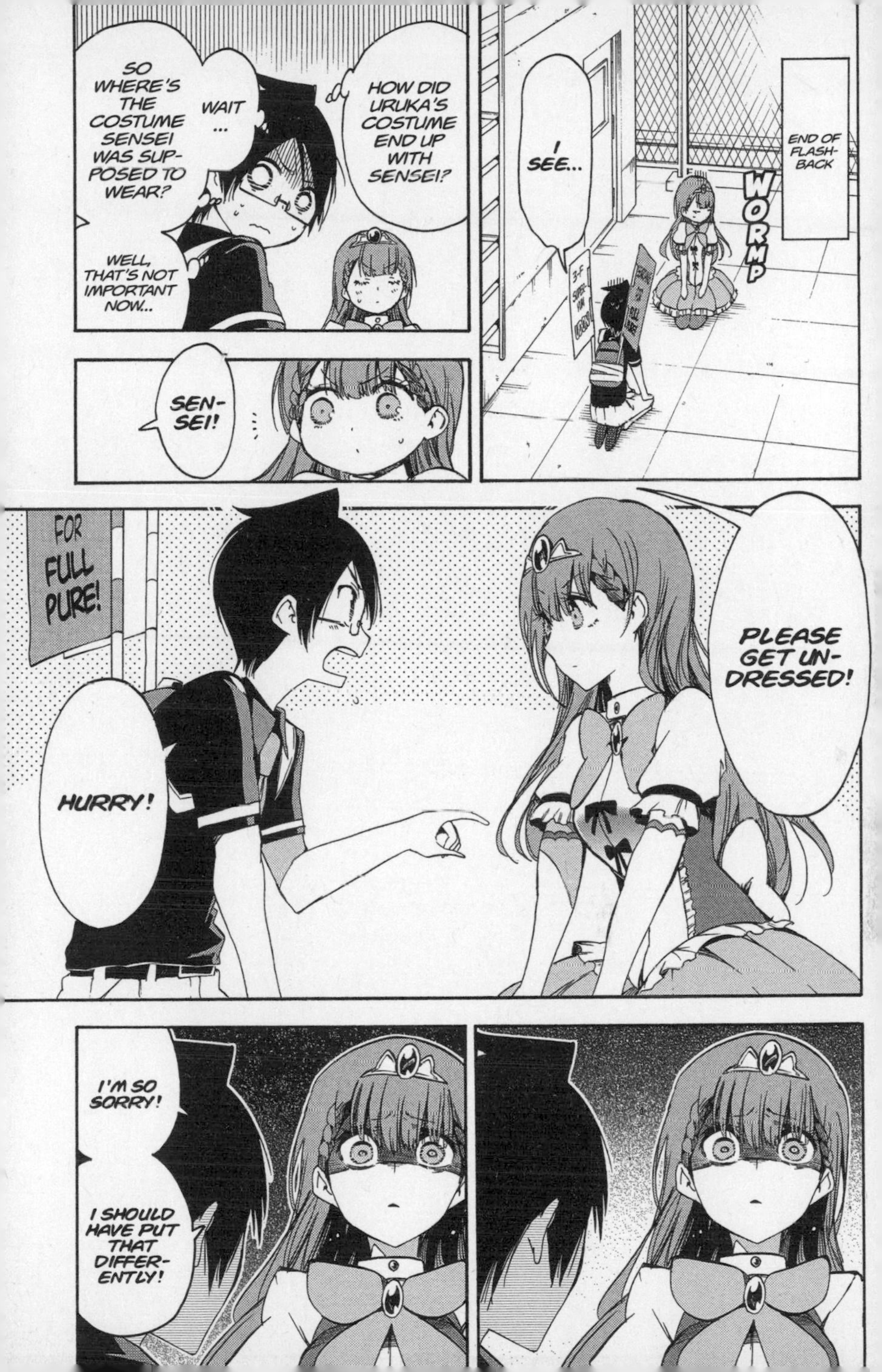
END OF FLASHBACK
WORMP
I SEE...
HOW DID URUKA'S COSTUME END UP WITH SENSEI?
WAIT ...
SO WHERE'S THE COSTUME SENSEI WAS SUPPOSED TO WEAR?
WELL, THAT'S NOT IMPORTANT NOW...
SENSEI!
PLEASE GET UNDRESSED!
FOR FULL PURE!
HURRY!
I'M SO SORRY!
I SHOULD HAVE PUT THAT DIFFERENTLY!

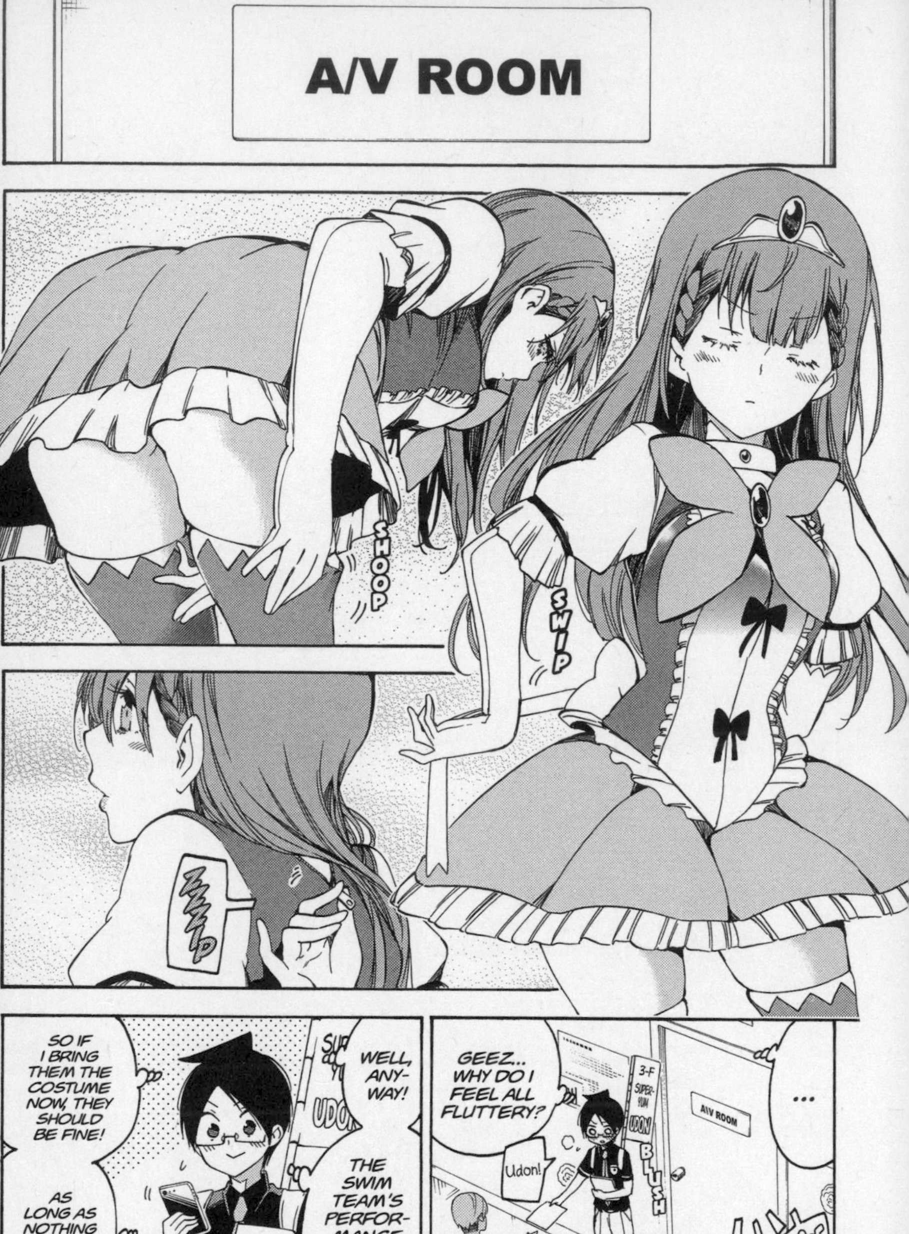
A/V ROOM
SWIP
SHOOP
ZZZIP
GEEZ... WHY DO I FEEL ALL FLUTTERY?
...
A/V ROOM
3-F SUPER-YUM UDON
Udon!
BLUSH
SHOOF
WELL, ANYWAY!
THE SWIM TEAM'S PERFORMANCE IS AT NOON...
SO IF I BRING THEM THE COSTUME NOW, THEY SHOULD BE FINE!
AS LONG AS NOTHING ELSE GOES WRONG...

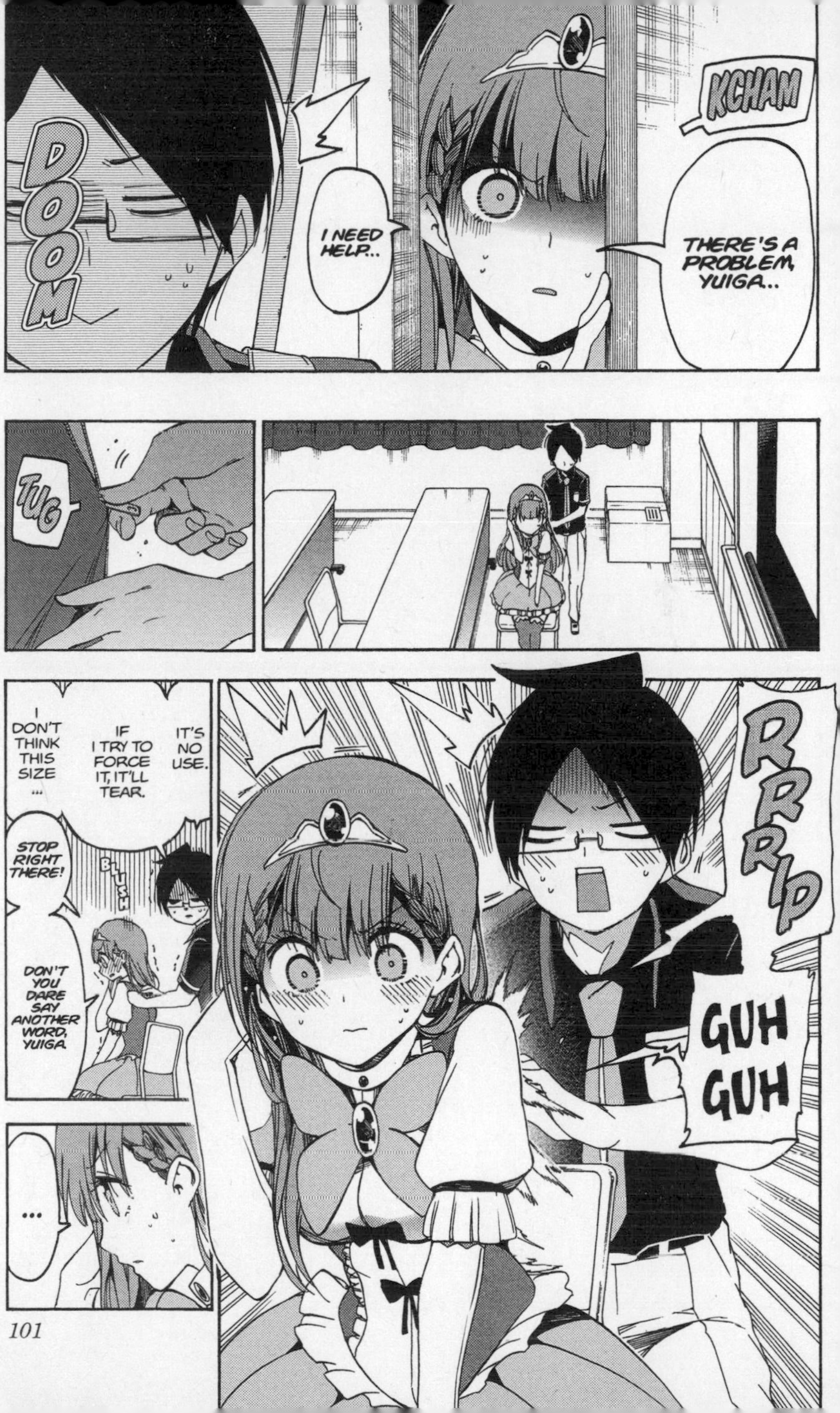
KCHAM
THERE'S A PROBLEM, YUIGA...
I NEED HELP...
DOOM
TUG
RRRIP
GUH GUH
IT'S NO USE.
IF I TRY TO FORCE IT, IT'LL TEAR.
I DON'T THINK THIS SIZE...
STOP RIGHT THERE!
BLUSH
DON'T YOU DARE SAY ANOTHER WORD, YUIGA.
...

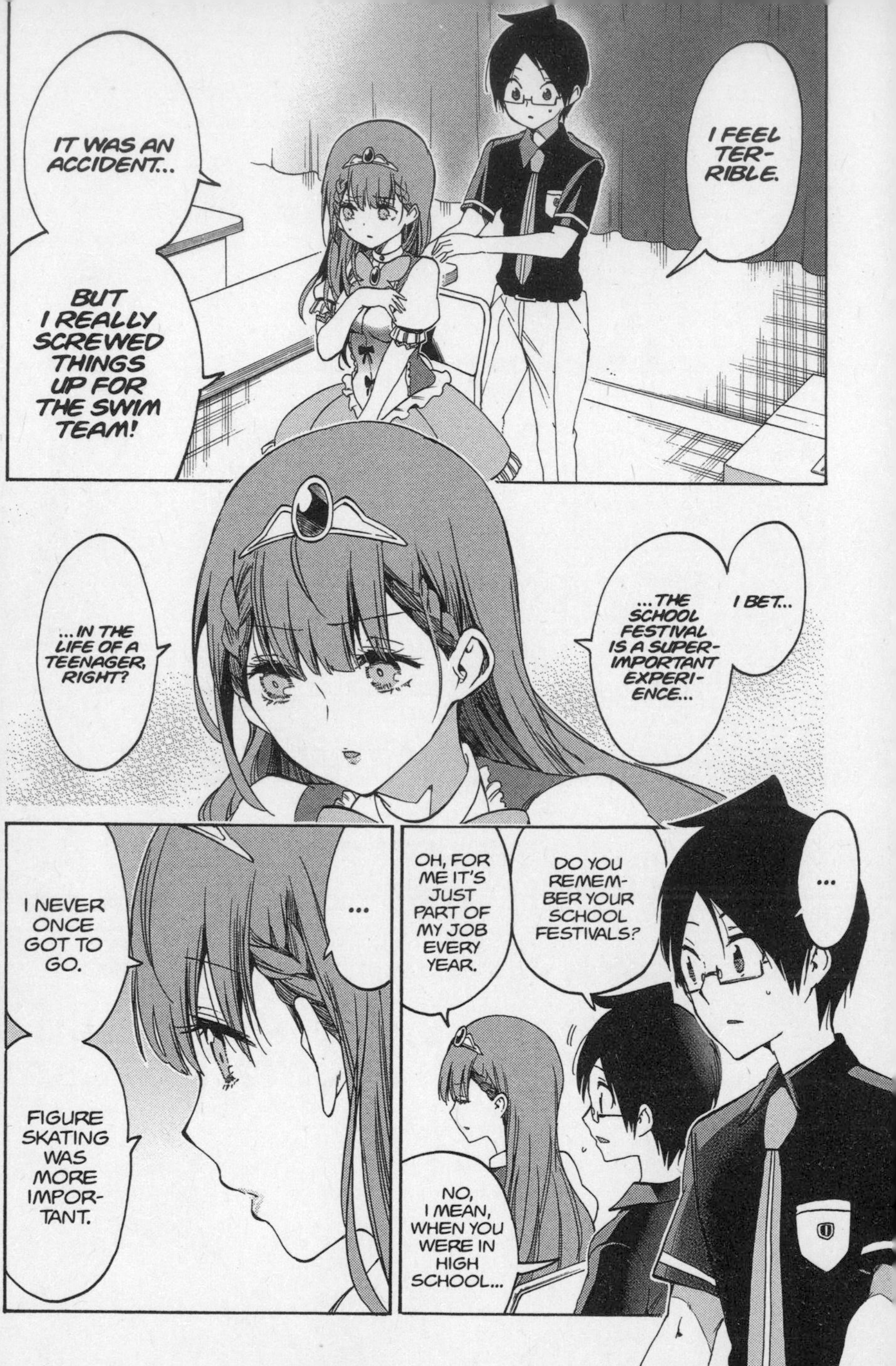
I FEEL TER-RIBLE.
IT WAS AN ACCIDENT...
BUT I REALLY SCREWED THINGS UP FOR THE SWIM TEAM!
I BET...
...THE SCHOOL FESTIVAL IS A SUPER-IMPORTANT EXPERI-ENCE...
...IN THE LIFE OF A TEENAGER, RIGHT?
...
DO YOU REMEM-BER YOUR SCHOOL FESTIVALS?
OH, FOR ME IT'S JUST PART OF MY JOB EVERY YEAR.
NO, I MEAN, WHEN YOU WERE IN HIGH SCHOOL...
...
I NEVER ONCE GOT TO GO.
FIGURE SKATING WAS MORE IMPOR-TANT.

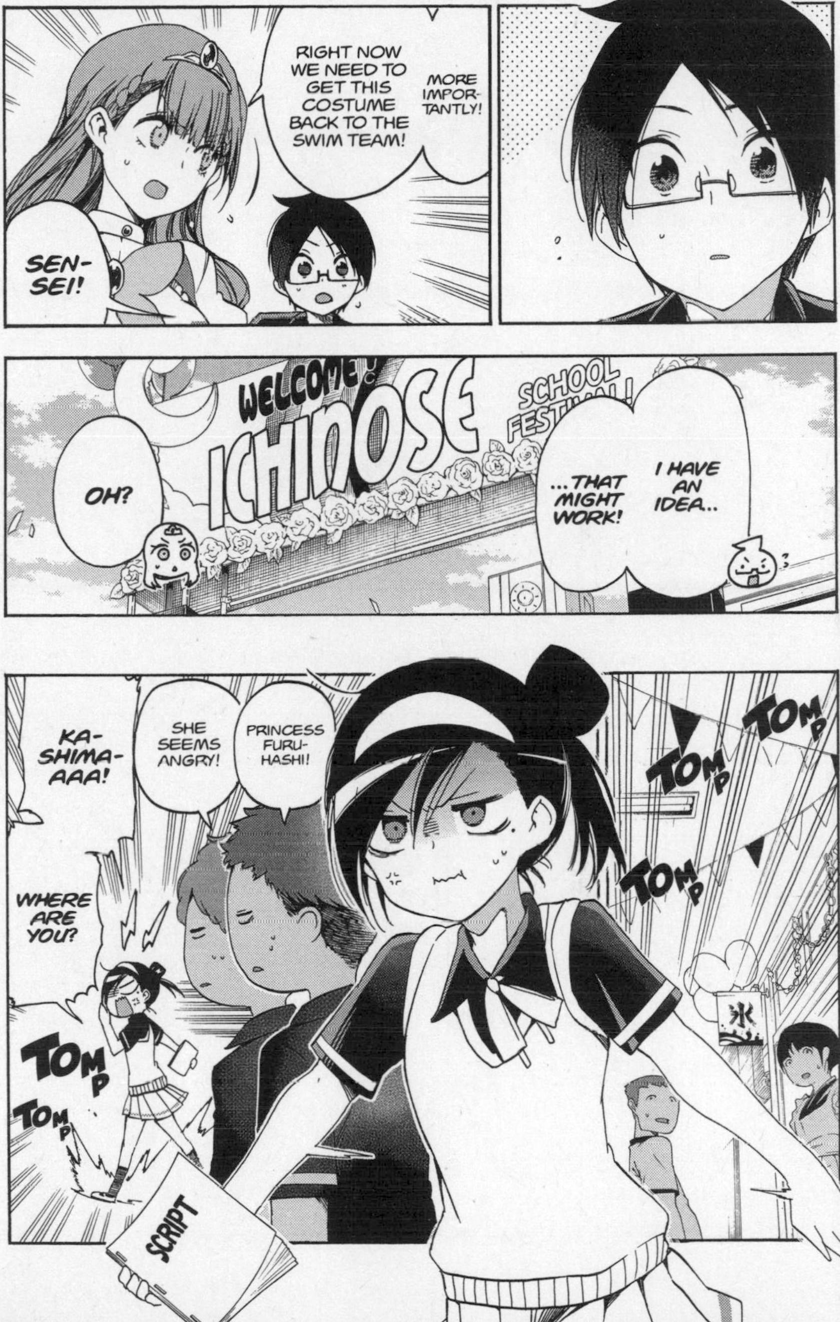
MORE IMPOR-TANTLY!
RIGHT NOW WE NEED TO GET THIS COSTUME BACK TO THE SWIM TEAM!
SEN-SEI!
SCHOOL
WELCOME
ICHINOSE
I HAVE AN IDEA...
...THAT MIGHT WORK!
OH?
TOMP
TOMP
TOMP
PRINCESS FURU-HASHI!
SHE SEEMS ANGRY!
KA-SHIMA-AAA!
WHERE ARE YOU?
TOMP
TOMP
SCRIPT

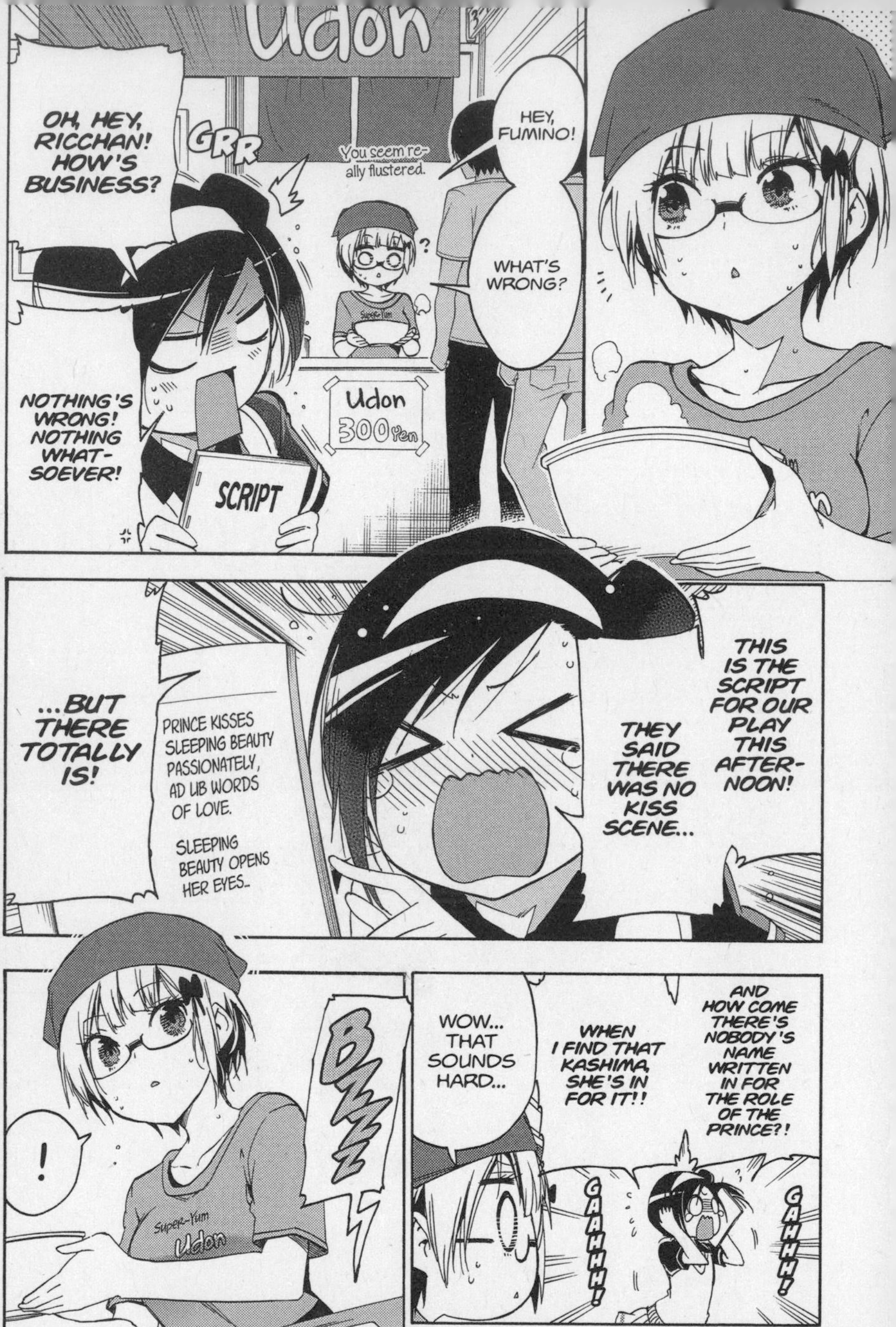
Udon
HEY, FUMINO!
WHAT'S WRONG?
You seem really flustered.
GRR
OH, HEY, RICCHAN! HOW'S BUSINESS?
Super-Yum
Udon 300 Yen
NOTHING'S WRONG! NOTHING WHATSOEVER!
SCRIPT
THIS IS THE SCRIPT FOR OUR PLAY THIS AFTERNOON!
THEY SAID THERE WAS NO KISS SCENE...
...BUT THERE TOTALLY IS!
PRINCE KISSES SLEEPING BEAUTY PASSIONATELY, AD LIB WORDS OF LOVE.
SLEEPING BEAUTY OPENS HER EYES..
AND HOW COME THERE'S NOBODY'S NAME WRITTEN IN FOR THE ROLE OF THE PRINCE?!
WHEN I FIND THAT KASHIMA, SHE'S IN FOR IT!!
WOW... THAT SOUNDS HARD...
GAHHH!
GAAHHH!
BZZZZ
!
Super-Yum Udon

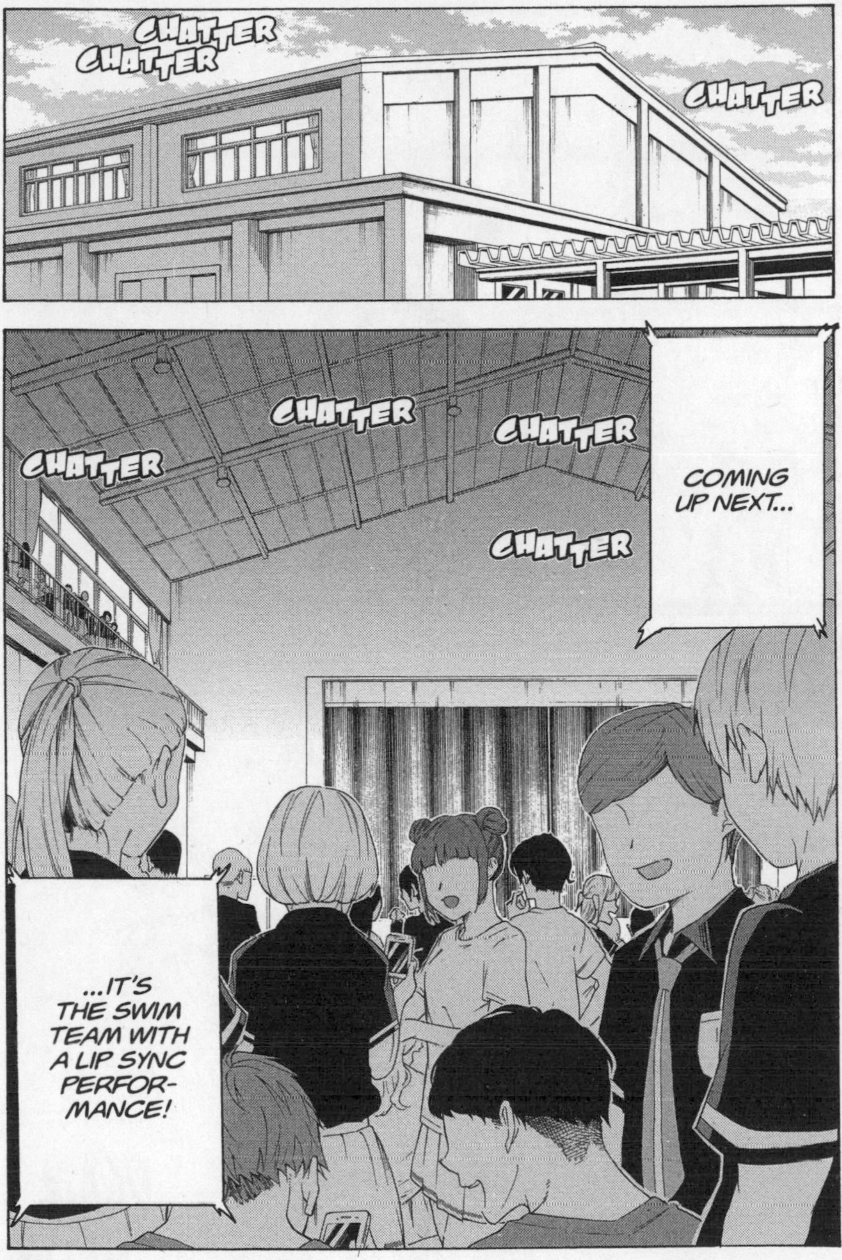
CHATTER
CHATTER
CHATTER
COMING UP NEXT...
CHATTER
CHATTER
CHATTER
CHATTER
...IT'S THE SWIM TEAM WITH A LIP SYNC PERFORMANCE!

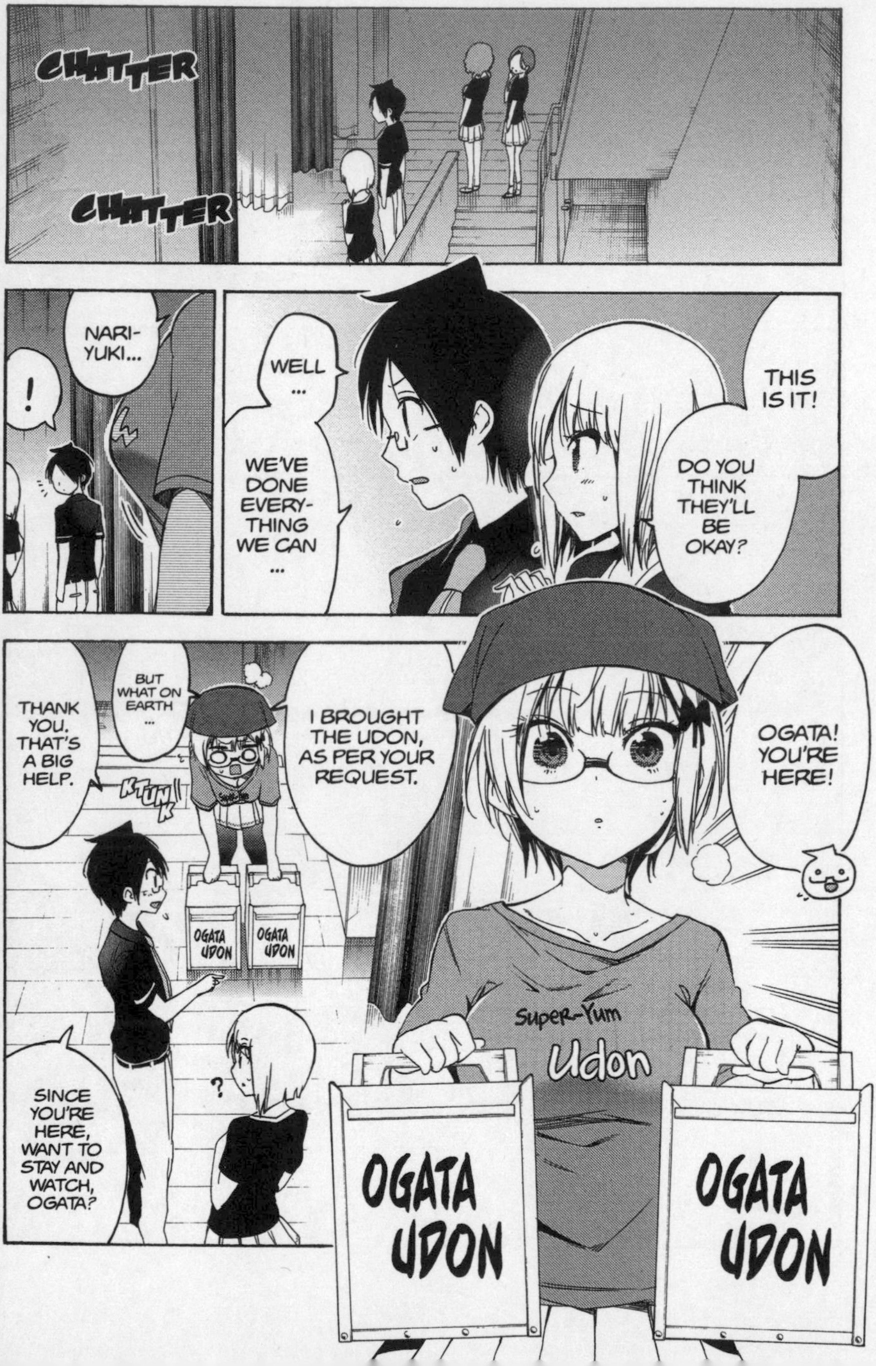
CHATTER
CHATTER
THIS IS IT!
DO YOU THINK THEY'LL BE OKAY?
WELL ...
WE'VE DONE EVERY-THING WE CAN ...
NARI-YUKI...
!
OGATA! YOU'RE HERE!
Super-Yum Udon
OGATA UDON
OGATA UDON
I BROUGHT THE UDON, AS PER YOUR REQUEST.
BUT WHAT ON EARTH ...
KTUNK
OGATA UDON
OGATA UDON
THANK YOU. THAT'S A BIG HELP.
?
SINCE YOU'RE HERE, WANT TO STAY AND WATCH, OGATA?

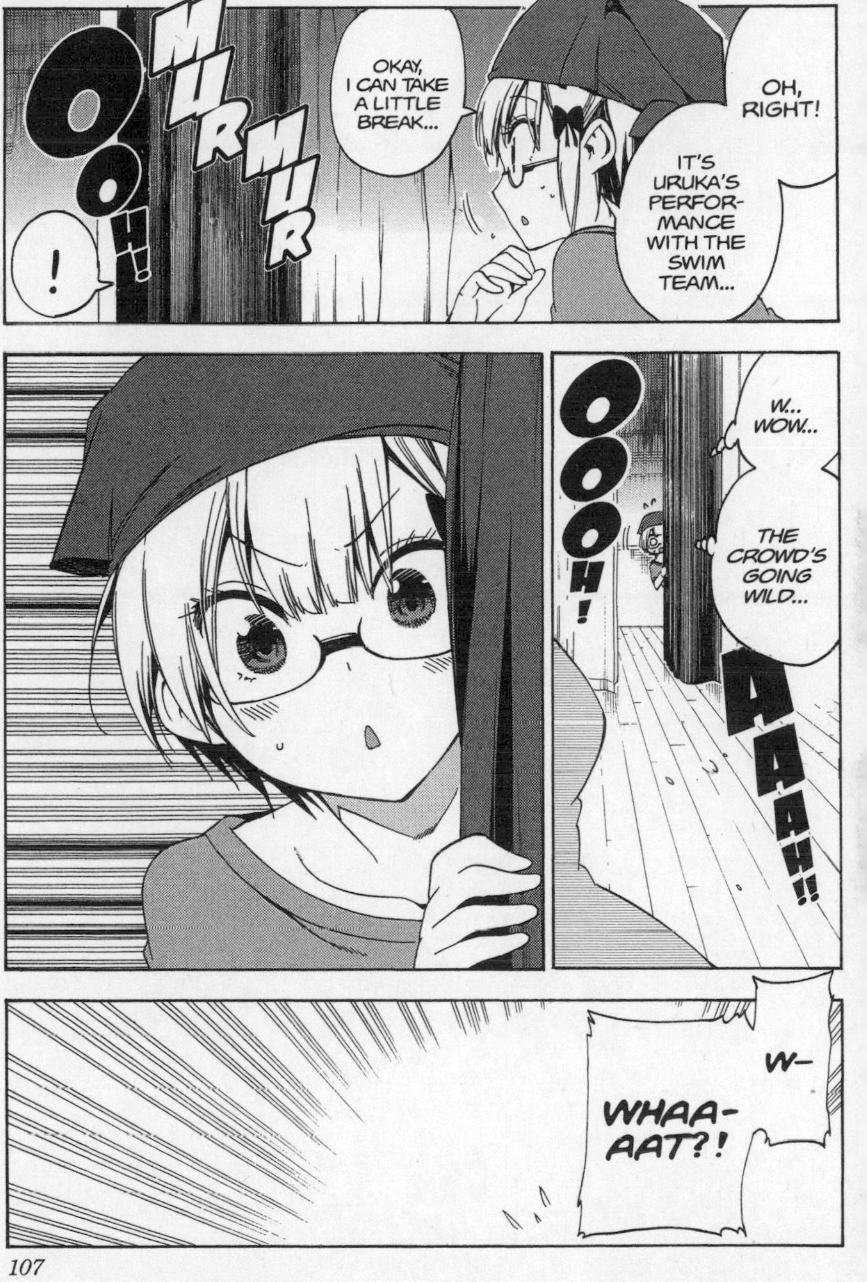
OH, RIGHT!
IT'S URUKA'S PERFORMANCE WITH THE SWIM TEAM...
OKAY, I CAN TAKE A LITTLE BREAK...
MURMUR
OOOH!
!
W... WOW...
THE CROWD'S GOING WILD...
OOOOOH!
AAAAH!!
W-
WHAA-AAT?!

After all, I'm your best friend!
I'll fill in for you when you're making deliveries, Rizu Ogata!
Our class will take care of it...
Um...
SUPER-YUM UDON
SUPER-YUM UDON

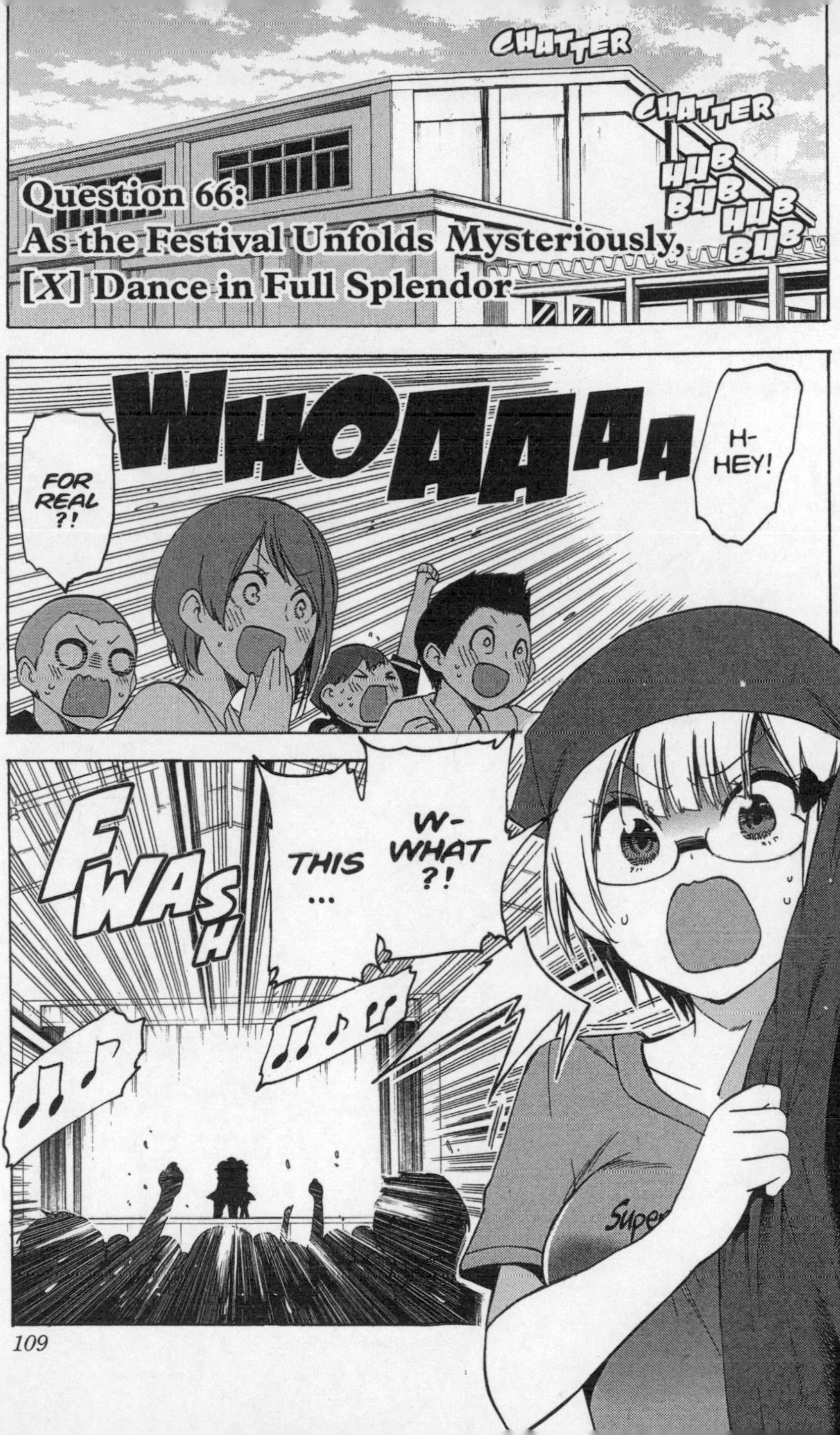
Question 66:
As the Festival Unfolds Mysteriously, [X] Dance in Full Splendor
CHATTER
CHATTER
HUB BUB HUB BUB
H-HEY!
WHOAAAA
FOR REAL?!
W-WHAT?!
THIS...
FWASH
Super

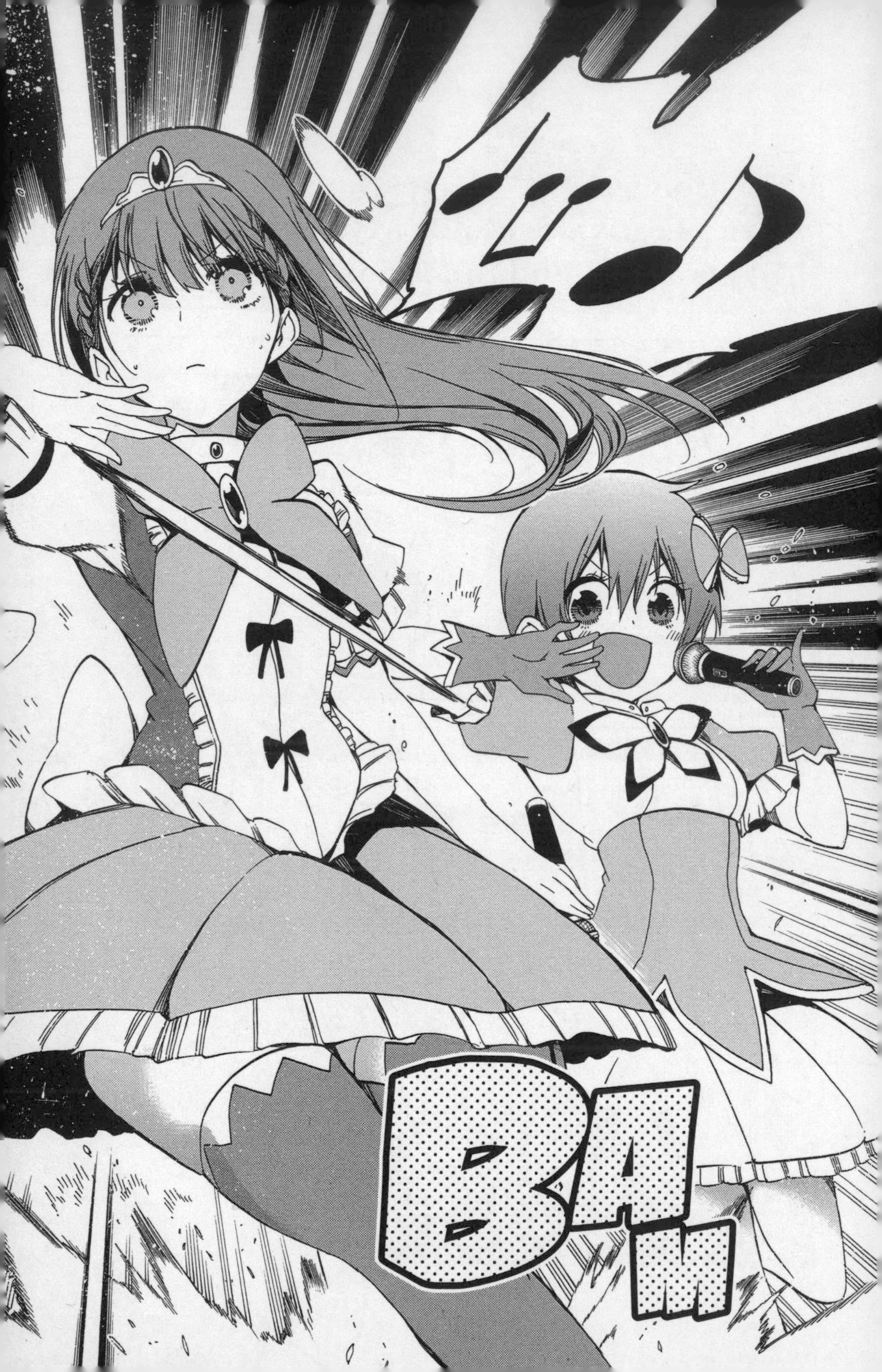
BAM

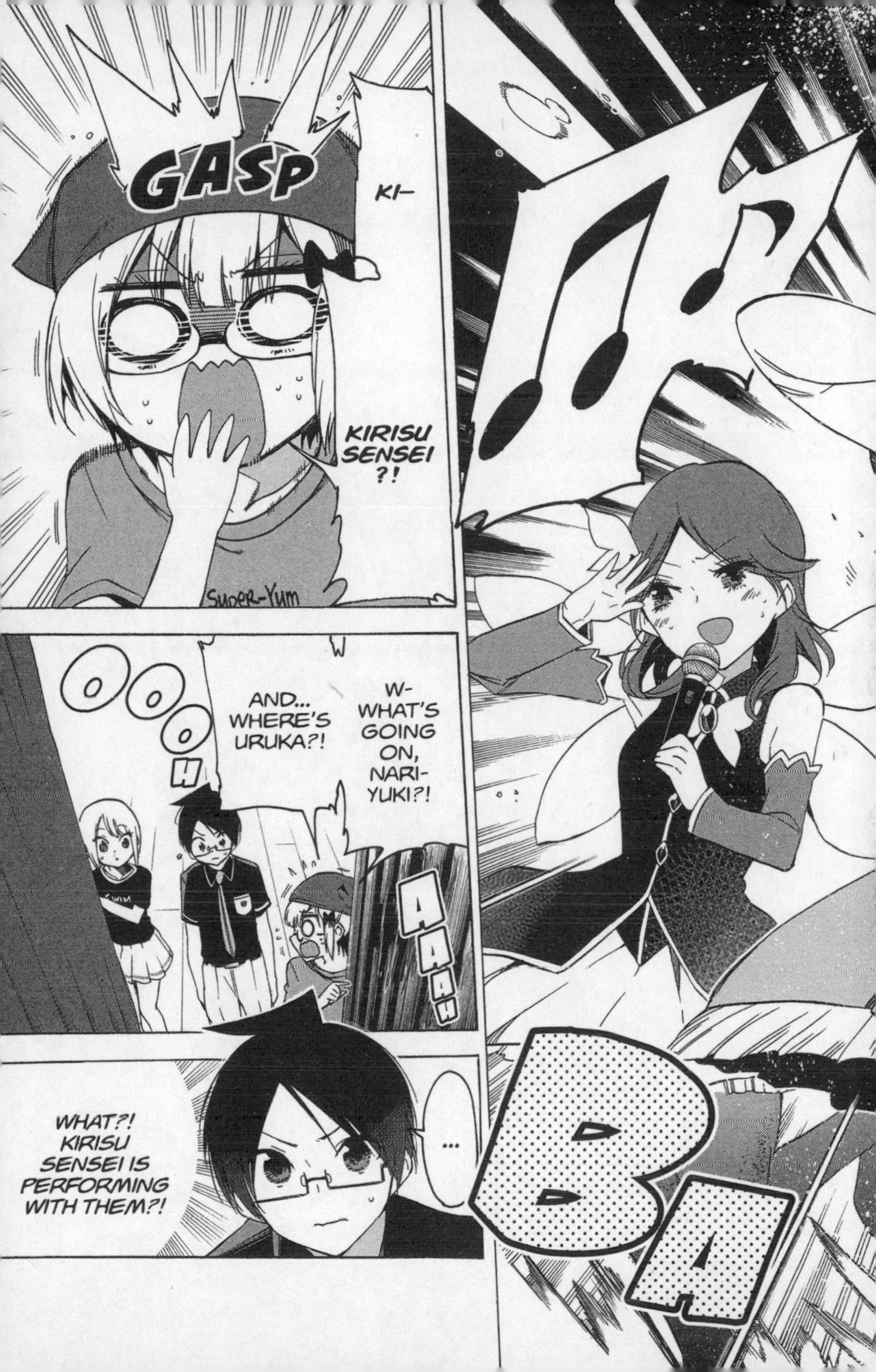
BA
GASP
KI—
KIRISU SENSEI?!
Super-Yum
W- WHAT'S GOING ON, NARI-YUKI?!
AND... WHERE'S URUKA?!
OOOOH
AAAAH
...
WHAT?! KIRISU SENSEI IS PERFORMING WITH THEM?!

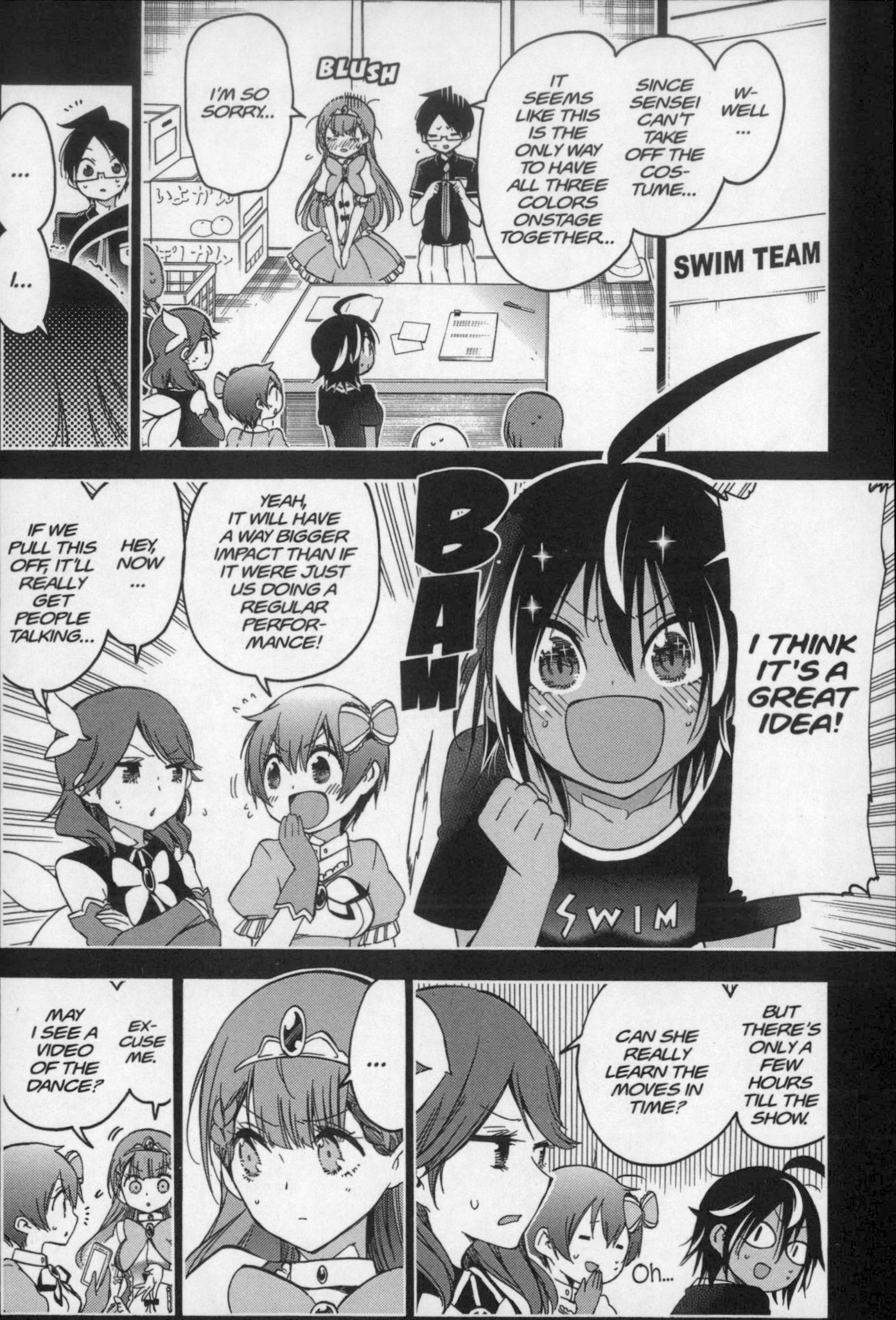
W-WELL ...
SINCE SENSEI CAN'T TAKE OFF THE COSTUME...
IT SEEMS LIKE THIS IS THE ONLY WAY TO HAVE ALL THREE COLORS ONSTAGE TOGETHER...
SWIM TEAM
BLUSH
I'M SO SORRY...
...
I...
I THINK IT'S A GREAT IDEA!
BAM
SWIM
YEAH, IT WILL HAVE A WAY BIGGER IMPACT THAN IF IT WERE JUST US DOING A REGULAR PERFORMANCE!
HEY, NOW ...
IF WE PULL THIS OFF, IT'LL REALLY GET PEOPLE TALKING...
BUT THERE'S ONLY A FEW HOURS TILL THE SHOW.
CAN SHE REALLY LEARN THE MOVES IN TIME?
Oh...
...
EXCUSE ME.
MAY I SEE A VIDEO OF THE DANCE?

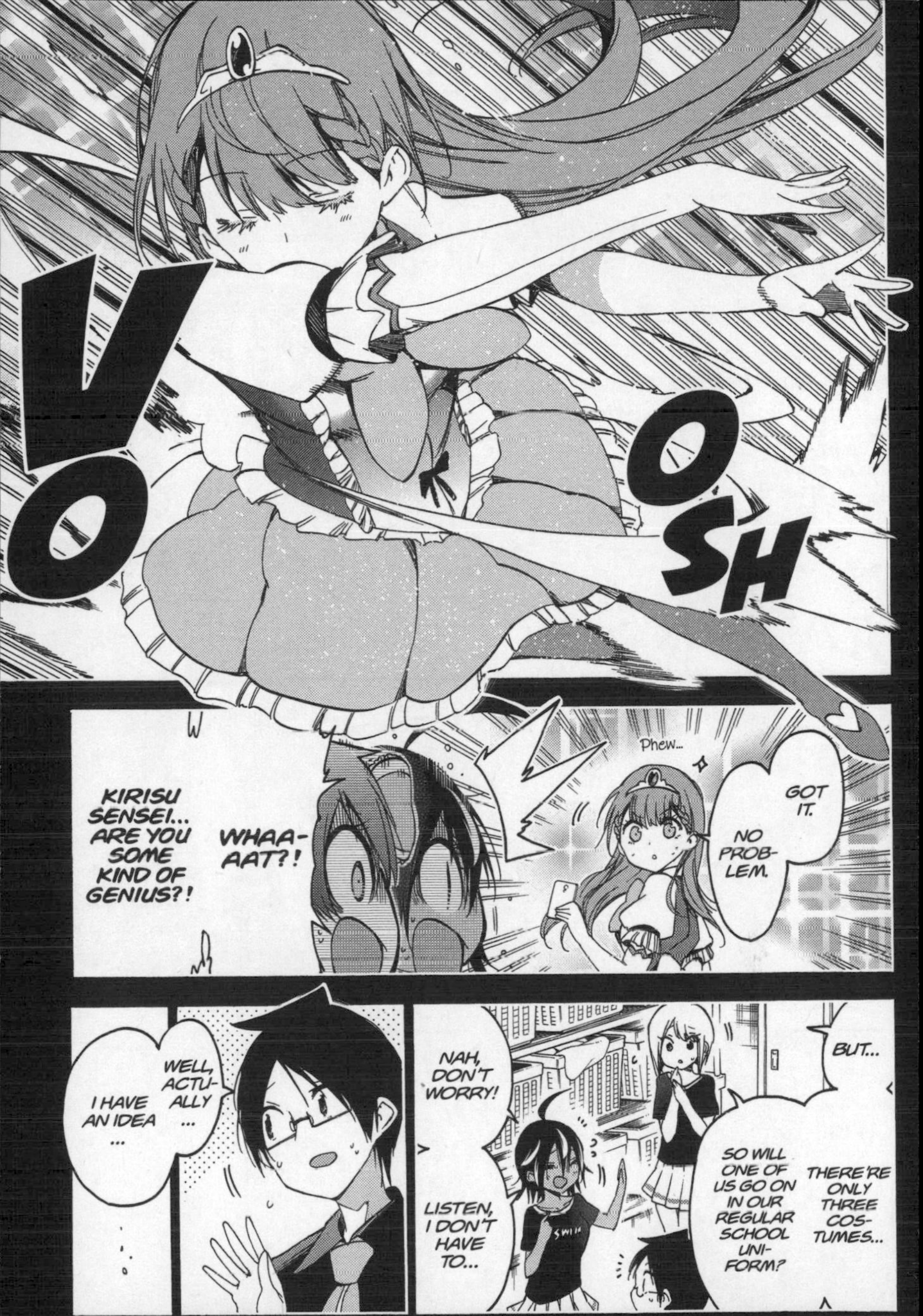
VOOSH
Phew...
GOT IT.
NO PROBLEM.
WHAA-AAT?!
KIRISU SENSEI... ARE YOU SOME KIND OF GENIUS?!
BUT...
THERE'RE ONLY THREE COS-TUMES...
SO WILL ONE OF US GO ON IN OUR REGULAR SCHOOL UNI-FORM?
NAH, DON'T WORRY!
LISTEN, I DON'T HAVE TO...
WELL, ACTU-ALLY...
I HAVE AN IDEA...

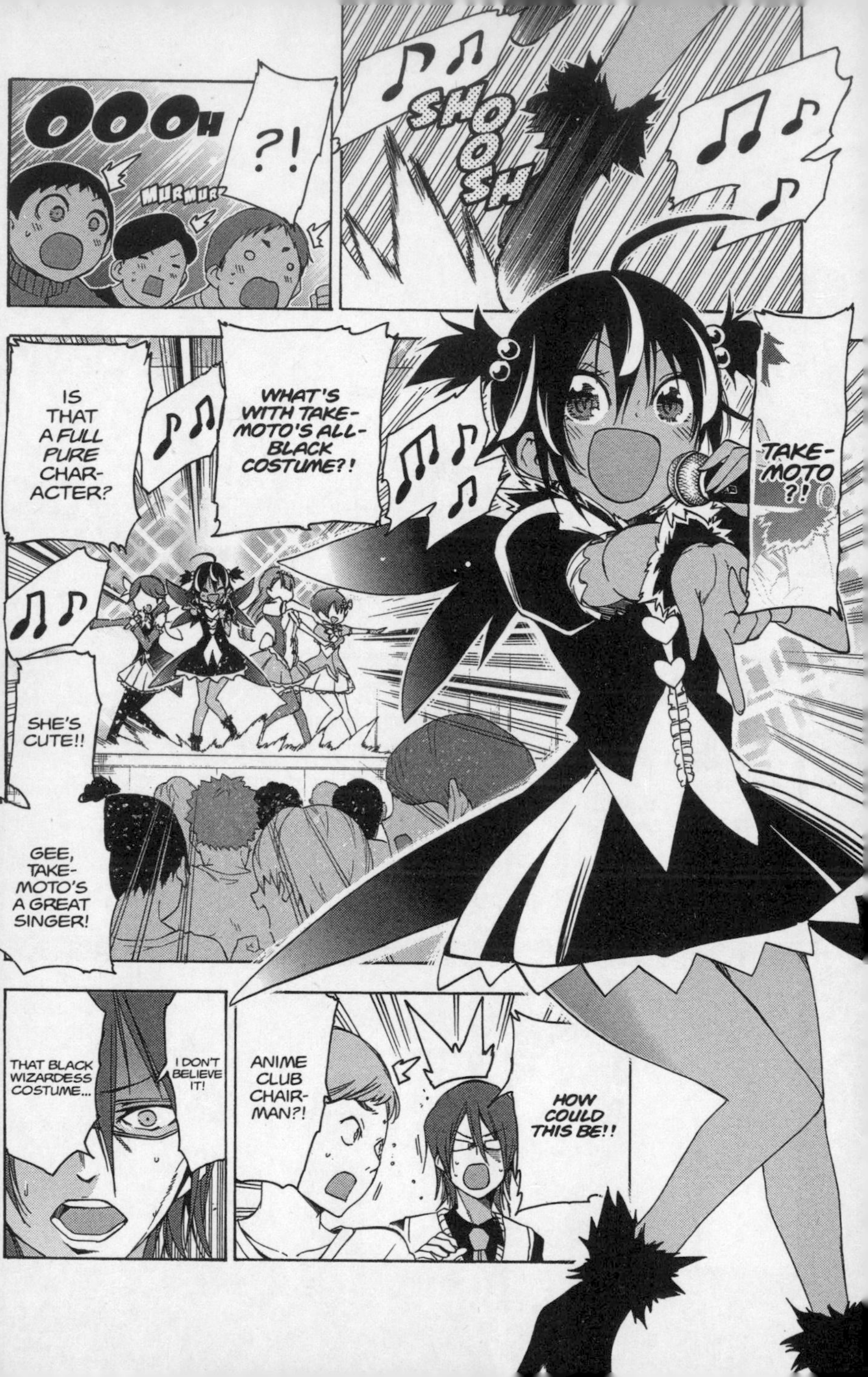
SHOOSH
?!
OOOH
MURMUR
TAKE-MOTO?!
WHAT'S WITH TAKE-MOTO'S ALL-BLACK COSTUME?!
IS THAT A FULL PURE CHAR-ACTER?
SHE'S CUTE!!
GEE, TAKE-MOTO'S A GREAT SINGER!
HOW COULD THIS BE!!
ANIME CLUB CHAIR-MAN?!
I DON'T BELIEVE IT!
THAT BLACK WIZARDESS COSTUME...

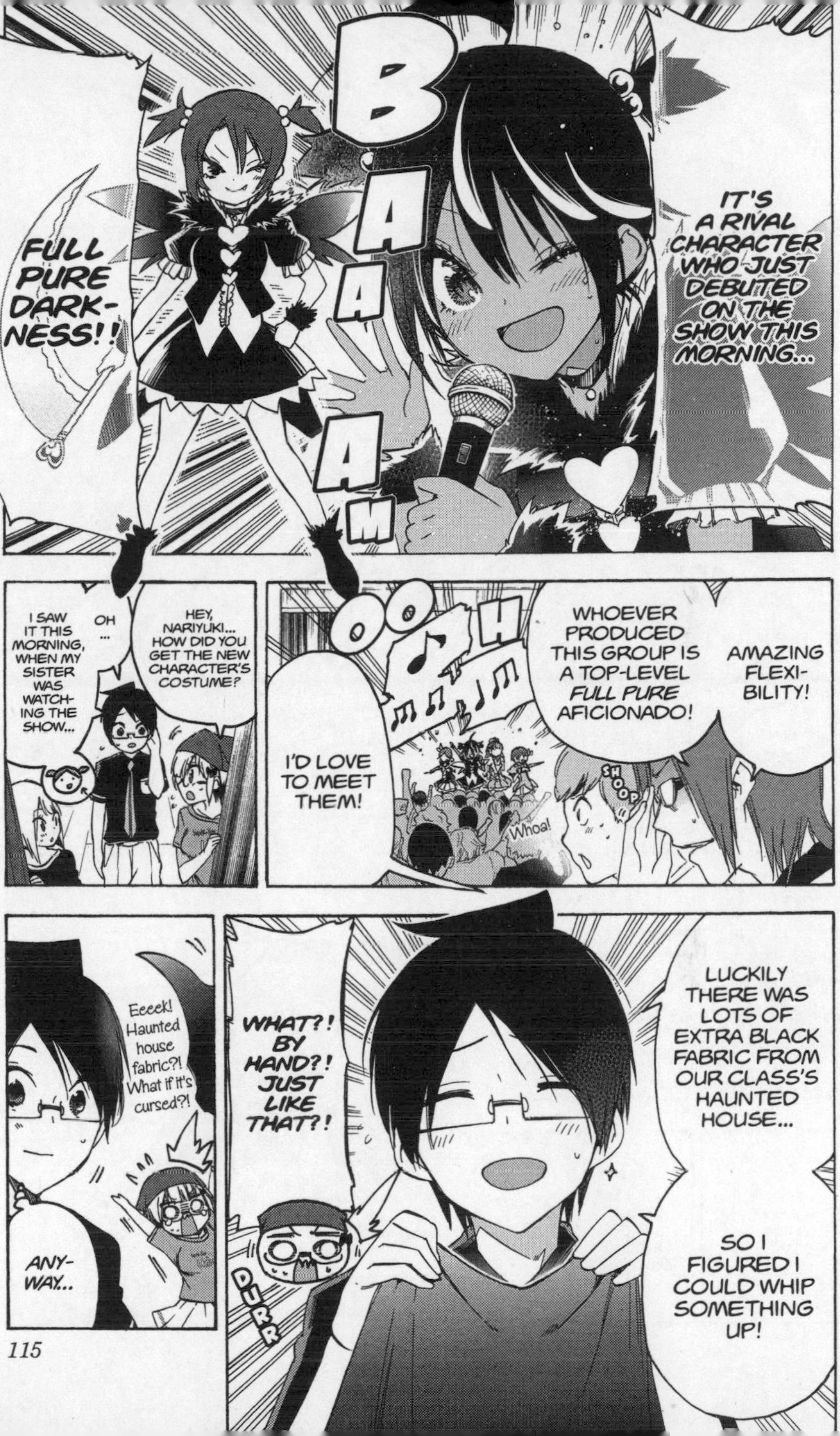
IT'S A RIVAL CHARACTER WHO JUST DEBUTED ON THE SHOW THIS MORNING...
BAAAAM
FULL PURE DARK-NESS!!
AMAZING FLEXI-BILITY!
WHOEVER PRODUCED THIS GROUP IS A TOP-LEVEL FULL PURE AFICIONADO!
OOOH
I'D LOVE TO MEET THEM!
SHOOP
Whoa!
HEY, NARIYUKI... HOW DID YOU GET THE NEW CHARACTER'S COSTUME?
OH ...
I SAW IT THIS MORNING, WHEN MY SISTER WAS WATCHING THE SHOW...
LUCKILY THERE WAS LOTS OF EXTRA BLACK FABRIC FROM OUR CLASS'S HAUNTED HOUSE...
SO I FIGURED I COULD WHIP SOMETHING UP!
WHAT?! BY HAND?! JUST LIKE THAT?!
DURR
Eeeek! Haunted house fabric?! What if it's cursed?!
ANY-WAY...

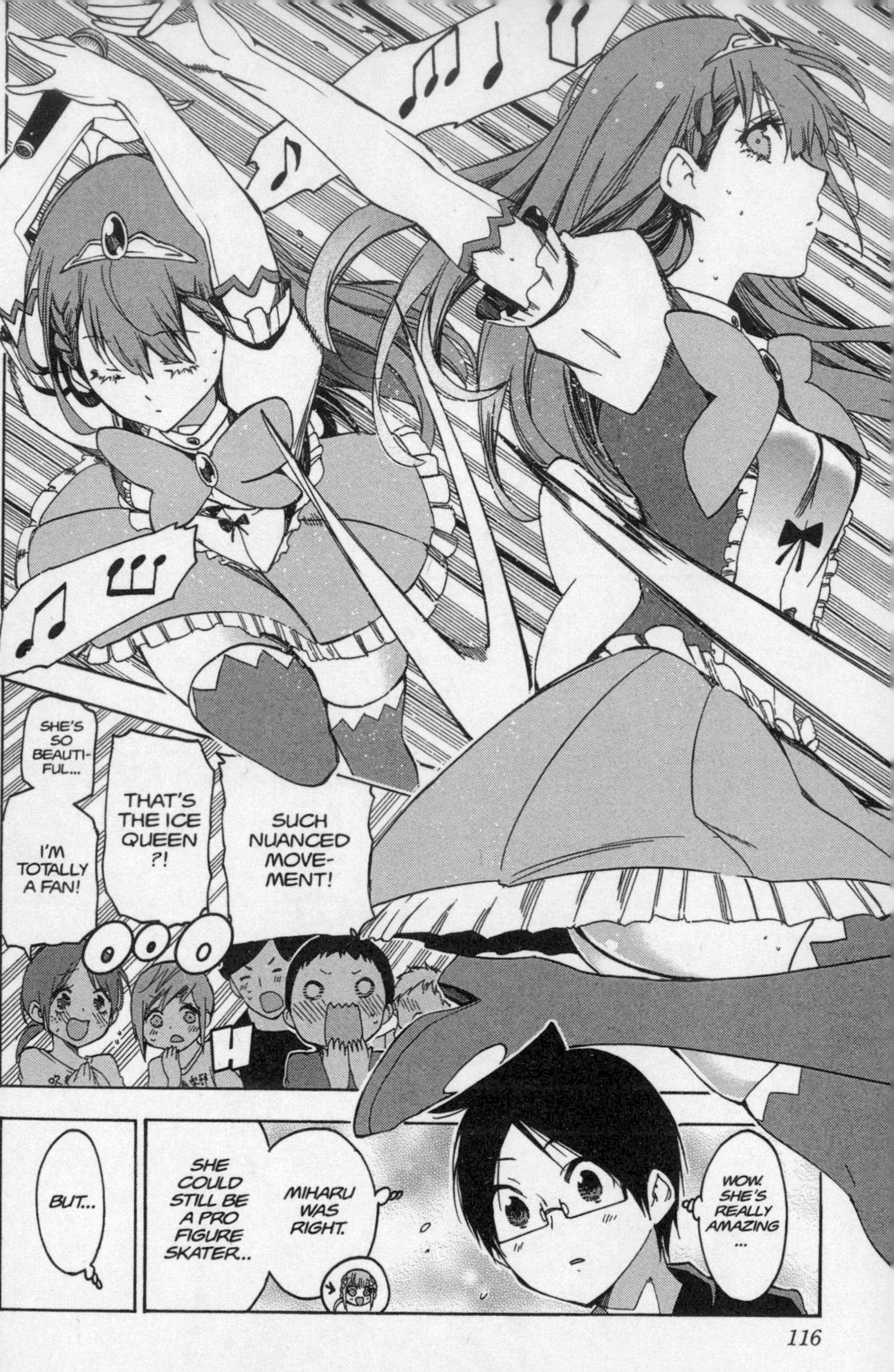
SUCH NUANCED MOVEMENT!
THAT'S THE ICE QUEEN ?!
SHE'S SO BEAUTIFUL... I'M TOTALLY A FAN!
H
WOW. SHE'S REALLY AMAZING ...
MIHARU WAS RIGHT.
SHE COULD STILL BE A PRO FIGURE SKATER...
BUT...

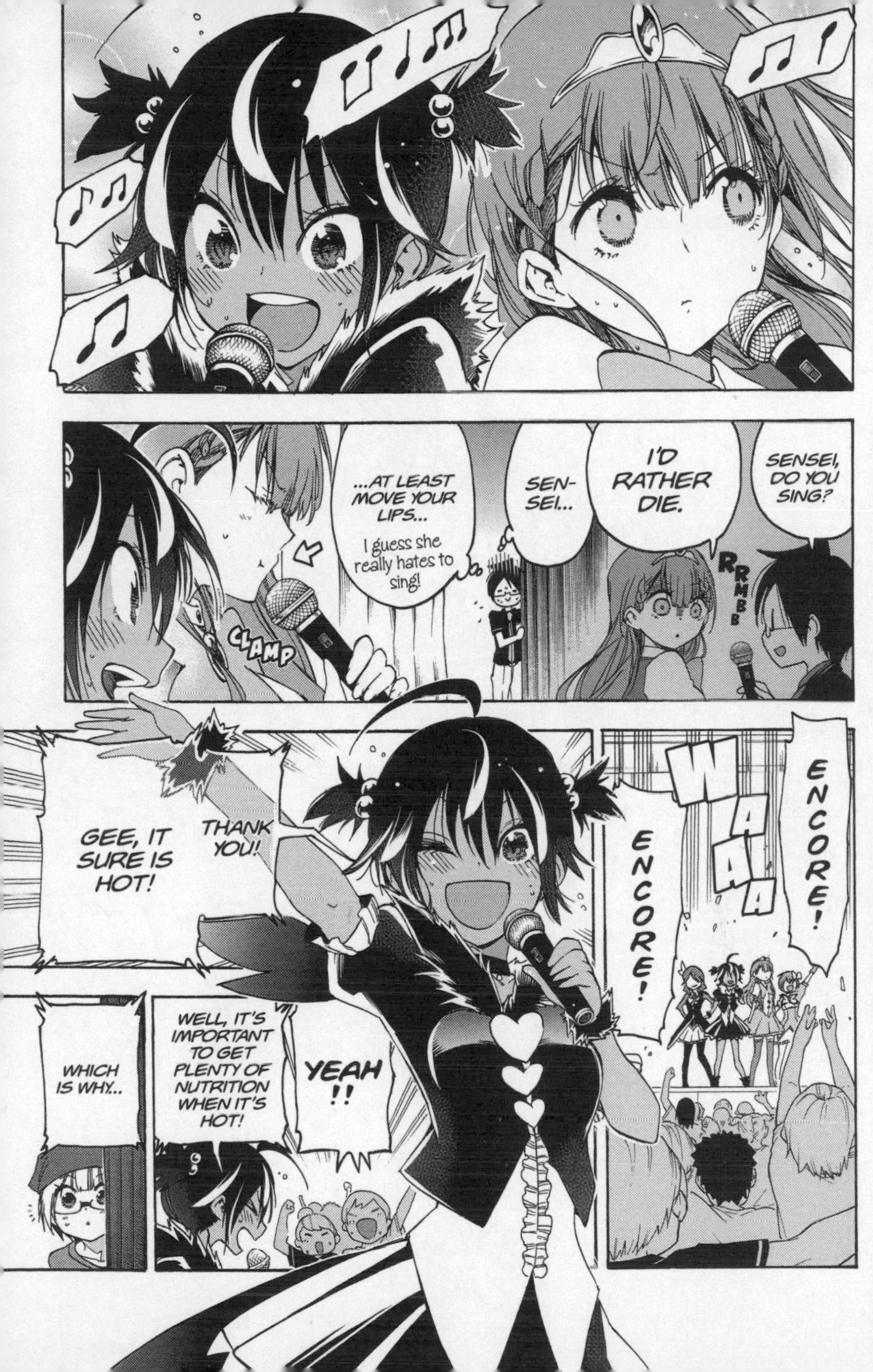
SENSEI, DO YOU SING?
RRMBB
I'D RATHER DIE.
SEN-SEI...
...AT LEAST MOVE YOUR LIPS...
I guess she really hates to sing!
CLAMP
ENCORE!
WAAAA
ENCORE!
THANK YOU!
GEE, IT SURE IS HOT!
YEAH!!
WELL, IT'S IMPORTANT TO GET PLENTY OF NUTRITION WHEN IT'S HOT!
WHICH IS WHY...

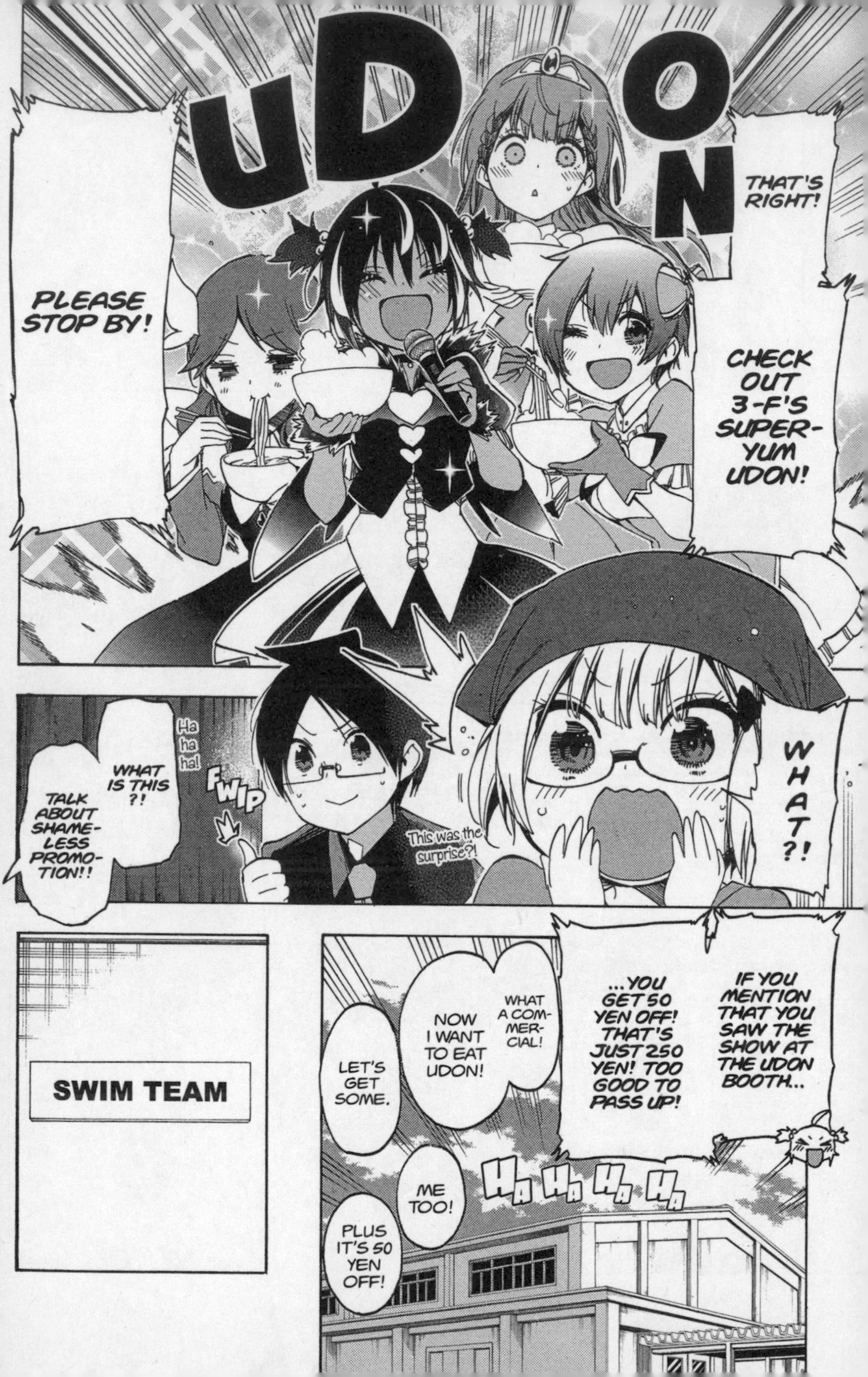
UDON
THAT'S RIGHT!
CHECK OUT 3-F'S SUPER-YUM UDON!
PLEASE STOP BY!
WHAT?!
This was the surprise?!
FWIP
Ha ha ha!
WHAT IS THIS?!
TALK ABOUT SHAMELESS PROMOTION!!
IF YOU MENTION THAT YOU SAW THE SHOW AT THE UDON BOOTH...
...YOU GET 50 YEN OFF! THAT'S JUST 250 YEN! TOO GOOD TO PASS UP!
WHAT A COMMERCIAL!
NOW I WANT TO EAT UDON!
LET'S GET SOME.
HA HA HA HA
ME TOO!
PLUS IT'S 50 YEN OFF!
SWIM TEAM

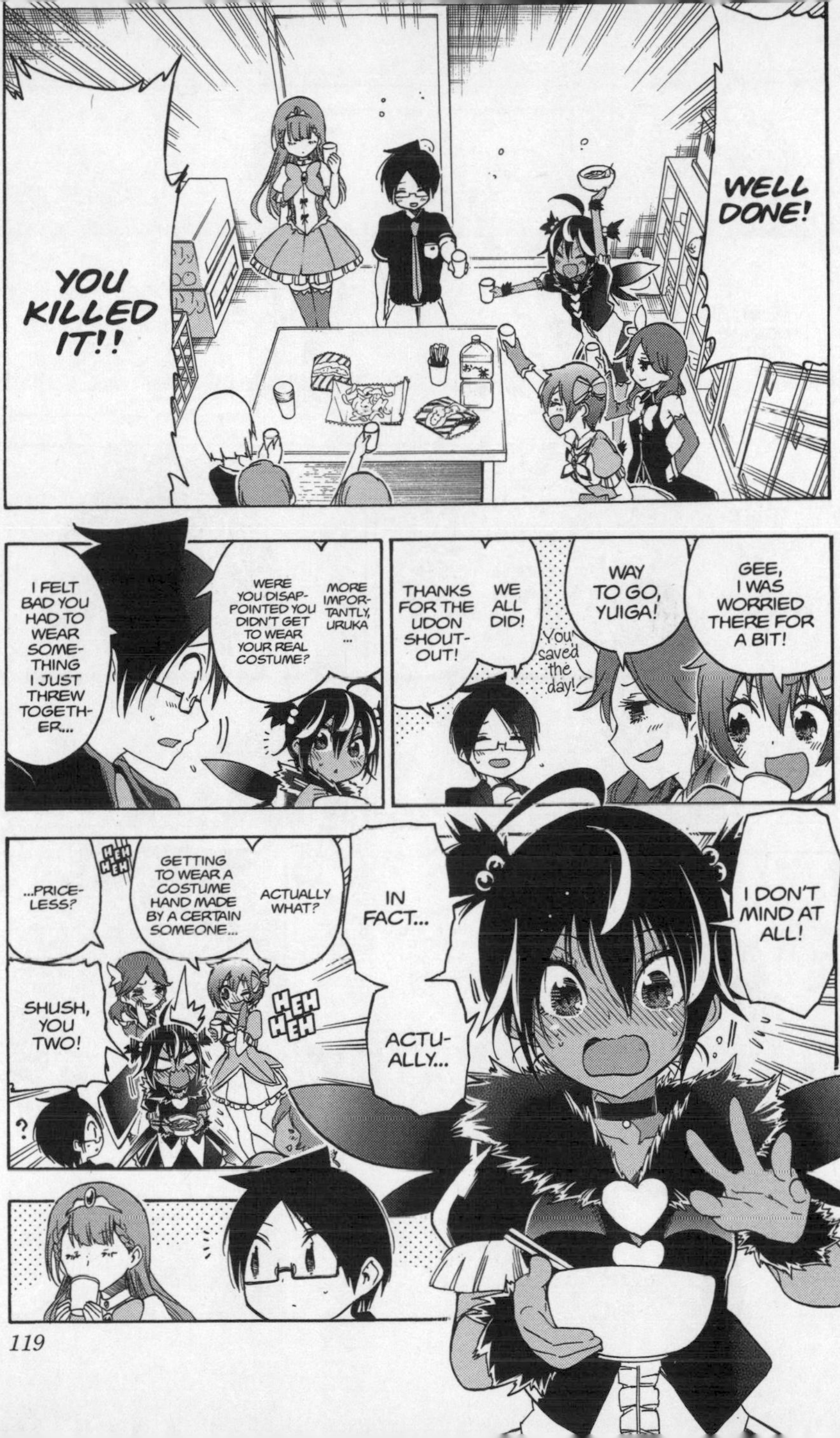
WELL DONE!
YOU KILLED IT!!
GEE, I WAS WORRIED THERE FOR A BIT!
WAY TO GO, YUIGA!
You saved the day!
WE ALL DID!
THANKS FOR THE UDON SHOUT-OUT!
MORE IMPORTANTLY, URUKA...
WERE YOU DISAPPOINTED YOU DIDN'T GET TO WEAR YOUR REAL COSTUME?
I FELT BAD YOU HAD TO WEAR SOMETHING I JUST THREW TOGETHER...
I DON'T MIND AT ALL!
IN FACT...
ACTUALLY...
ACTUALLY WHAT?
GETTING TO WEAR A COSTUME HAND MADE BY A CERTAIN SOMEONE...
HEH HEH
...PRICELESS?
HEH HEH
SHUSH, YOU TWO!
?

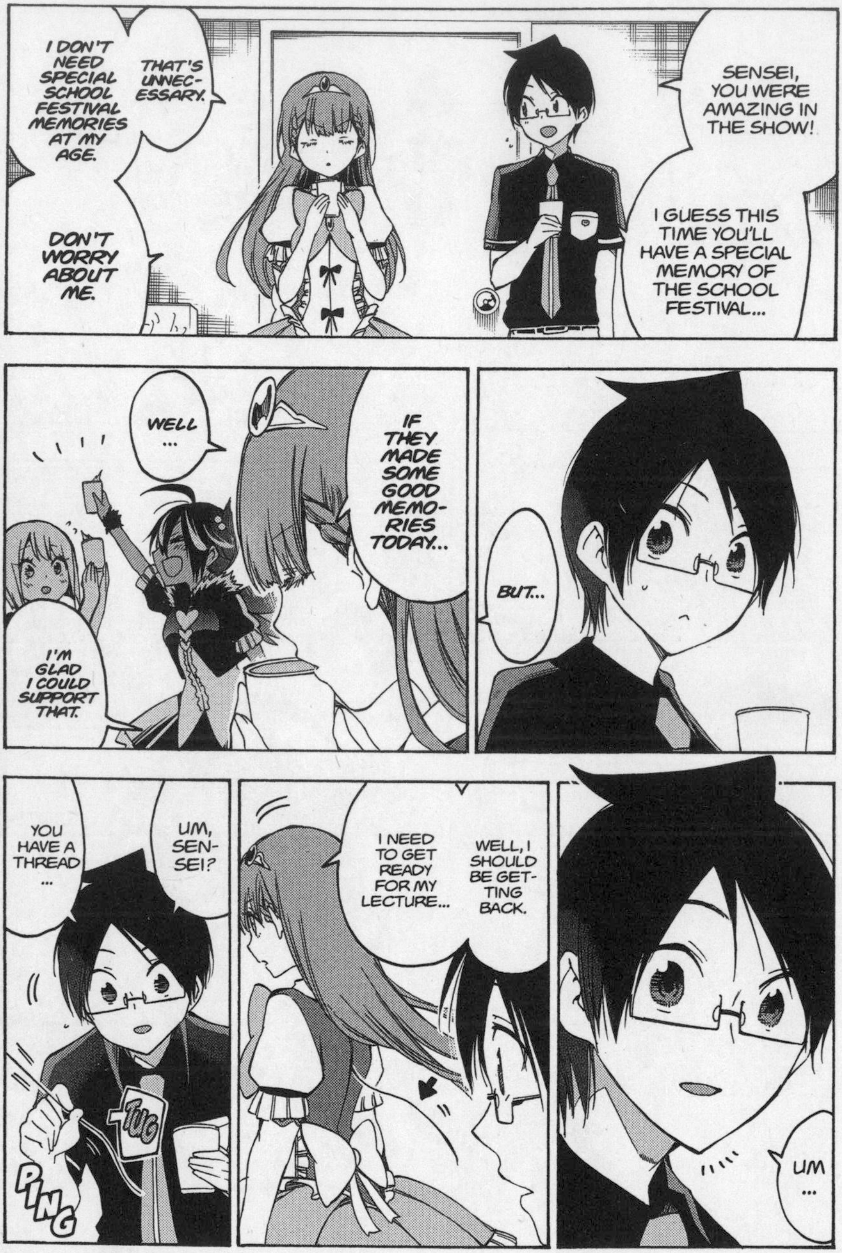
SENSEI, YOU WERE AMAZING IN THE SHOW!
I GUESS THIS TIME YOU'LL HAVE A SPECIAL MEMORY OF THE SCHOOL FESTIVAL...
THAT'S UNNEC-ESSARY.
I DON'T NEED SPECIAL SCHOOL FESTIVAL MEMORIES AT MY AGE.
DON'T WORRY ABOUT ME.
BUT...
IF THEY MADE SOME GOOD MEMO-RIES TODAY...
WELL ...
I'M GLAD I COULD SUPPORT THAT.
UM ...
WELL, I SHOULD BE GET-TING BACK.
I NEED TO GET READY FOR MY LECTURE...
UM, SEN-SEI?
YOU HAVE A THREAD ...
TUG
PING

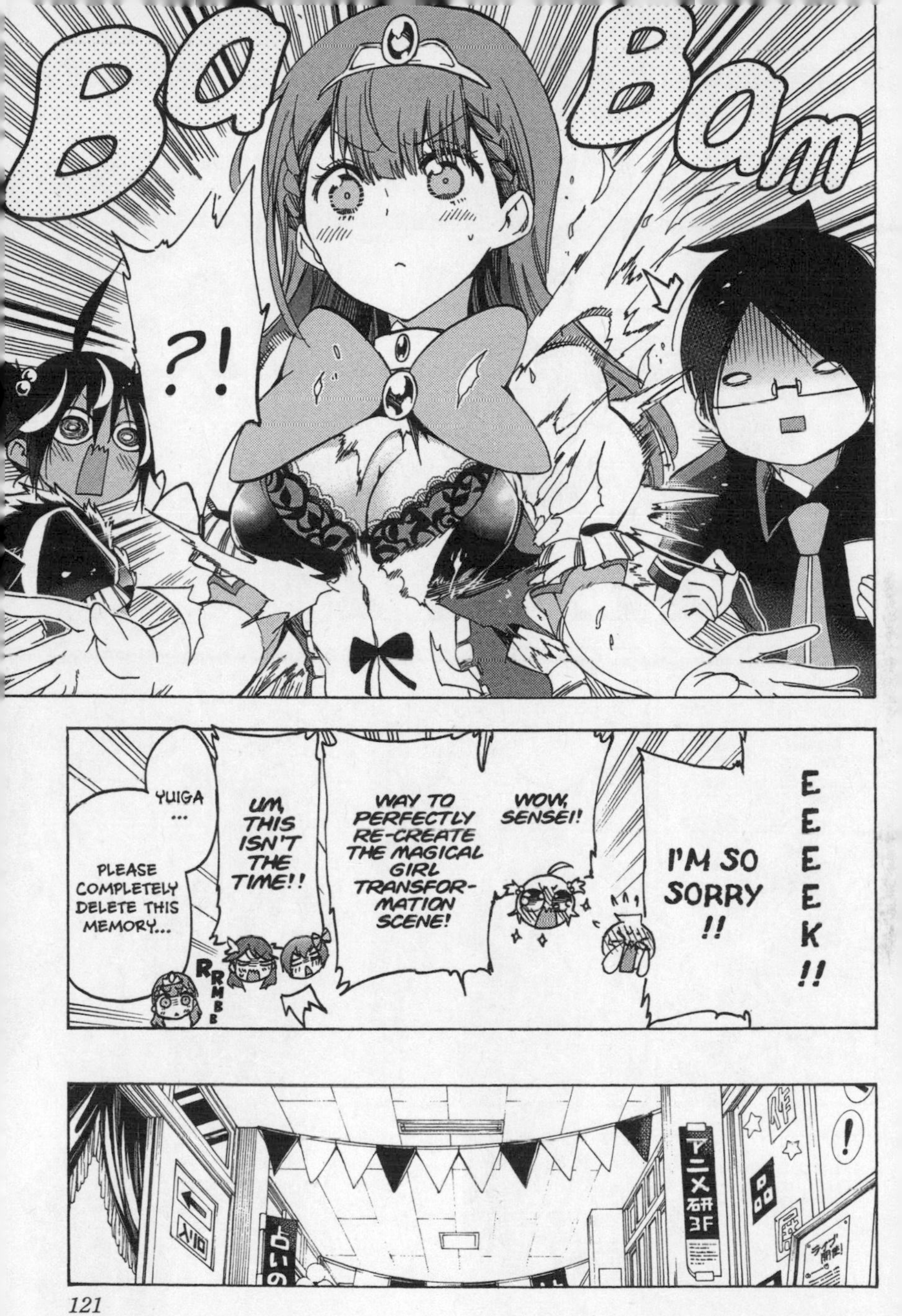
Ba Bam
?!
EEEEK!!
I'M SO SORRY!!
WOW, SENSEI!
WAY TO PERFECTLY RE-CREATE THE MAGICAL GIRL TRANSFORMATION SCENE!
UM, THIS ISN'T THE TIME!!
RRMBB
YUIGA...
PLEASE COMPLETELY DELETE THIS MEMORY...
アニメ研 3F
占いの
!

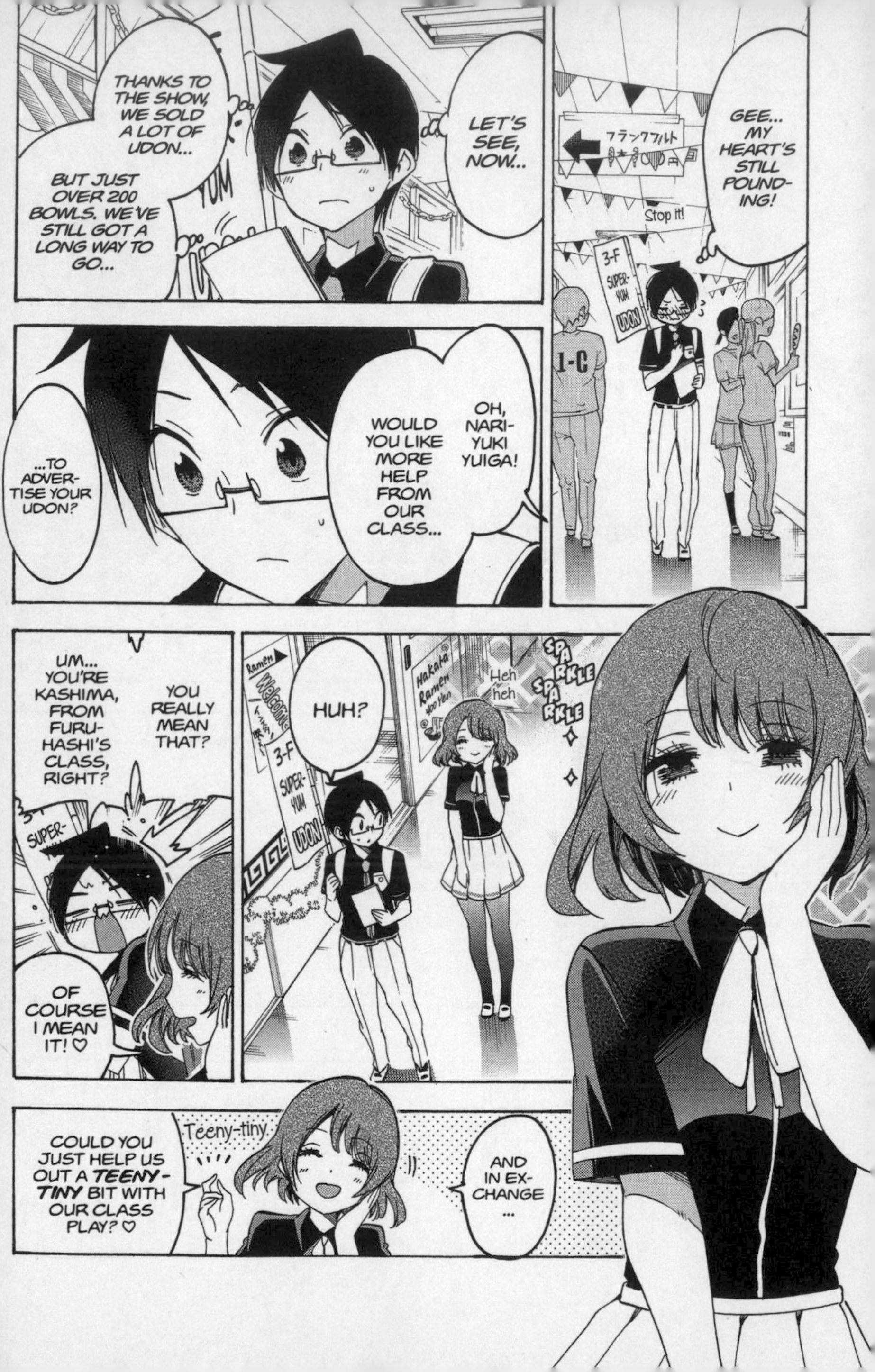

GEE... MY HEART'S STILL POUNDING!
Stop it!
フランクフルト
3-F SUPER-YUM UDON
1-C
LET'S SEE, NOW...
THANKS TO THE SHOW, WE SOLD A LOT OF UDON...
BUT JUST OVER 200 BOWLS. WE'VE STILL GOT A LONG WAY TO GO...
YUM
OH, NARI-YUKI YUIGA!
WOULD YOU LIKE MORE HELP FROM OUR CLASS...
...TO ADVERTISE YOUR UDON?
SPARKLE SPARKLE
Heh heh
HUH?
Ramen
Welcome
Hakata Ramen 400 Yen
3-F SUPER-YUM UDON
YOU REALLY MEAN THAT?
UM... YOU'RE KASHIMA, FROM FURU-HASHI'S CLASS, RIGHT?
SUPER-
OF COURSE I MEAN IT! ♡
AND IN EXCHANGE...
COULD YOU JUST HELP US OUT A ***TEENY-TINY*** BIT WITH OUR CLASS PLAY? ♡
Teeny-tiny.

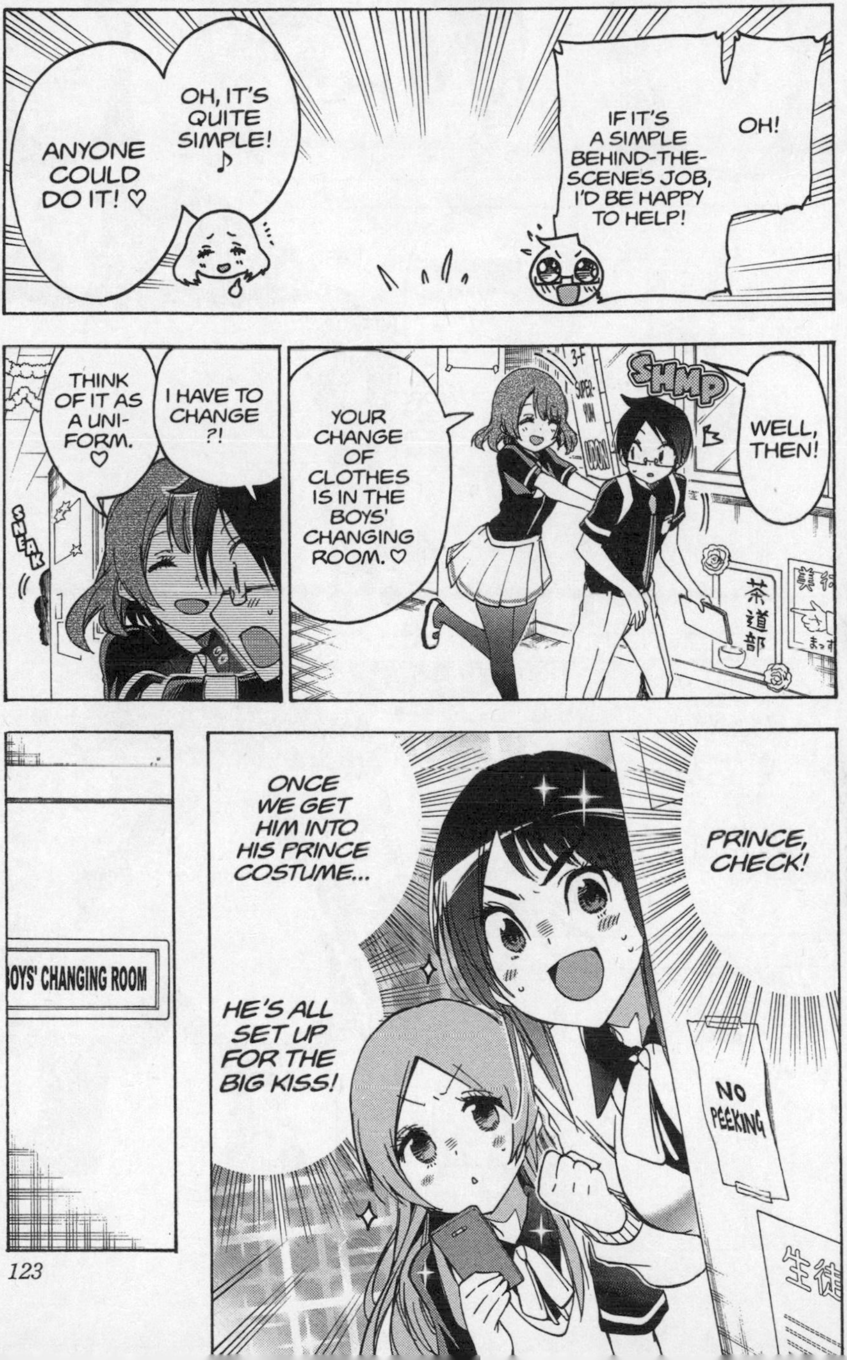
OH!
IF IT'S A SIMPLE BEHIND-THE-SCENES JOB, I'D BE HAPPY TO HELP!
OH, IT'S QUITE SIMPLE! ♪
ANYONE COULD DO IT! ♡
WELL, THEN!
SHMP
YOUR CHANGE OF CLOTHES IS IN THE BOYS' CHANGING ROOM. ♡
I HAVE TO CHANGE?!
THINK OF IT AS A UNIFORM. ♡
SNEAK
PRINCE, CHECK!
ONCE WE GET HIM INTO HIS PRINCE COSTUME...
HE'S ALL SET UP FOR THE BIG KISS!
NO PEEKING
BOYS' CHANGING ROOM

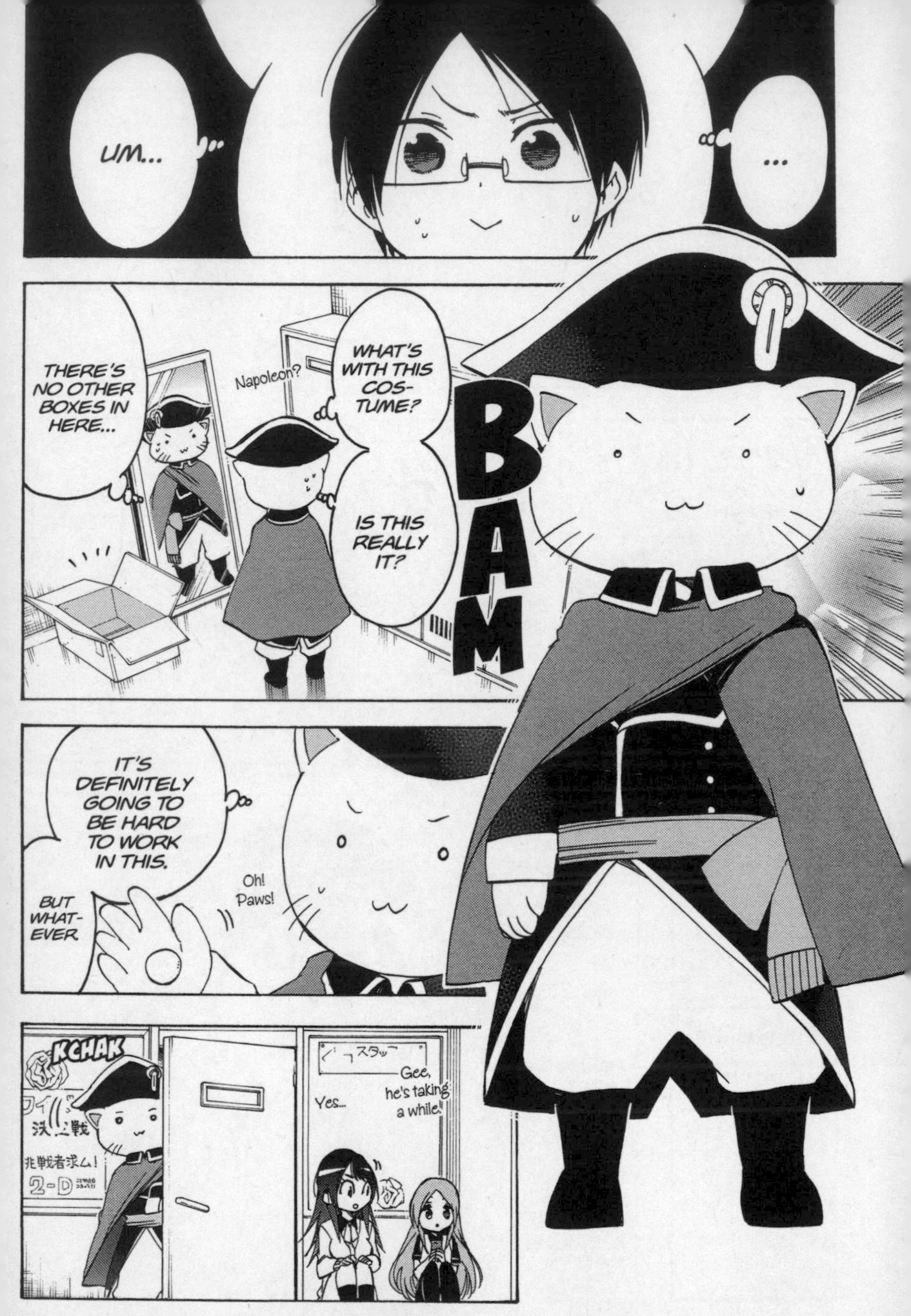

...
UM...
BAM
WHAT'S WITH THIS COSTUME?
IS THIS REALLY IT?
Napoleon?
THERE'S NO OTHER BOXES IN HERE...
Oh! Paws!
IT'S DEFINITELY GOING TO BE HARD TO WORK IN THIS.
BUT WHATEVER.
Gee, he's taking a while!
Yes...
KCHAK
2-D

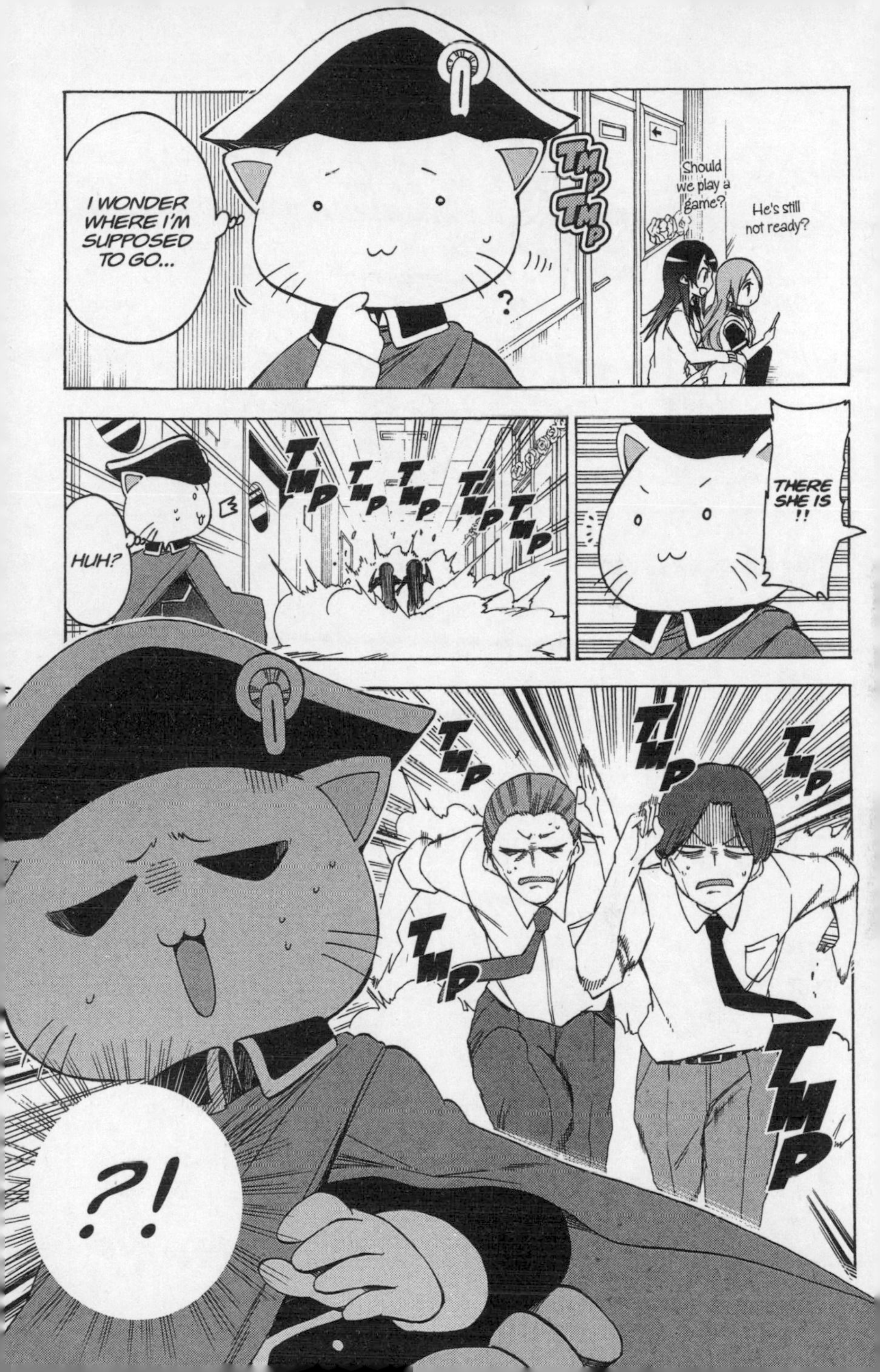
He's still not ready?
Should we play a game?
TMP TMP
I WONDER WHERE I'M SUPPOSED TO GO...
THERE SHE IS!!
TMP TMP TMP TMP TMP
HUH?
TMP
TMP
TMP
TMP
TMP
?!

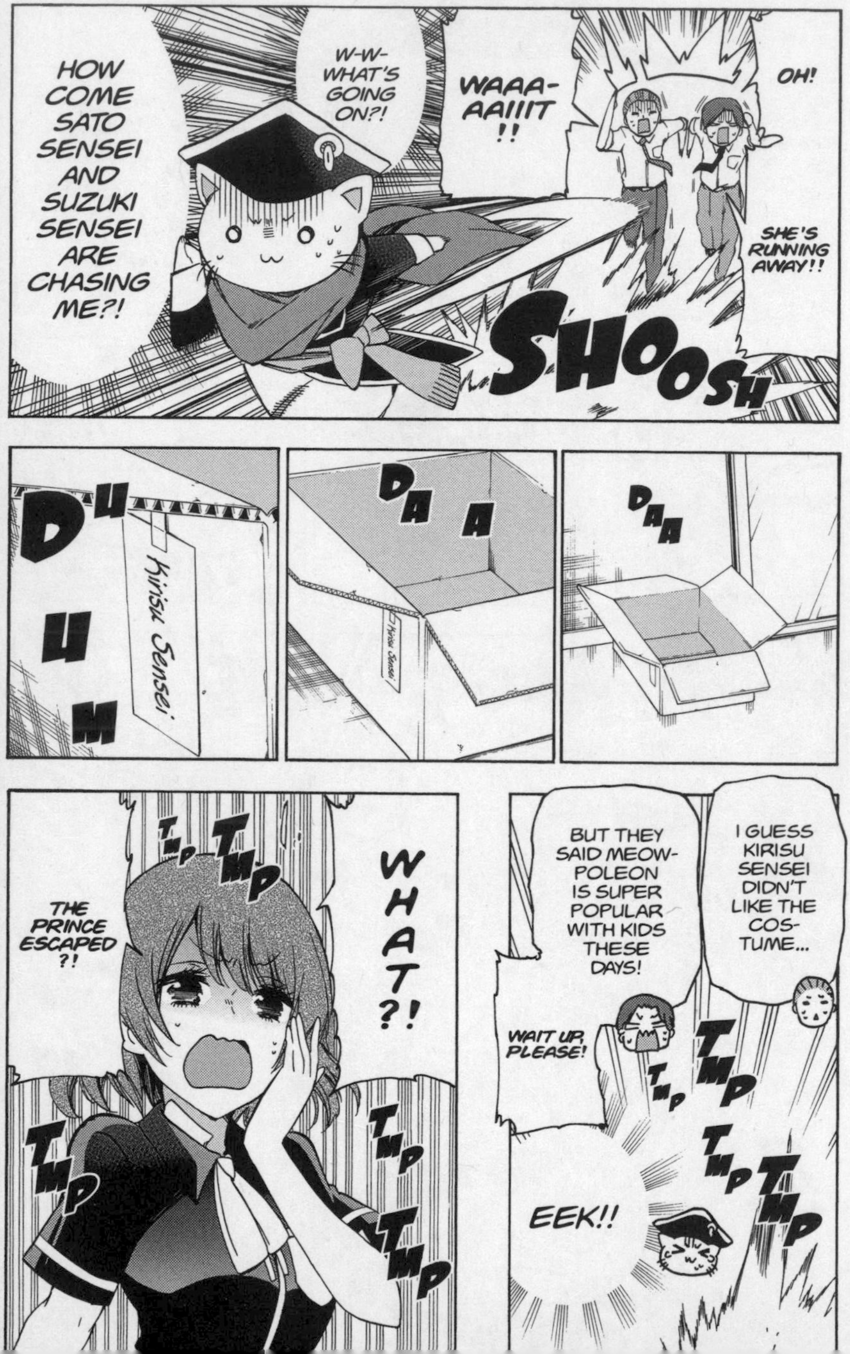
OH!
WAAAA-AAIIIT!!
SHE'S RUNNING AWAY!!
W-W-WHAT'S GOING ON?!
HOW COME SATO SENSEI AND SUZUKI SENSEI ARE CHASING ME?!
SHOOSH
DAA
DA A
Kirisu Sensei
DUUM
Kirisu Sensei
I GUESS KIRISU SENSEI DIDN'T LIKE THE COS-TUME...
BUT THEY SAID MEOW-POLEON IS SUPER POPULAR WITH KIDS THESE DAYS!
WAIT UP, PLEASE!
TMP TMP
TMP TMP
EEK!!
WHAT?!
TMP TMP
THE PRINCE ESCAPED?!
TMP TMP
TMP

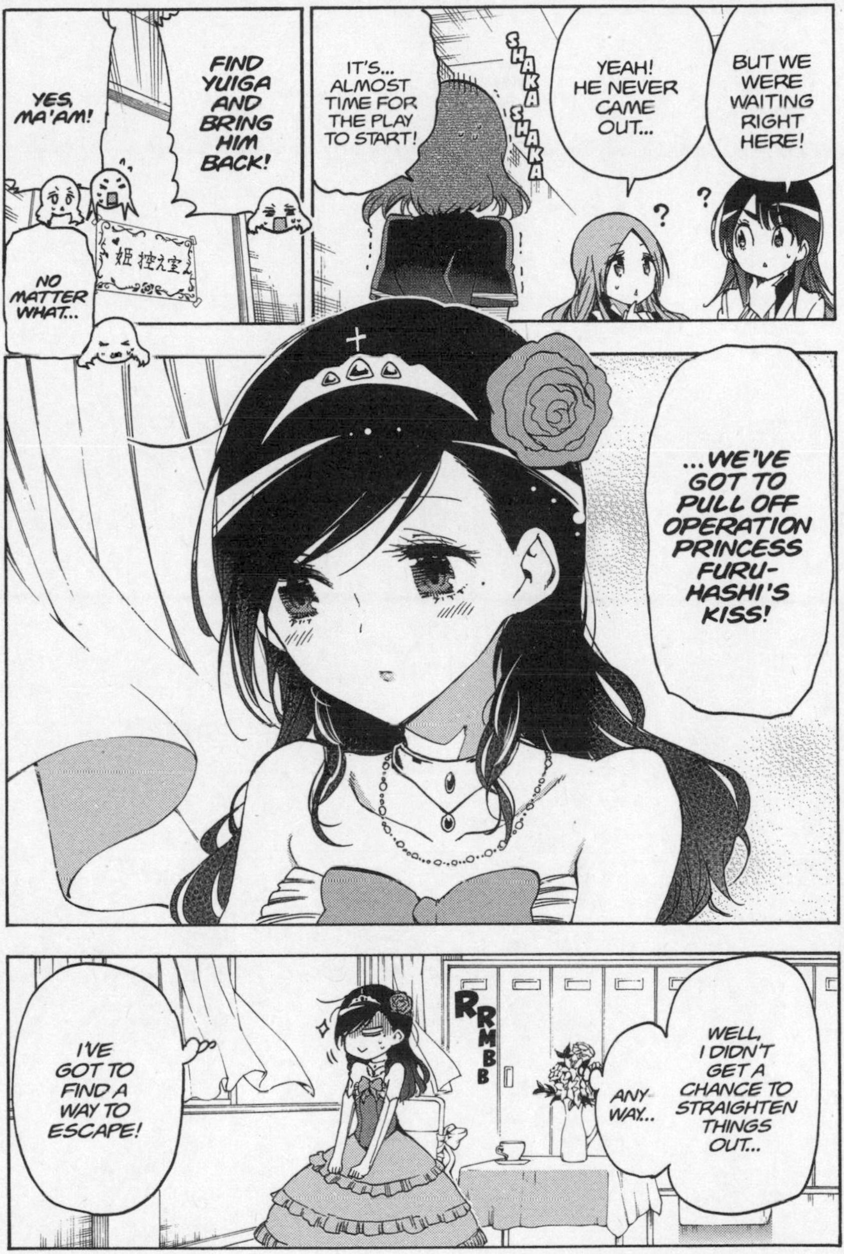
BUT WE WERE WAITING RIGHT HERE!
YEAH! HE NEVER CAME OUT...
SHAKA SHAKA
IT'S... ALMOST TIME FOR THE PLAY TO START!
FIND YUIGA AND BRING HIM BACK!
YES, MA'AM!
姫控え室
NO MATTER WHAT...
...WE'VE GOT TO PULL OFF OPERATION PRINCESS FURU-HASHI'S KISS!
WELL, I DIDN'T GET A CHANCE TO STRAIGHTEN THINGS OUT...
ANY-WAY...
RRRMBB
I'VE GOT TO FIND A WAY TO ESCAPE!

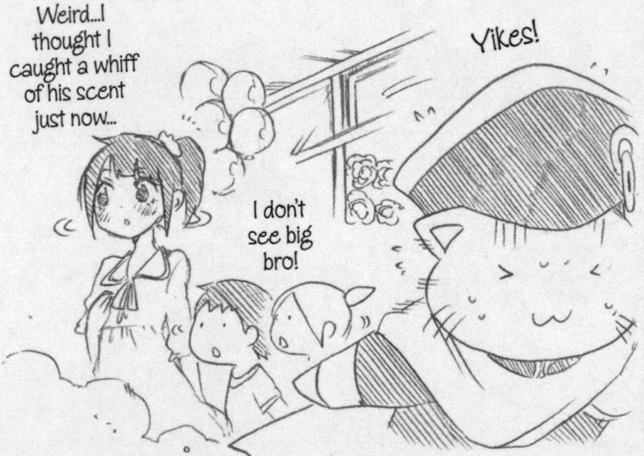
Yikes!
I don't see big bro!
Weird...I thought I caught a whiff of his scent just now...

Question 67: The [*X*] Tread a Thorny Path as the Festivities Continue…

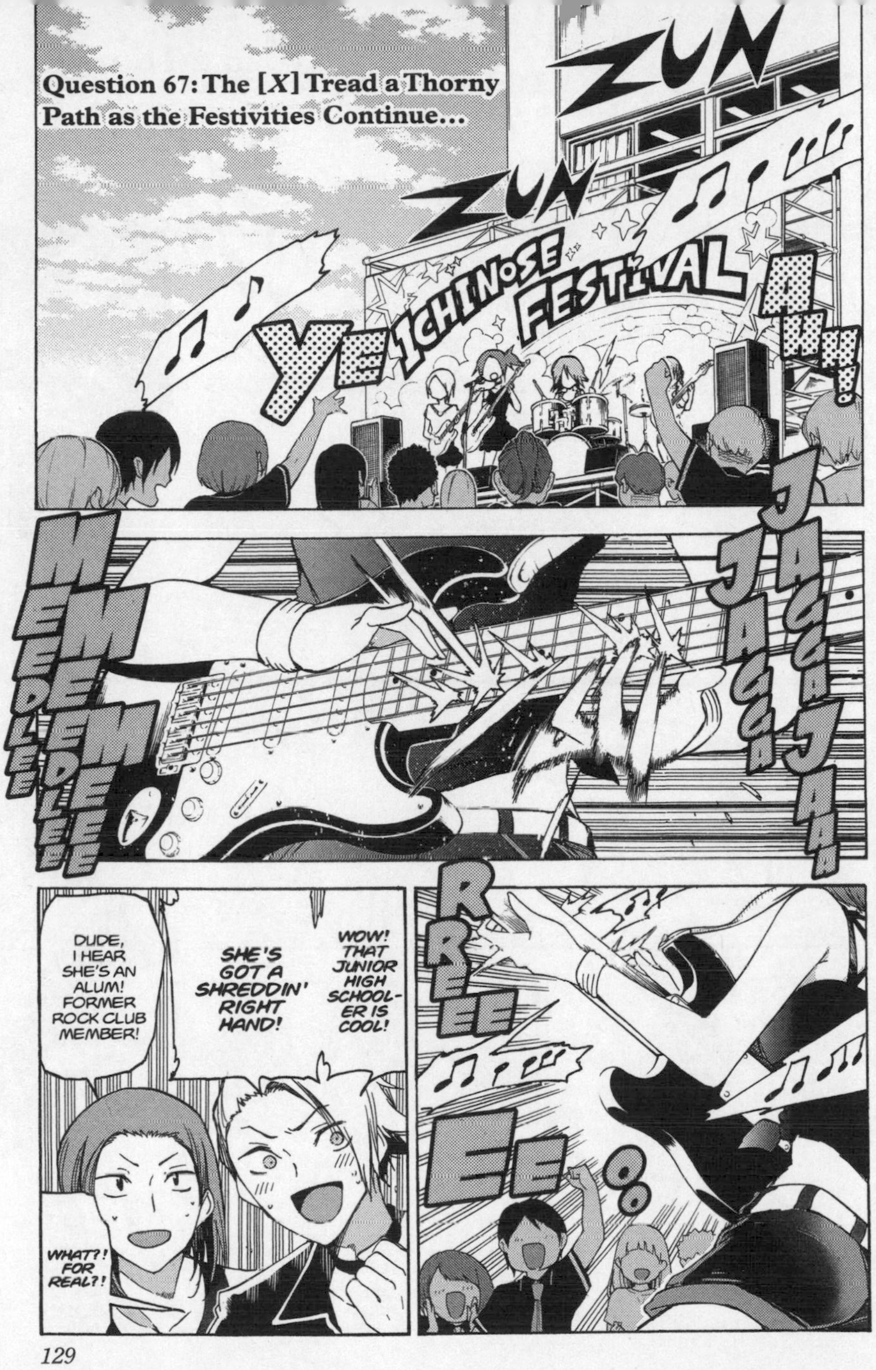
ZUN
ZUN
ICHINOSE FESTIVAL
YE
AHH!
RREEEE
EE
WOW! THAT JUNIOR HIGH SCHOOLER IS COOL!
SHE'S GOT A SHREDDIN' RIGHT HAND!
DUDE, I HEAR SHE'S AN ALUM! FORMER ROCK CLUB MEMBER!
WHAT?! FOR REAL?!

Question 67: The [X] Tread a Thorny Path as the Festivities Continue...

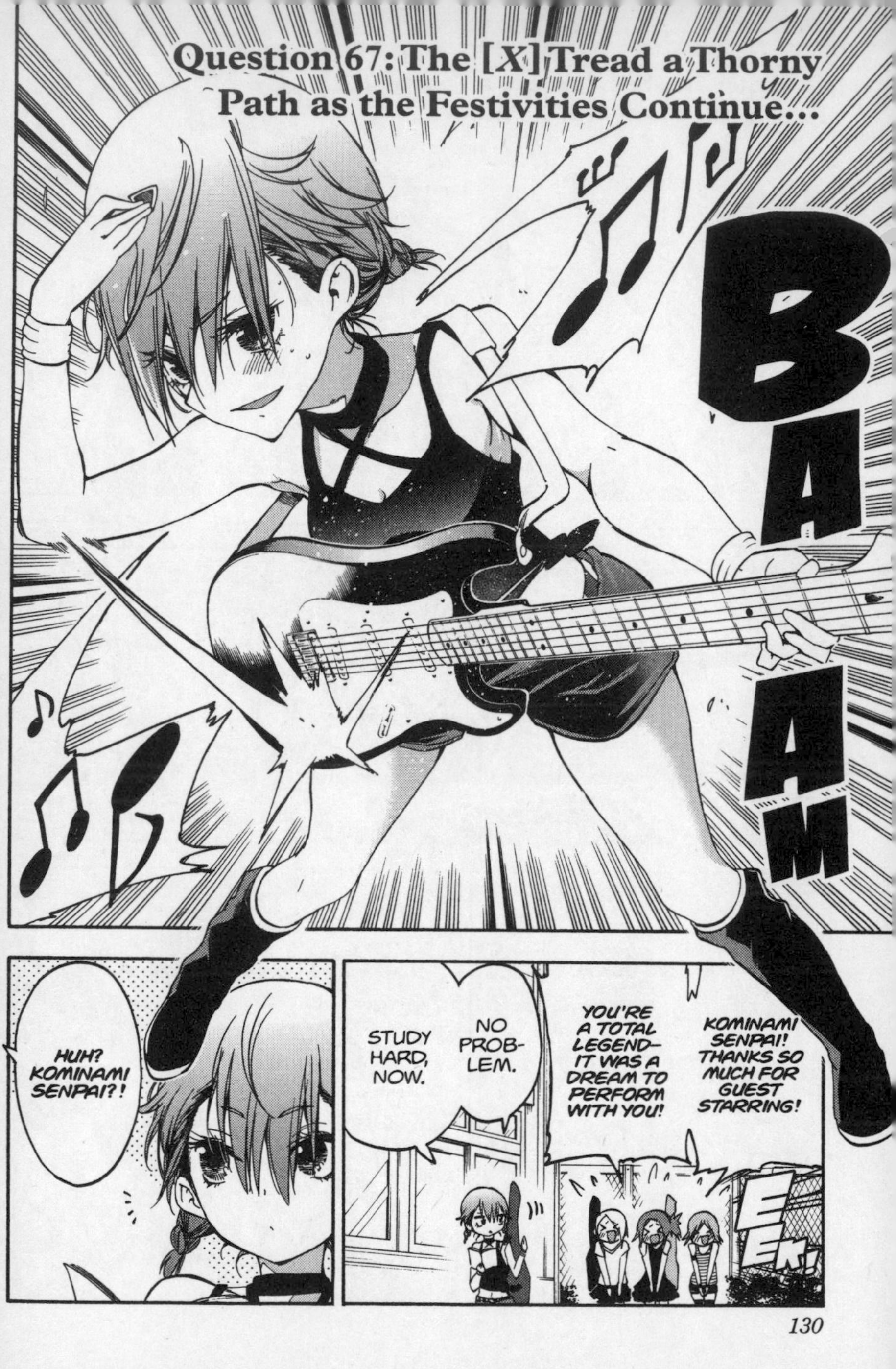

BAAM
KOMINAMI SENPAI! THANKS SO MUCH FOR GUEST STARRING!
YOU'RE A TOTAL LEGEND—IT WAS A DREAM TO PERFORM WITH YOU!
NO PROB-LEM.
STUDY HARD, NOW.
EEK!
HUH? KOMINAMI SENPAI?!

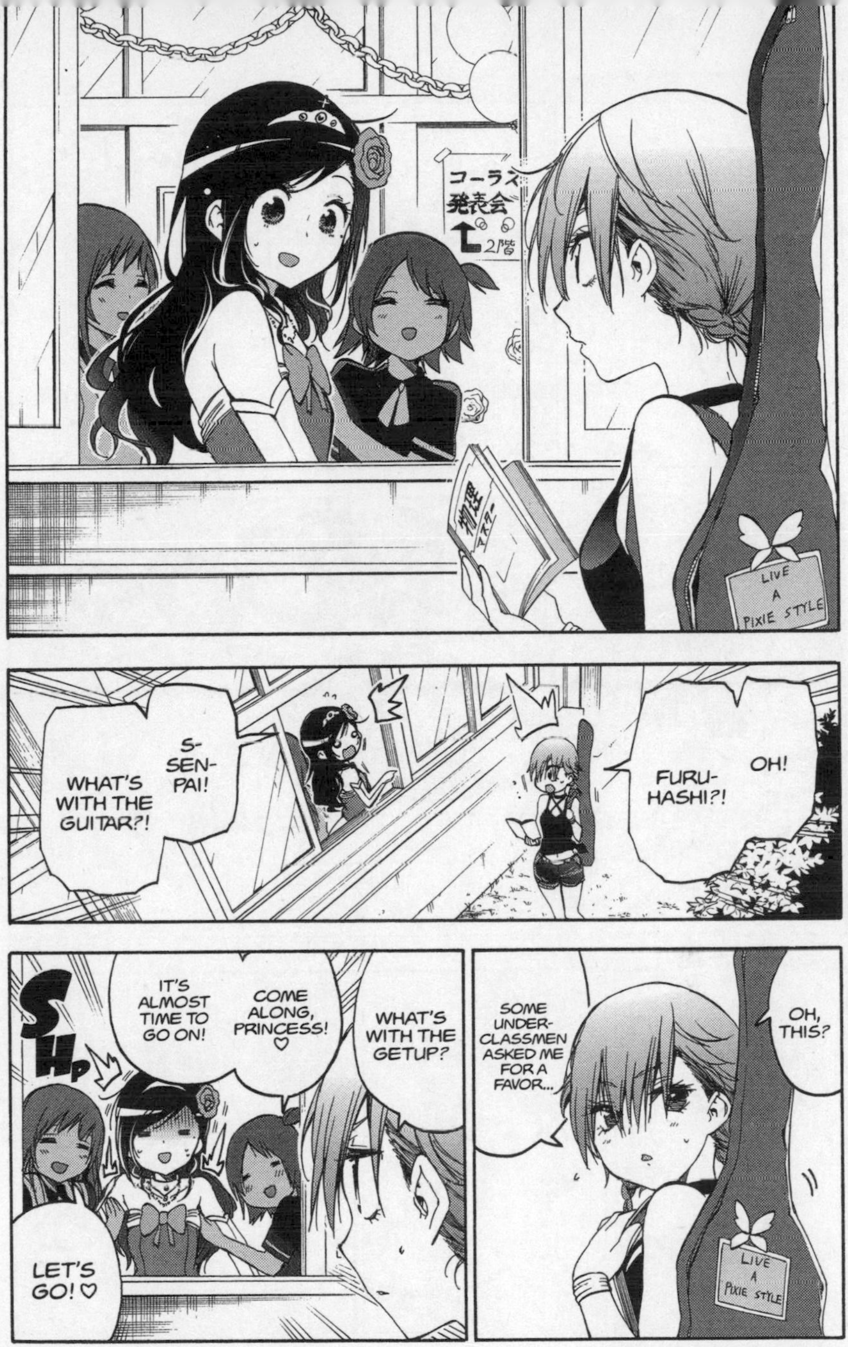

コーラス
発表会
2階
物理
LIVE A PIXIE STYLE
OH!
FURU-HASHI?!
S-SENPAI!
WHAT'S WITH THE GUITAR?!
OH, THIS?
SOME UNDERCLASSMEN ASKED ME FOR A FAVOR...
LIVE A PIXIE STYLE
WHAT'S WITH THE GETUP?
COME ALONG, PRINCESS! ♡
IT'S ALMOST TIME TO GO ON!
SHP
LET'S GO! ♡

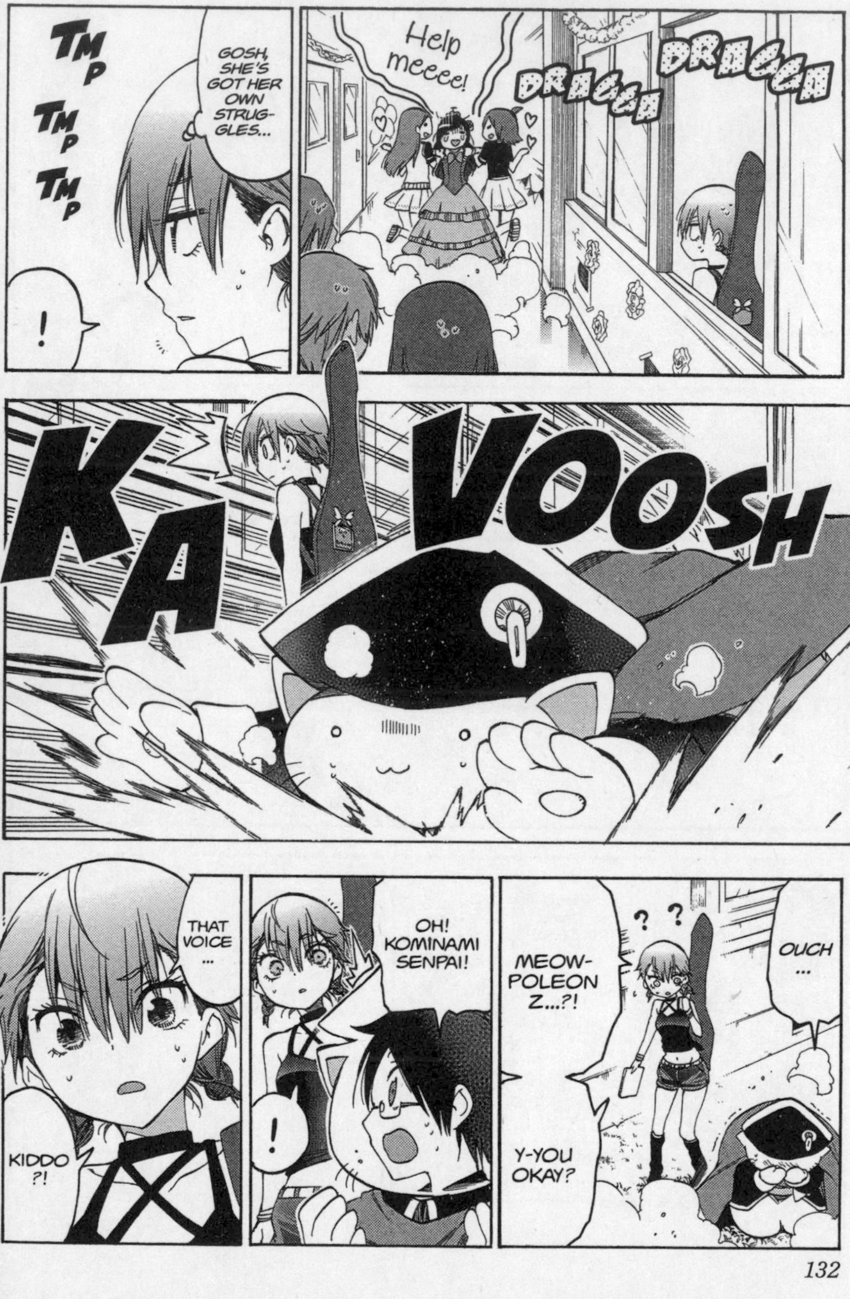

Help meeee!
DRAGGH DRAGGH
GOSH, SHE'S GOT HER OWN STRUG-GLES...
TMP TMP TMP
!
KA VOOSH
OUCH ...
MEOW-POLEON Z...?!
Y-YOU OKAY?
OH! KOMINAMI SENPAI!
!
THAT VOICE ...
KIDDO ?!

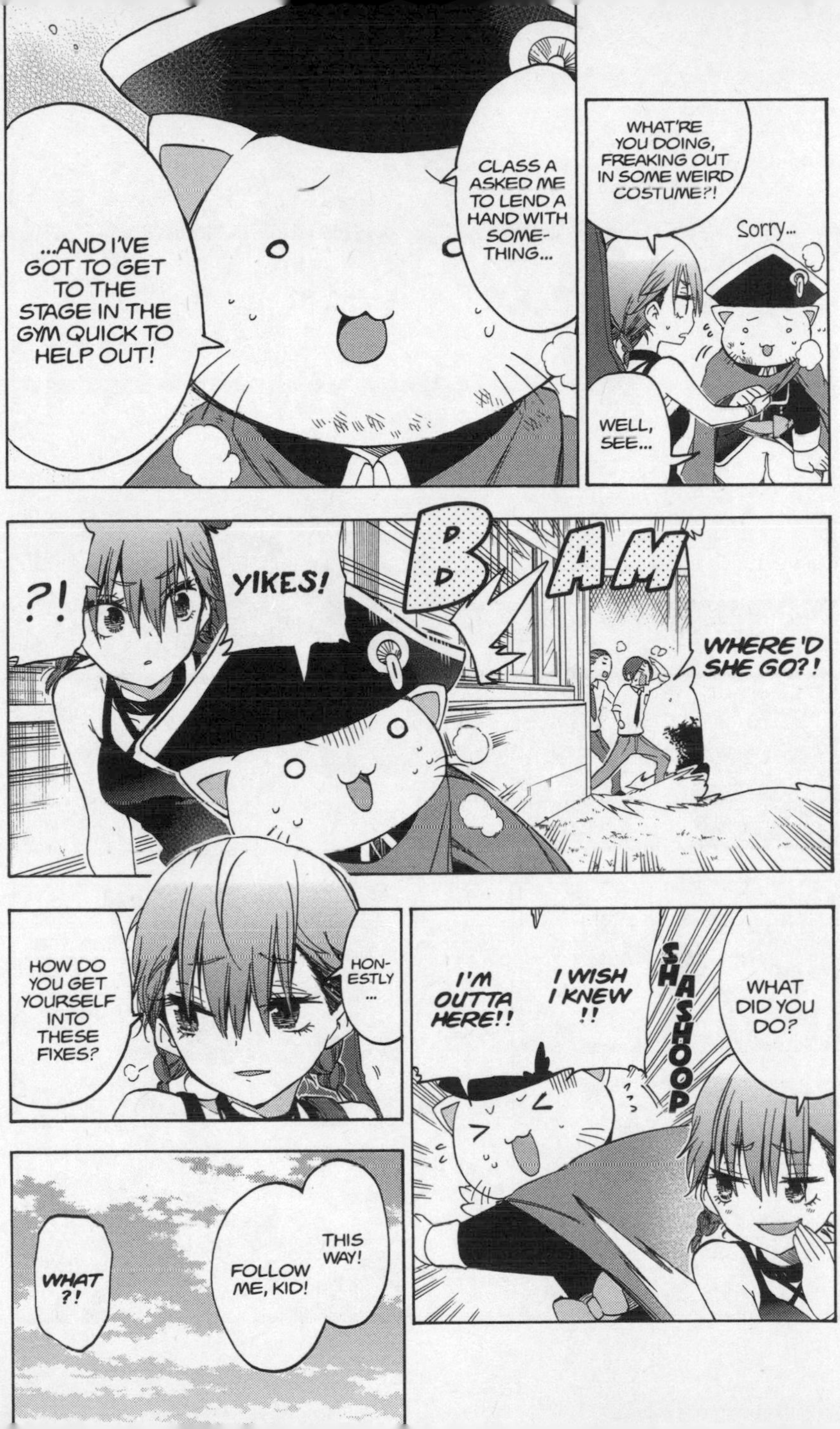
WHAT'RE YOU DOING, FREAKING OUT IN SOME WEIRD COSTUME?!
Sorry...
WELL, SEE...
CLASS A ASKED ME TO LEND A HAND WITH SOME-THING...
...AND I'VE GOT TO GET TO THE STAGE IN THE GYM QUICK TO HELP OUT!
BAM
WHERE'D SHE GO?!
YIKES!
?!
WHAT DID YOU DO?
SHASHOOP
I WISH I KNEW!!
I'M OUTTA HERE!!
HON-ESTLY...
HOW DO YOU GET YOURSELF INTO THESE FIXES?
THIS WAY!
FOLLOW ME, KID!
WHAT?!

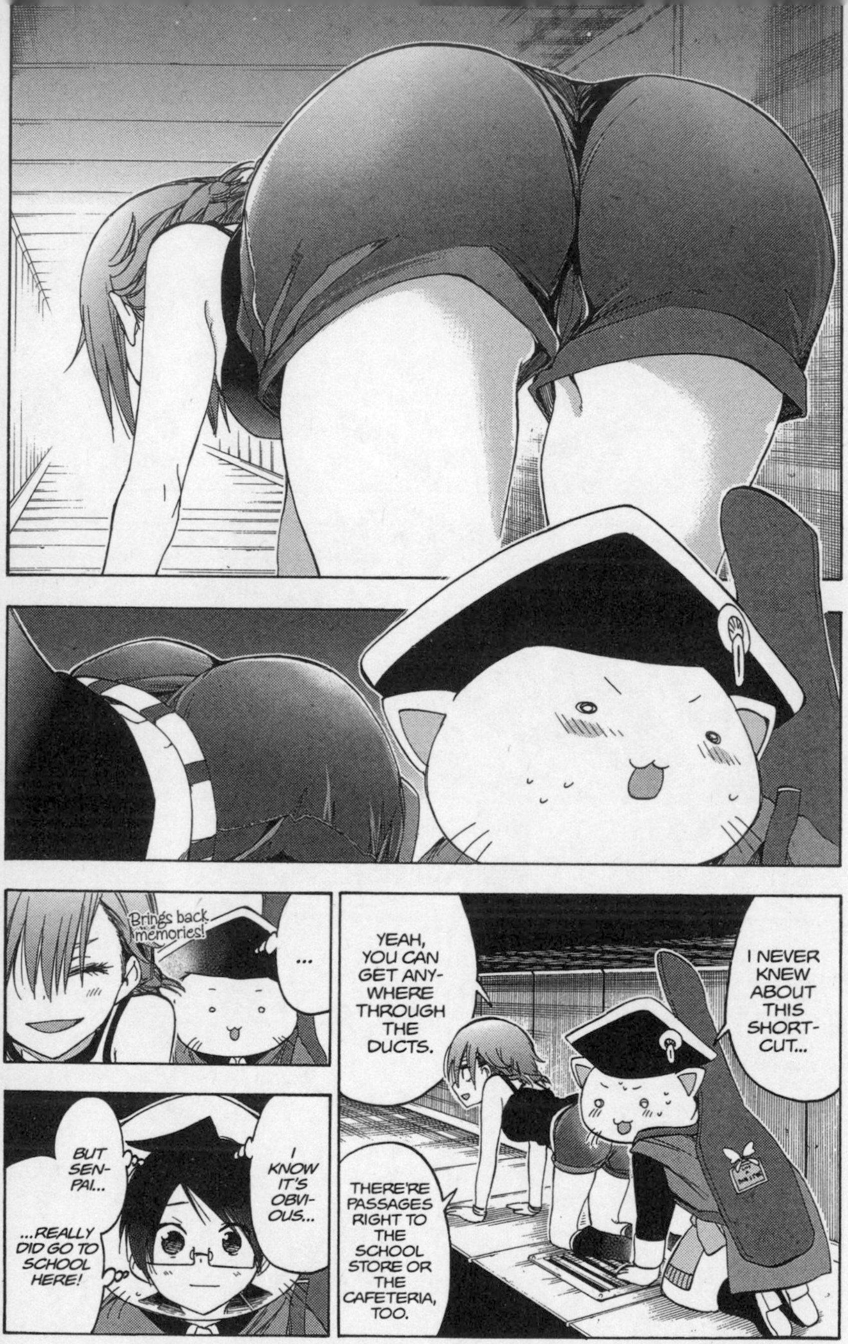
I NEVER KNEW ABOUT THIS SHORT-CUT...
YEAH, YOU CAN GET ANY-WHERE THROUGH THE DUCTS.
THERE'RE PASSAGES RIGHT TO THE SCHOOL STORE OR THE CAFETERIA, TOO.
...
Brings back memories!
I KNOW IT'S OBVI-OUS...
BUT SEN-PAI...
...REALLY DID GO TO SCHOOL HERE!

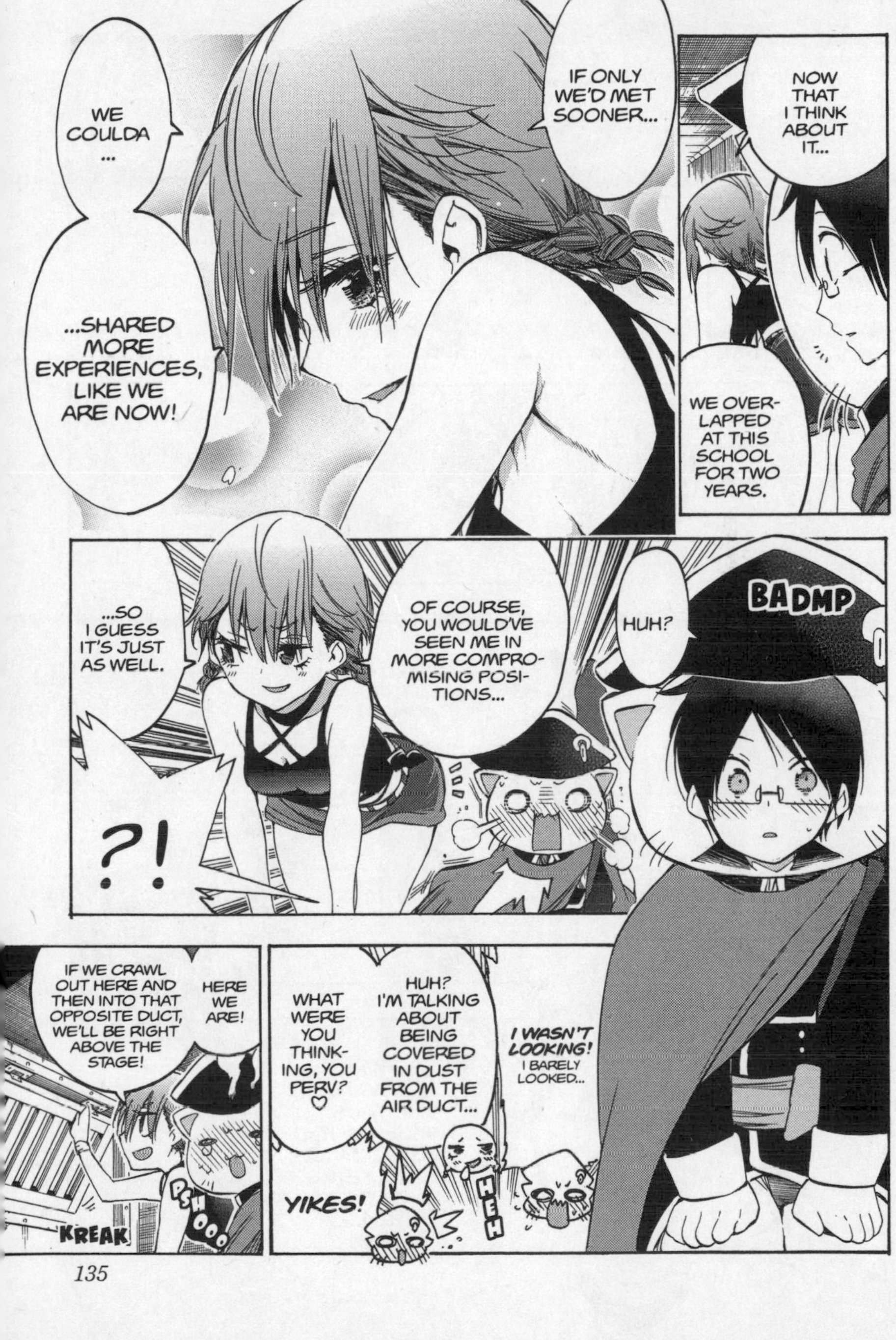
NOW THAT I THINK ABOUT IT...
WE OVER-LAPPED AT THIS SCHOOL FOR TWO YEARS.
IF ONLY WE'D MET SOONER...
WE COULDA ...
...SHARED MORE EXPERIENCES, LIKE WE ARE NOW!
BADMP
HUH?
OF COURSE, YOU WOULD'VE SEEN ME IN MORE COMPRO-MISING POSI-TIONS...
...SO I GUESS IT'S JUST AS WELL.
?!
I WASN'T LOOKING! I BARELY LOOKED...
HUH? I'M TALKING ABOUT BEING COVERED IN DUST FROM THE AIR DUCT...
WHAT WERE YOU THINK-ING, YOU PERV? ♡
HEH
YIKES!
HERE WE ARE!
IF WE CRAWL OUT HERE AND THEN INTO THAT OPPOSITE DUCT, WE'LL BE RIGHT ABOVE THE STAGE!
PSHOOO
KREAK

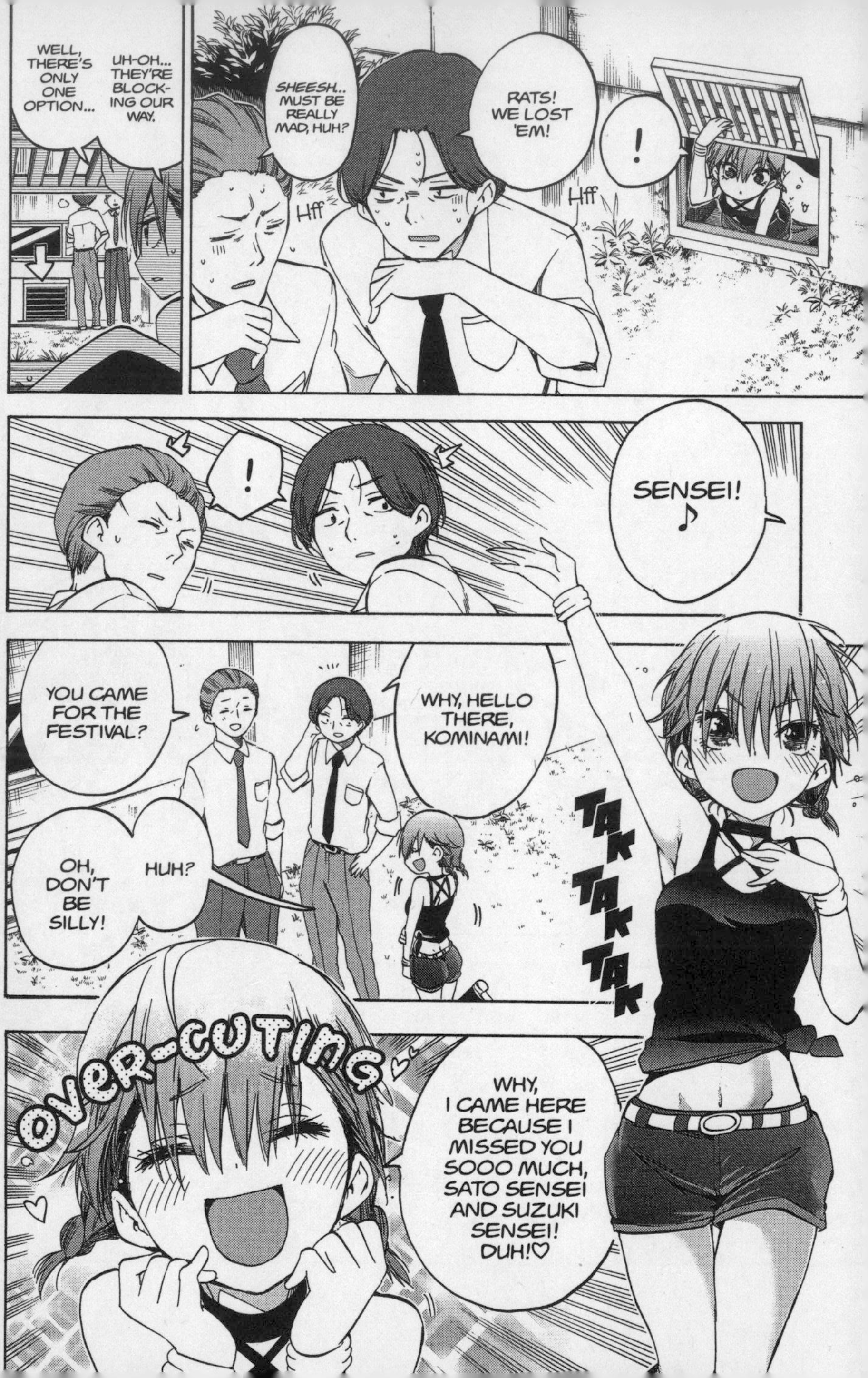
!
RATS! WE LOST 'EM!
SHEESH... MUST BE REALLY MAD, HUH?
Hff
Hff
UH-OH... THEY'RE BLOCK-ING OUR WAY.
WELL, THERE'S ONLY ONE OPTION...
SENSEI! ♪
!
TAK TAK TAK TAK
WHY, HELLO THERE, KOMINAMI!
YOU CAME FOR THE FESTIVAL?
HUH?
OH, DON'T BE SILLY!
WHY, I CAME HERE BECAUSE I MISSED YOU SOOO MUCH, SATO SENSEI AND SUZUKI SENSEI! DUH!♡
OVER-CUTING

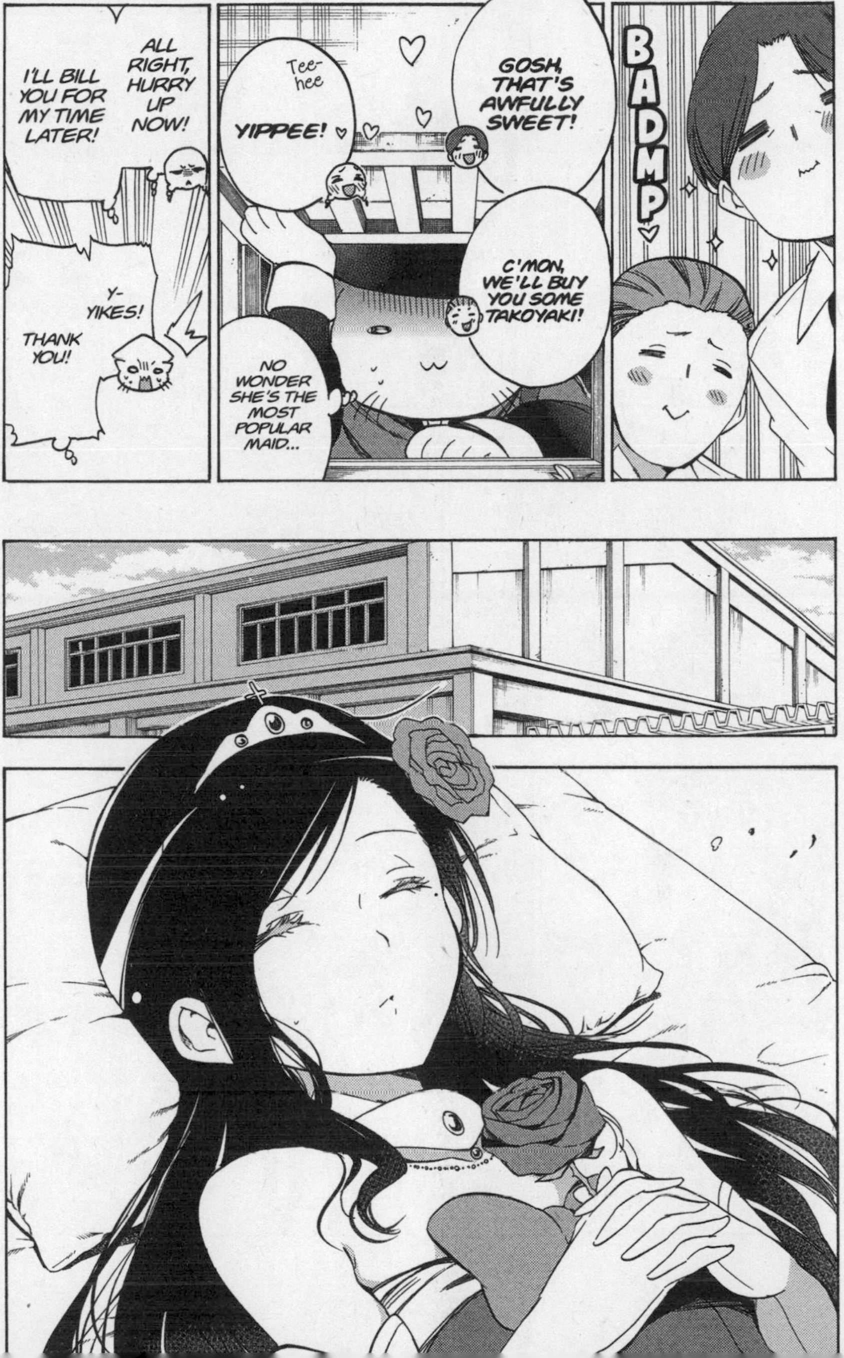
BADMP
GOSH, THAT'S AWFULLY SWEET!
Tee-hee
YIPPEE!
C'MON, WE'LL BUY YOU SOME TAKOYAKI!
NO WONDER SHE'S THE MOST POPULAR MAID...
ALL RIGHT, HURRY UP NOW!
I'LL BILL YOU FOR MY TIME LATER!
Y-YIKES!
THANK YOU!

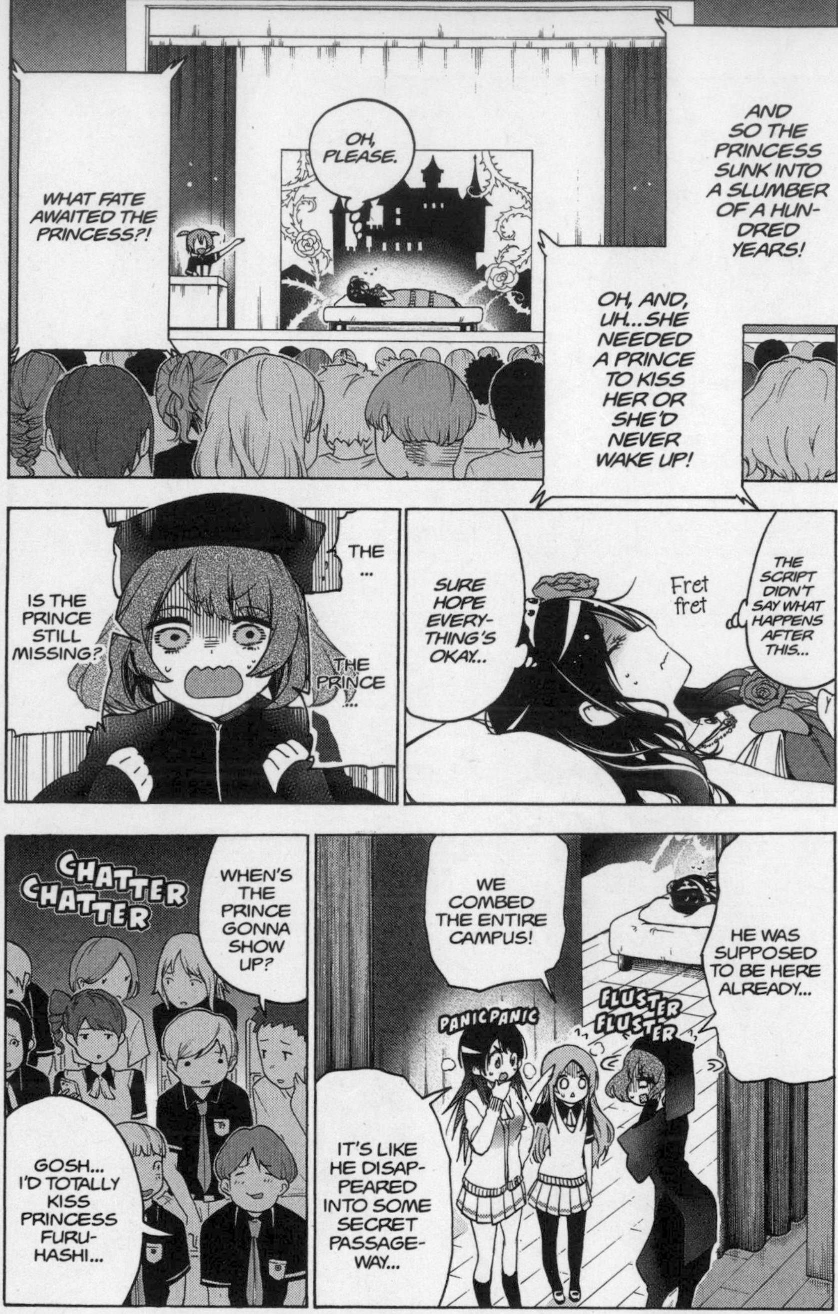
AND SO THE PRINCESS SUNK INTO A SLUMBER OF A HUN-DRED YEARS!
OH, AND, UH...SHE NEEDED A PRINCE TO KISS HER OR SHE'D NEVER WAKE UP!
OH, PLEASE.
WHAT FATE AWAITED THE PRINCESS?!
THE SCRIPT DIDN'T SAY WHAT HAPPENS AFTER THIS...
Fret fret
SURE HOPE EVERY-THING'S OKAY...
THE ...
THE PRINCE ...
IS THE PRINCE STILL MISSING?
HE WAS SUPPOSED TO BE HERE ALREADY...
WE COMBED THE ENTIRE CAMPUS!
FLUSTER FLUSTER
PANIC PANIC
IT'S LIKE HE DISAP-PEARED INTO SOME SECRET PASSAGE-WAY...
WHEN'S THE PRINCE GONNA SHOW UP?
CHATTER CHATTER
GOSH... I'D TOTALLY KISS PRINCESS FURU-HASHI...

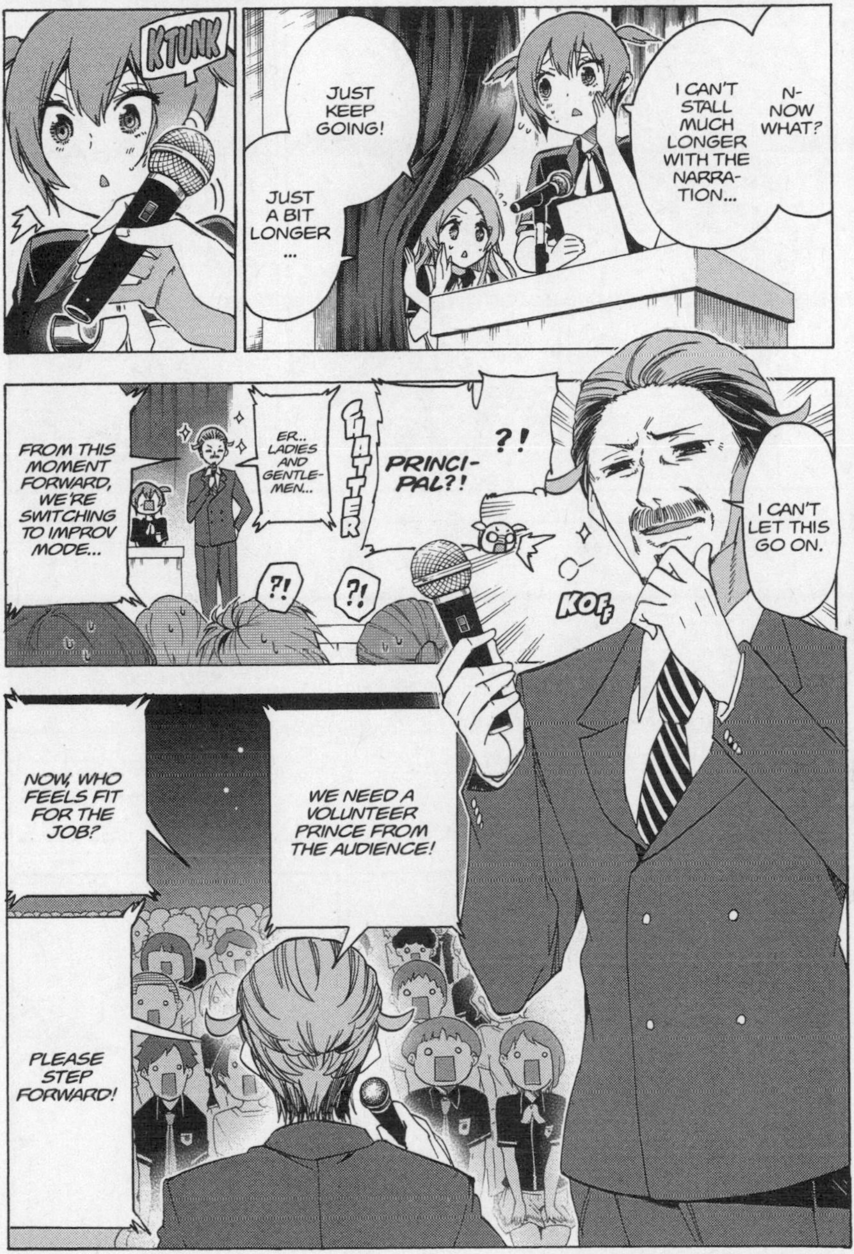
N-NOW WHAT?
I CAN'T STALL MUCH LONGER WITH THE NARRATION...
JUST KEEP GOING!
JUST A BIT LONGER...
KTUNK
I CAN'T LET THIS GO ON.
KOFF
?!
PRINCIPAL?!
CHATTER
ER.. LADIES AND GENTLEMEN...
?!
?!
FROM THIS MOMENT FORWARD, WE'RE SWITCHING TO IMPROV MODE...
WE NEED A VOLUNTEER PRINCE FROM THE AUDIENCE!
NOW, WHO FEELS FIT FOR THE JOB?
PLEASE STEP FORWARD!

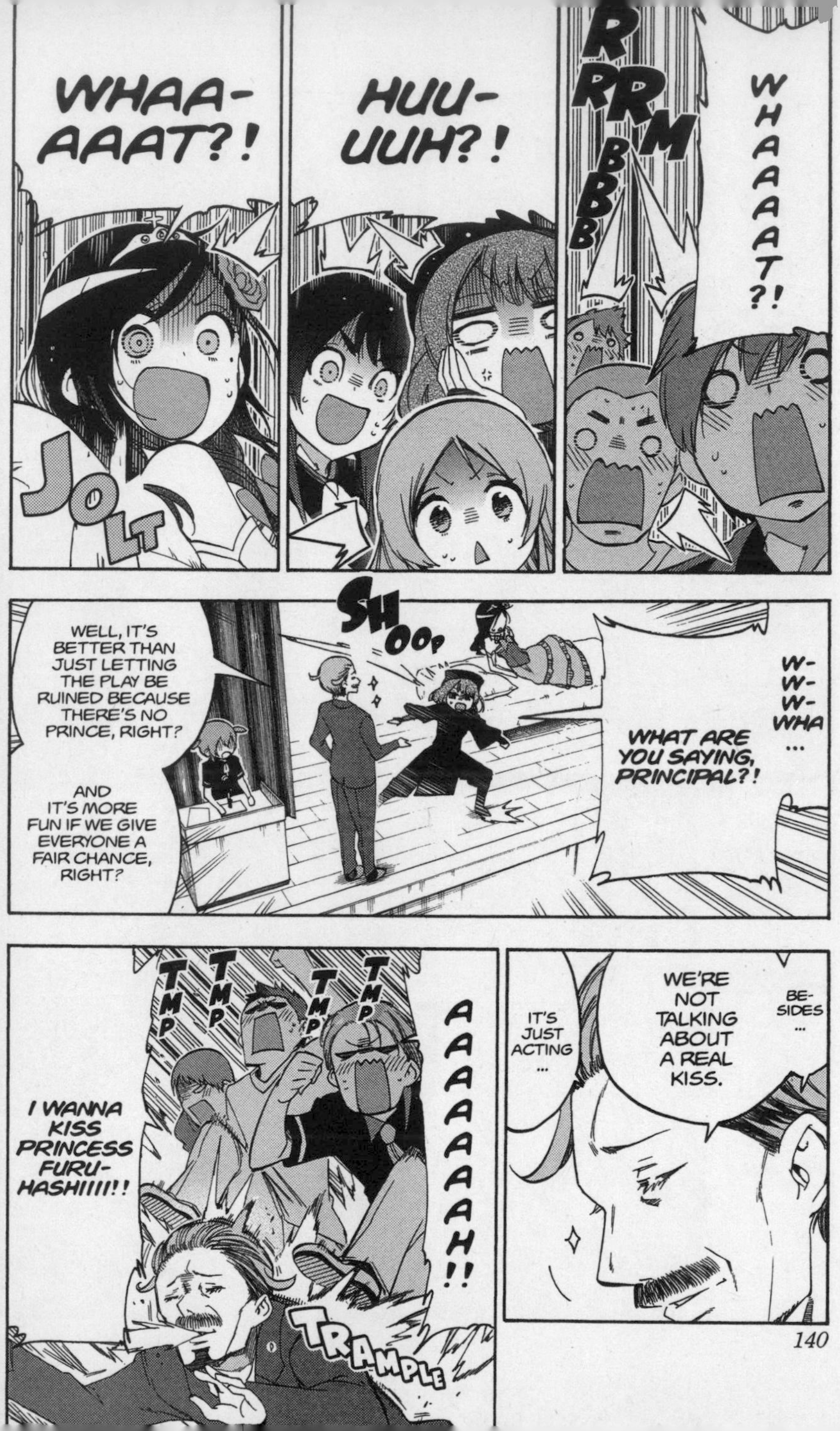
RRRMBBBB
WHAAAAAT?!
HUUU-UUH?!
WHAA-AAAT?!
JOLT
W-W-W-WHA...
WHAT ARE YOU SAYING, PRINCIPAL?!
SHOOP
WELL, IT'S BETTER THAN JUST LETTING THE PLAY BE RUINED BECAUSE THERE'S NO PRINCE, RIGHT?
AND IT'S MORE FUN IF WE GIVE EVERYONE A FAIR CHANCE, RIGHT?
BE-SIDES...
WE'RE NOT TALKING ABOUT A REAL KISS.
IT'S JUST ACTING...
AAAAAAAAAH!!
TMP
TMP
TMP
TMP
I WANNA KISS PRINCESS FURU-HASHIIIII!!
TRAMPLE

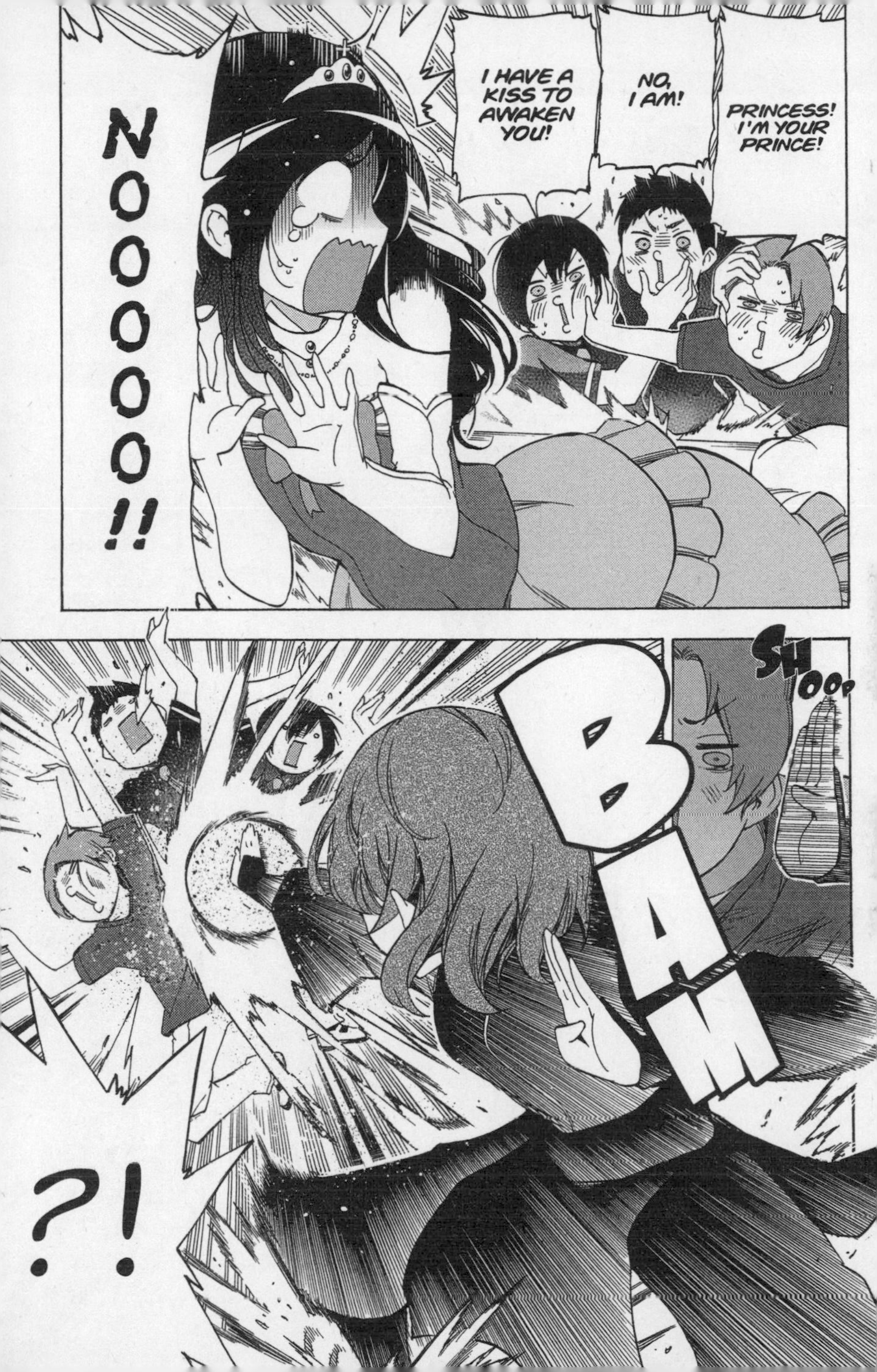
PRINCESS! I'M YOUR PRINCE!
NO, I AM!
I HAVE A KISS TO AWAKEN YOU!
NOOOOOO!!
SHOOP
BAM
?!

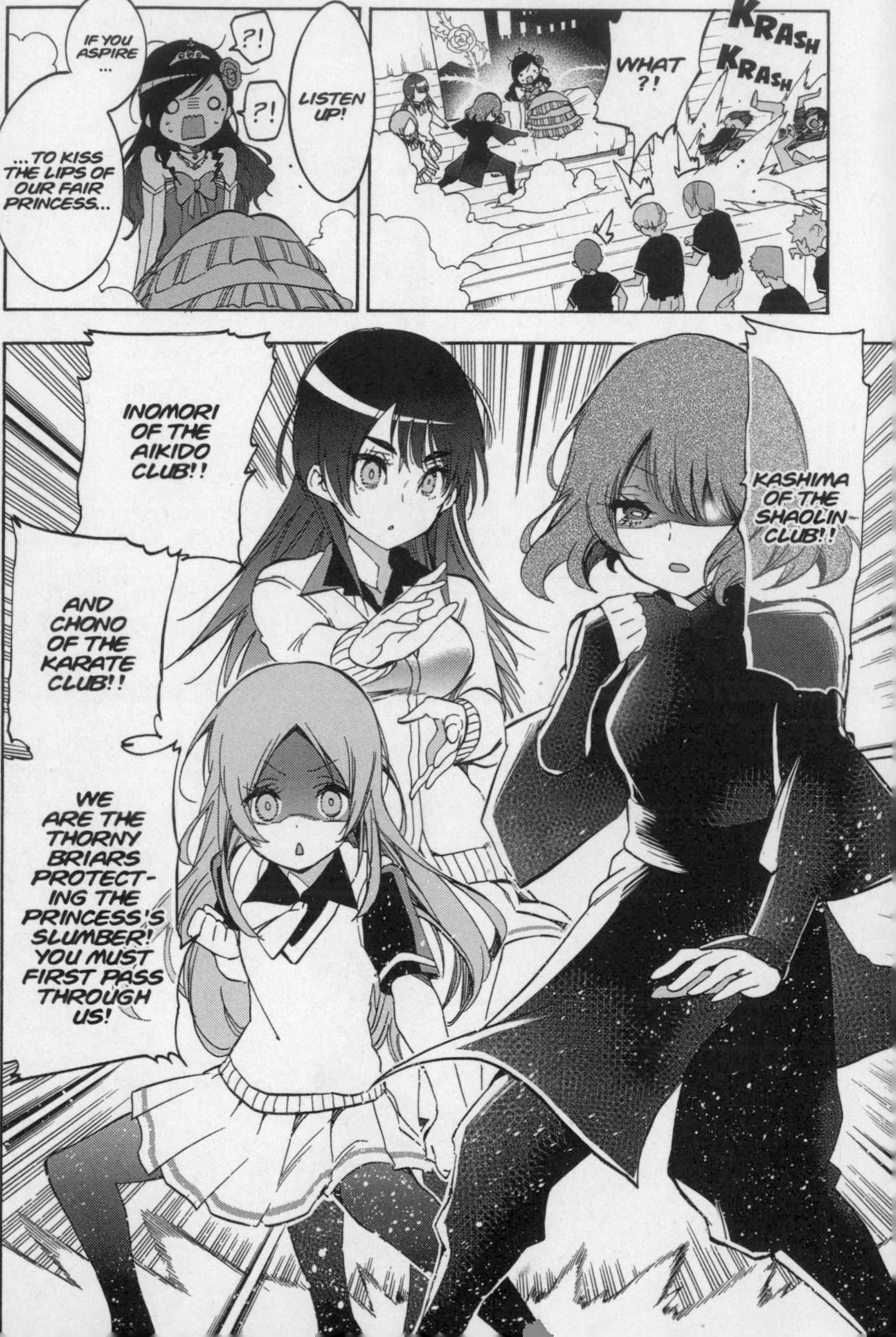
KRASH
KRASH
WHAT?!
LISTEN UP!
?!
?!
IF YOU ASPIRE...
...TO KISS THE LIPS OF OUR FAIR PRINCESS...
KASHIMA OF THE SHAOLIN CLUB!!
INOMORI OF THE AIKIDO CLUB!!
AND CHONO OF THE KARATE CLUB!!
WE ARE THE THORNY BRIARS PROTECTING THE PRINCESS'S SLUMBER! YOU MUST FIRST PASS THROUGH US!

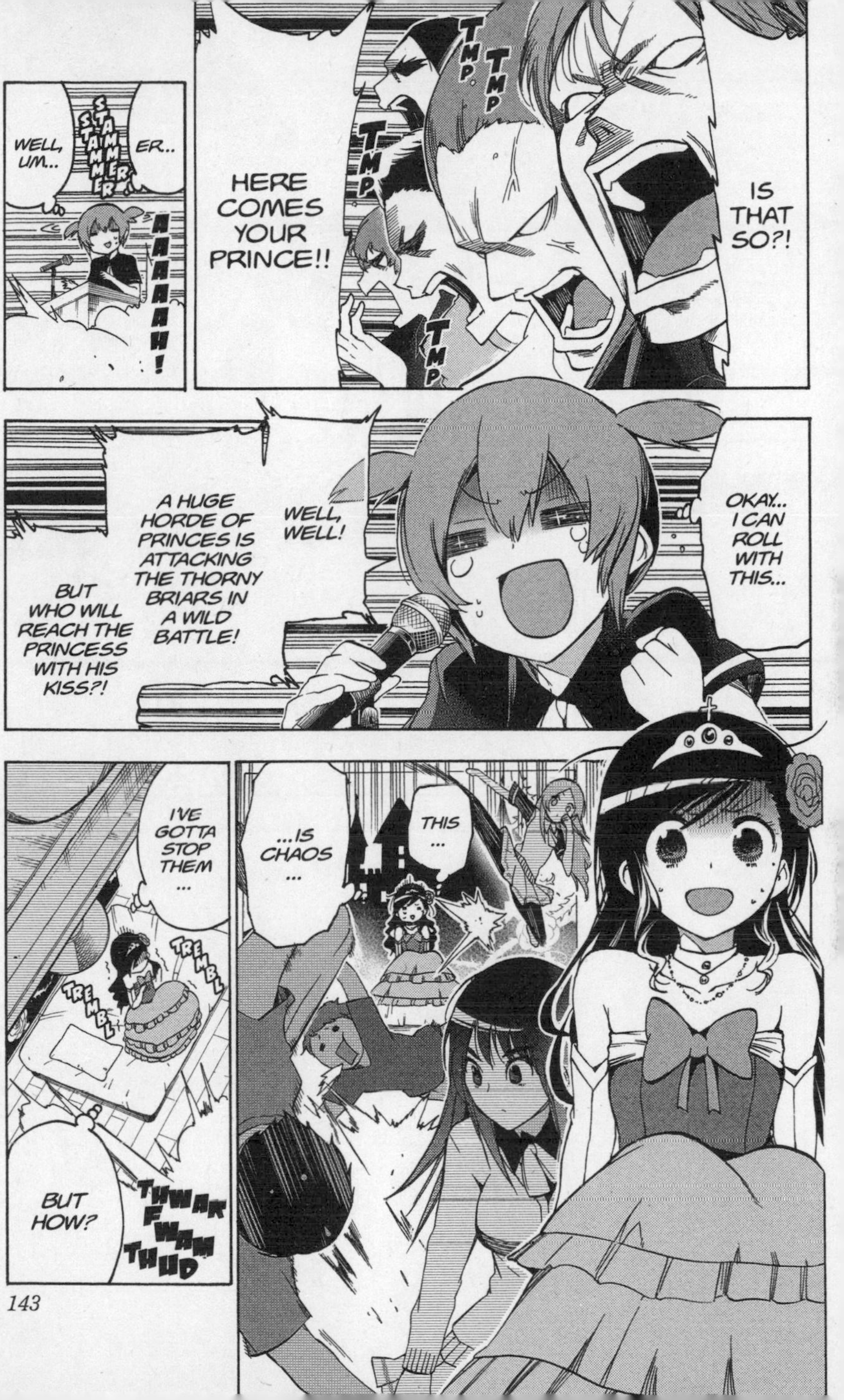
IS THAT SO?!
TMP TMP
HERE COMES YOUR PRINCE!!
TMP
TMP
ER...
STAMMER STAMMER
WELL, UM...
AAAAAAH!
OKAY... I CAN ROLL WITH THIS...
WELL, WELL!
A HUGE HORDE OF PRINCES IS ATTACKING THE THORNY BRIARS IN A WILD BATTLE!
BUT WHO WILL REACH THE PRINCESS WITH HIS KISS?!
THIS ...
...IS CHAOS ...
I'VE GOTTA STOP THEM ...
TREMBL
TREMBL
BUT HOW?
THWAK FWAM THUD

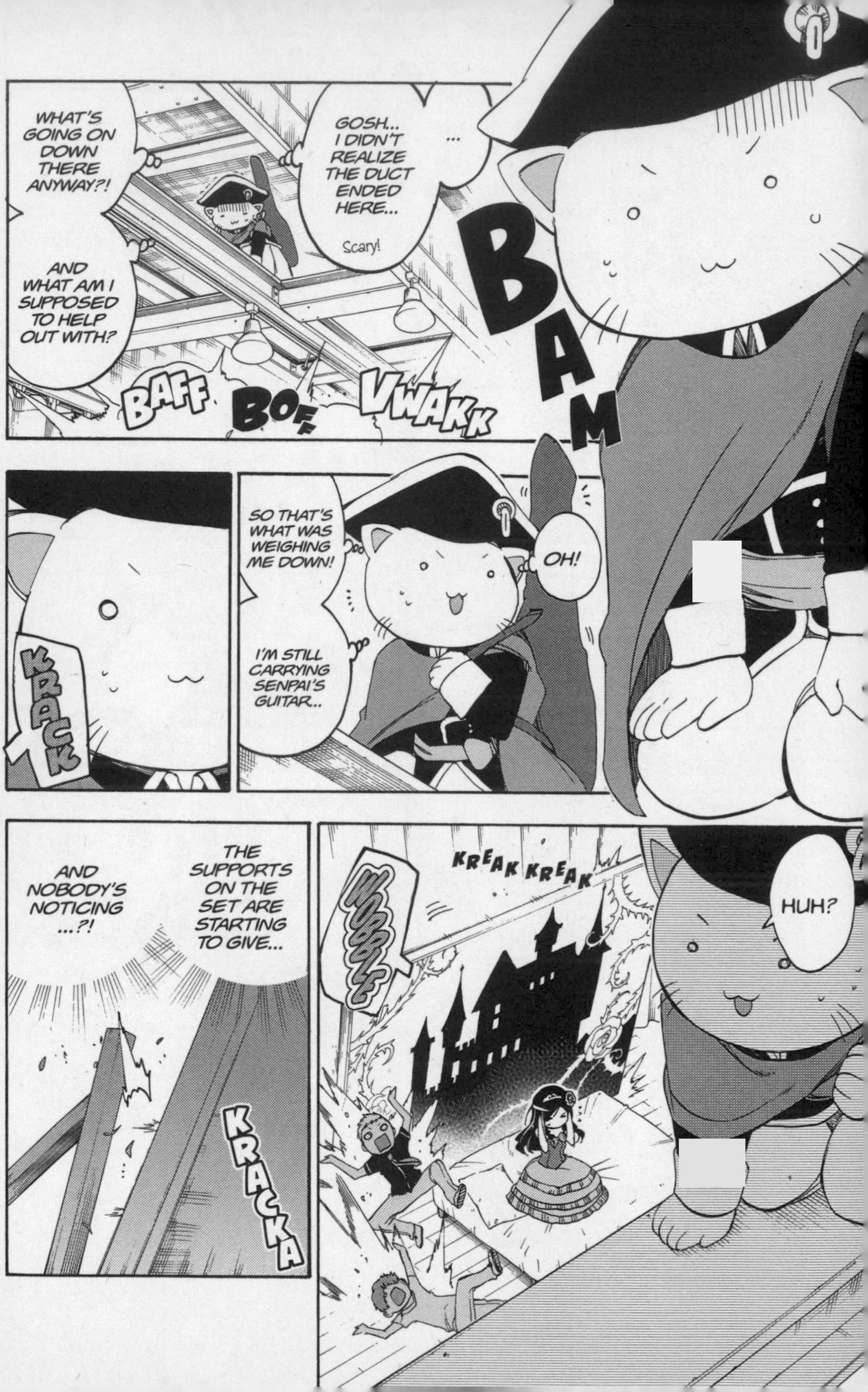
BAM
GOSH... I DIDN'T REALIZE THE DUCT ENDED HERE...
Scary!
...
WHAT'S GOING ON DOWN THERE ANYWAY?!
AND WHAT AM I SUPPOSED TO HELP OUT WITH?
BAFF
BOFF
VWAKK
OH!
SO THAT'S WHAT WAS WEIGHING ME DOWN!
I'M STILL CARRYING SENPAI'S GUITAR..
KRACK
HUH?
KREAK KREAK
WOBBLE
THE SUPPORTS ON THE SET ARE STARTING TO GIVE...
AND NOBODY'S NOTICING ...?!
KRACKA

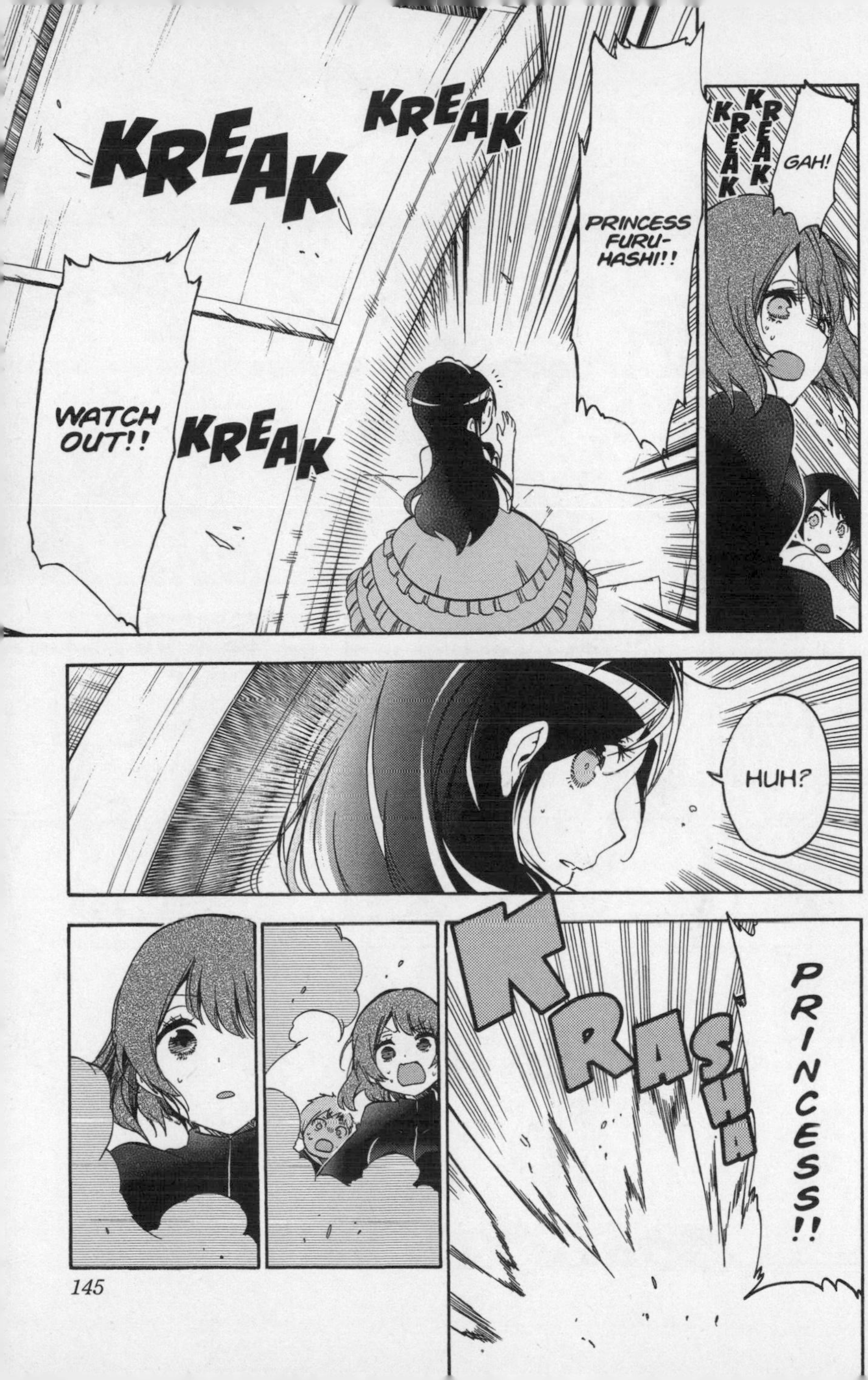
KREAK
KREAK
GAH!
PRINCESS FURU-HASHI!!
KREAK
KREAK
WATCH OUT!!
KREAK
HUH?
KRASH
PRINCESS!!

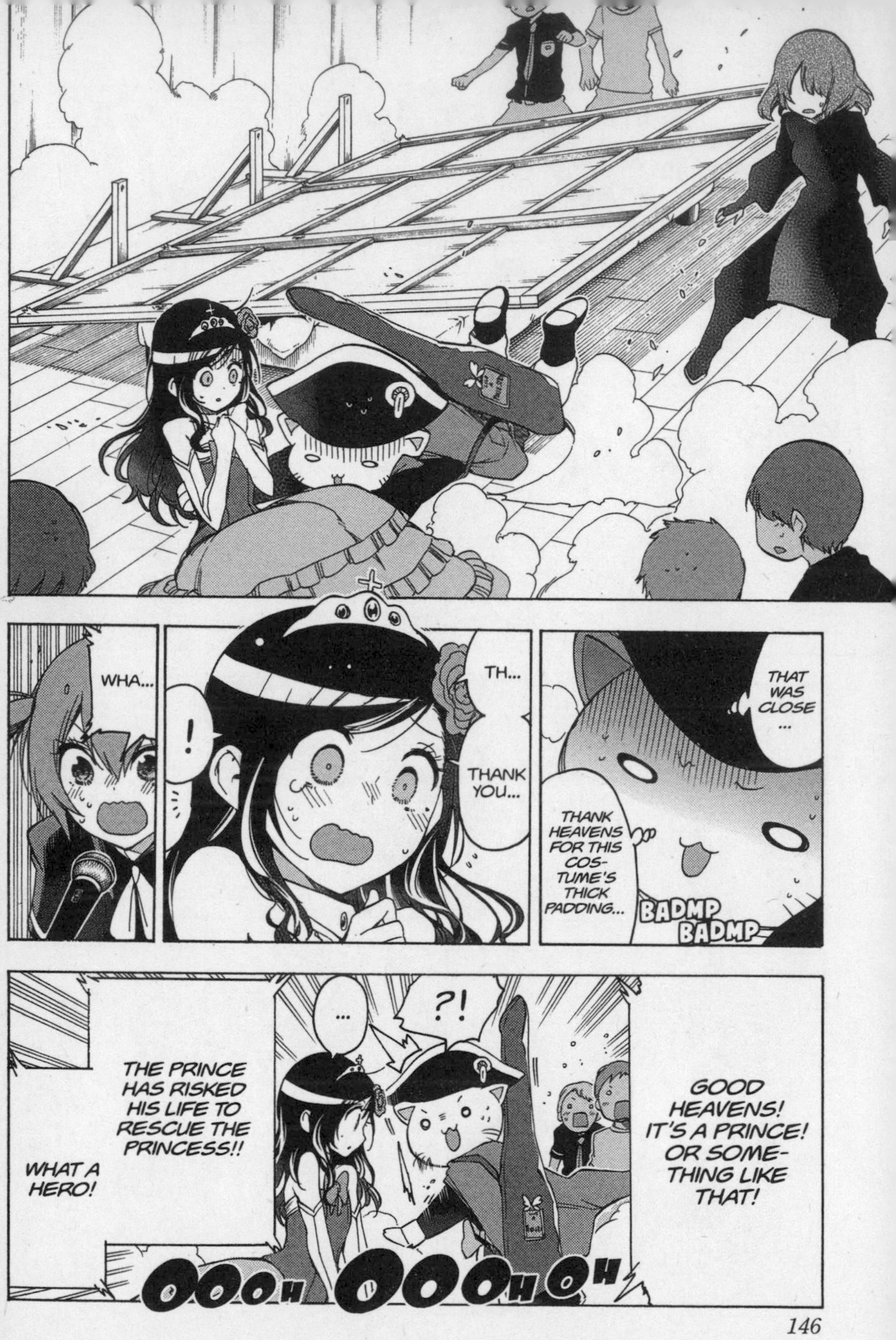
THAT WAS CLOSE ...
THANK HEAVENS FOR THIS COS-TUME'S THICK PADDING...
BADMP BADMP
TH...
THANK YOU...
!
WHA...
GOOD HEAVENS! IT'S A PRINCE! OR SOME-THING LIKE THAT!
?!
...
THE PRINCE HAS RISKED HIS LIFE TO RESCUE THE PRINCESS!!
WHAT A HERO!
OOOH OOOOH OH

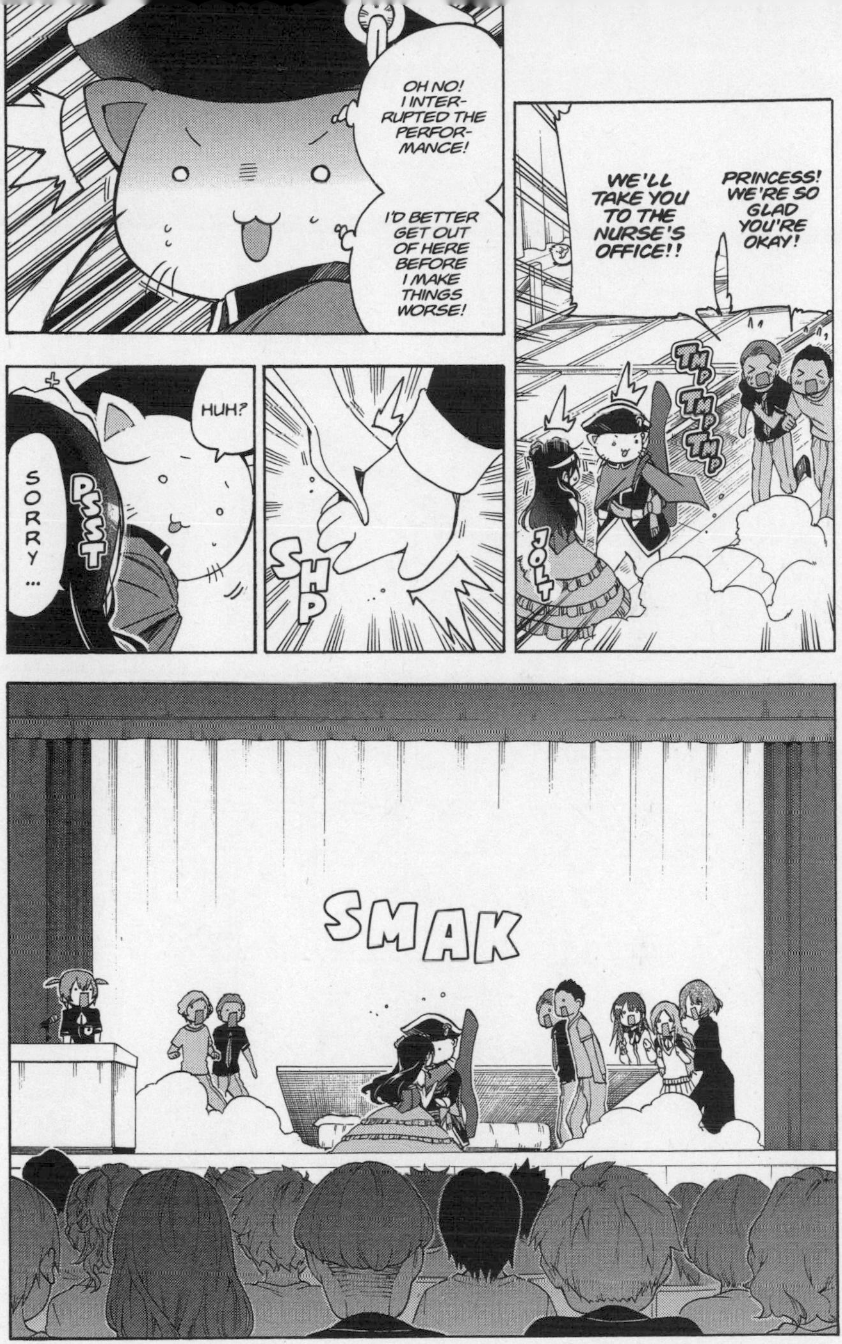
PRINCESS! WE'RE SO GLAD YOU'RE OKAY!
WE'LL TAKE YOU TO THE NURSE'S OFFICE!!
TMP TMP TMP
JOLT
OH NO! I INTER-RUPTED THE PERFOR-MANCE!
I'D BETTER GET OUT OF HERE BEFORE I MAKE THINGS WORSE!
SHP
HUH?
PSSST
SORRY...
SMAK

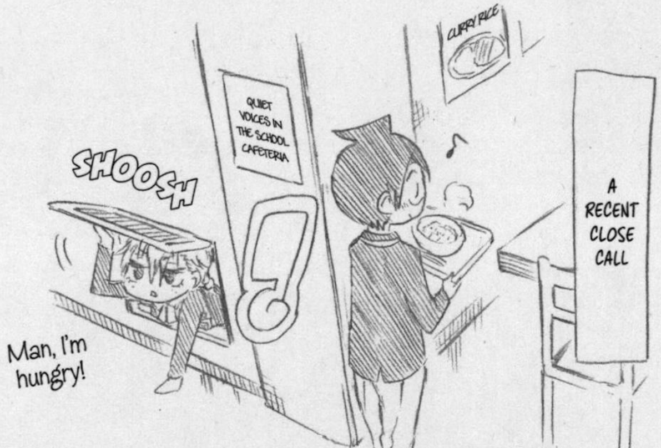
A RECENT CLOSE CALL
CURRY RICE
QUIET VOICES IN THE SCHOOL CAFETERIA
SHOOSH
Man, I'm hungry!

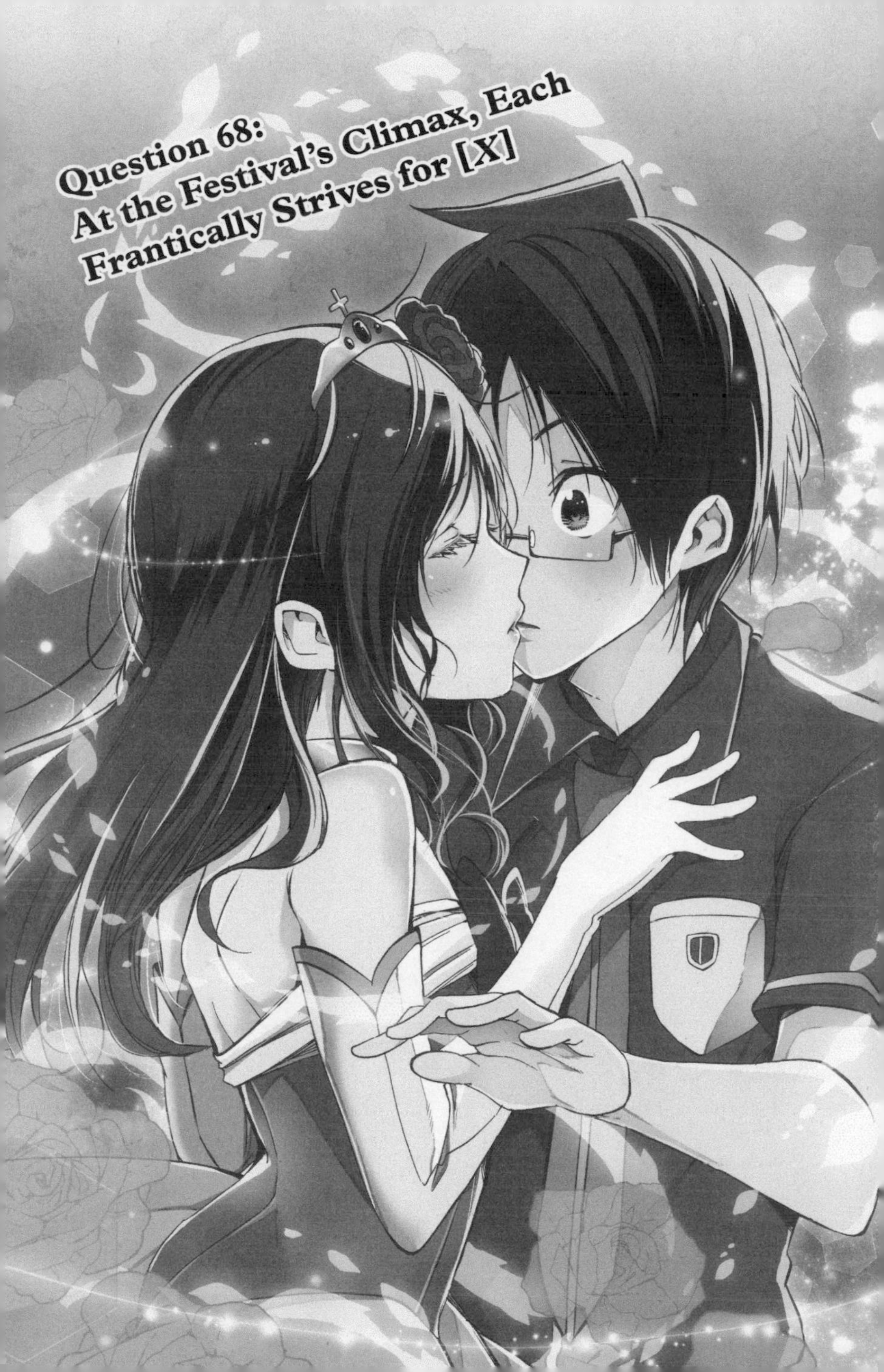
Question 68:
At the Festival's Climax, Each
Frantically Strives for [X]

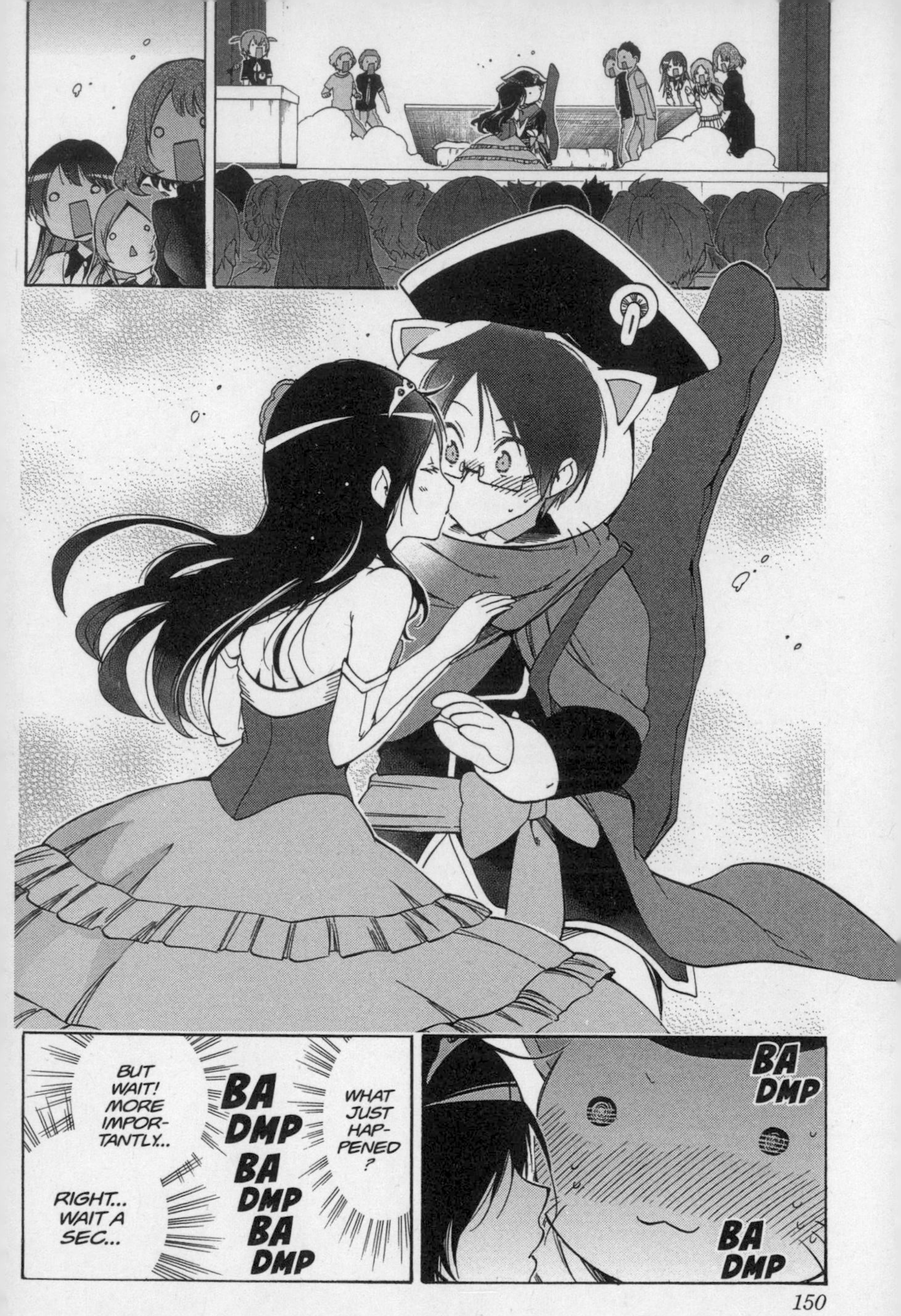
BA DMP
BA DMP
WHAT JUST HAP-PENED?
BA DMP BA DMP BA DMP
BUT WAIT! MORE IMPOR-TANTLY...
RIGHT... WAIT A SEC...

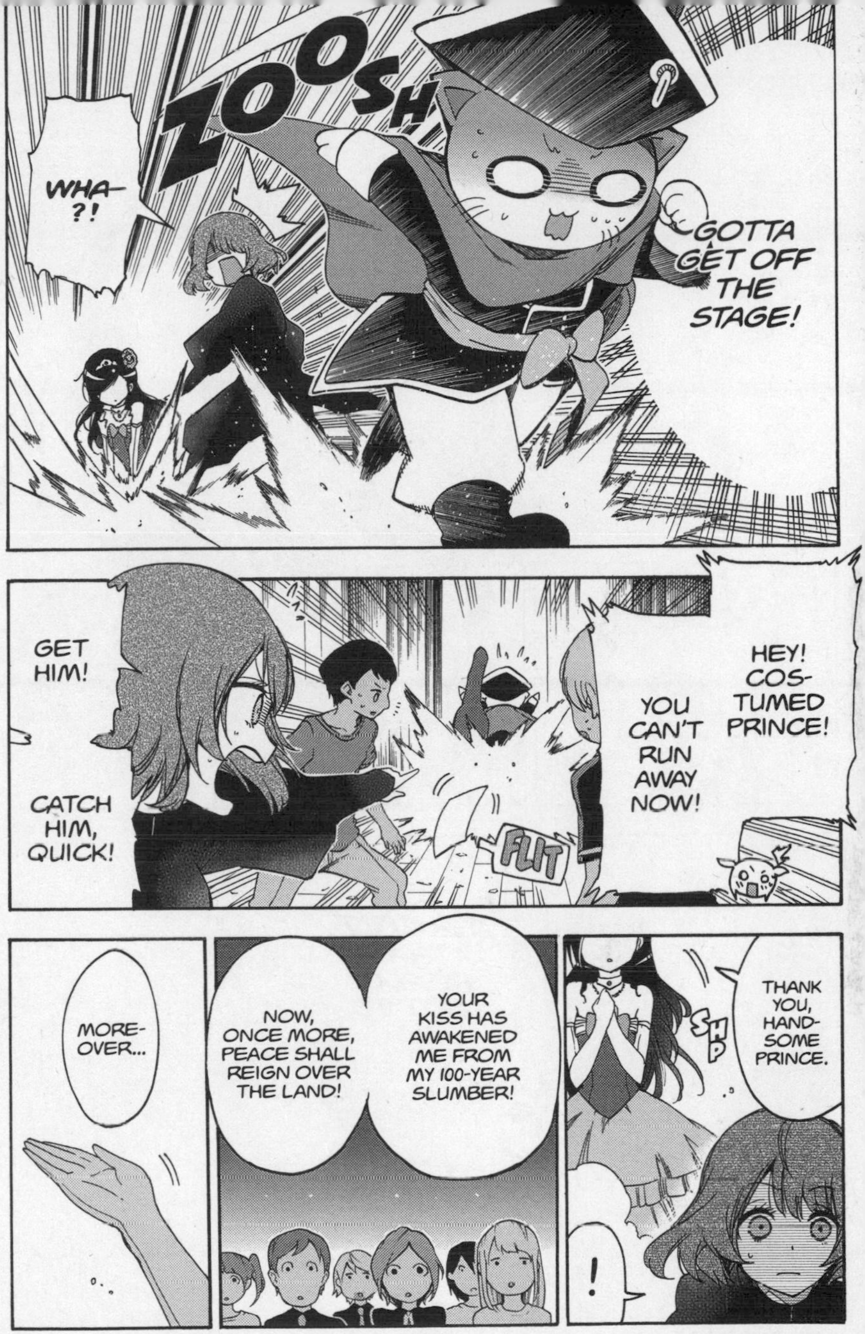
ZOOSH
GOTTA GET OFF THE STAGE!
WHA-?!
HEY! COS-TUMED PRINCE!
YOU CAN'T RUN AWAY NOW!
FLIT
GET HIM!
CATCH HIM, QUICK!
THANK YOU, HAND-SOME PRINCE.
SHP
!
YOUR KISS HAS AWAKENED ME FROM MY 100-YEAR SLUMBER!
NOW, ONCE MORE, PEACE SHALL REIGN OVER THE LAND!
MORE-OVER...

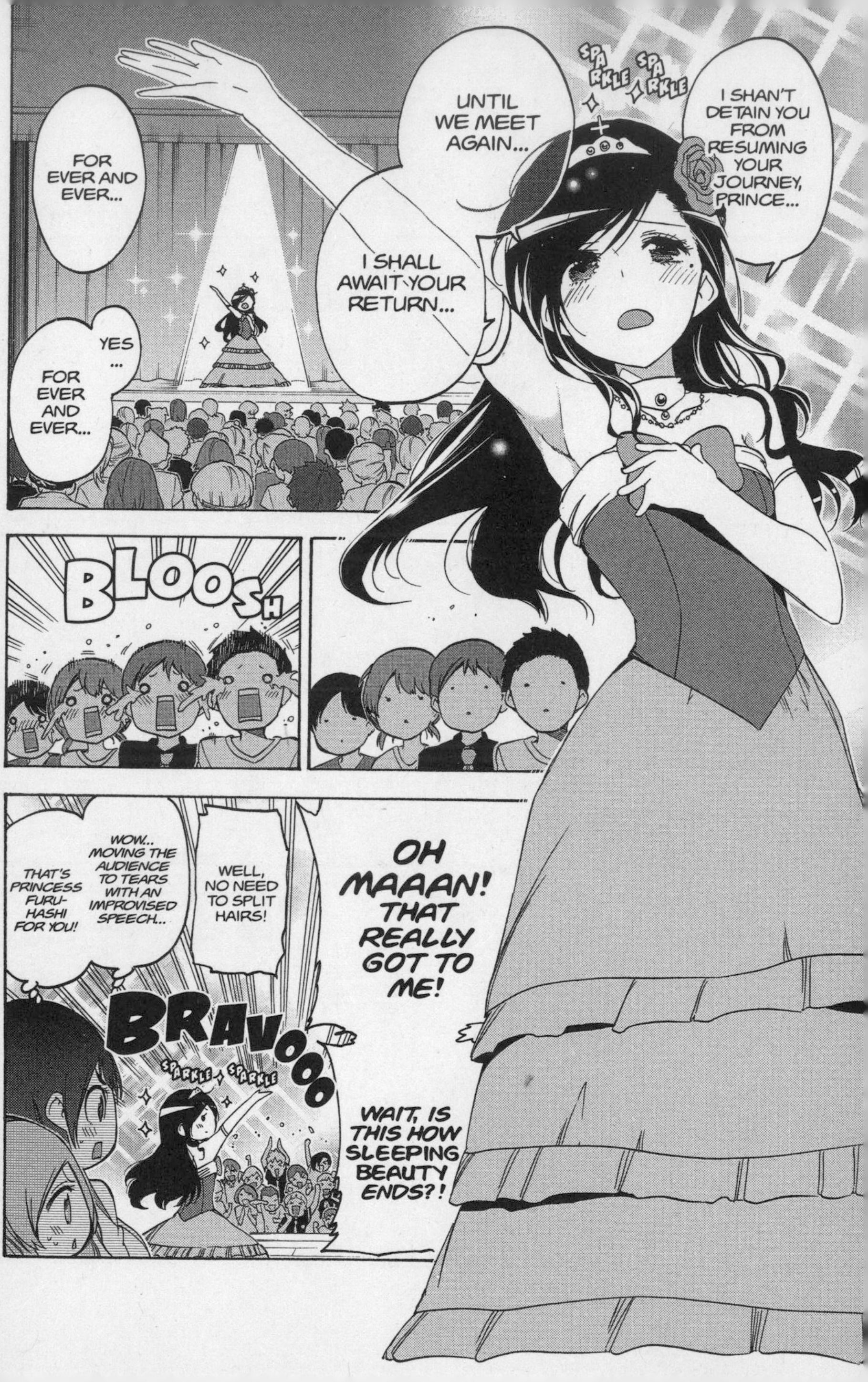
SPARKLE SPARKLE
I SHAN'T DETAIN YOU FROM RESUMING YOUR JOURNEY, PRINCE...
UNTIL WE MEET AGAIN...
I SHALL AWAIT YOUR RETURN...
FOR EVER AND EVER...
YES... FOR EVER AND EVER...
BLOOSH
OH MAAAN! THAT REALLY GOT TO ME!
WAIT, IS THIS HOW SLEEPING BEAUTY ENDS?!
WELL, NO NEED TO SPLIT HAIRS!
WOW... MOVING THE AUDIENCE TO TEARS WITH AN IMPROVISED SPEECH...
THAT'S PRINCESS FURUHASHI FOR YOU!
BRAVOOO
SPARKLE SPARKLE

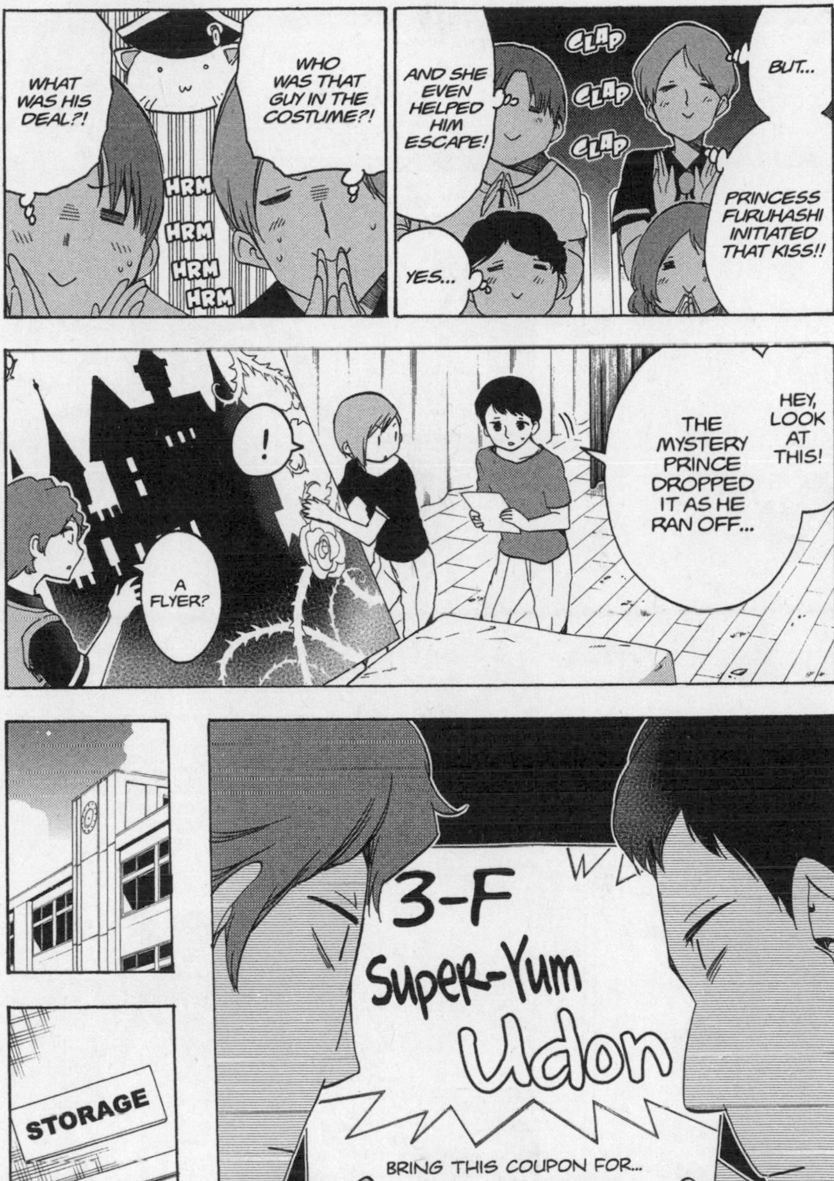
BUT...
PRINCESS FURUHASHI INITIATED THAT KISS!!
CLAP
CLAP
CLAP
AND SHE EVEN HELPED HIM ESCAPE!
YES...
WHO WAS THAT GUY IN THE COSTUME?!
WHAT WAS HIS DEAL?!
HRM
HRM
HRM
HRM
HEY, LOOK AT THIS!
THE MYSTERY PRINCE DROPPED IT AS HE RAN OFF...
!
A FLYER?
3-F
Super-Yum
Udon
BRING THIS COUPON FOR...
300 Yen ⇨ 250 Yen
WHATTA DEAL!!
STORAGE

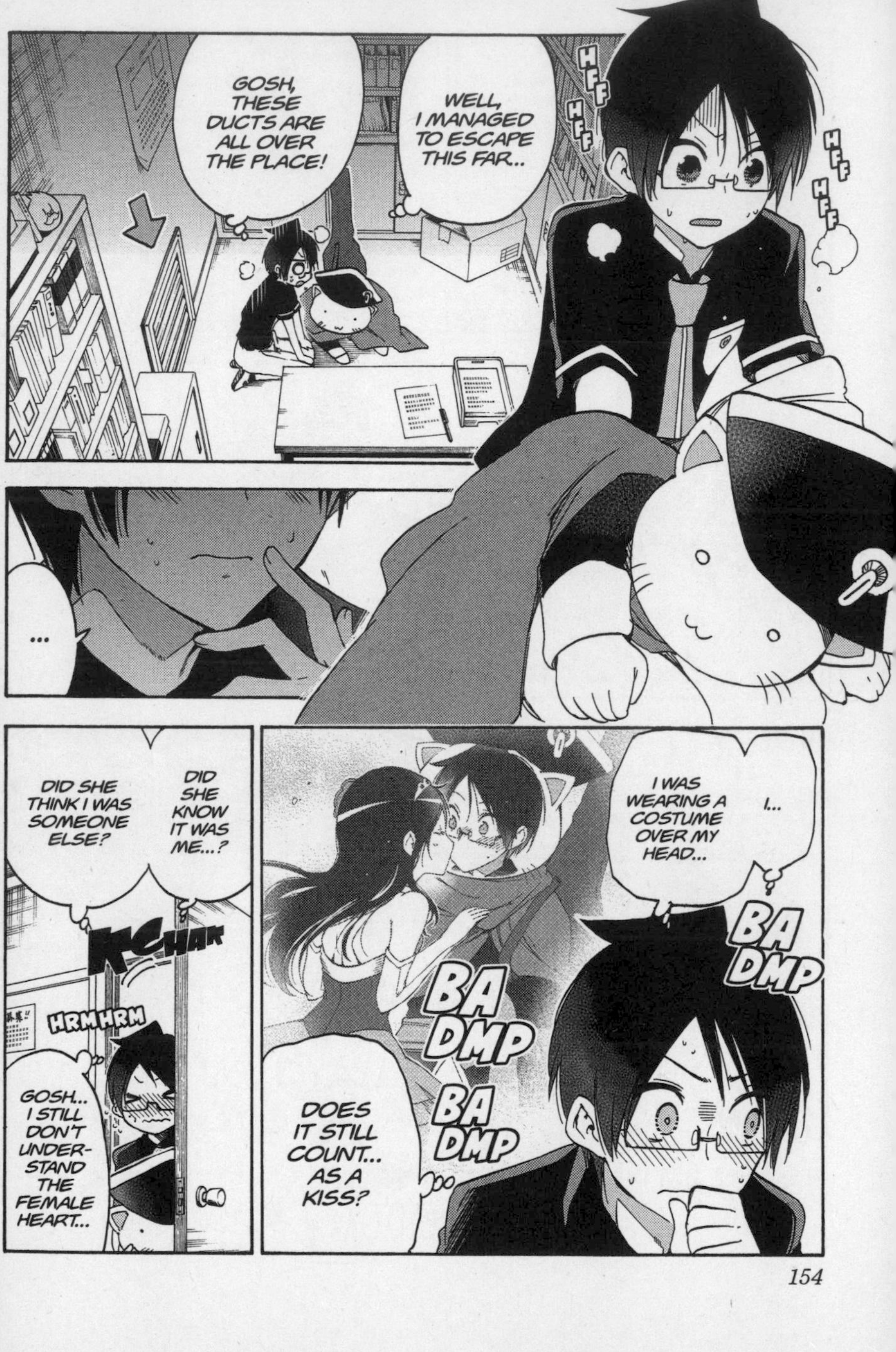
HFF HFF
HFF HFF
WELL, I MANAGED TO ESCAPE THIS FAR..
GOSH, THESE DUCTS ARE ALL OVER THE PLACE!
...
I...
I WAS WEARING A COSTUME OVER MY HEAD...
BA DMP
BA DMP
DOES IT STILL COUNT... AS A KISS?
BA DMP
DID SHE KNOW IT WAS ME...?
DID SHE THINK I WAS SOMEONE ELSE?
KCHAK
HRMHRM
GOSH... I STILL DON'T UNDER-STAND THE FEMALE HEART...

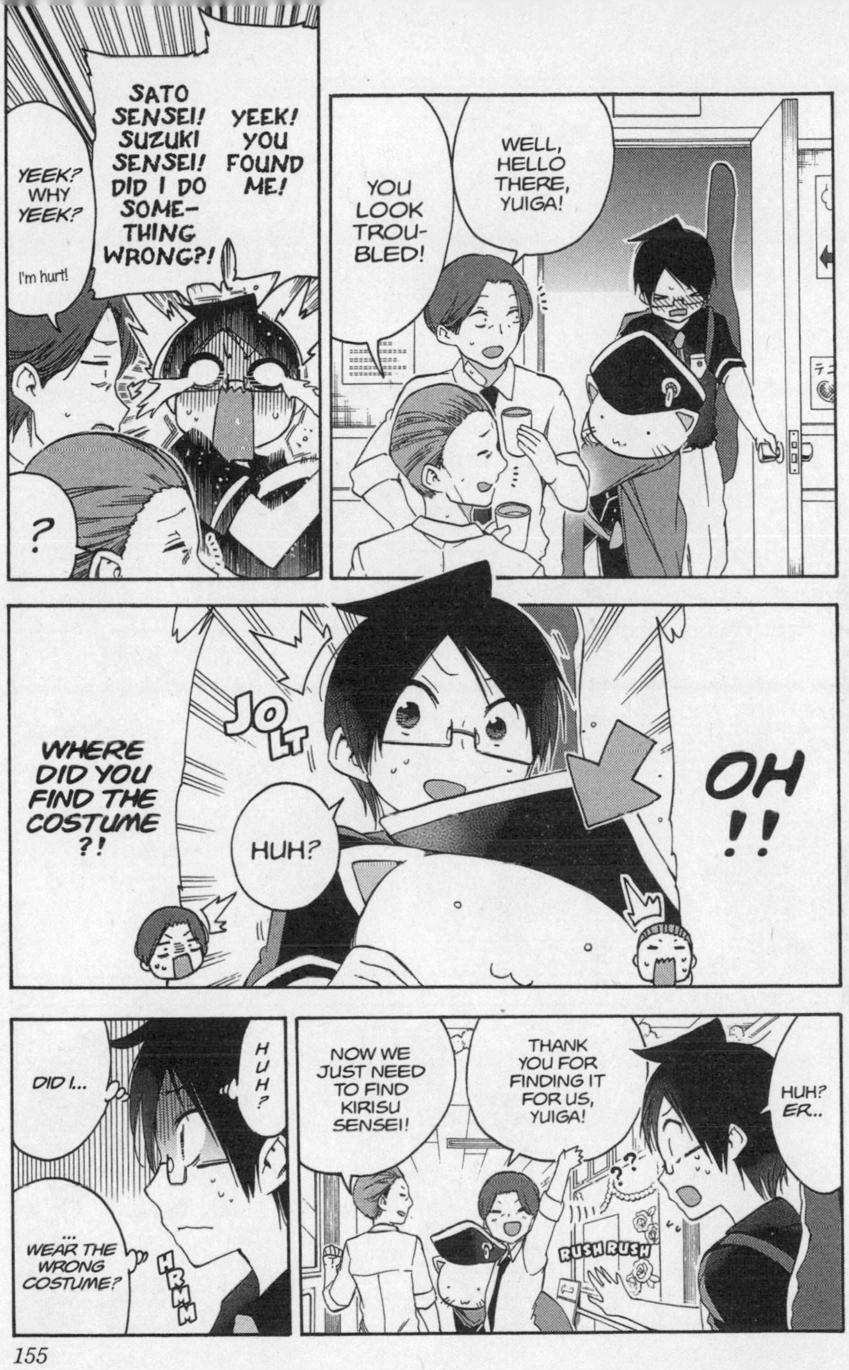
WELL, HELLO THERE, YUIGA!
YOU LOOK TROU-BLED!
YEEK! YOU FOUND ME!
SATO SENSEI! SUZUKI SENSEI! DID I DO SOME-THING WRONG?!
YEEK? WHY YEEK?
I'm hurt!
?
OH !!
JOLT
HUH?
WHERE DID YOU FIND THE COSTUME ?!
HUH? ER...
THANK YOU FOR FINDING IT FOR US, YUIGA!
NOW WE JUST NEED TO FIND KIRISU SENSEI!
RUSH RUSH
HUH?
DID I...
... WEAR THE WRONG COSTUME?
HRMM

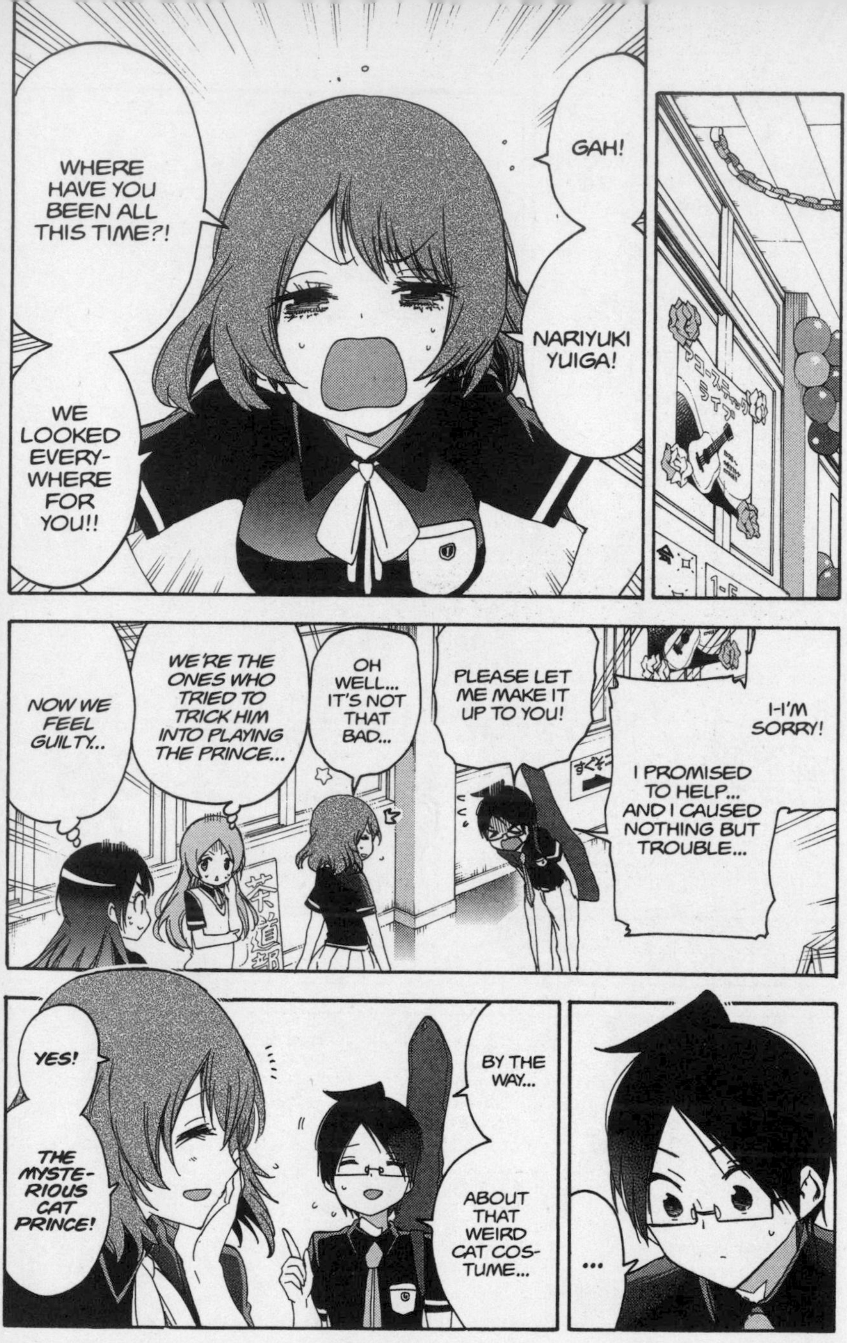
GAH!
NARIYUKI YUIGA!
WHERE HAVE YOU BEEN ALL THIS TIME?!
WE LOOKED EVERY-WHERE FOR YOU!!
I-I'M SORRY!
I PROMISED TO HELP... AND I CAUSED NOTHING BUT TROUBLE...
PLEASE LET ME MAKE IT UP TO YOU!
OH WELL... IT'S NOT THAT BAD...
WE'RE THE ONES WHO TRIED TO TRICK HIM INTO PLAYING THE PRINCE...
NOW WE FEEL GUILTY...
...
BY THE WAY...
ABOUT THAT WEIRD CAT COS-TUME...
YES!
THE MYSTE-RIOUS CAT PRINCE!

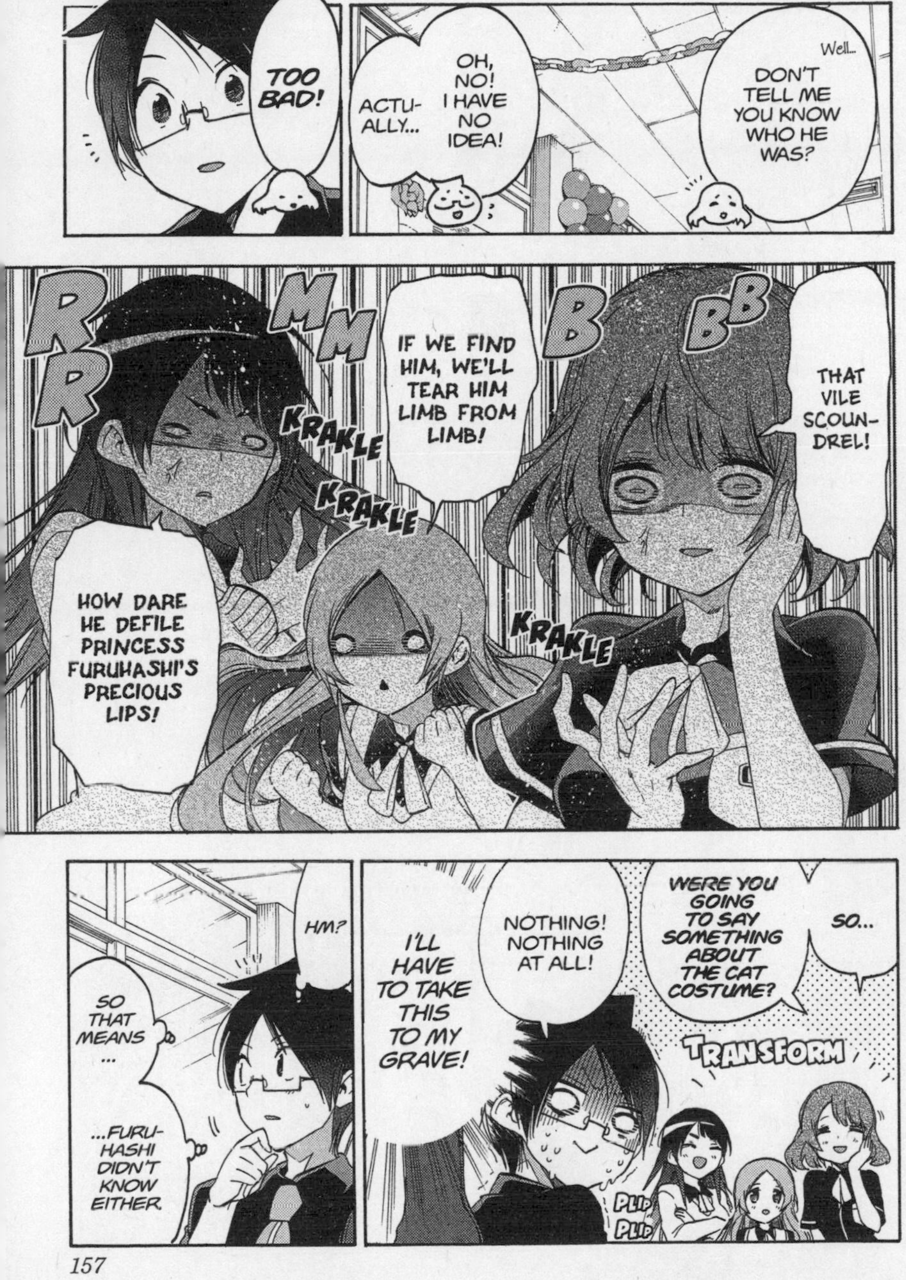
Well...
DON'T TELL ME YOU KNOW WHO HE WAS?
OH, NO! I HAVE NO IDEA!
ACTU-ALLY...
TOO BAD!
THAT VILE SCOUN-DREL!
BBB
IF WE FIND HIM, WE'LL TEAR HIM LIMB FROM LIMB!
MM
RR
KRAKLE
KRAKLE
KRAKLE
HOW DARE HE DEFILE PRINCESS FURUHASHI'S PRECIOUS LIPS!
SO...
WERE YOU GOING TO SAY SOMETHING ABOUT THE CAT COSTUME?
NOTHING! NOTHING AT ALL!
I'LL HAVE TO TAKE THIS TO MY GRAVE!
TRANSFORM
PLIP
PLIP
HM?
SO THAT MEANS ...
...FURU-HASHI DIDN'T KNOW EITHER.

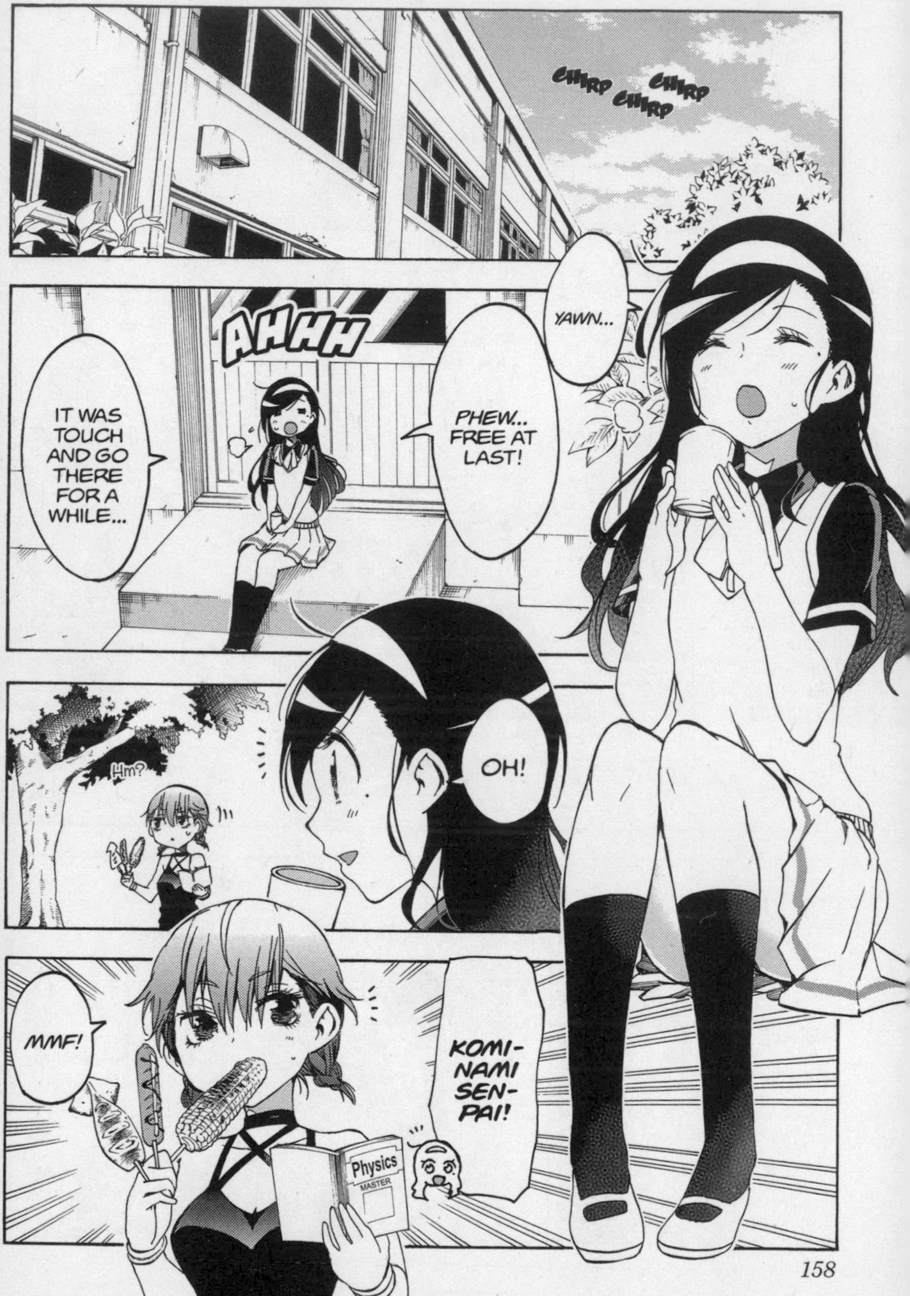
CHIRP
CHIRP
CHIRP
YAWN...
AHHH
PHEW... FREE AT LAST!
IT WAS TOUCH AND GO THERE FOR A WHILE...
OH!
Hm?
KOMI-NAMI SEN-PAI!
MMF!
Physics
MASTER

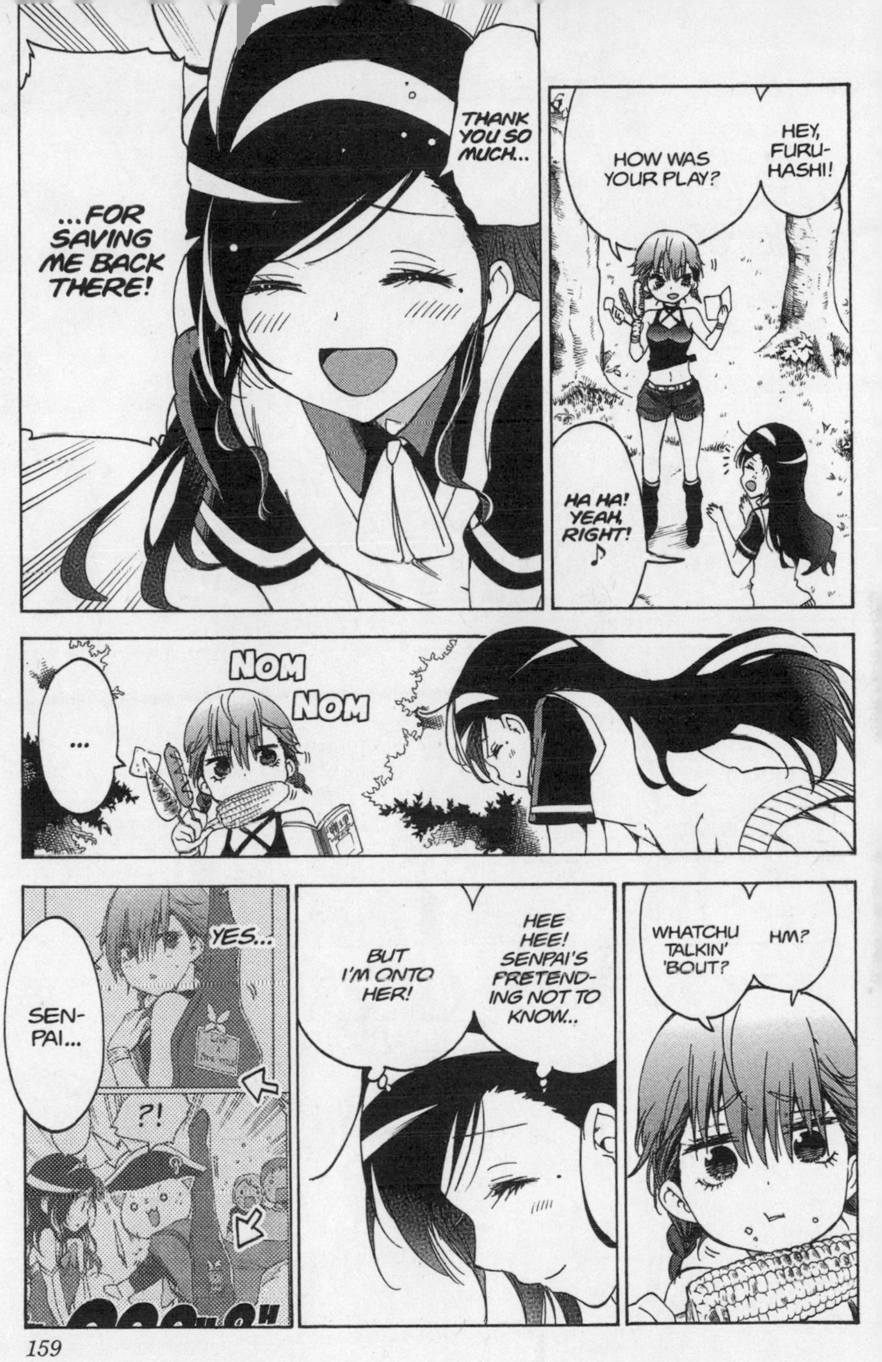
HEY, FURU-HASHI!
HOW WAS YOUR PLAY?
HA HA! YEAH, RIGHT! ♪
THANK YOU SO MUCH...
...FOR SAVING ME BACK THERE!
NOM NOM
...
HM?
WHATCHU TALKIN' 'BOUT?
HEE HEE! SENPAI'S PRETEND-ING NOT TO KNOW...
BUT I'M ONTO HER!
YES...
SEN-PAI...
?!

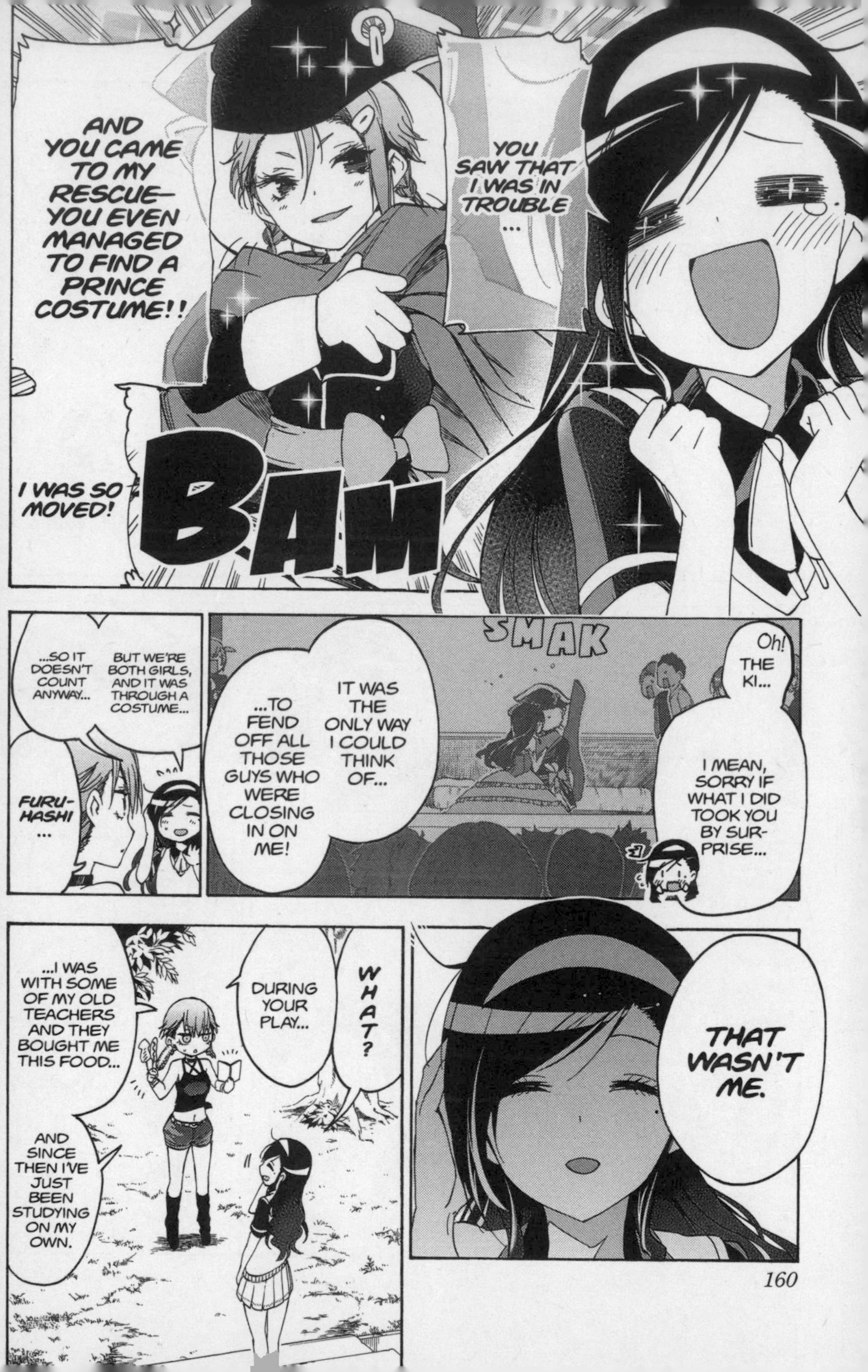
YOU SAW THAT I WAS IN TROUBLE ...
AND YOU CAME TO MY RESCUE— YOU EVEN MANAGED TO FIND A PRINCE COSTUME!!
BAM
I WAS SO MOVED!
SMAK
Oh! THE KI...
I MEAN, SORRY IF WHAT I DID TOOK YOU BY SUR-PRISE...
IT WAS THE ONLY WAY I COULD THINK OF...
...TO FEND OFF ALL THOSE GUYS WHO WERE CLOSING IN ON ME!
BUT WE'RE BOTH GIRLS, AND IT WAS THROUGH A COSTUME...
...SO IT DOESN'T COUNT ANYWAY...
FURU-HASHI ...
THAT WASN'T ME.
WHAT?
DURING YOUR PLAY...
...I WAS WITH SOME OF MY OLD TEACHERS AND THEY BOUGHT ME THIS FOOD...
AND SINCE THEN I'VE JUST BEEN STUDYING ON MY OWN.

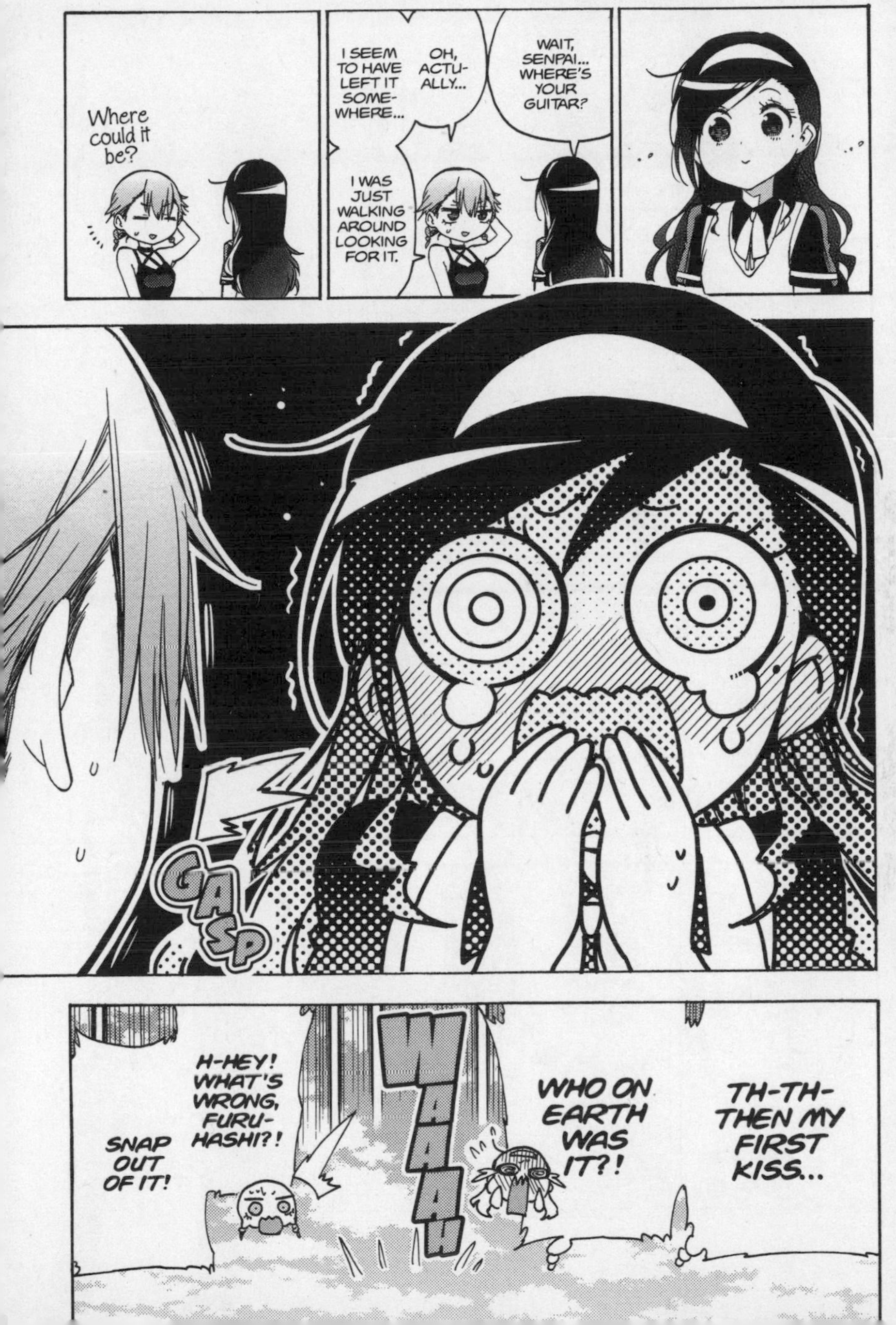
WAIT, SENPAI... WHERE'S YOUR GUITAR?
OH, ACTUALLY...
I SEEM TO HAVE LEFT IT SOMEWHERE...
I WAS JUST WALKING AROUND LOOKING FOR IT.
Where could it be?
GASP
TH-TH-THEN MY FIRST KISS...
WHO ON EARTH WAS IT?!
WAAAAH
H-HEY! WHAT'S WRONG, FURUHASHI?!
SNAP OUT OF IT!

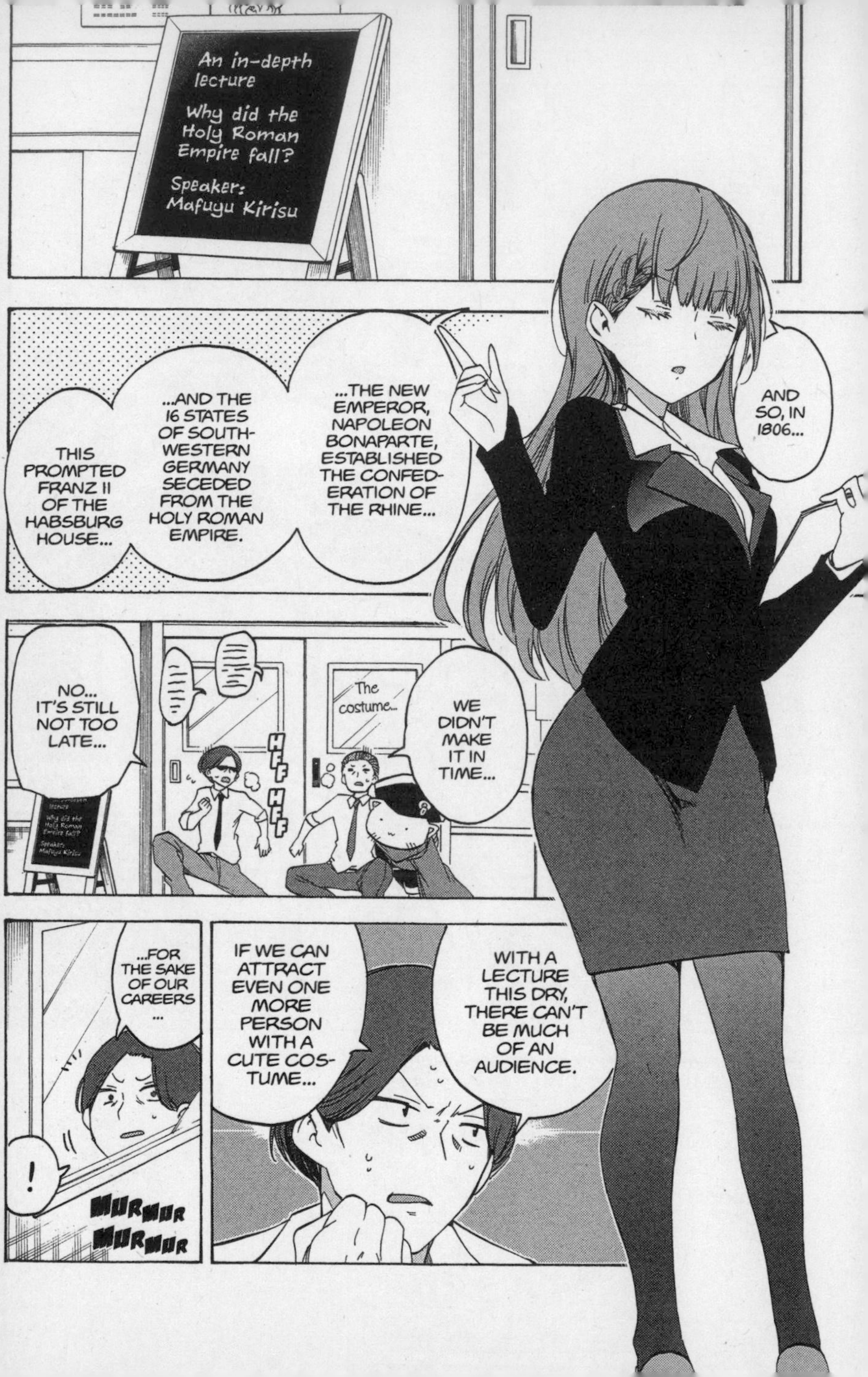

An in-depth lecture
Why did the Holy Roman Empire fall?
Speaker: Mafuyu Kirisu
AND SO, IN 1806...
...THE NEW EMPEROR, NAPOLEON BONAPARTE, ESTABLISHED THE CONFEDERATION OF THE RHINE...
...AND THE 16 STATES OF SOUTH-WESTERN GERMANY SECEDED FROM THE HOLY ROMAN EMPIRE.
THIS PROMPTED FRANZ II OF THE HABSBURG HOUSE...
WE DIDN'T MAKE IT IN TIME...
The costume...
HFF HFF
NO... IT'S STILL NOT TOO LATE...
WITH A LECTURE THIS DRY, THERE CAN'T BE MUCH OF AN AUDIENCE.
IF WE CAN ATTRACT EVEN ONE MORE PERSON WITH A CUTE COSTUME...
...FOR THE SAKE OF OUR CAREERS...
!
MURMUR MURMUR

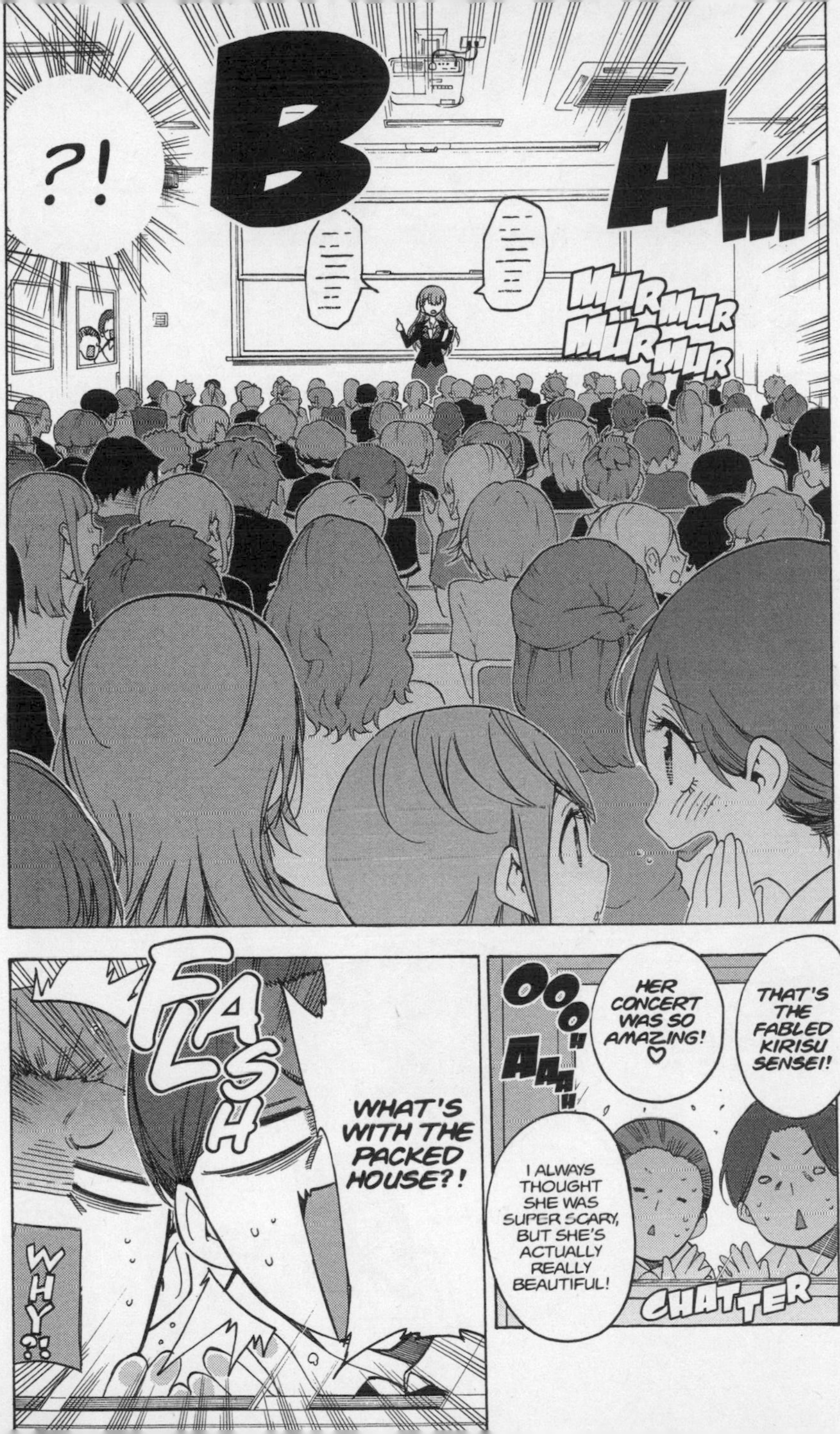
BAM
MURMUR MURMUR
MURMUR MURMUR
?!
THAT'S THE FABLED KIRISU SENSEI!
HER CONCERT WAS SO AMAZING! ♡
OOOOH AAAAH
I ALWAYS THOUGHT SHE WAS SUPER SCARY, BUT SHE'S ACTUALLY REALLY BEAUTIFUL!
CHATTER
FLASH
WHAT'S WITH THE PACKED HOUSE?!
WHY?!

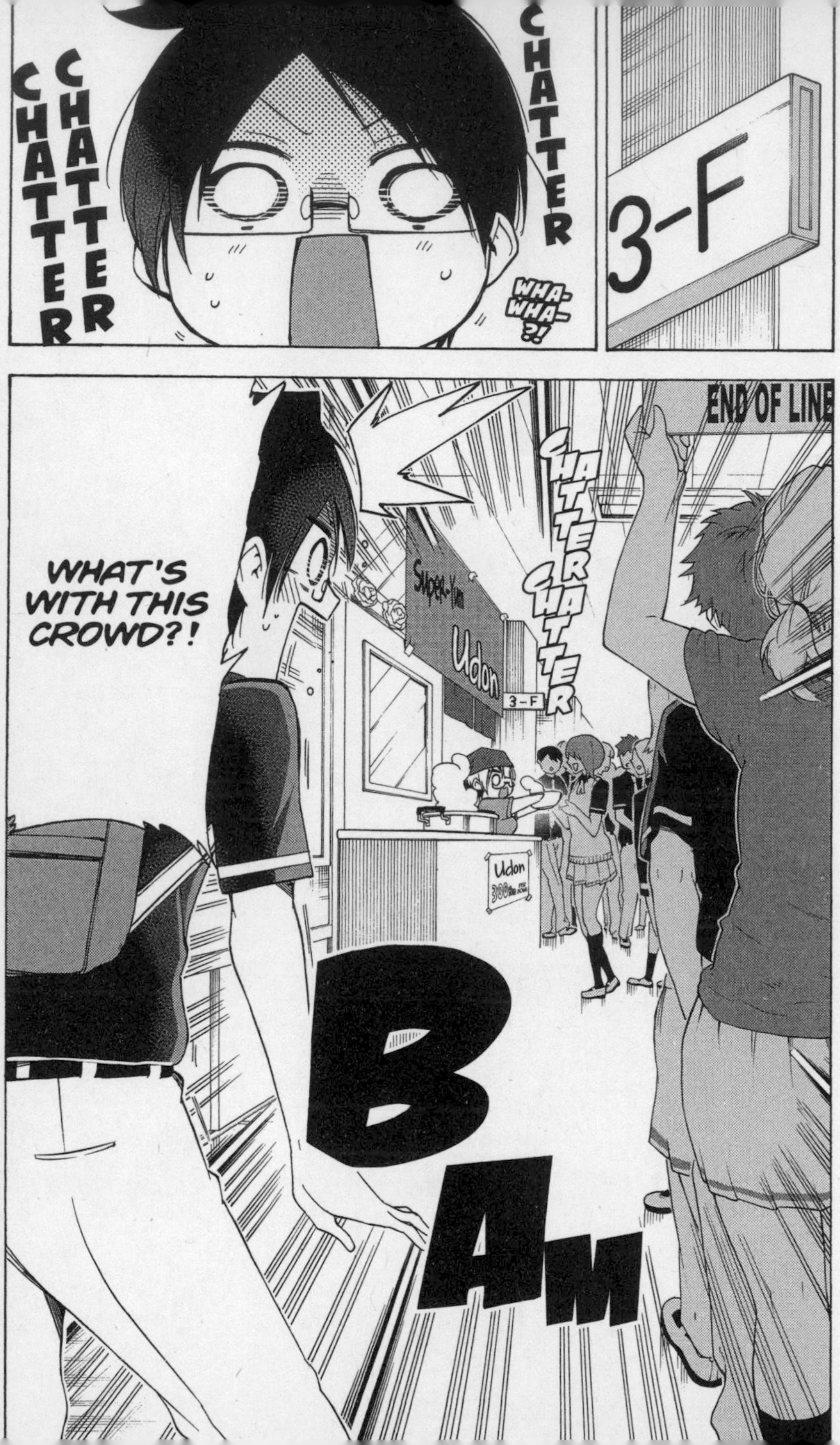
3-F
CHATTER
WHA-WHA-?!
CHATTER
CHATTER
END OF LINE
CHATTER CHATTER
Udon
3-F
WHAT'S WITH THIS CROWD?!
Udon
BAM

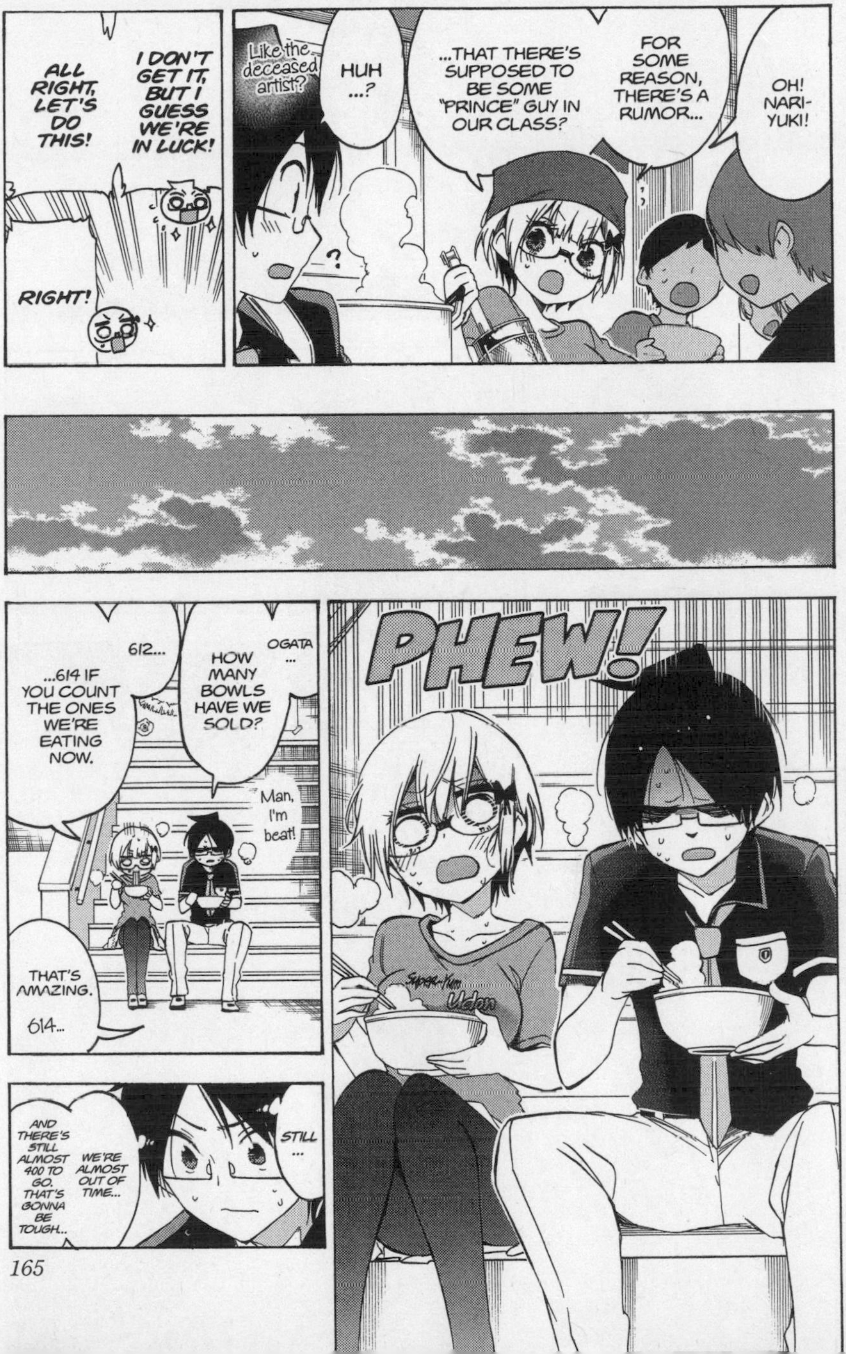
OH! NARI-YUKI!
FOR SOME REASON, THERE'S A RUMOR...
...THAT THERE'S SUPPOSED TO BE SOME "PRINCE" GUY IN OUR CLASS?
HUH ...?
Like the deceased artist?
I DON'T GET IT, BUT I GUESS WE'RE IN LUCK!
ALL RIGHT, LET'S DO THIS!
RIGHT!
PHEW!
OGATA ...
HOW MANY BOWLS HAVE WE SOLD?
612...
...614 IF YOU COUNT THE ONES WE'RE EATING NOW.
Man, I'm beat!
THAT'S AMAZING.
614...
Super-Yum Udon
STILL ...
WE'RE ALMOST OUT OF TIME...
AND THERE'S STILL ALMOST 400 TO GO. THAT'S GONNA BE TOUGH...

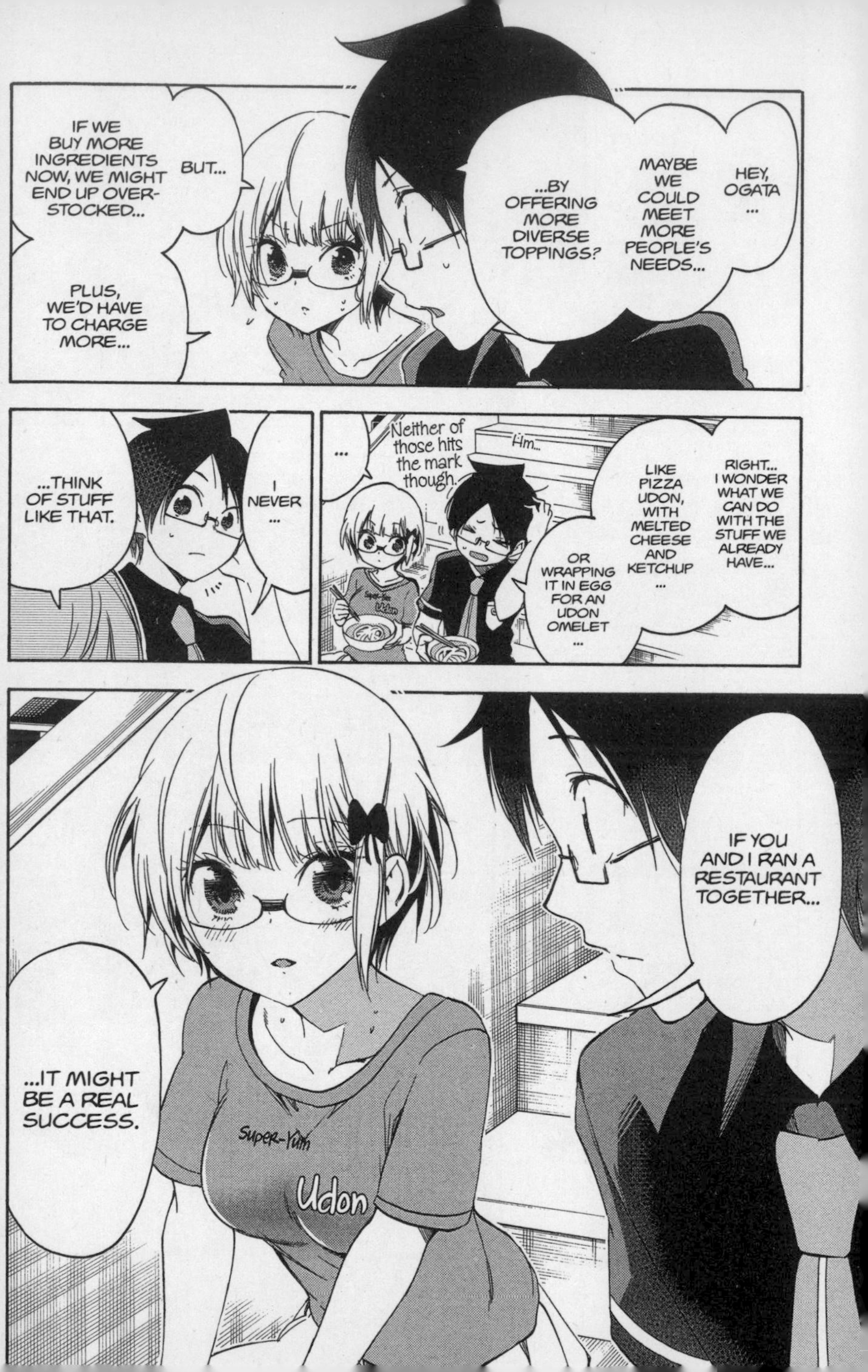
HEY, OGATA ...
MAYBE WE COULD MEET MORE PEOPLE'S NEEDS...
...BY OFFERING MORE DIVERSE TOPPINGS?
BUT...
IF WE BUY MORE INGREDIENTS NOW, WE MIGHT END UP OVER-STOCKED...
PLUS, WE'D HAVE TO CHARGE MORE...
RIGHT... I WONDER WHAT WE CAN DO WITH THE STUFF WE ALREADY HAVE...
LIKE PIZZA UDON, WITH MELTED CHEESE AND KETCHUP ...
OR WRAPPING IT IN EGG FOR AN UDON OMELET ...
Hm...
Neither of those hits the mark though.
...
I NEVER ...
...THINK OF STUFF LIKE THAT.
IF YOU AND I RAN A RESTAURANT TOGETHER...
...IT MIGHT BE A REAL SUCCESS.
Super-Yum
Udon

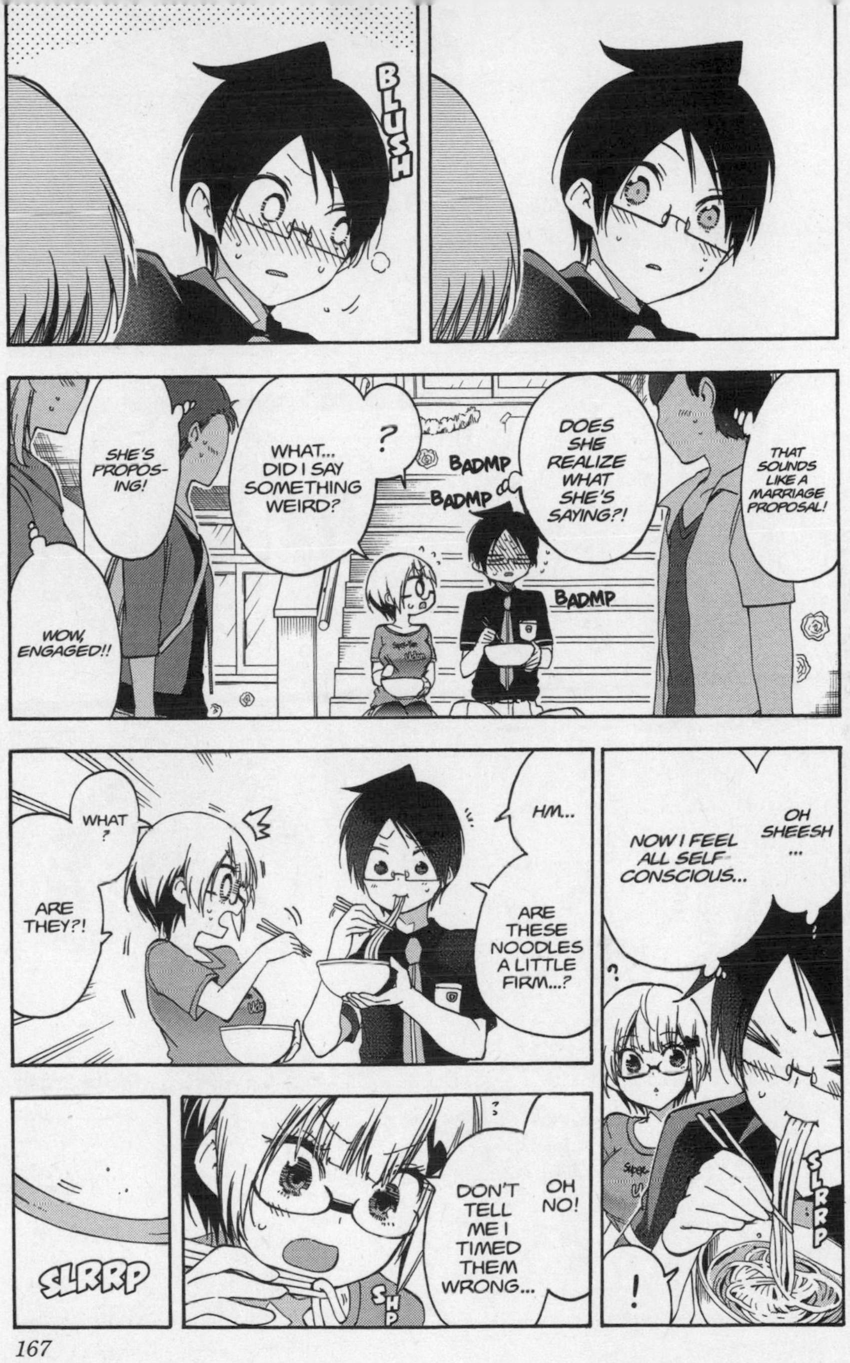
BLUSH
THAT SOUNDS LIKE A MARRIAGE PROPOSAL!
DOES SHE REALIZE WHAT SHE'S SAYING?!
BADMP
BADMP
BADMP
?
WHAT... DID I SAY SOMETHING WEIRD?
SHE'S PROPOS-ING!
WOW, ENGAGED!!
OH SHEESH...
NOW I FEEL ALL SELF-CONSCIOUS...
?
SLRRP
!
HM...
ARE THESE NOODLES A LITTLE FIRM...?
WHAT?
ARE THEY?!
OH NO!
DON'T TELL ME I TIMED THEM WRONG...
SHP
SLRRP

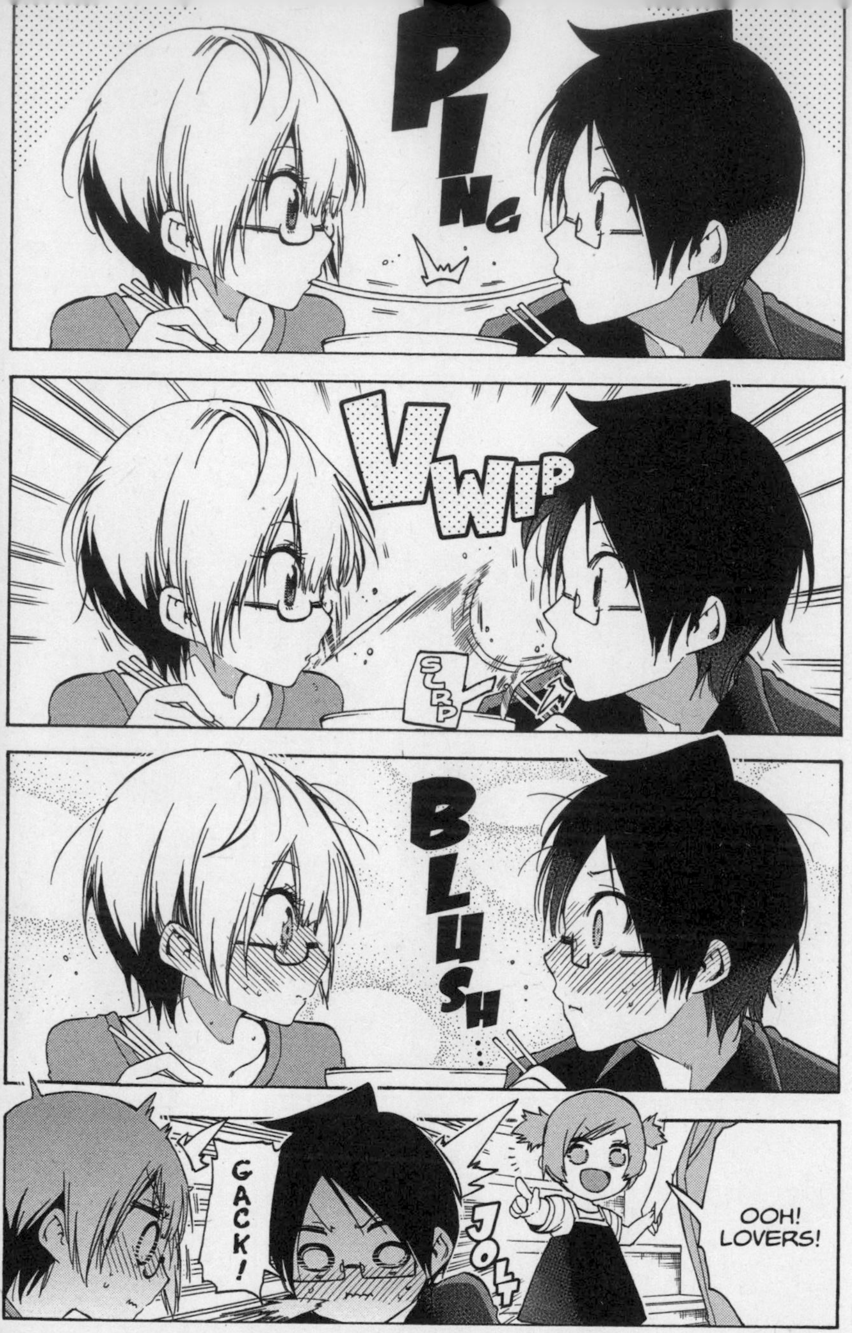
PING
VWIP
SLRP
BLUSH
OOH! LOVERS!
JOLT
GACK!

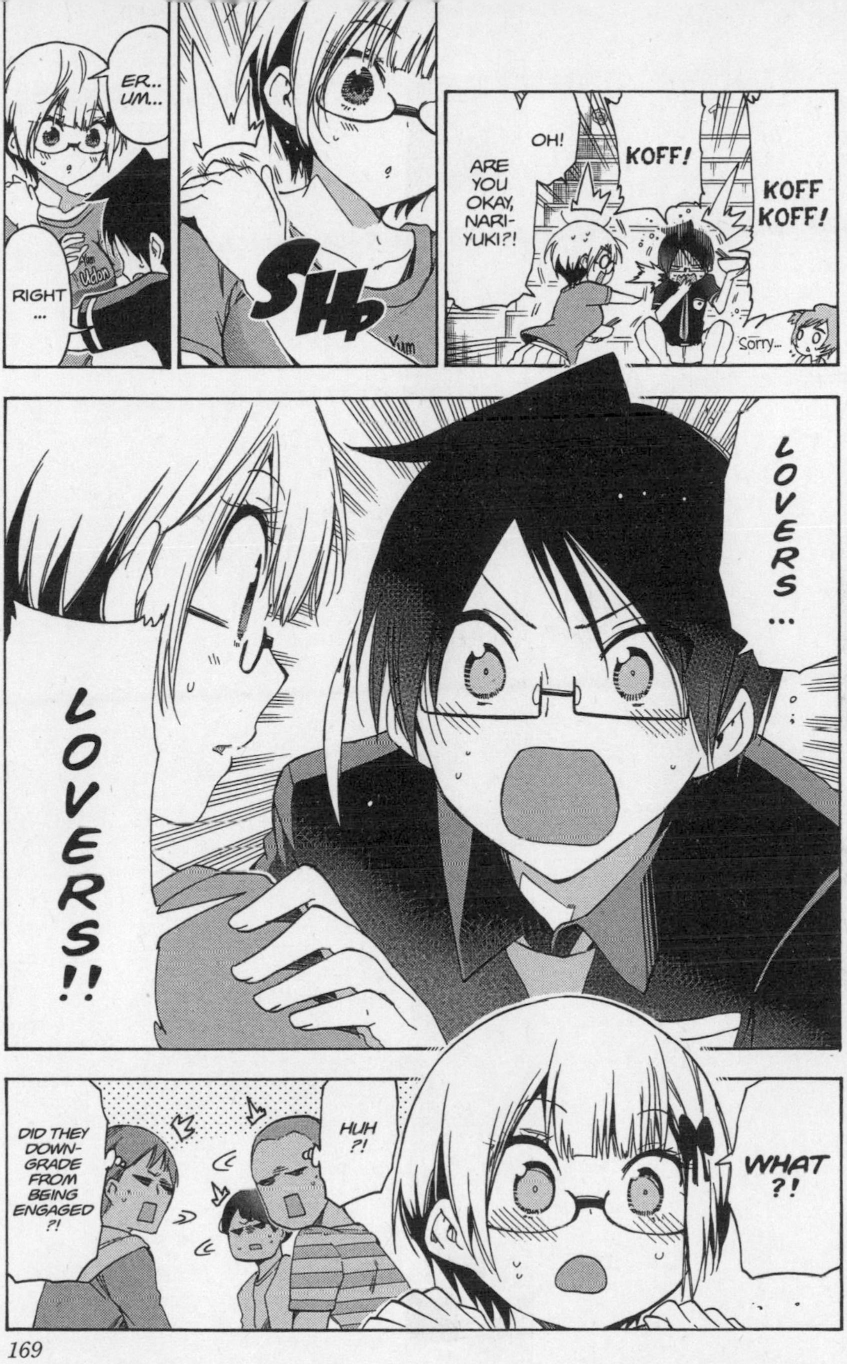
KOFF KOFF!
KOFF!
OH!
ARE YOU OKAY, NARI-YUKI?!
Sorry...
SHP
Yum
ER.. UM...
RIGHT ...
LOVERS ...
LOVERS!!
WHAT ?!
HUH ?!
DID THEY DOWN-GRADE FROM BEING ENGAGED ?!

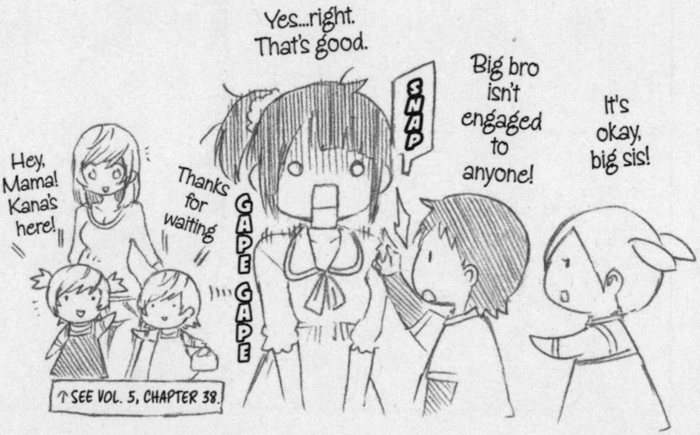
It's okay, big sis!
Big bro isn't engaged to anyone!
SNAP
Yes...right. That's good.
GAPE GAPE
Thanks for waiting
Hey, Mama! Kana's here!
↑SEE VOL. 5, CHAPTER 38.

Question 69: A Post-Festival Celebration of [X], both Dazzling and Lonely

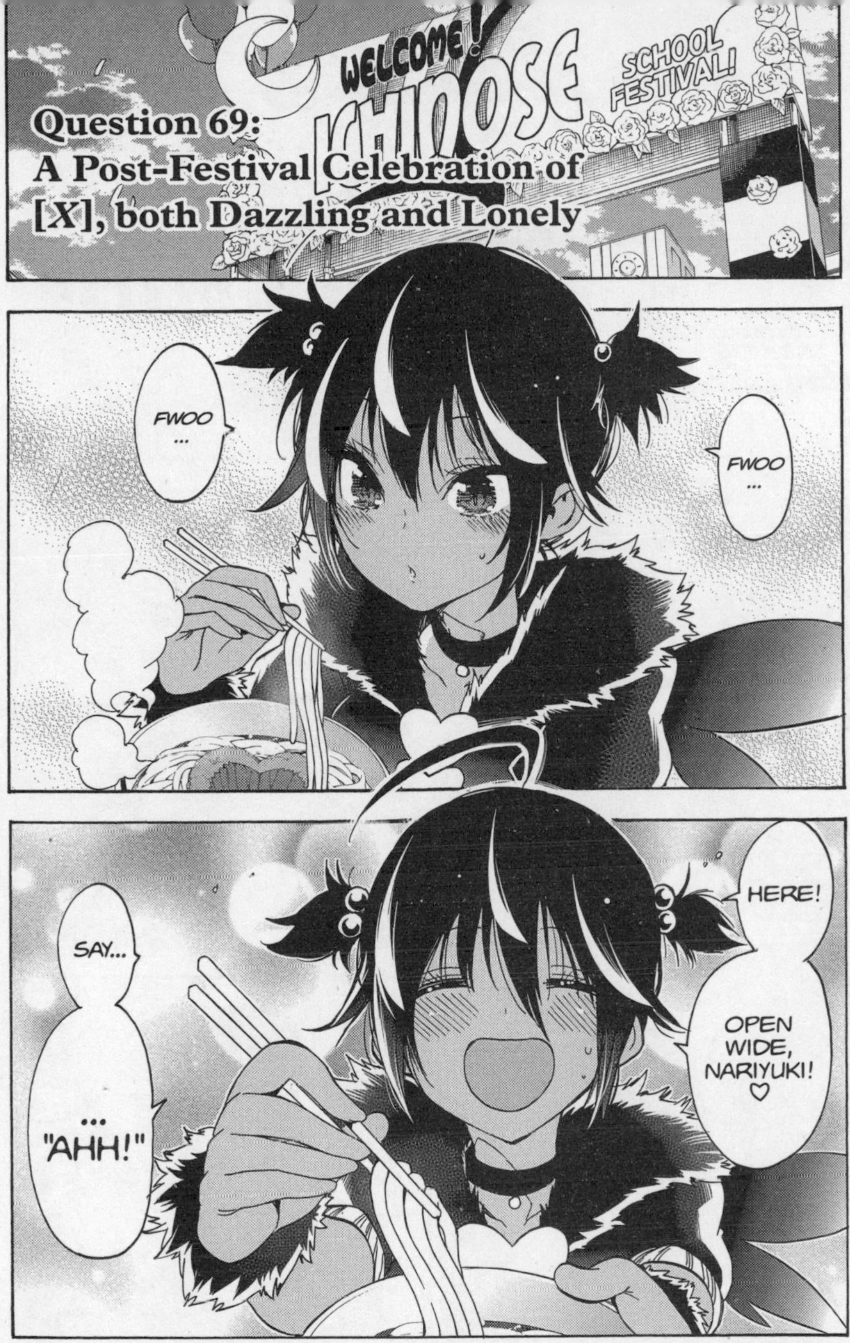
WELCOME! ICHINOSE SCHOOL FESTIVAL!
FWOO ...
FWOO ...
HERE!
OPEN WIDE, NARIYUKI! ♡
SAY...
... "AHH!"

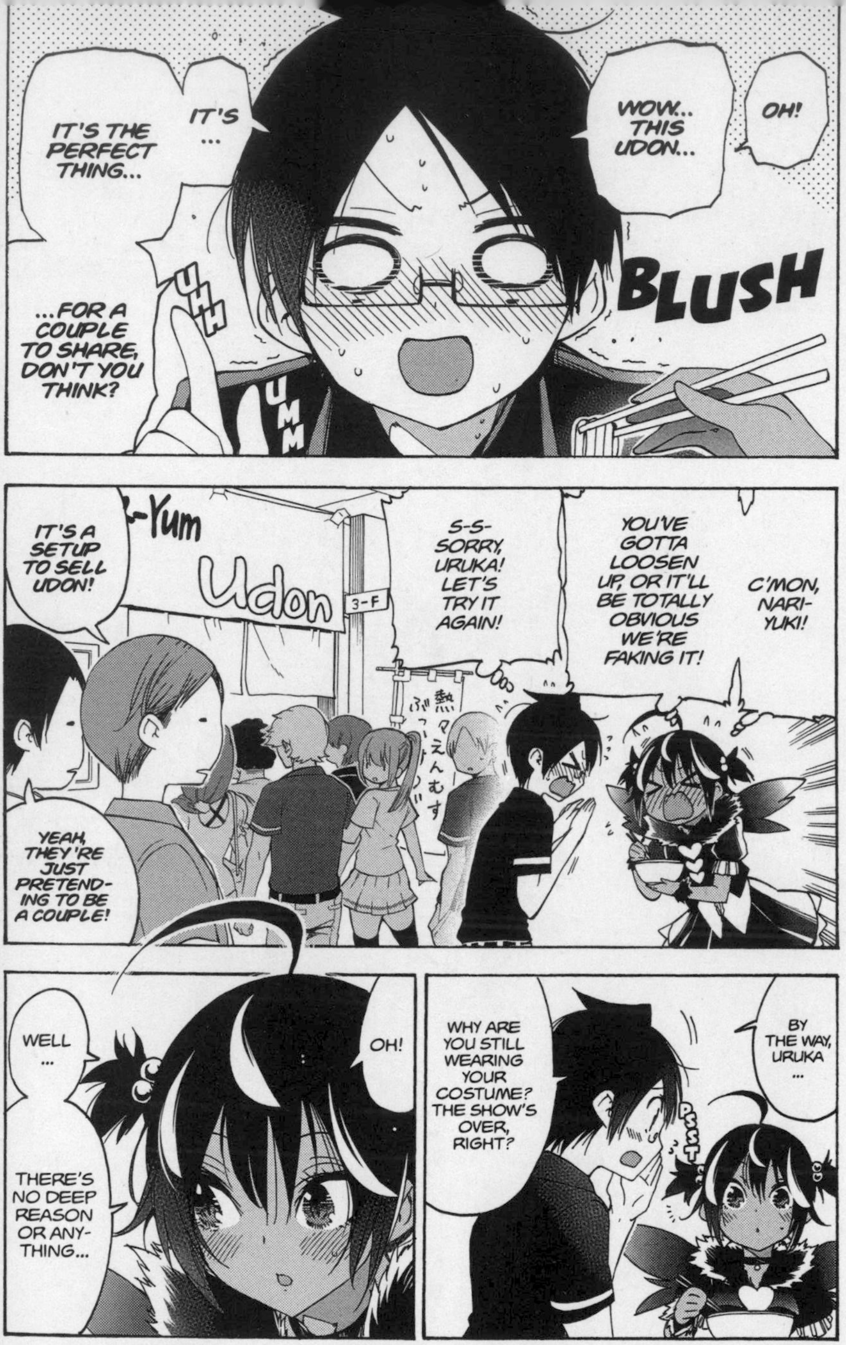
OH!
WOW... THIS UDON...
BLUSH
IT'S ...
IT'S THE PERFECT THING...
...FOR A COUPLE TO SHARE, DON'T YOU THINK?
UHH
UMM
C'MON, NARI-YUKI!
YOU'VE GOTTA LOOSEN UP, OR IT'LL BE TOTALLY OBVIOUS WE'RE FAKING IT!
S-S-SORRY, URUKA! LET'S TRY IT AGAIN!
-Yum
Udon
3-F
熱々えんむす
IT'S A SETUP TO SELL UDON!
YEAH, THEY'RE JUST PRETEND-ING TO BE A COUPLE!
BY THE WAY, URUKA ...
PSST
WHY ARE YOU STILL WEARING YOUR COSTUME? THE SHOW'S OVER, RIGHT?
OH!
WELL ...
THERE'S NO DEEP REASON OR ANY-THING...

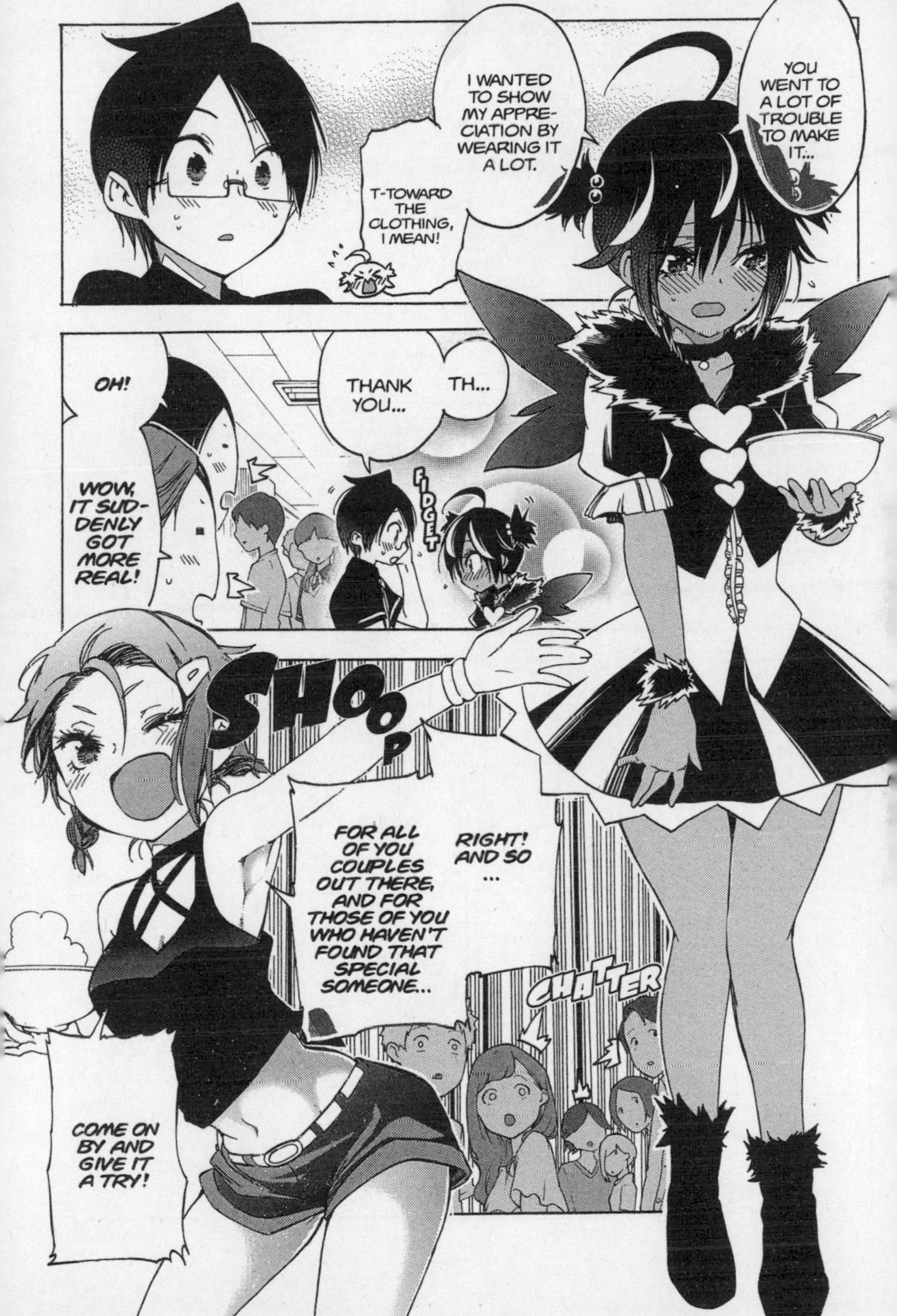
YOU WENT TO A LOT OF TROUBLE TO MAKE IT...
I WANTED TO SHOW MY APPRECIATION BY WEARING IT A LOT.
T-TOWARD THE CLOTHING, I MEAN!
TH...
THANK YOU...
FIDGET
OH!
WOW, IT SUDDENLY GOT MORE REAL!
SHOOP
RIGHT! AND SO ...
FOR ALL OF YOU COUPLES OUT THERE, AND FOR THOSE OF YOU WHO HAVEN'T FOUND THAT SPECIAL SOMEONE...
CHATTER
COME ON BY AND GIVE IT A TRY!

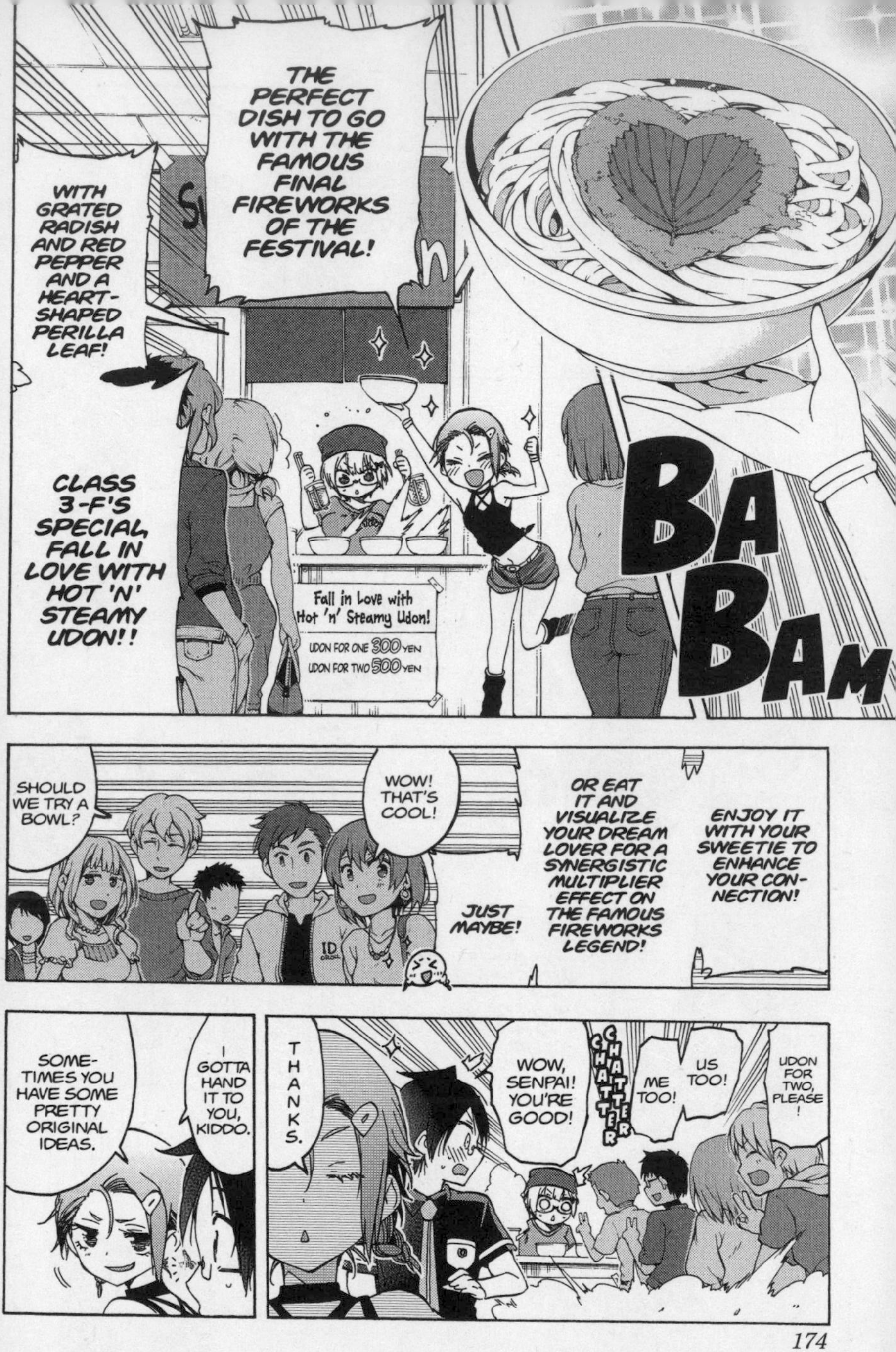
BA BA BAM
THE PERFECT DISH TO GO WITH THE FAMOUS FINAL FIREWORKS OF THE FESTIVAL!
WITH GRATED RADISH AND RED PEPPER AND A HEART-SHAPED PERILLA LEAF!
Fall in Love with Hot 'n' Steamy Udon!
UDON FOR ONE 300 YEN
UDON FOR TWO 500 YEN
CLASS 3-F'S SPECIAL, FALL IN LOVE WITH HOT 'N' STEAMY UDON!!
ENJOY IT WITH YOUR SWEETIE TO ENHANCE YOUR CONNECTION!
OR EAT IT AND VISUALIZE YOUR DREAM LOVER FOR A SYNERGISTIC MULTIPLIER EFFECT ON THE FAMOUS FIREWORKS LEGEND!
JUST MAYBE!
WOW! THAT'S COOL!
SHOULD WE TRY A BOWL?
UDON FOR TWO, PLEASE!
US TOO!
ME TOO!
CHATTER CHATTER
WOW, SENPAI! YOU'RE GOOD!
THANKS.
I GOTTA HAND IT TO YOU, KIDDO.
SOMETIMES YOU HAVE SOME PRETTY ORIGINAL IDEAS.

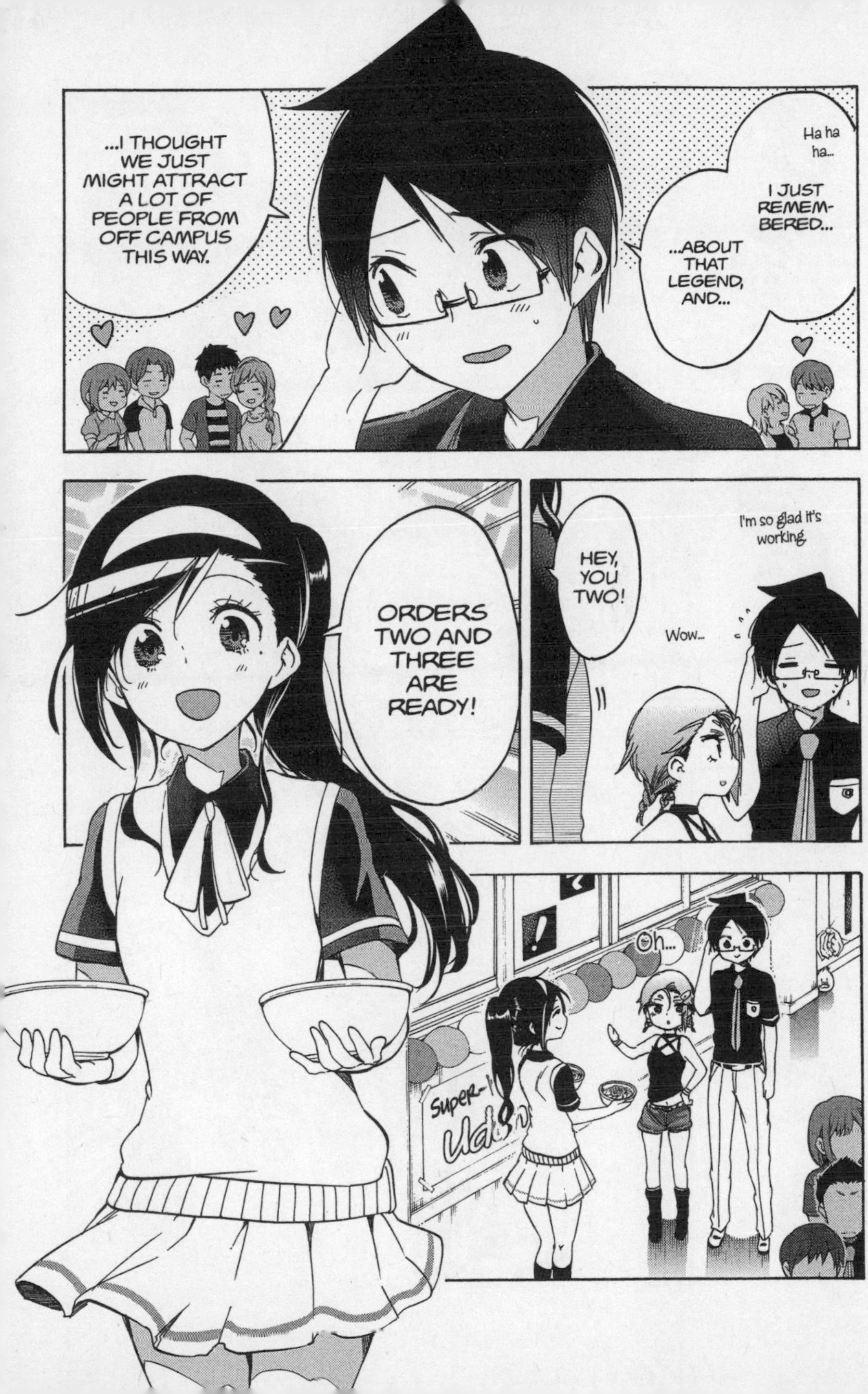
Ha ha ha...
I JUST REMEMBERED...
...ABOUT THAT LEGEND, AND...
...I THOUGHT WE JUST MIGHT ATTRACT A LOT OF PEOPLE FROM OFF CAMPUS THIS WAY.
I'm so glad it's working.
HEY, YOU TWO!
Wow...
ORDERS TWO AND THREE ARE READY!
Oh...
Super-

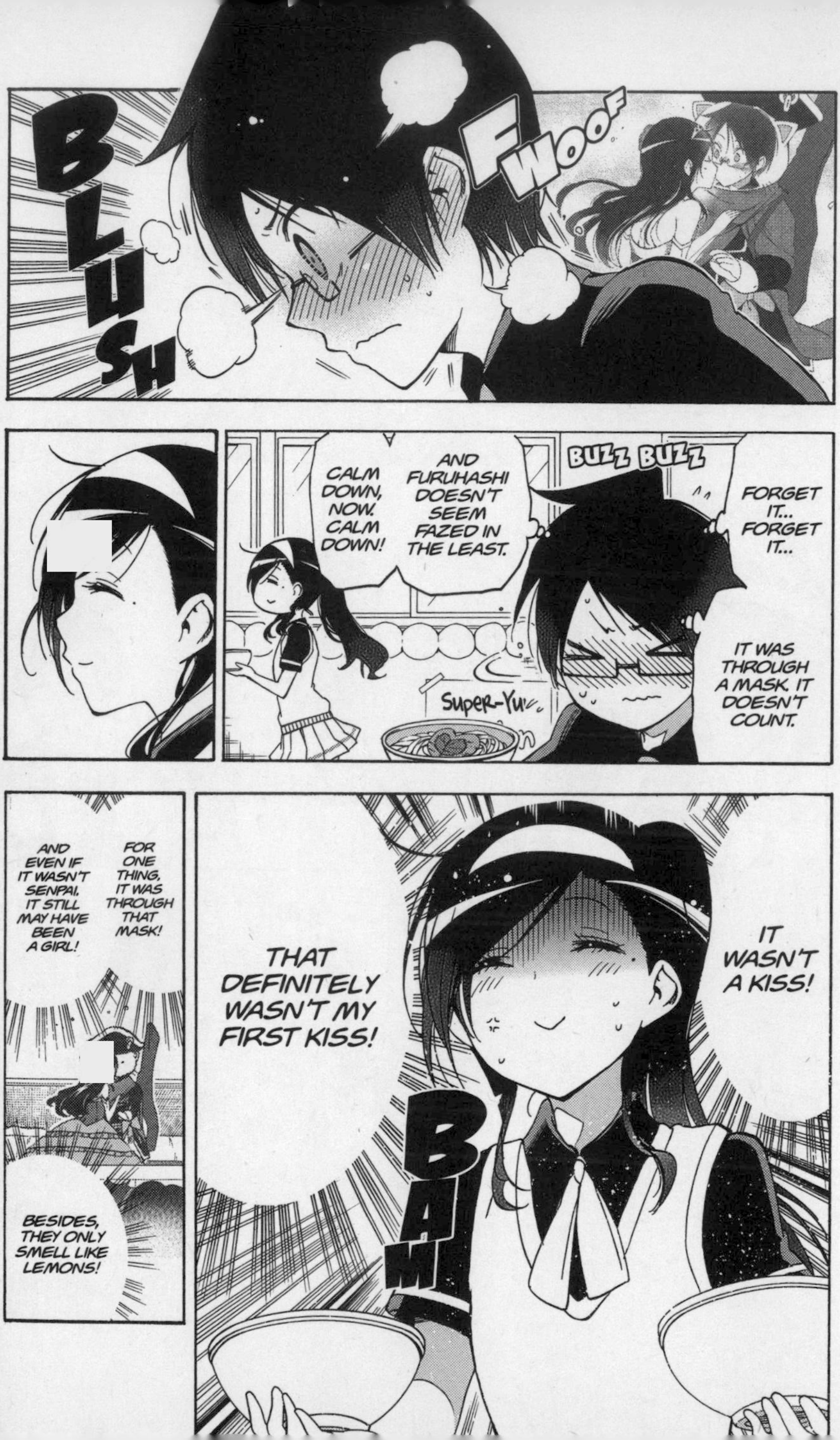
FWOOF
BLUSH
FORGET IT... FORGET IT...
IT WAS THROUGH A MASK. IT DOESN'T COUNT.
BUZZ BUZZ
AND FURUHASHI DOESN'T SEEM FAZED IN THE LEAST.
CALM DOWN, NOW. CALM DOWN!
Super-Yu
IT WASN'T A KISS!
THAT DEFINITELY WASN'T MY FIRST KISS!
BAM
FOR ONE THING, IT WAS THROUGH THAT MASK!
AND EVEN IF IT WASN'T SENPAI, IT STILL MAY HAVE BEEN A GIRL!
BESIDES, THEY ONLY SMELL LIKE LEMONS!

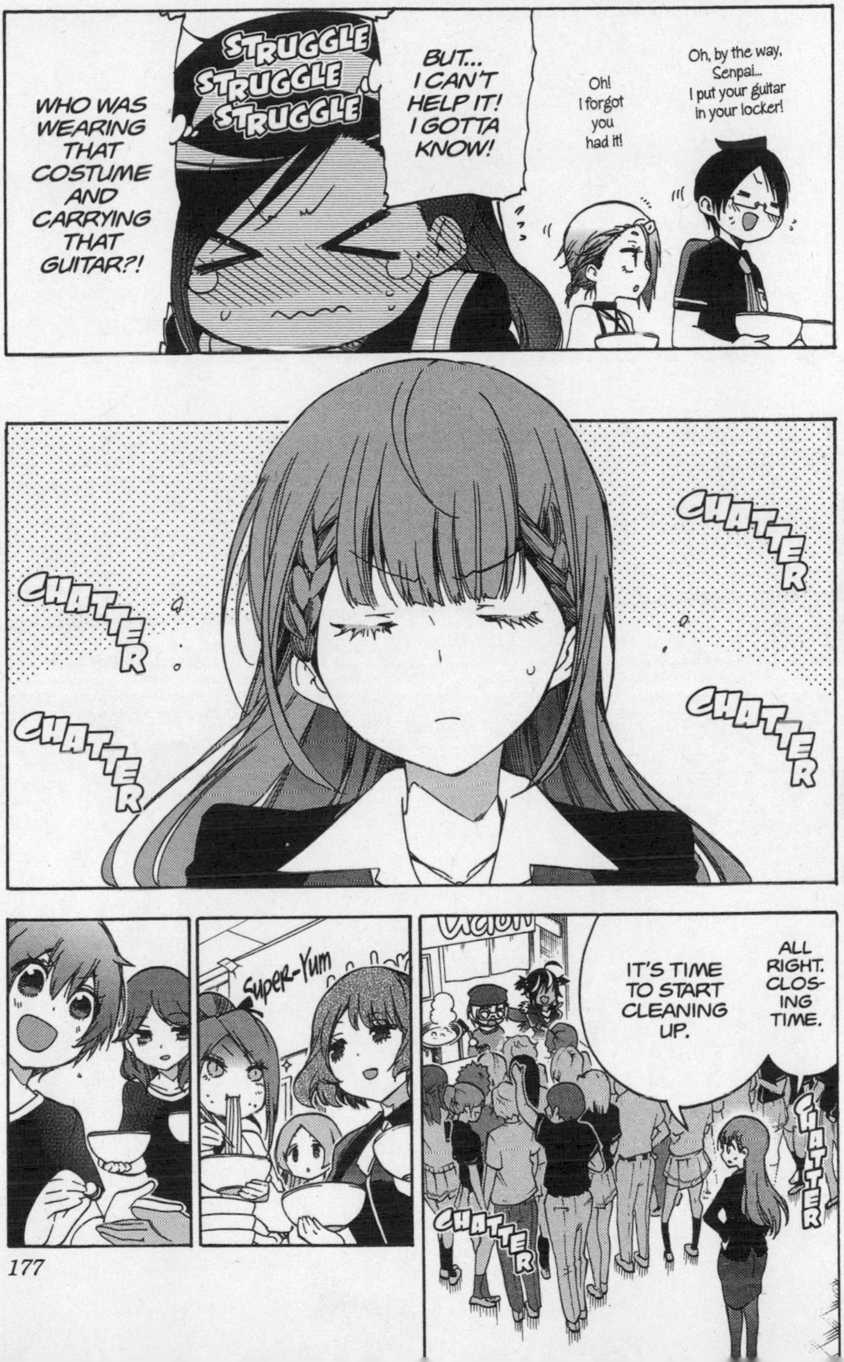
Oh, by the way, Senpai... I put your guitar in your locker!
Oh! I forgot you had it!
BUT... I CAN'T HELP IT! I GOTTA KNOW!
STRUGGLE STRUGGLE STRUGGLE
WHO WAS WEARING THAT COSTUME AND CARRYING THAT GUITAR?!
CHATTER
CHATTER
CHATTER
CHATTER
ALL RIGHT. CLOSING TIME.
IT'S TIME TO START CLEANING UP.
CHATTER
CHATTER
Super-Yum

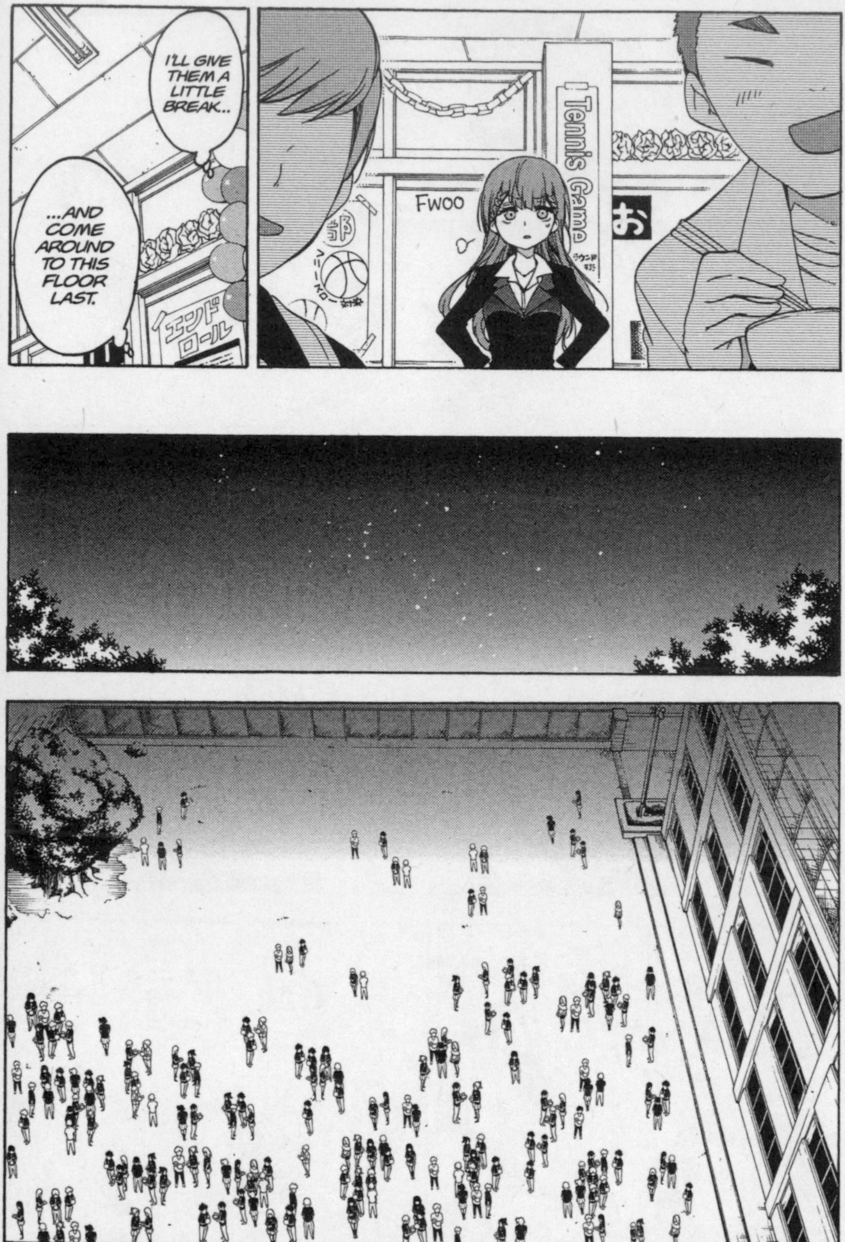
Tennis Game
Fwoo
I'LL GIVE THEM A LITTLE BREAK..
...AND COME AROUND TO THIS FLOOR LAST.

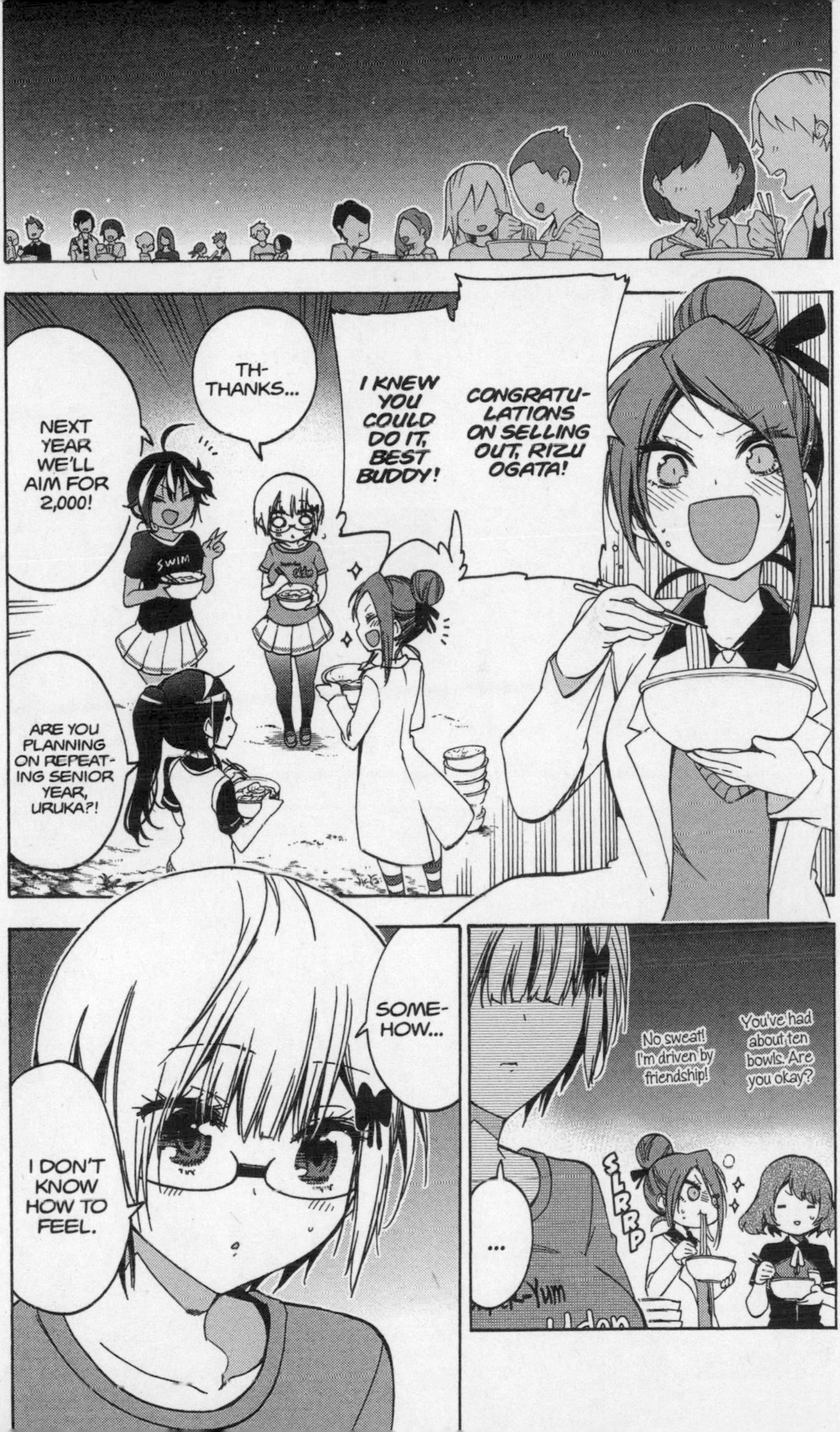
CONGRATULATIONS ON SELLING OUT, RIZU OGATA!
I KNEW YOU COULD DO IT, BEST BUDDY!
TH-THANKS...
NEXT YEAR WE'LL AIM FOR 2,000!
ARE YOU PLANNING ON REPEATING SENIOR YEAR, URUKA?!
You've had about ten bowls. Are you okay?
No sweat! I'm driven by friendship!
SLRRP
...
SOMEHOW...
I DON'T KNOW HOW TO FEEL.

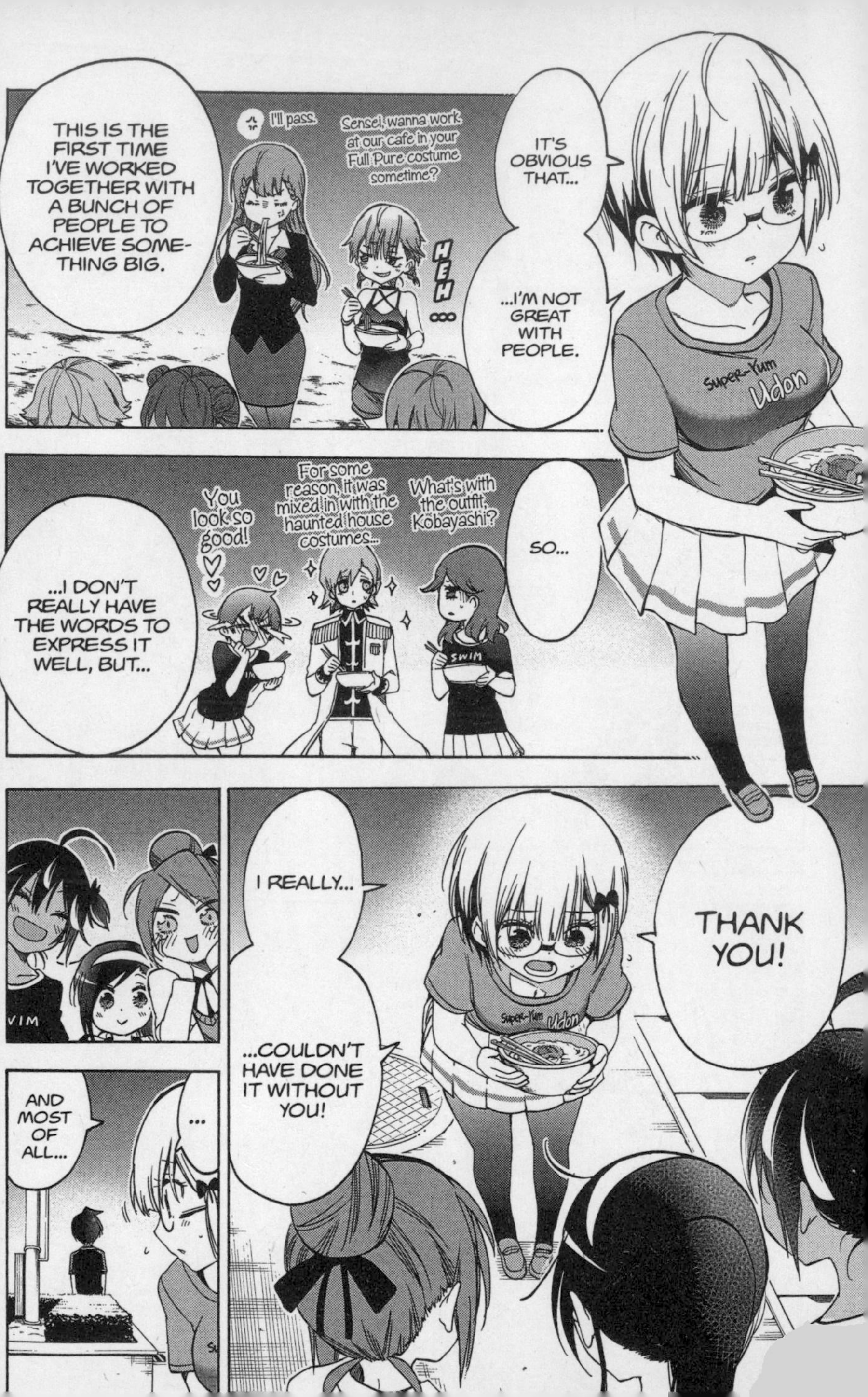
IT'S OBVIOUS THAT...
...I'M NOT GREAT WITH PEOPLE.
Sensei, wanna work at our cafe in your Full Pure costume sometime?
HEH...
I'll pass.
THIS IS THE FIRST TIME I'VE WORKED TOGETHER WITH A BUNCH OF PEOPLE TO ACHIEVE SOME-THING BIG.
Super-Yum Udon
SO...
What's with the outfit, Kobayashi?
For some reason, it was mixed in with the haunted house costumes...
You look so good!
SWIM
...I DON'T REALLY HAVE THE WORDS TO EXPRESS IT WELL, BUT...
I REALLY...
...COULDN'T HAVE DONE IT WITHOUT YOU!
THANK YOU!
Super-Yum Udon
SWIM
...
AND MOST OF ALL...

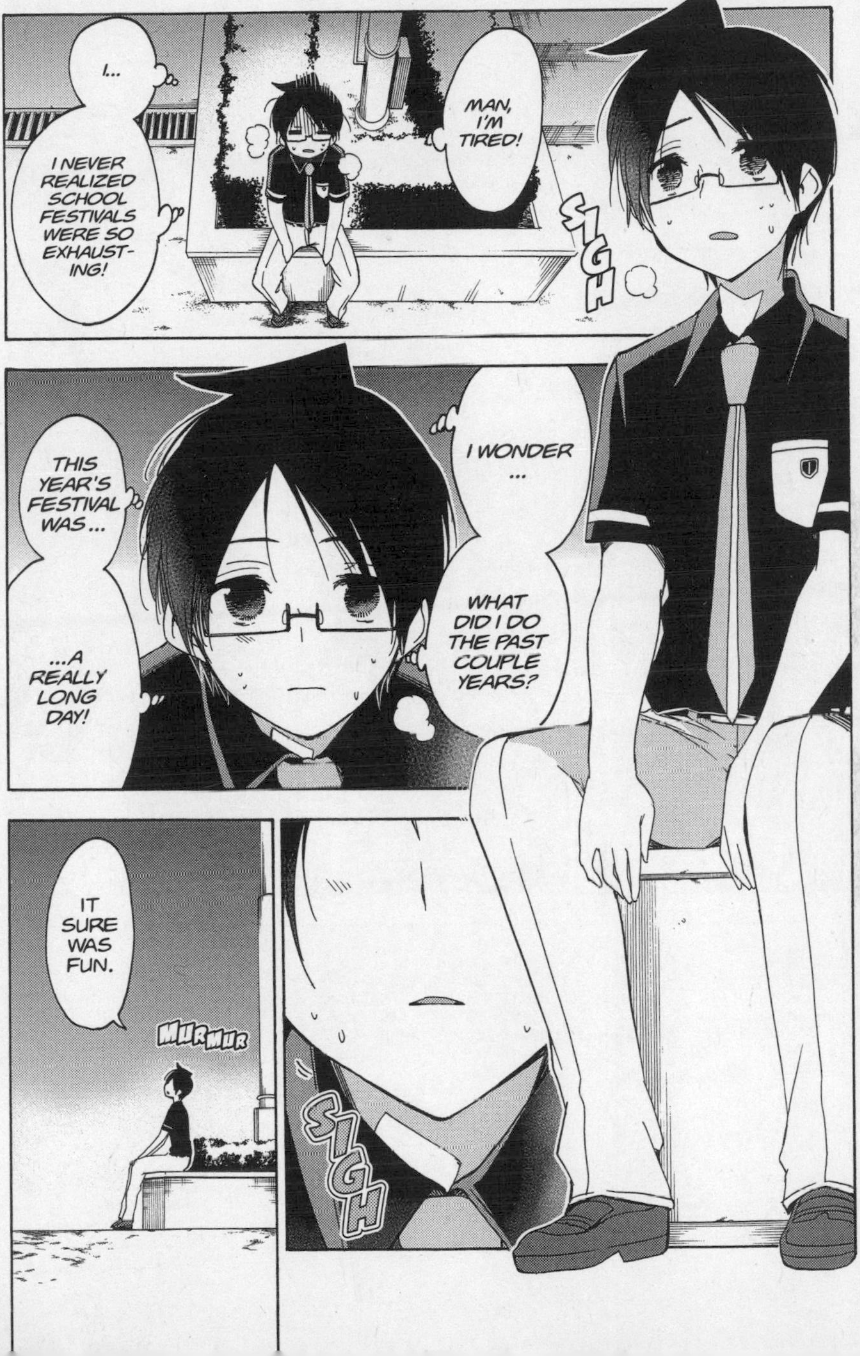
SIGH
MAN, I'M TIRED!
I...
I NEVER REALIZED SCHOOL FESTIVALS WERE SO EXHAUST-ING!
I WONDER ...
WHAT DID I DO THE PAST COUPLE YEARS?
THIS YEAR'S FESTIVAL WAS...
...A REALLY LONG DAY!
SIGH
IT SURE WAS FUN.
MURMUR

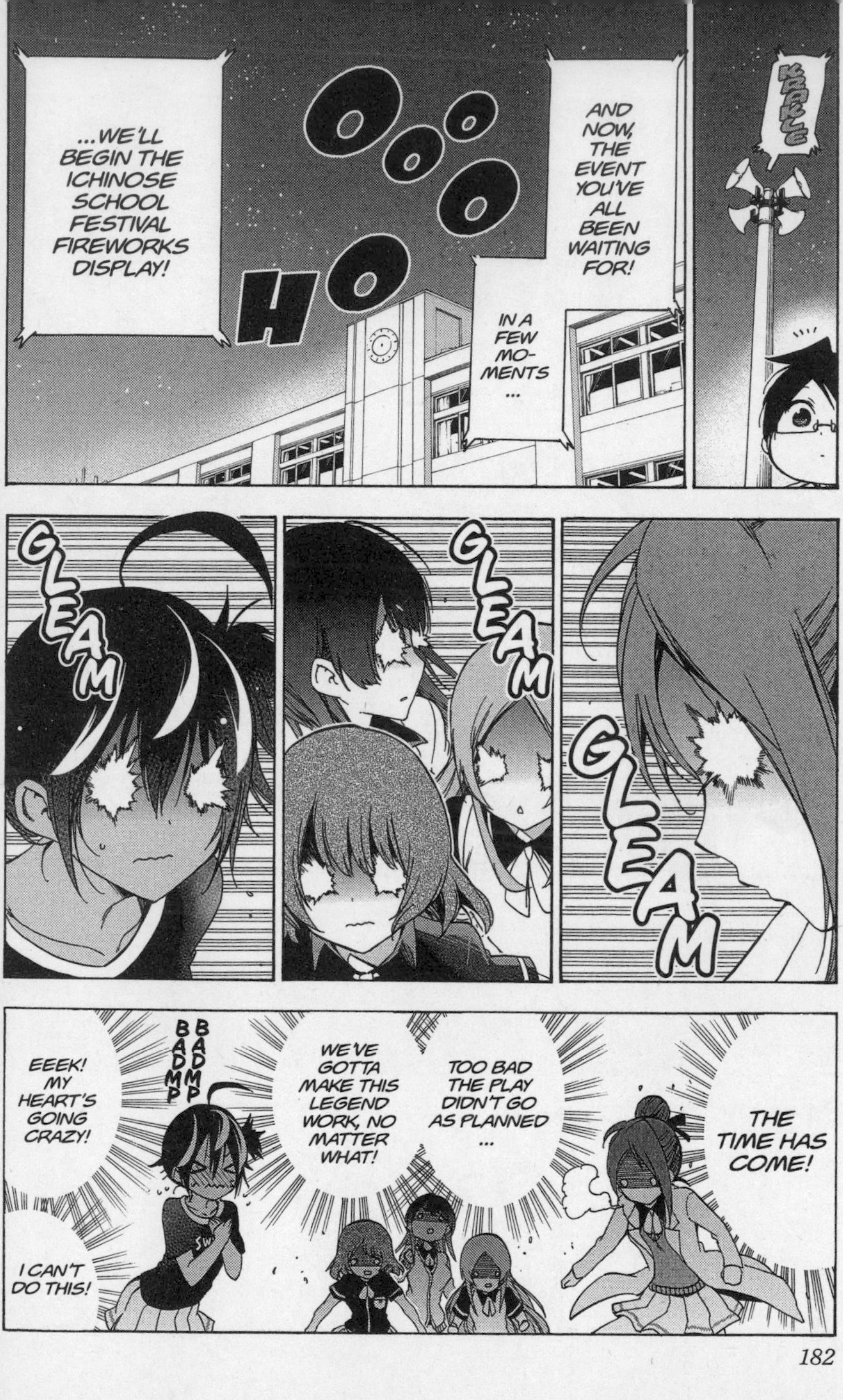
KRAKLE
AND NOW, THE EVENT YOU'VE ALL BEEN WAITING FOR!
IN A FEW MOMENTS...
...WE'LL BEGIN THE ICHINOSE SCHOOL FESTIVAL FIREWORKS DISPLAY!
HOOOOO
GLEAM GLEAM
GLEAM
GLEAM
THE TIME HAS COME!
TOO BAD THE PLAY DIDN'T GO AS PLANNED...
WE'VE GOTTA MAKE THIS LEGEND WORK, NO MATTER WHAT!
BADMP BADMP
EEEK! MY HEART'S GOING CRAZY!
I CAN'T DO THIS!

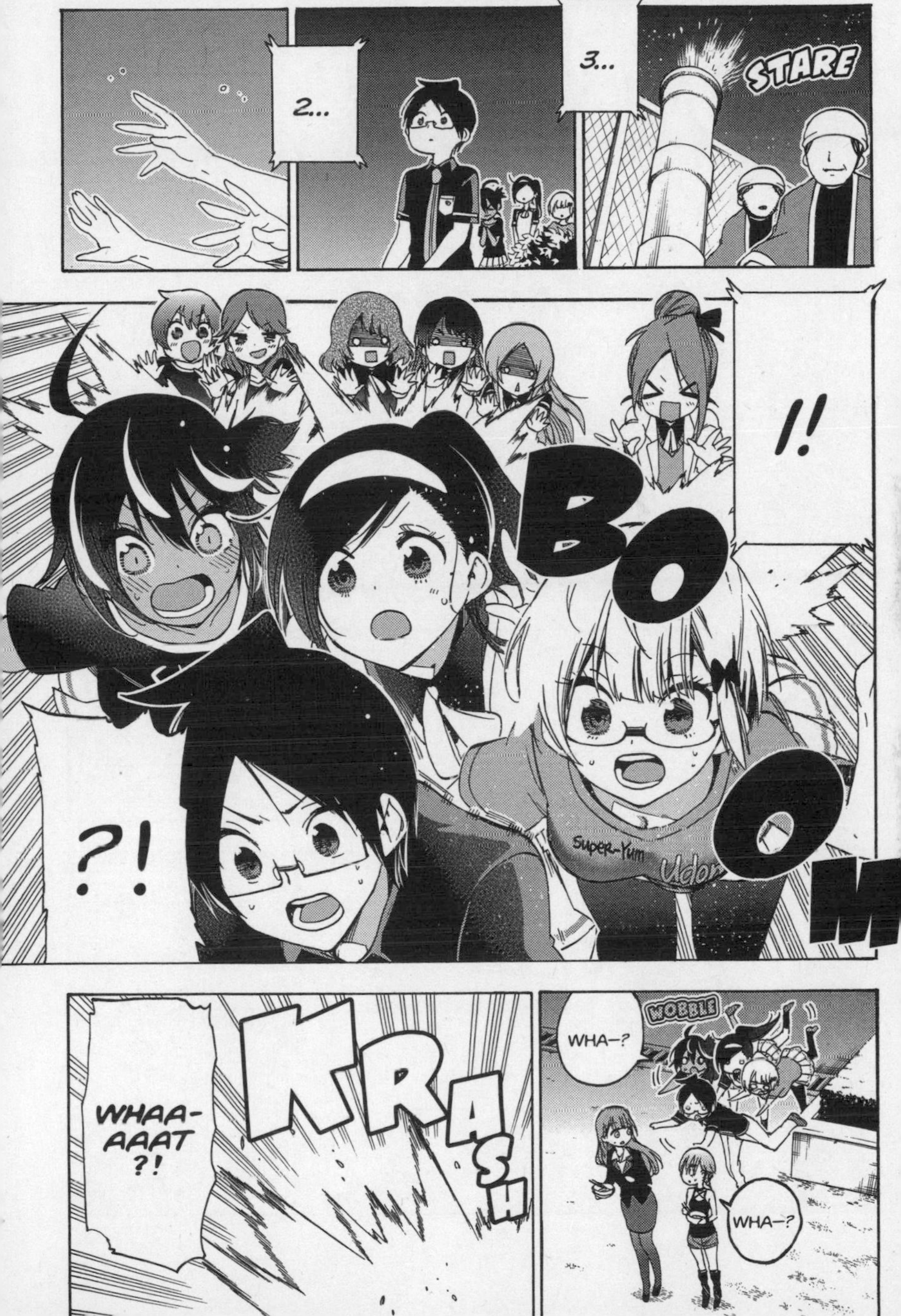
3...
STARE
2...
!!
BOOOM
?!
Super-Yum
Udon
WOBBLE
WHA-?
WHA-?
KRASH
WHAA-
AAAT
?!

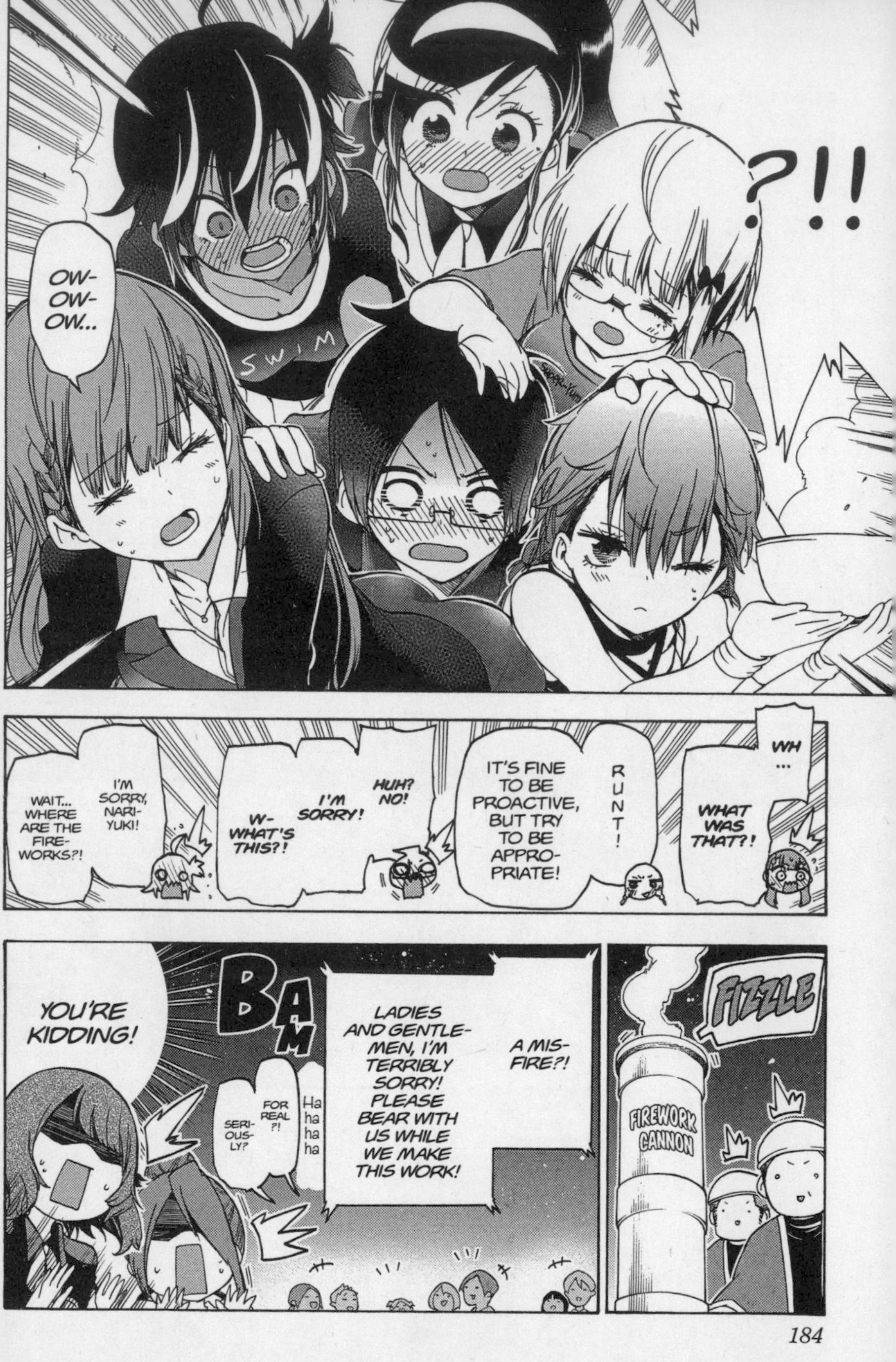
?!!
OW-OW-OW...
WH... WHAT WAS THAT?!
RUNT!
IT'S FINE TO BE PROACTIVE, BUT TRY TO BE APPROPRIATE!
HUH? NO!
I'M SORRY!
W-WHAT'S THIS?!
I'M SORRY, NARI-YUKI!
WAIT... WHERE ARE THE FIRE-WORKS?!
FIZZLE
FIREWORK CANNON
A MIS-FIRE?!
LADIES AND GENTLE-MEN, I'M TERRIBLY SORRY! PLEASE BEAR WITH US WHILE WE MAKE THIS WORK!
BAM
Ha ha ha ha
FOR REAL?!
SERI-OUSLY?
YOU'RE KIDDING!

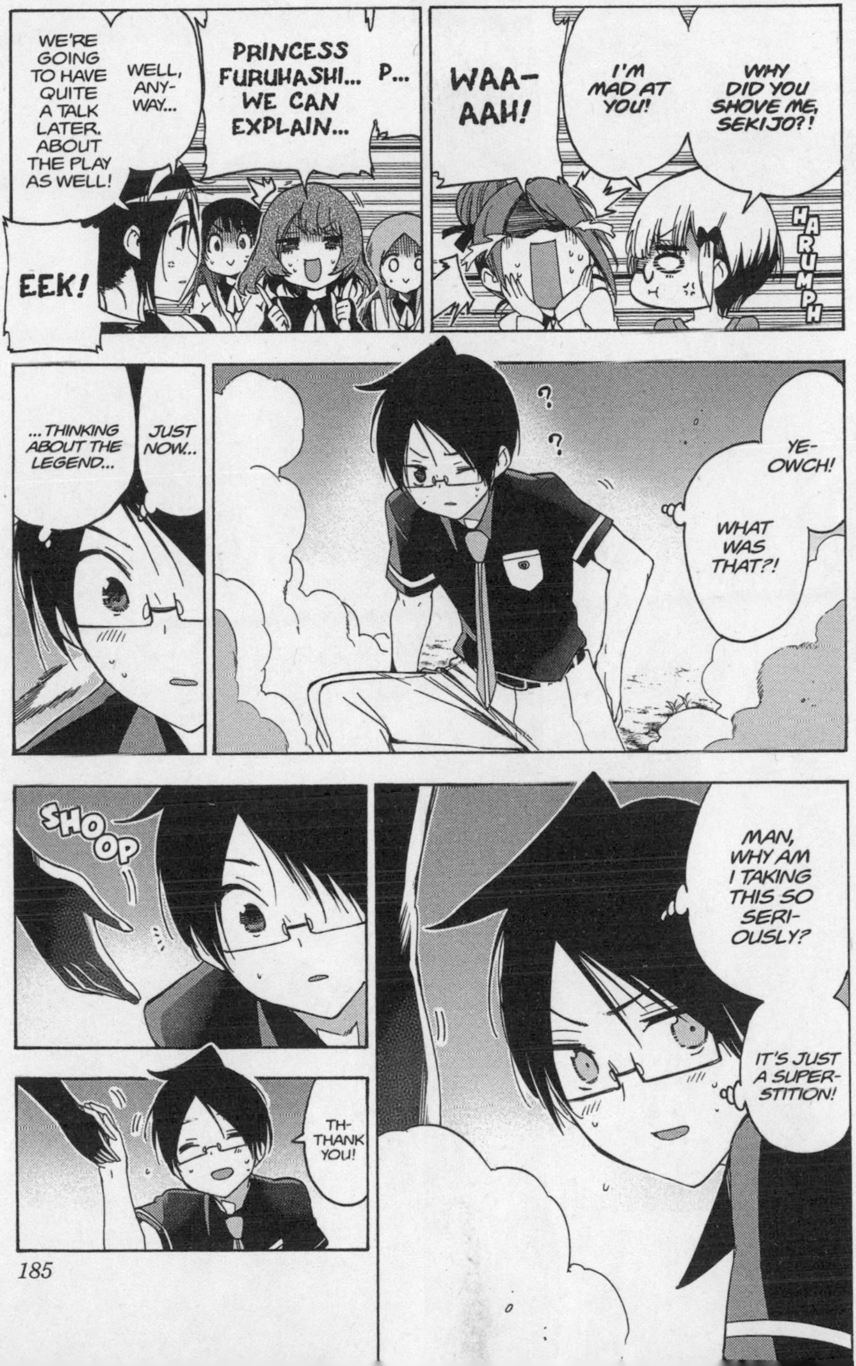
WHY DID YOU SHOVE ME, SEKIJO?!
I'M MAD AT YOU!
WAA-AAH!
HARUMPH
P...
PRINCESS FURUHASHI... WE CAN EXPLAIN...
WELL, ANYWAY...
WE'RE GOING TO HAVE QUITE A TALK LATER. ABOUT THE PLAY AS WELL!
EEK!
YE-OWCH!
WHAT WAS THAT?!
JUST NOW...
...THINKING ABOUT THE LEGEND...
MAN, WHY AM I TAKING THIS SO SERIOUSLY?
IT'S JUST A SUPERSTITION!
SHOOP
TH-THANK YOU!

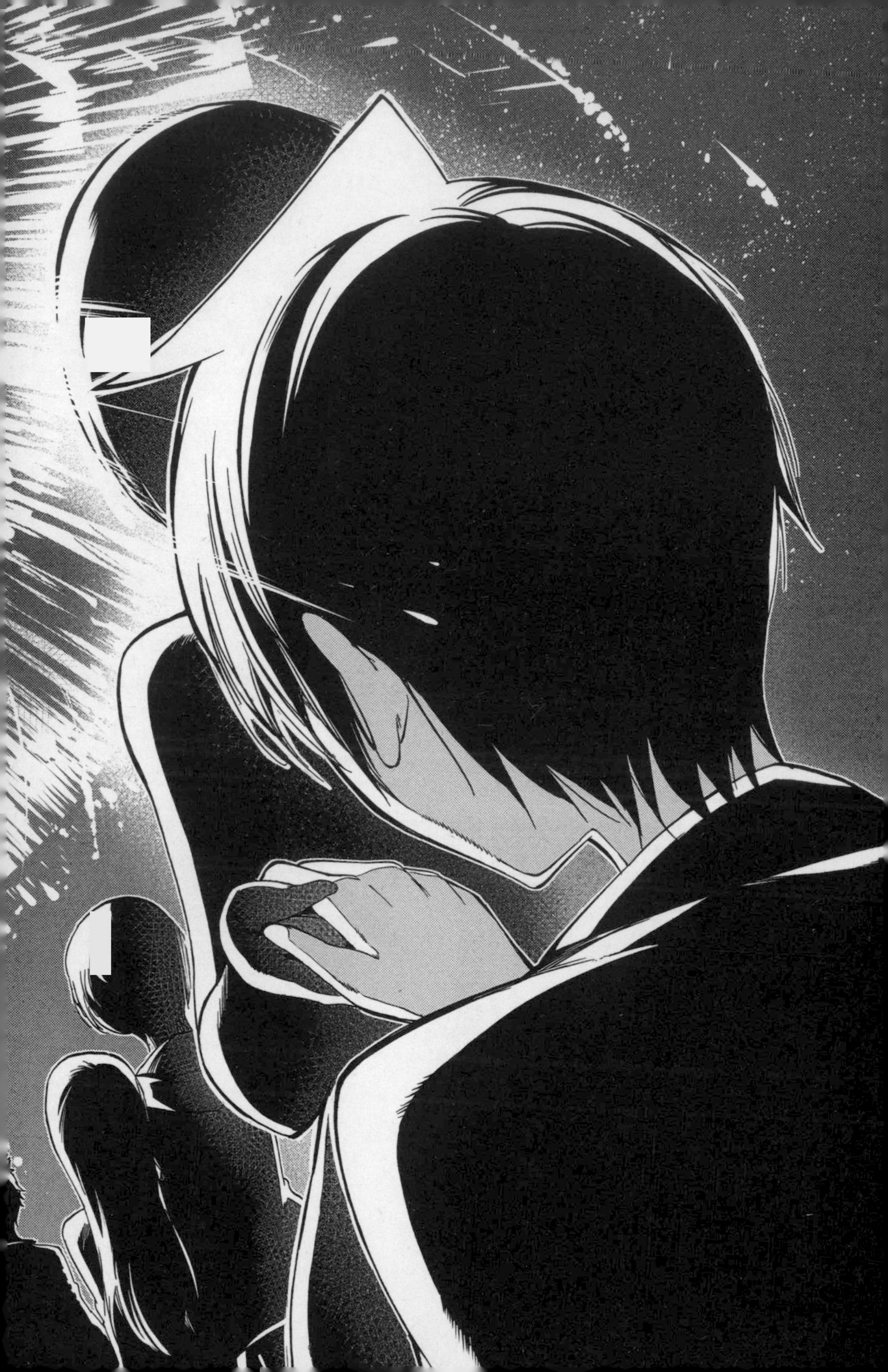

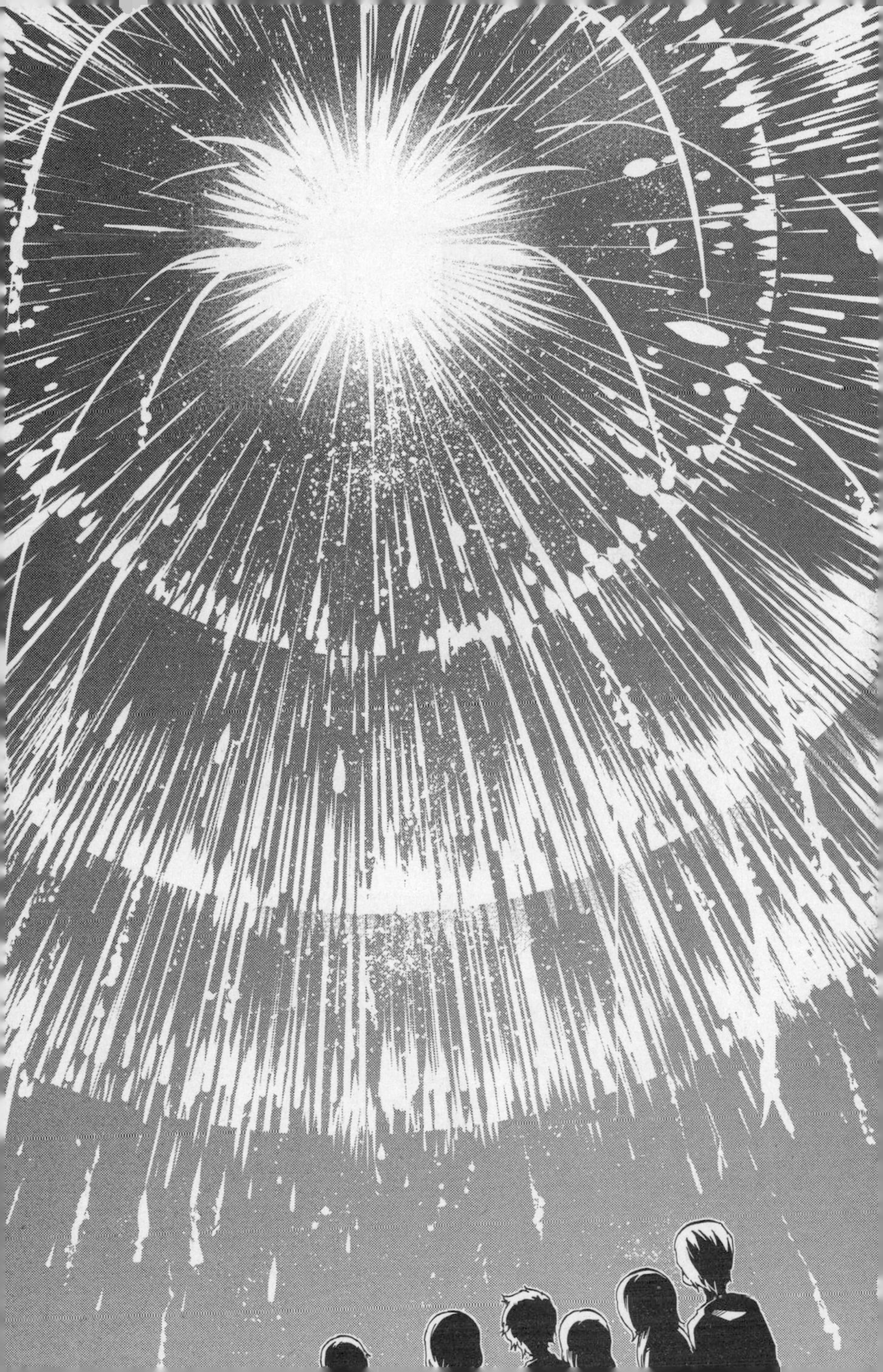

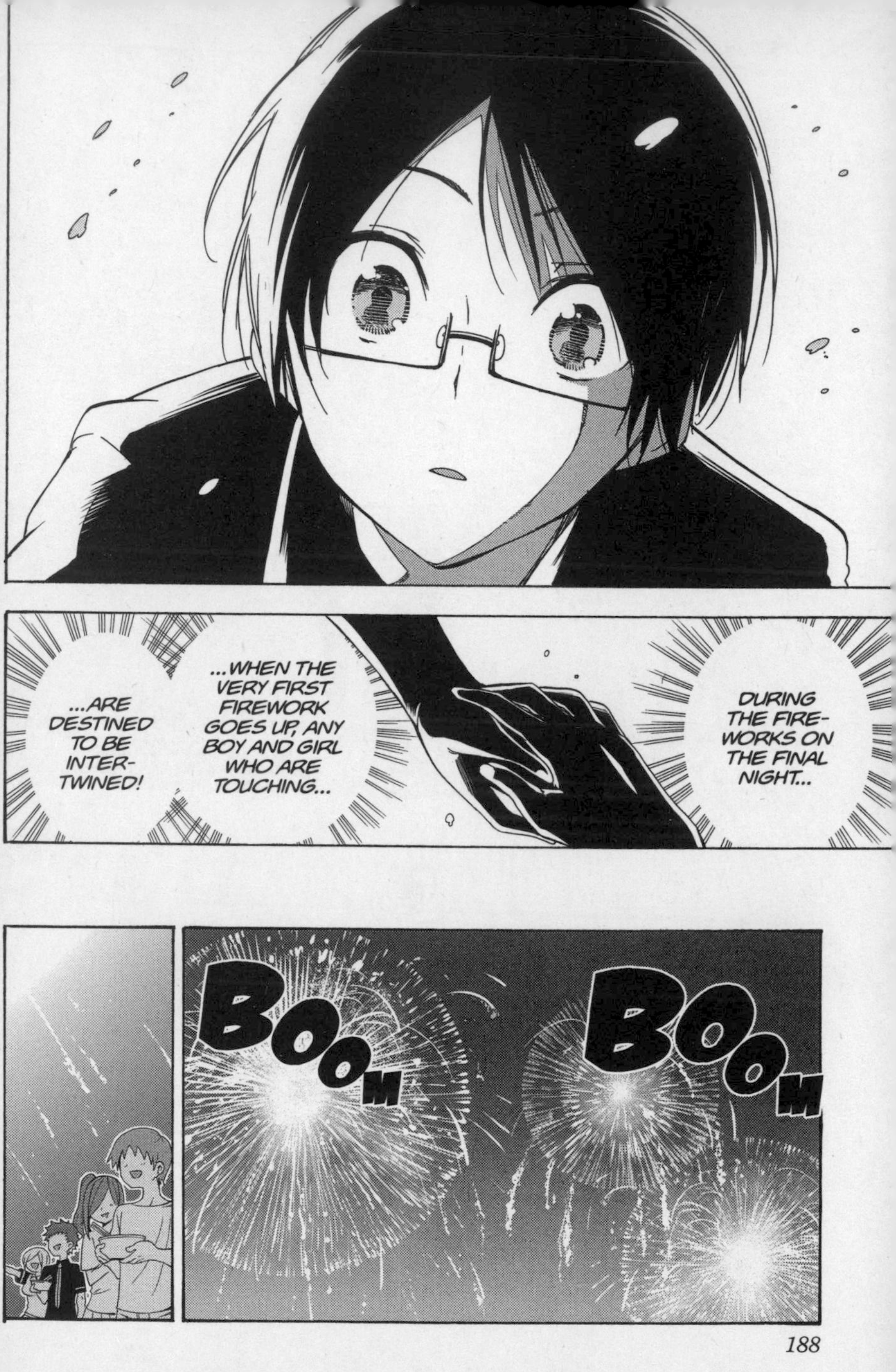
DURING THE FIRE-WORKS ON THE FINAL NIGHT...
...WHEN THE VERY FIRST FIREWORK GOES UP, ANY BOY AND GIRL WHO ARE TOUCHING...
...ARE DESTINED TO BE INTER-TWINED!
BOOM
BOOM

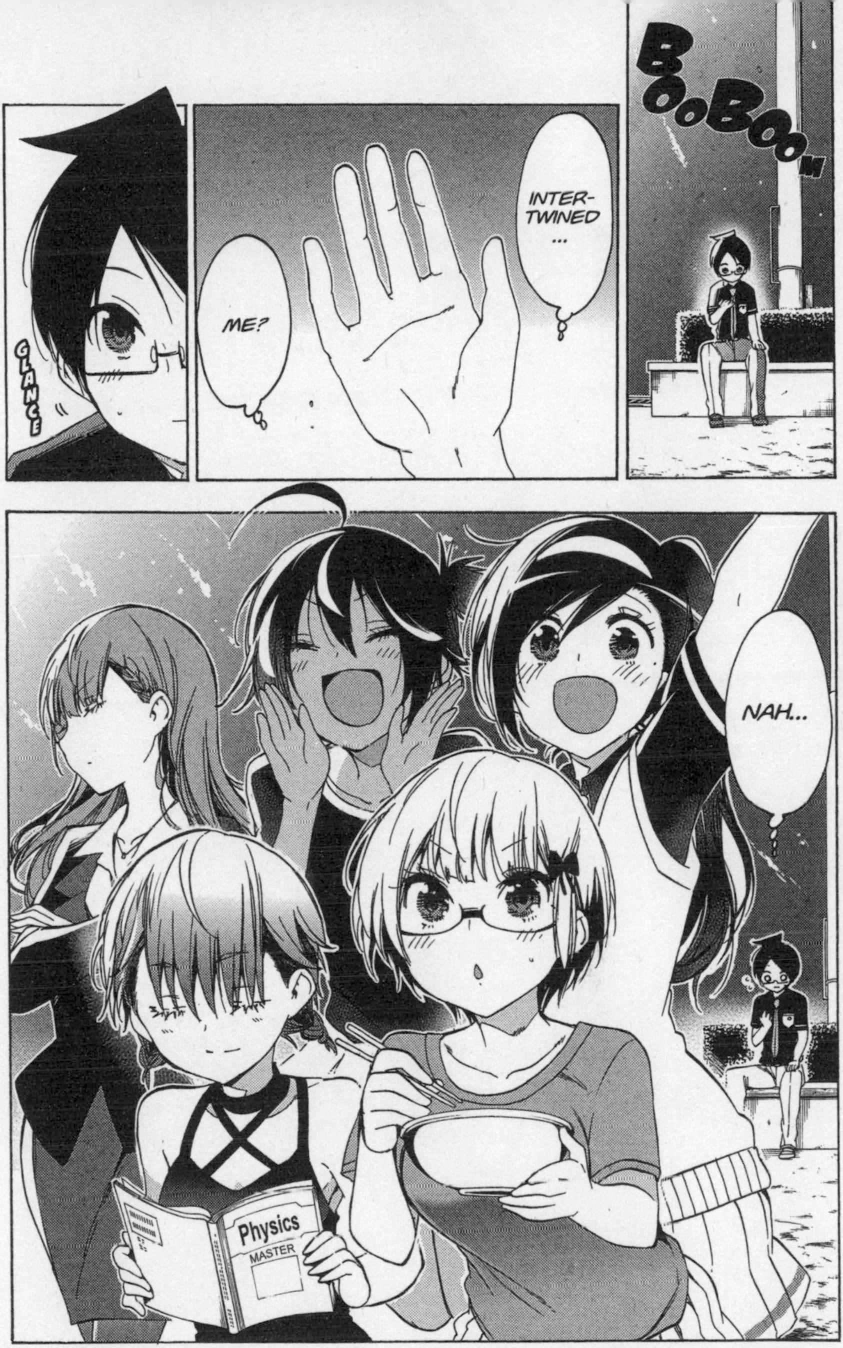
BOOBOOM
INTER-TWINED...
ME?
GLANCE
NAH...
Physics
MASTER

LATER
THE STRANGE UDON PRINCE WOULD GO DOWN IN ICHINOSE ACADEMY HISTORY AS AN UNSOLVED MYSTERY.
ALSO, THE SCHOOL FESTIVAL LEGEND...
...WAS MODIFIED TO INCLUDE THE PHRASE "WHILE EATING UDON." BUT THAT'S ANOTHER STORY.

[x] We + Never ÷ × Learn

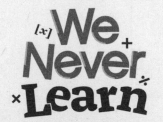

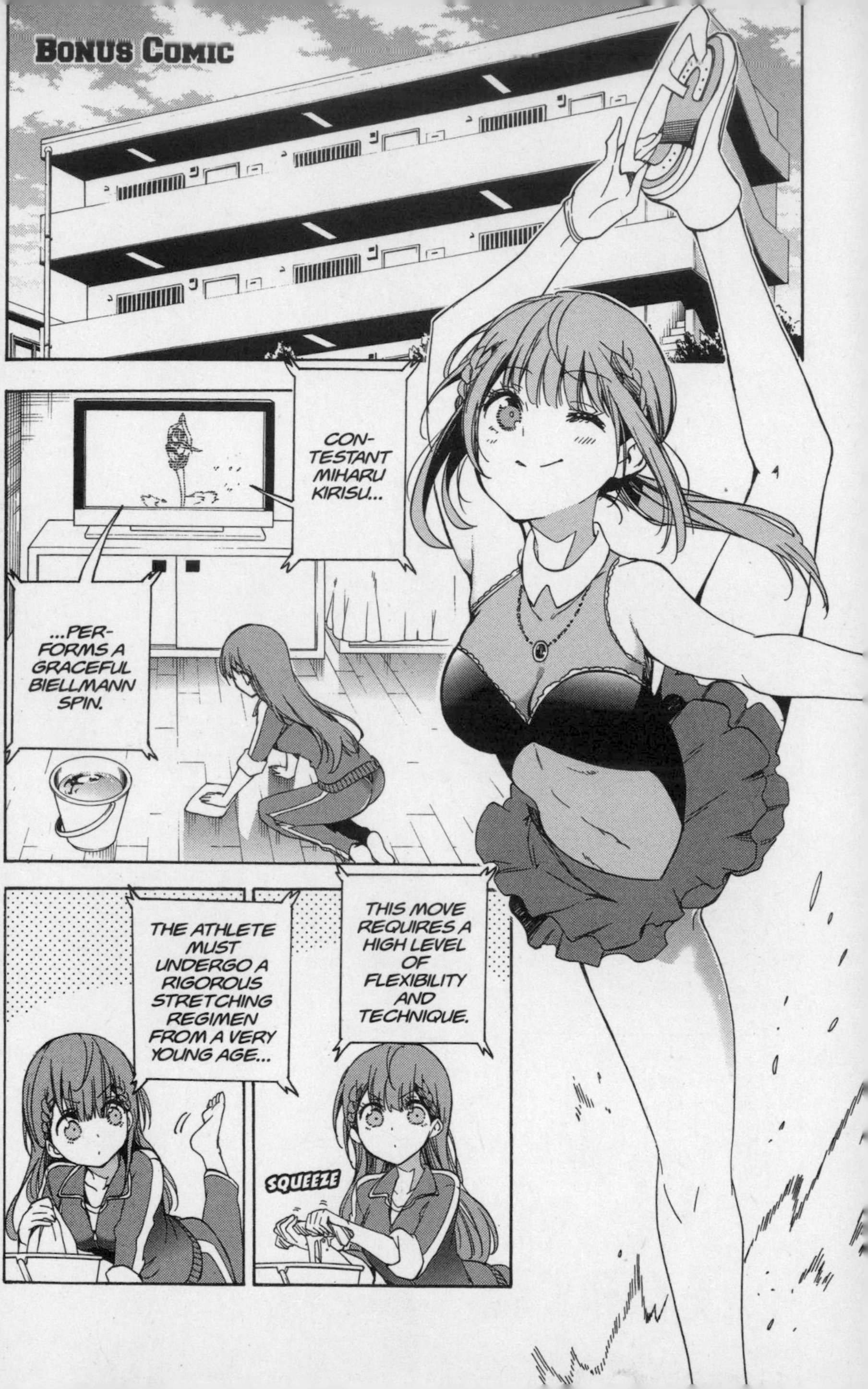
BONUS COMIC
CON-TESTANT MIHARU KIRISU...
...PER-FORMS A GRACEFUL BIELLMANN SPIN.
THIS MOVE REQUIRES A HIGH LEVEL OF FLEXIBILITY AND TECHNIQUE.
SQUEEZE
THE ATHLETE MUST UNDERGO A RIGOROUS STRETCHING REGIMEN FROM A VERY YOUNG AGE...

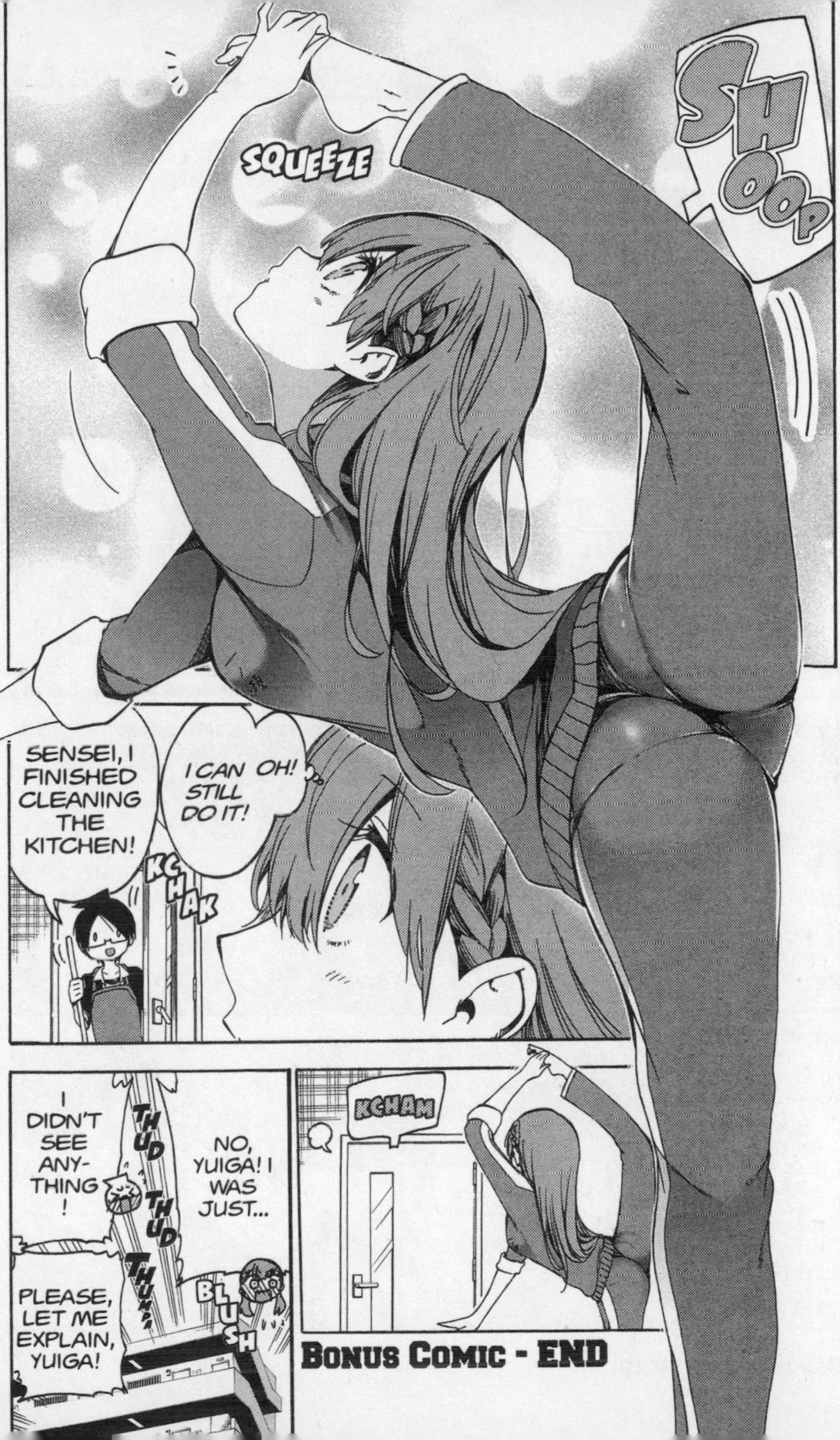
SHOOOP
SQUEEZE
OH!
I CAN STILL DO IT!
SENSEI, I FINISHED CLEANING THE KITCHEN!
KCHAK
KCHAM
NO, YUIGA! I WAS JUST...
I DIDN'T SEE ANYTHING!
THUD
THUD
THUD
THUMP
BLUSH
PLEASE, LET ME EXPLAIN, YUIGA!
BONUS COMIC - END

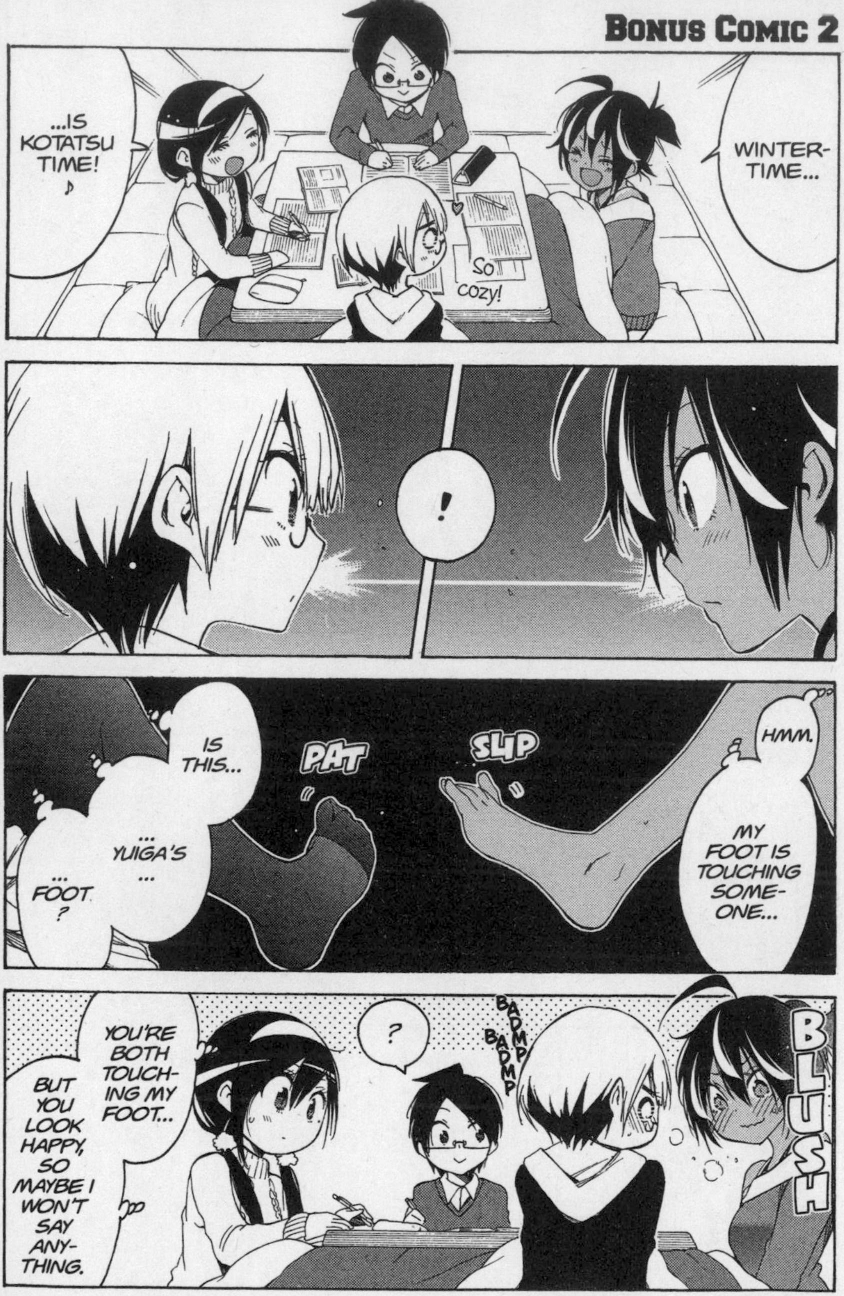
WINTER-TIME...
...IS KOTATSU TIME! ♪
So cozy!
!
HMM.
MY FOOT IS TOUCHING SOME-ONE...
SLIP
PAT
IS THIS...
...YUIGA'S...
...FOOT?
BLUSH
BADMP BADMP
?
YOU'RE BOTH TOUCHING MY FOOT...
BUT YOU LOOK HAPPY, SO MAYBE I WON'T SAY ANYTHING.

BONUS COMIC 2 - END

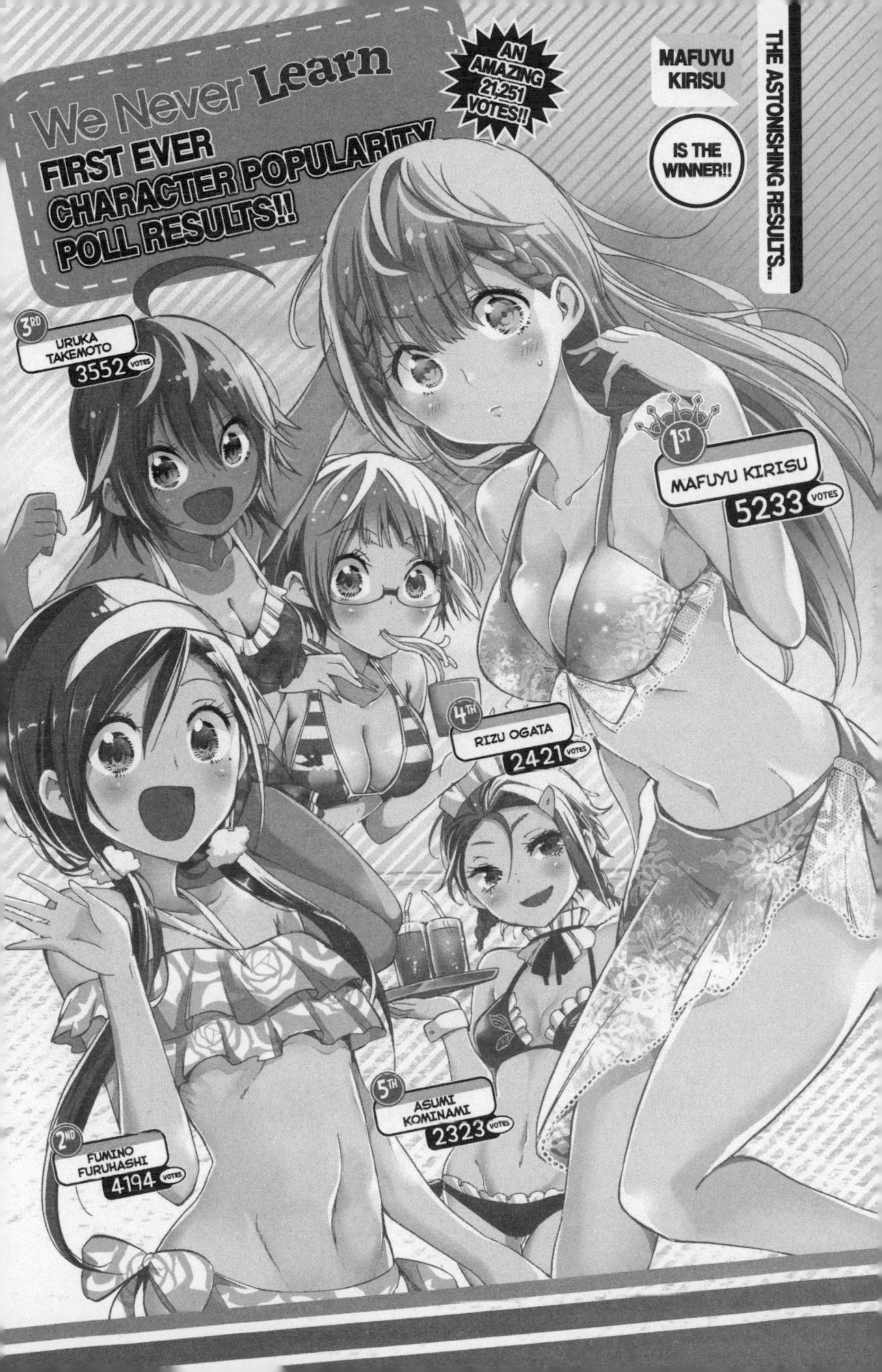

We Never Learn
FIRST EVER CHARACTER POPULARITY POLL RESULTS!!
AN AMAZING 21,251 VOTES!!
THE ASTONISHING RESULTS...
MAFUYU KIRISU
IS THE WINNER!!
1ST MAFUYU KIRISU 5233 VOTES
2ND FUMINO FURUHASHI 4194 VOTES
3RD URUKA TAKEMOTO 3552 VOTES
4TH RIZU OGATA 2421 VOTES
5TH ASUMI KOMINAMI 2323 VOTES

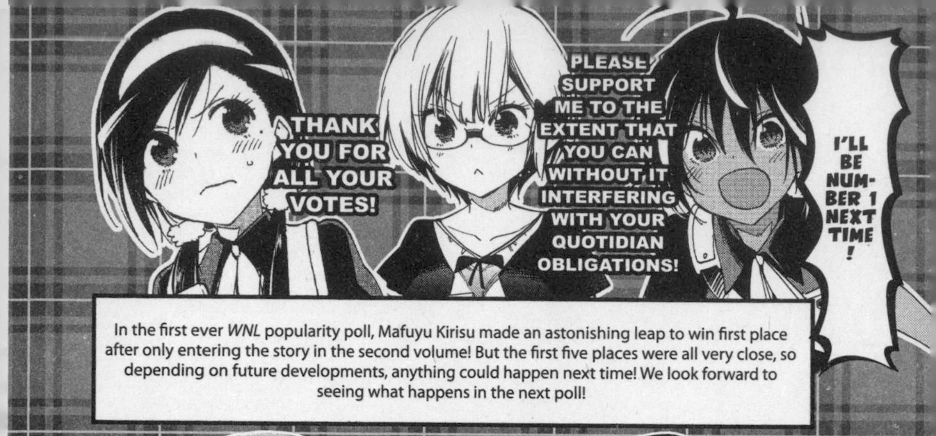
I'LL BE NUMBER 1 NEXT TIME!
PLEASE SUPPORT ME TO THE EXTENT THAT YOU CAN WITHOUT IT INTERFERING WITH YOUR QUOTIDIAN OBLIGATIONS!
THANK YOU FOR ALL YOUR VOTES!

In the first ever *WNL* popularity poll, Mafuyu Kirisu made an astonishing leap to win first place after only entering the story in the second volume! But the first five places were all very close, so depending on future developments, anything could happen next time! We look forward to seeing what happens in the next poll!

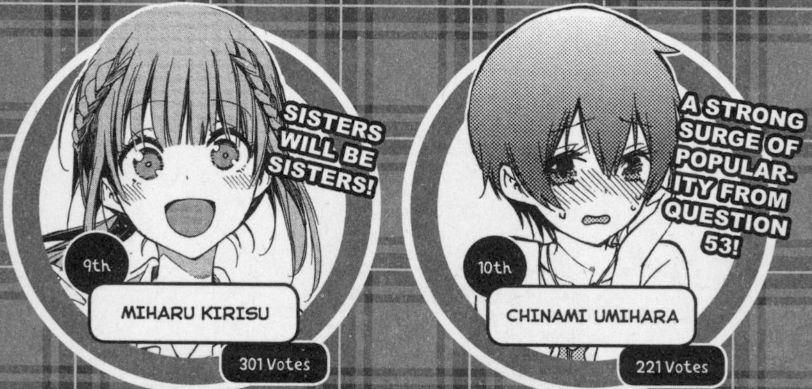
SISTERS WILL BE SISTERS!
9th
MIHARU KIRISU
301 Votes
A STRONG SURGE OF POPULARITY FROM QUESTION 53!
10th
CHINAMI UMIHARA
221 Votes

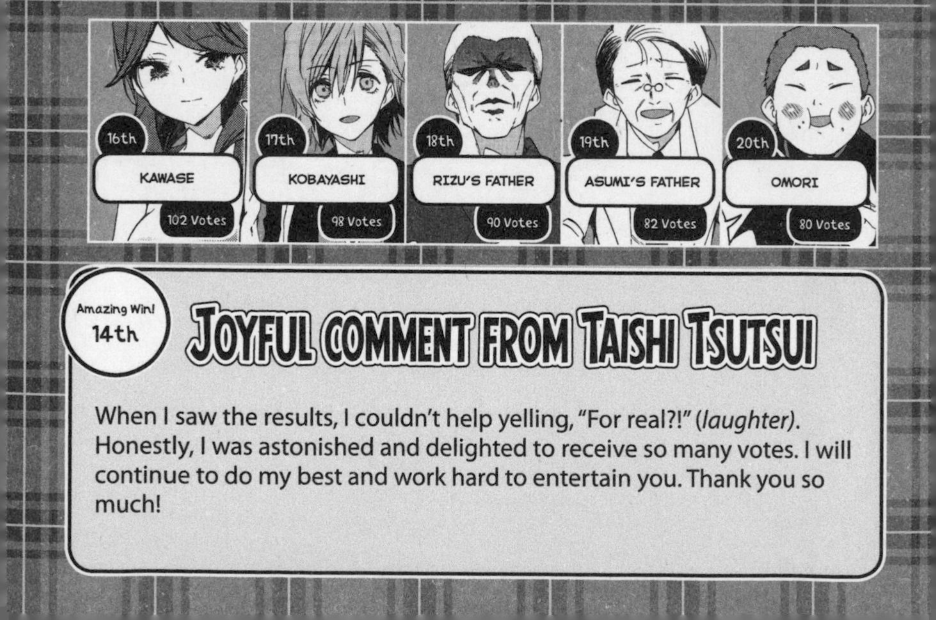
16th
KAWASE
102 Votes
17th
KOBAYASHI
98 Votes
18th
RIZU'S FATHER
90 Votes
19th
ASUMI'S FATHER
82 Votes
20th
OMORI
80 Votes

Amazing Win! 14th

JOYFUL COMMENT FROM TAISHI TSUTSUI

When I saw the results, I couldn't help yelling, "For real?!" (*laughter*). Honestly, I was astonished and delighted to receive so many votes. I will continue to do my best and work hard to entertain you. Thank you so much!

We Never Learn

FIRST EVER CHARACTER POPULARITY POLL RESULTS!!

COMIC INTERLUDES ARE MINE!

6th
MIZUKI YUIGA
446 Votes

THE STANDARD RANKING OF A LOVE COMIC HERO!

7th
YUIGA NARIYUKI
437 Votes

PONYTAIL POWER!

8th
SAWAKO SEKIJO
365 Votes

11th
INOMORI
(THORN CLUB MEMBER)
220 Votes

12th
KASHIMA
(THORN CLUB MEMBER)
193 Votes

13th
CHONO
(THORN CLUB MEMBER)
180 Votes

14th
TAISHI TSUTSUI
128 Votes

15th
FUMINO YUIGA
(ONLY APPEARED IN QUESTION 39)
121 Votes

Miscellaneous riffraff?! The confusing mess of characters in 21st place and beyond!!*

Ikeda, Cage Case (Esprit), Uruka Takemoto in junior high, Magical Patissier Onodera Kosaki, Gariole Doll, Nariyuki-merged-with-Fumino in Question 52, Kei Yonagi of *Act-Age*, Machiko of the maid cafe, Himura of the maid *cafe*, Mikuni of the maid cafe, Lieutenant General P. Fluletei of *Samone Is Samona,* Yu Mikonami of *Spring Weapon Number One,* Kazuki Yuiga, Uruka's mother, the almost-a-size-B size-A bra, Jino Yokozuna of *Hinomaru Sumo,* Star Clone of *The Promised Neverland,* Tomohiro Hasegawa Sensei, the principal, Hanae Yuiga, Hanako Woof-Woof, the lingerie shop manager, Perro the Kirisu family dog, Sachie Umino of *Spring Weapon Number One,* Hazuki Yuiga, Yoshida of the cram school stupid trio, Fumino's mother, Tsutsui Sensei's wife, Rizu Ogata's spare glasses, Nariyuki Yuiga's glasses, Pixie Maid Ashumi, Rizu's language arts notebook enscribed densely with pi, school uniform version of Kirisu Sensei, Y of Chiba, Seishiro Tsugumi of *Nisekoi*
(*Listed in random order!)

[x] We + Never ÷ × Learn

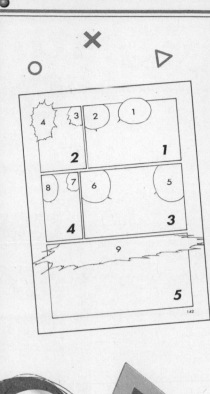

We Never Learn reads from right to left, starting in the upper-right corner. Japanese is read from right to left, meaning that action, sound effects and word-balloon order are completely reversed from English order.

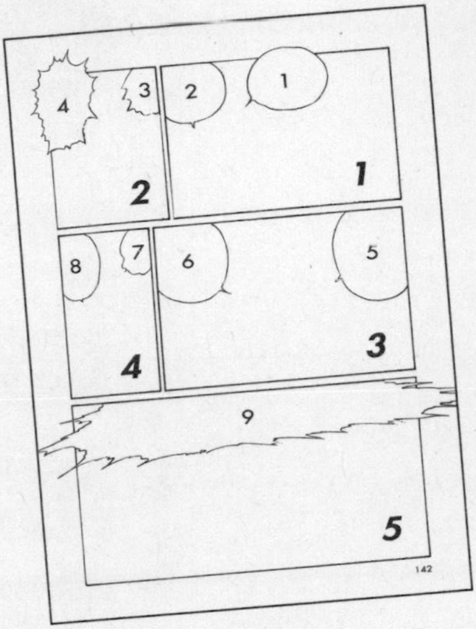
1
2
3
4
1
2
5
6
7
8
3
4
9
5
142

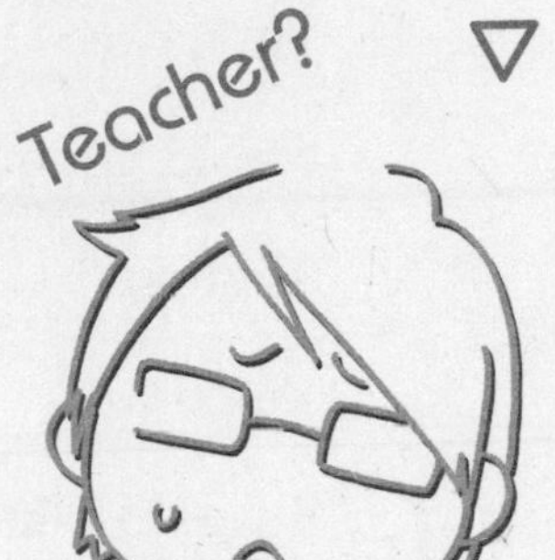
Teacher?

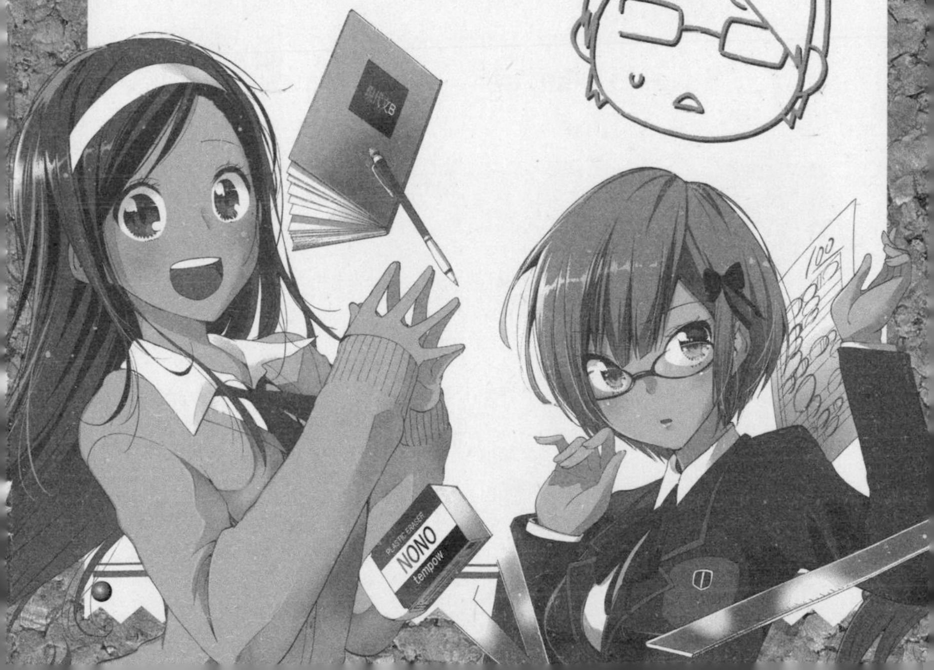
PLASTIC ERASER
NONO
tempow

We Never Learn 8

STAFF LIST

STAFF

Taishi Tsutsui

Yu Kato

Naoki Ochiai

Sachiko

Yukki

Satoshi Okazaki

HELP

Paripoi

Shinobu Irooki

Chikomichi